ALSO BY LYNNE OLSON

A Question of Honor:
The Kosciuszko Squadron: Forgotten Heroes of World War II
(with Stanley Cloud)

Freedom's Daughters:
The Unsung Heroines of the Civil Rights Movement
from 1830 to 1970

The Murrow Boys:
Pioneers on the Front Lines of Broadcast Journalism
(with Stanley Cloud)

TROUBLESOME
YOUNG MEN

TROUBLESOME YOUNG MEN

THE REBELS WHO BROUGHT

CHURCHILL TO POWER

AND HELPED SAVE ENGLAND

LYNNE OLSON

FARRAR, STRAUS AND GIROUX · NEW YORK

Farrar, Straus and Giroux
18 West 18th Street, New York 10011

Grateful acknowledgment is made to the following for permission to reprint excerpts from selected material:

Quotations from the letters and papers of Lady Violet Bonham Carter are reprinted by permission of the Bonham Carter family and the Bodleian Library, Oxford.

Quotations from the letters of Neville Chamberlain are reprinted by permission of the Special Collections Department, University Library, University of Birmingham.

Quotations from the letters of Anthony Eden (Lord Avon) are reprinted by permission of Lady Avon.

Quotations from the letters and papers of Paul Emrys-Evans are reprinted by permission of Carline Henderson.

Quotations from the papers of Richard Law (Lord Coleraine) are reprinted by permission of the second Lord Coleraine.

Quotations from the letters and papers of the fourth and fifth marquesses of Salisbury are reprinted by permission of the seventh Marquess of Salisbury.

Quotations from the letters and papers of James P. L. Thomas (Lord Cilcennin) are reprinted by permission of the Carmarthenshire Archives Service.

The Library of Congress has cataloged the hardcover edition as follows:

Olson, Lynne.
    Troublesome young men : the rebels who brought Churchill to power and helped save England / Lynn Olson—1st ed.
        p. cm.
    Includes bibliographical references and index.
    ISBN-13: 978-0-374-17954-0 (hardcover : alk. paper)
    ISBN-10: 0-374-17954-9 (hardcover : alk. paper)
    1. Great Britain—Politics and government—1936–1945. 2. Churchill, Winston, Sir, 1874–1965. 3. Chamberlain, Neville, 1869–1940. 4. Conservative Party (Great Britain). I. Title.

DA587.047 2007
941.084—dc22   2006017905

Paperback ISBN-13: 978-0-374-53133-1
Paperback ISBN-10: 0-374-53133-1

Designed by Jonathan D. Lippincott

www.fsgbooks.com

1 3 5 7 9 10 8 6 4 2 1

Cover photographs: (*front*) Budget Day © Hulton Archive / Getty Images; (*spine*) courtesy of the Library of Congress, Prints and Photographs Division, FSA/OWI Collection; (*back, left to right*) Leo Amery © Empics, Robert Boothby © Empics, Harold Macmillan © Hulton Archive / Getty Images, Ronald Cartland © Hulton-Deutsch Collection / CORBIS

FOR STAN AND CARLY

You have always been most kind to those of us who are ordinarily classed merely as troublesome young men.

—Harold Macmillan to Winston Churchill, January 1928

Thirty resolute men in your House of Commons could save the world.

—Felix Frankfurter to Richard Law, July 1939

CONTENTS

TROUBLESOME
YOUNG MEN

INTRODUCTION

They were schooled at Eton and Harrow, Cambridge and Oxford. They lived in Belgravia and Mayfair and spent their weekends at sprawling country houses in Kent, Sussex, and Oxfordshire. They were part of the small, clubby network that dominated English society. And now, in May 1940, these Tory members of Parliament were doing the unthinkable: trying to topple Prime Minister Neville Chamberlain, the leader of their own party, from power.

They knew they were courting political suicide. They were challenging a powerful, authoritarian prime minister who equated criticism of his policies with treason and employed a full complement of dirty tricks to stamp out dissent. Opponents branded the rebels as unpatriotic. Sir Samuel Hoare, the home secretary, denounced them as "jitterbugs" and claimed that their "alarm-and-scare-mongering" had thwarted a new "golden age of tranquility" in Europe.

Like other former public-school boys, the small band of backbenchers had been taught to value loyalty. But in the current crisis, they believed, they owed loyalty to their country, not to their party or prime minister. For eight months Britain had been at war with Germany, a war that Chamberlain and his government clearly had no interest in fighting, a war being waged, as one Tory rebel said, "without arms, without faith, and without heart."

Defending Poland was the ostensible reason why Britain and France had declared war on Hitler's Germany the previous September. But Poland had been quickly devastated by the German invasion, and its Western allies, despite all the treaties and all the promises to that shattered country, did nothing to save it. Was there any other justification for continuing this putative conflict? If so, Chamberlain's government never said what it was. The government declined to declare its war aims and seemed to prefer a token war, waged as cheaply as possible. The British Army was undermanned, ill equipped, and badly organized. Mobilization was lethargic; able-bodied men were still working as chauffeurs and as doormen at London's private clubs and luxury hotels. Armament production was proceeding at a snail's pace, and few, if any, controls had been imposed on civilian manufacturing.

Throughout Great Britain, there was doubt, cynicism, apathy, and distrust. When war was declared, the British braced themselves to bear the shock, believing their cause was just. But when their leaders turned their backs on Poland and nothing more happened, the sense of mission evaporated. More than a million city dwellers had been evacuated to the countryside; a blackout had been imposed, causing tremendous disruption and danger—and for what? Where were the bombs? What was the rationale for turning everyone's life upside down? Why were the wealthy still throwing lavish parties and drinking champagne at posh nightclubs while workers struggled with shortages and skyrocketing costs? To his radio listeners in America, the CBS correspondent Edward R. Murrow reported that the people of Britain felt "the machine is out of control, that we are all passengers on an express train traveling at high speed through a dark tunnel toward an unknown destiny. The suspicion recurs that the train may have no engineer, no one who can handle it."

Hitler, meanwhile, had no doubts about where *he* was heading. His forces had taken full advantage of the inertia of Britain and France, knifing through Poland the previous autumn, then, in April, invading Denmark and routing the British Army and Royal Navy from Norway. German troops were now poised to launch a lightning sweep through the heart of Western Europe, striking toward the English Channel.

Socially and militarily, Britain teetered on the edge of disaster. Yet there appeared to be little hope for change. Chamberlain was determined to stay in power, and most of the massive Tory majority in the House of Commons seemed determined to support him. So were the BBC and the nation's newspapers. Such support was in the national interest, editors rationalized. Criticizing the government in time of war would be disloyal, they declared, splitting the country further and only helping the Germans.

This, then, was what the Tory insurgents faced as they plotted to oust Neville Chamberlain. It was the climax of a two-year struggle against his policy of appeasement of Nazi Germany that had begun with the resignation of Anthony Eden as foreign secretary in February 1938. The fight had been bitter and intensely personal. The rebels were challenging men who had been their comrades in school, who belonged to the same clubs, who in some cases were members of their own families. They were violating the gentlemanly norms of their society; for that, they were vilified as traitors to their party, government, class, and country. Among the rebels themselves, there were deep divisions and dissension. They had trouble finding a leader; only after the war had begun did a senior colleague finally step forward with the courage and conviction to head the revolt.

That leader was not Winston Churchill. Indeed, the Tory dissidents had been given no help at all by the man who once had been the foremost critic of Chamberlain's appeasement policy. When war was declared, Churchill joined the cabinet as first lord of the admiralty. In the months that followed, although he pressed hard in government councils for a more vigorous prosecution of the war, he remained loyal to the prime minister. To the dismay of his anti-appeasement colleagues, Churchill made clear he would do nothing to help bring Chamberlain down. If the prime minister was to be toppled, it must be their doing, not his.

The climax of the anti-Chamberlain movement would come on a soft, golden spring afternoon in early May, when members of the House of Commons gathered to debate Britain's humiliating defeat in Norway. It was the final showdown between the prime minister and the Tory rebels, joined by their newfound Labour, Liberal, and Independent allies. As they worked feverishly before the debate to line up last-minute support, the rebels knew that the odds of their succeeding were regarded as slim to none. According to *Time* magazine, "nobody thought on that first afternoon of debate that there was more than an outside chance of dislodging Chamberlain."

Yet three days later Neville Chamberlain was gone, and Winston Churchill was prime minister. This is the story of how that came to be—and the men who made it happen.

The idea for *Troublesome Young Men* grew out of research for two previous books that I wrote with my husband, Stanley Cloud, both of them touching on the climactic summer of 1940 in Britain. It was during those terrible yet glorious days that the epic of Winston Churchill really began. "You ask what is our aim?" he declared to the House of Commons on May 13, three days after replacing Chamberlain. "I can answer in one word: victory." That word remained his touchstone, even as France fell, British troops retreated to Dunkirk, and a German invasion of Britain seemed to loom on the horizon. When Luftwaffe bombers began their assault on Britain later that summer, the new prime minister rallied his countrymen to greatness.

The story of Winston Churchill in 1940 is, without question, one of the most compelling dramas in modern British history. But as I researched the period in more detail, it seemed to me that the behind-the-scenes story leading to Churchill's accession—that of the Tory rebels defying their party and prime minister—is, in its way, no less significant or engrossing. For if it hadn't been for those MPs, and for the parliamentary colleagues who joined their ranks in the Norway debate, Churchill would never have been given the chance to rise so magnificently to the challenge, and Britain might well have negotiated for peace with Hitler or even gone down to defeat.

In the past six decades the emergence of Churchill as savior of Britain has come to be viewed almost as a preordained event. He is such a monumental figure, sweeping everyone else from center stage and claiming history's spotlight, that it's easy to believe, as many people do, that he stood virtually alone in opposing appeasement before the war and that his rise to power was inevitable. Neither assumption is true. As the historian Paul Addison has noted, "Looking back on the crisis of May 1940 with the benefit of hindsight, we must remark how uninevitable the 'inevitable' seemed to be at the time."

As prime minister, Neville Chamberlain possessed an overwhelming parliamentary majority. He and his men were masters of the House of Commons, manipulating and dominating that body just as they did the other traditional overseer of the government, the press. Using tactics that have striking resonance today, Chamberlain and his subordinates restricted journalists' access to government sources, badgered the BBC and newspapers to follow the government's line, and claimed that critics of their policies—in both the press and Parliament—were guilty of damaging the national interest.

Because of Chamberlain's seemingly impregnable position, the rebels encountered frustration after frustration in their two-year struggle. Fighting appeasement, one of them observed, was "like battering one's head against a stone wall." They were forced to wait for a major military setback before they could finally make their move. But once that reversal occurred, the foundation for revolt was firmly in place. Although some historians have argued that Chamberlain's downfall in the Norway debate was the consequence of "parliamentary political spontaneous combustion," it was, in fact, the result of the rebels' actions. "Rebellion," as the biographer Catherine Drinker Bowen observed, "does not come by sudden chance." The Tory dissidents pressed for the debate and urged the Labour Party to call for what turned out to be a vote of confidence in Chamberlain. And it was their leader, a former close friend of the prime minister's, who, in one of the most electrifying speeches ever heard in Parliament, persuaded a number of his colleagues that Chamberlain must go.

On the eve of Hitler's invasion of Western Europe, the House of Commons, prompted by the dissidents, reasserted itself as the guardian of democracy and took the first critical step toward victory. With their action, the rebels underscored the truth of a comment made by Ronald Cartland, the youngest member of their group, who himself would suffer the consequences of the government's failure to prepare properly for war.

"No government can change men's souls," Cartland said. "The souls of men change governments."

CHAPTER ONE

"WE MAY BE GOING TO DIE"

———⟡———

It had been a brilliant summer. On that point everyone agreed.

Children floated toy boats on the Serpentine in Hyde Park, while young lovers lay on deck chairs nearby and basked in the sunshine. At the Ritz, middle-aged women in flowered hats lunched on salmon and strawberries. In the evenings, crowds gathered outside stately mansions in Knightsbridge and Belgravia, as debutantes in satin and silk and young men in white tie and tails emerged from taxis and rushed, laughing, into the houses' brightly lit interiors. In those brief seconds before the butler shut the door, spectators could hear the faint strains of "Love Walked In" or "Cheek to Cheek" and imagine, just for a moment, that they were young, titled, and rich, and whirling around on the dance floor.

There was racing at Goodwood and Ascot, cricket at Lord's, tennis at Wimbledon, the regatta at Henley. There were dances and dinners, nightclub outings, and house parties in the country. But the highlight of the 1939 London season, in the opinion of those fortunate enough to have been invited, was the gala coming-out ball at Blenheim Palace for the seventeen-year-old Lady Sarah Spencer-Churchill, daughter of the Duke of Marlborough. The palace's massive stone facade had been floodlit for the occasion, its baroque beauty visible for miles. Tiny colored lights twinkled in the trees and shrubs of Blenheim's twenty acres of gardens; its lake, also floodlit, seemed bathed in gold. A band played in a pavilion on the vast lawn, as footmen in powdered wigs and yellow and blue Marlborough livery handed out champagne to more than seven hundred guests, including Winston Churchill, who had been born at Blenheim and was a first cousin of the honored debutante's late grandfather Sunny Marlborough. Most of those present danced until dawn. The scene, said one dazzled guest, was "gay, young, brilliant, in short, perfection."

In that magical setting it was easy to forget that half a continent away, hundreds of thousands of German troops were massing on the borders of Poland, that in Warsaw residents were digging zigzag trenches in their parks while loudspeakers boomed out practice air-raid warnings. Europe stood on the brink of war. If Hitler invaded Poland, as seemed likely now, Britain had pledged to take up arms in defense of the Poles.

Yet as the summer wound down, there was little sense of crisis in that sea-girted country. Foreign visitors marveled at the calm of the British, their seeming insouciance in the face of peril. "Taxi-cab drivers, waiters and porters went about their work as though they were oblivious to the fact that soon they would be caught up in one of the greatest storms the world had ever known," recalled Virginia Cowles, a young Boston socialite who had just begun work as a reporter for *The Sunday Times*, London. "The most you could get out of anyone was a short comment such as 'Things aren't too bright, are they?' and you suddenly felt guilty of bad taste for having referred to it."

For Helen Kirkpatrick, another young American reporter, living in England in the summer of 1939 was akin to driving a car and realizing you were about to crash. "Afterwards, when they pick you out of the wreck, you can tell them so clearly how you saw the other car coming headlong towards you, how you tried to turn aside but couldn't quite make it," Kirkpatrick, a correspondent for the *Chicago Daily News*, wrote. "We knew it was coming—there it was ahead. Nothing could stop it. But life went on just the same as usual."

Even with war looming, there would be no disruption of the social routine. The final days of July marked the end of the glittering season. By August 2 the annual late-summer exodus from London was well under way. Brighton and the other English seaside resorts were already jammed. Members of the upper class were en route to their country estates for a bit of grouse shooting or to the beaches and casinos of southern France. As one society matron explained to her debutante granddaughter, "Darling, the thing is: one [shouldn't] be seen in London after July 31."

Neville Chamberlain prepared to follow his countrymen's example. Bone-weary, the seventy-year-old British prime minister was looking forward to a few weeks of salmon fishing in the Scottish Highlands. But before he could make his escape, he had one last duty on his schedule: to preside over the formal adjournment of Parliament for its traditional two-month summer break.

A number of members of Parliament, however, were appalled at the idea of a long vacation. This was not, after all, a typical desultory August. War could break out at any moment. What on earth was the prime minister thinking? Was he trying to get Parliament out of the way so he could renege on Britain's promises to the Poles? Chamberlain had seemed unequivocal in March, when he pledged to defend Poland against German aggression. Yet disquieting reports were circulating of intense British pressure on the Poles to make concessions to Germany, of secret talks with German officials about a possible deal. According to *The New York Times*, London and Paris were now privately warning Poland not to antagonize Hitler. And earlier in the summer, when Polish officials sought credits from Britain for arms, they were told by the Treasury that the matter was not considered "of great urgency."

To some MPs, such reports were unpleasantly reminiscent of Chamberlain's appeasement of Germany a year earlier. Was he now preparing to betray the Poles as he had betrayed the Czechs at the Munich Conference the year before? The prime minister's decision to embark on his personal diplomatic missions to Hitler in September 1938 had violated all precedent, having been made without consulting his own cabinet, much less the House of Commons. Indeed, when Chamberlain began his pilgrimages to Germany, Parliament was in its two-month summer recess, a fact that anti-appeasement MPs remembered only too well in August 1939. The House of Commons, representing the British people, was supposed to guide and control the executive. Instead, complained the Conservative MP Harold Macmillan, "we are being treated more and more like a Reichstag, to meet only to hear the orations and to register the decrees of the government of the day."

The forty-four-year-old Macmillan was one of a small group of Tory MPs who had been scathingly critical of the Munich agreement and who had banded together, under the ostensible leadership of former foreign secretary Anthony Eden, to resist any further appeasement. At a meeting in late July the dissidents, whom Chamberlain and his men dismissively referred to as the "glamour boys," decided to oppose the long summer recess. Separately, Winston Churchill, the best-known Tory foe of Chamberlain's foreign policy, made the same decision. Over lunch at Chartwell, his country house in Kent, Churchill told Edward Spears, an old friend and a member of the Eden group, that the prime minister's adjournment plans would simply encourage Hitler in the belief that Britain would not go to war if Germany invaded Poland.

Chamberlain brushed off Churchill's opposition—indeed, the opposition of all those who had resisted appeasement—as casually as he would flick away an ant at a picnic. What did he have to fear from Winston, a controversial and divisive figure, with no bedrock of support in Parliament or the Conservative Party? Even Eden shied away from cooperating with him. As for Eden's "glamour boys," how could they make problems for him when their own leader was doing his best to reinstate himself in Chamberlain's good graces and get back into the cabinet? At their meeting in July, Eden had told the others that "if there were ever an issue upon which our group should affirm our identity and vote against the Government, it is this issue." Within days, however, he was having second thoughts.

Chamberlain had no intention of taking Eden back into his government—once a rebel, always a rebel—but he was not averse to keeping him dangling. And even if the handsome ex-foreign secretary suddenly developed a backbone, it would accomplish nothing. Chamberlain was sure he had the Tory insurgents firmly under control. They had been attacked as disloyal by the prime minister's many supporters in the press and government. Their phones had been tapped, their meetings spied on, their constituencies pressured to withdraw support from them at the next election.

Most members of the huge Tory majority in the Commons whole-heartedly supported Chamberlain. So did the king and the House of Lords. The Labour Party, weak and divided, offered no threat. The other Opposition party, the Liberals, with only twenty-one members, was a joke.

No, Chamberlain was convinced, he had nothing to worry about at all.

In midafternoon on August 2 the House of Commons was set to begin its debate on the government's adjournment motion. The House chamber, beneath its vaulted, timbered ceiling, was filling up fast, with the noise level rising as MPs streamed in from the lobbies and smoking room. Once the debate was under way, the dimly lit chamber would be stuffy and jammed, as it always was when an important issue was being discussed. The Commons lacked enough seating for its more than six hundred members; in their first days in the House, new MPs invariably expressed amazement at how small this cradle of democracy really was. On occasions like this, some MPs were forced to stand or sit in the gangways or cluster around the Speaker's canopied chair. Those who were seated were packed close together on the tiered dark green leather benches.

The cramped, spare quarters were no accident. When the Palace of Westminster, which contains the Houses of Parliament, was rebuilt after a disastrous fire in 1834, its architect and interior designer viewed it more as a setting for royal ceremonial occasions than as the center of a democratic government. While the scarlet and gold House of Lords chamber was outfitted with stained glass windows, a magnificent throne, opulent furnishings, and frescoes depicting medieval sovereigns, the Commons chamber was small and austere, with terrible acoustics and tiny galleries for visitors and the press. Unlike the Lords' quarters, it was not intended as a theater of state. Yet the anger, passion, and drama displayed in the little oak-paneled hall over the past century had at times bordered on the operatic. In the view of David Lloyd George, one of the Commons' most accomplished showmen, nothing could compete with the excitement and electricity of the House. When the young son of a parliamentary colleague told the former prime minister that he planned to go into the Royal Navy, Lloyd George frowned and shook his white-maned head. "There are much greater storms in politics," he declared. "If it's piracy you want, with broadsides, boarding parties, walking the plank, and blood on the deck, this is the place." The two thin red lines on the floor in front of each of the front benches underscored that sense of confrontation and combat. According to Commons tradition, no member was allowed to step over the lines during a debate; the distance between the two was supposed to be the exact distance between two outstretched arms brandishing swords.

The August 2 debate held the promise of considerable confrontation, and MPs took their seats with the eagerness of a first-night audience at the Old Vic. The day was sultry and hot, but as usual, Neville Chamberlain made no concessions to the weather. Wearing his usual black waistcoat, tailcoat, striped pants, and starched high white collar, the prime minister rose from his seat on the government's front bench at precisely 2:45 p.m., and, in his reedy voice, proposed that the Commons adjourn until October 3. On the opposite side of the House, just a few feet away, Arthur Greenwood, the lanky deputy Labour leader, stood to face Chamberlain. Greenwood immediately made clear that he and other Labour members suspected Chamberlain of having another Munich in mind. "Last September the House reassembled to witness a funeral pyre," Greenwood said. "A great people had their independence taken from them. I believe that an overwhelming majority of the public in this country would wish Parliament to be on alert at this critical time." With that, he introduced an amendment limiting the House's summer recess to less than three weeks. Members, he declared, should be called back no later than August 21.

When Winston Churchill stood to be recognized, the air was alive with the expectation of verbal fireworks. Churchill did not disappoint. His shoulders hunched, his head thrust forward, Churchill talked of the crush of German troops on Poland's borders, of German arms and supplies steadily moving east. "At this moment in its long history," he thundered, "it would be disastrous, it would be pathetic, it would be shameful for the House of Commons to write itself off as an effective and potent factor . . . It is a very hard thing . . . for the Government to say to the House, 'Begone! Run off and play. Take your [gas] masks with you. Do not worry about public affairs. Leave them to the gifted and experienced Ministers.'"

Churchill supported Greenwood's amendment, as did Macmillan and several other Tories. (Despite his fiery words less than a week earlier, Anthony Eden did not speak in the debate.) Just before Chamberlain was set to respond, Leo Amery, an old friend of the prime minister's, appealed to him to take the lead in uniting the Commons and the nation behind him in this time of national emergency.

Compromise, however, was far from Neville Chamberlain's mind. He was furious at Churchill and the other Tory renegades, at Amery for joining them. The prime minister had always been a man of great determination and obstinacy, but in the past year, after being acclaimed throughout the world as the savior of peace following Munich, he had become increasingly intolerant of any criticism or disagreement. He "suffers from a curious vanity and self-esteem which were born at Munich and have flourished ever since," John Colville, one of his private secretaries, noted in his diary. Now the savior of peace would make clear how very personally he took these attacks on the government, how he regarded them as intolerable slurs against himself.

Chamberlain stood, his jaw clenched, his face flushed. Removing his pince-nez from his nose, he rested one arm on the Treasury dispatch box on the table in front of him and stared at Labour MPs across the chamber. Then he turned halfway around to face his party's backbenchers. Very well, he announced, if "you distrust the Government and show it by your vote," he would treat such opposition as "a vote of no confidence in the Government, and no confidence in the Prime Minister in particular." Murmurs of surprise rippled through the chamber. In making the vote one of confidence in himself, Chamberlain was in effect demanding total party loyalty from the Conservative MPs, issuing an implicit order to refrain from criticizing further the adjournment proposal. It was clear, Chamberlain added acidly, that his critics were "very badly in need of a holiday . . . their reasoning faculties wanted a little freshening up at the seaside."

Sitting a few yards away from the prime minister, on the second bench below the gangway, thirty-two-year-old Ronald Cartland was seething. Cartland had been in Parliament less than four years, representing King's Norton, a constituency in Birmingham adjacent to Chamberlain's own district. Indeed, the Chamberlain family's powerful party machine in Birmingham had approved his selection as a Conservative candidate and helped him win his seat. But that had not stopped him from becoming one of the most outspoken Tory critics of the prime minister's appeasement policy.

Cartland had wanted to be an MP ever since he could remember. As a small boy he would sit at a table in his nursery, scribble furiously on sheets of paper, mount a box, and deliver campaign speeches to his nanny and older sister, Barbara. Sometimes he told them to heckle; other times he demanded applause. He was that rare creature: a young politician who combined great ambition with a determination to speak his mind, regardless of the consequences. He "had very little of the diffidence that the House of Commons expects from those who seek its approval," said a Tory colleague. "But that was one of Ronald's most marked characteristics. He never did seek the approval of anybody."

The slim dark-haired MP understood why the British system of government demanded such loyalty from parliamentary members of the party in power. Rejection by the House of Commons of a major government measure might bring about the resignation of the prime minister and his cabinet. But Chamberlain enjoyed such a huge majority in the House that the likelihood of his losing a vote was all but nonexistent. Nonetheless, he demanded total support and as a result, in Cartland's view, had turned Parliament into a lapdog legislature, existing only to do the will of the prime minister. The BBC and most newspapers had become just as servile. "We are near to press censorship," Cartland remarked shortly before the debate. "Film censorship already exists. But it is the dictatorship over the mind which causes me alarm. The right to one's own opinions is being constantly and openly challenged."

Especially if one was a Tory MP. Cartland, who knew from personal experience what he was talking about, had recently written: "Men who hold views contrary to their Party leaders are termed rebels, and subservience is held of more account than originality. Members who are not in step with their Party Whips are threatened with expulsion and attempts are made to undermine their position in their constituency. Measures are taken to prevent their voicing their opinions, both inside and outside the House of Commons." The Commons, he told a friend, had become nothing more than "a cross between Madame Tussaud's and a marionette show." In a message to his constituents that summer, he declared: "The liberty of every citizen in the country depends ultimately on whether we have freedom of speech and independence of judgment in the House . . ."

Never, Cartland believed, was that freedom more important than now, with Britain on the verge of war. In 1937 he had joined the Territorial Army, a part-time civilian force similar to the National Guard in the United States; he now was a lieutenant in the Worcestershire and Oxfordshire Yeomanry. He would spend two weeks in late August at a training camp, preparing for combat, as would thousands of other young men in the Territorials. How could the House abandon its responsibilities to these soldiers and to the rest of the country?

Cartland decided he had heard enough of the debate. Jumping up, he left the chamber and, with Macmillan, the former diplomat Harold Nicolson, and other members of the Eden group, adjourned to the members' lobby to discuss how to respond to the prime minister's challenge. They were joined there by Robert Boothby, an ebullient Scot who belonged to Winston Churchill's small band of followers. A few moments later Churchill himself approached them. "Well," Cartland remarked dejectedly to the older man, "we can do no more about it." Churchill clapped an arm around Cartland's shoulders. "Do no more, my boy?" he boomed. "There is a lot more we can do! This is the time to fight—to speak—to attack!"

Cartland stood silently, mulling over Churchill's words. Just then another young dissident rushed up to the group. "You must speak at once," he told Cartland breathlessly. "The thing is blowing up [into] a real gale!" Cartland had not prepared any remarks; he'd been content to let the senior MPs take the lead in that day's debate. But Churchill's comment had changed his mind. It *was* the time to attack.

He turned on his heel and hurried back to the chamber. Within minutes he was recognized by the Speaker. "I am sorry to detain the House for a few moments, but I would like to say a few words as a backbencher of the Prime Minister's own party," he said. He was, he added, "profoundly disturbed" by Chamberlain's speech. Then, looking straight at Chamberlain, Cartland unleashed a thunderbolt. Did the prime minister realize that in many parts of the country he was considered a dictator? "I do not know how many meetings I have addressed in the last year," Cartland said, "but over and over again I have had to deny [that] impression . . ." Of course the idea was absurd, he added, but Chamberlain's "absolute refusal" to consider compromise on the issue of adjournment "will make it much more difficult for us to try and dispel that idea."

Indignant cries of "Nonsense!" and "No!" from the Tory side of the House mingled with boisterous cheers from the Labour benches. Chamberlain's despotic ways had long been a topic of conversation in the House smoking room and in the lobbies, not to mention around the table at London dinner parties. But a member of his own party calling him a dictator to his face, in open debate? "Cartland had committed the greatest of all heresies," Harold Nicolson later wrote. "He had dared not only to challenge the party whips but to affront the sacred name of Chamberlain himself."

Ignoring the rising chorus of anger around him, Cartland continued: "The right honorable gentleman is the head of a strong Government. He has an immense vote and he knows that he can carry anything through the Lobby . . . How easy it would be for him, when the whole of democracy is trying to stand together to resist aggression, to say that he had tremendous faith in this democratic institution." By now the jeering and catcalls from the Tory benches were so loud they nearly drowned out Cartland's words. He paused, fighting to keep his emotions in check. Then, raising his voice to be heard above the din, he declared: "We are in the situation that within a month we may be going to fight—and we may be going to die."

Behind him, Sir Patrick Hannon, the senior Tory MP from Birmingham and an ardent Chamberlain supporter, shouted, "No!" A close friend of Cartland's great-uncle, the florid, white-haired Hannon had been a key player in the younger man's selection to stand for Parliament by the formidable political machine controlled by the Chamberlain family. Cartland spun around to face his former mentor. "It is all very well for the honorable gentleman to say 'No,'" he declared. "There are thousands of young men at the moment in training . . . and the least that we can do here . . . is to show that we have immense faith in this democratic institution." Turning back, Cartland stared at Chamberlain. "It is much more important . . . to get the whole country behind you than to make jeering, pettifogging party speeches which divide the nation," he said. "Why cannot the Prime Minister ask for real confidence in himself as Prime Minister and as leader of the country rather than as leader of a party? I frankly say that I despair when I listen to speeches like that to which I have listened this afternoon." With that comment, Cartland sat down. A few moments later he left the chamber.

The place was in an uproar. MPs had come expecting drama, but no one had expected this. No other speech that day—and there had been many, in what turned out to be the sharpest parliamentary duel since Munich—had the impact of Cartland's passionate address, which Macmillan later described as coming from a man with a sense of impending doom. Harold Nicolson wrote in his diary: "Its effect was galvanic. I have seldom felt the temperature of the chamber rise so rapidly." Patrick Hannon rose in purple-faced rage to denounce the younger man's "poisonous" words. The people of Birmingham, he assured the prime minister, "had profound belief and confidence in Mr. Chamberlain." Sir Patrick added: "I want to make it clear to the House my regret and disappointment that I had anything to do with [Cartland's] selection as a Member of Parliament for his division." After the debate was over, a gleeful Churchill pumped Cartland's hand, exclaiming, "Well done, my boy, well done!" In the members' smoking room, a cabinet minister snorted, "Ronald Cartland!" and pointed his thumbs down.

In the end Chamberlain, as usual, triumphed. Nearly forty Conservatives, many of whom had opposed appeasement since well before Munich, did not take the extreme step that would make them pariahs in their party, of voting against the prime minister in this vote of confidence. They showed their disquiet in a milder way, by refusing to vote at all. Even Cartland abstained, as did Churchill, Macmillan, Boothby, Nicolson, Eden, and Amery. Their action had no effect on the flood tide of Tory support for the prime minister. He carried the House by a vote of 245–129.

The following day stories about Cartland's speech and the Tory dissidents' revolt were splashed across the front pages of the country's leading newspapers. "Forty Tories Rebel," proclaimed a large *Daily Mirror*
headline. "Mr. Cartland in Pillory," the *Manchester Guardian* declared.
The *Evening Standard*'s leading story was headlined: "Premier Calls for
List of MPs Who Did Not Vote Last Night. They Will All Be Black-
listed." The Tories who abstained were in great disfavor with the Conservative Party machine, and "their actions [will be] remembered against
them," the story reported. Yet most would see no official disciplinary
action, other than reprimands from the chief whip. "I understand,
however," wrote the article's unidentified author, "that the case of Mr.
Ronald Cartland is regarded as being different because of his criticism
of the Prime Minister."

Cartland was in the worst trouble of his political career. The morning after his speech he received a letter from another young MP: "An
attempt will be made, of course, to ruin you because of what you
said . . . I can assure you there will be an organized attempt by government supporters to prove their own virtue by assailing yours. The first
part of what you said last night will be widely and maliciously misrep-
resented." An *Evening News* story noted: "Mr. Ronald Cartland, the tall,
dark, good-looking young Conservative member, has leapt into fame,
or, if you like, notoriety overnight with his extraordinary attack on Mr.
Chamberlain . . . A member of the Birmingham political team can't hope
to use adjectives like 'jeering' and 'pettifogging' in relation to his leader,
the Prime Minister, and get completely away with it. Mr. Cartland is a
bold young man. He will need to be."

Soon after the debate some twenty Conservative MPs, among them
Patrick Hannon, demanded that the whips take "severe measures"
against Cartland, protesting that "it is not right that they should be expected to share even the nominal association with Mr. Cartland of be-
longing to the same party." The head of Birmingham's Tory machine
conferred with Neville Chamberlain on how to get rid of the young up-
start. "Ronald Cartland's latest speech has aroused great resentment in
Birmingham, and there is a strong feeling that he should not be allowed to continue," the party head wrote to Chamberlain on August 5.
"I have seen the chairman of King's Norton Division this morning and

he is in accord with the view that another candidate should be sought." That same day Chamberlain wrote to his sister: "As for Master Cartland, I hope that he has effectually blotted his copybook in King's Norton, and I am taking steps to stimulate local opposition. He has always been a disloyal member of the team . . . We may lose the seat as a result, but I would rather do that than have a traitor in the camp." Shortly thereafter Cartland was summoned to appear before his constituency association on September 4 to discuss whether he should be replaced as its candidate at the next election.

His political career might indeed be over, but "I regret nothing," Cartland told his sister. "I would say it again tomorrow—I stand by everything I said. And when war comes—and come it will—the Prime Minister will be unable to unite the House; they will never follow him. And without a united Parliament, you cannot have a united nation."

CHAPTER TWO

PLAYING THE GAME

Soon after Ronald Cartland had been elected to Parliament, he and the other new Tory MPs were summoned to a meeting with a lean, darkly handsome man named David Margesson. In drill sergeant tones, Margesson, the government's chief whip, lectured the fledgling parliamentarians on the vital importance of "playing the game" and "never batting against your own side."

Although Cartland would soon demonstrate how little he took those lessons to heart, neither he nor most of the other Conservative newcomers needed instruction in them from Margesson, for they were two of the cardinal rules drilled into new boys at England's elite public schools, which most Tory MPs had attended. More than a third of all Conservative members during this period, and a fair number of Liberals and Labourites, had gone to Eton and Harrow, the two most prestigious institutions. A good many more MPs had attended Rugby, Shrewsbury, Winchester, Westminster, and Charterhouse, which was Cartland's alma mater. Many had gone on to university at Oxford or Cambridge.

This public-school old boy network—small, tight-knit, and insular—dominated British government and society as it had for generations. Its members lived in the same London neighborhoods, belonged to the same clubs, went to the same parties, spoke with the same Oxbridge accent, used the same slang, married one another's sisters, had affairs with one another's wives.

Virginia Cowles, the young Bostonian who had become a reporter in London, had been welcomed into the capital's leading social and political circles and was a frequent guest at their dinner and house parties. "What surprised me most about these gatherings was that everyone seemed to have known everyone else since childhood," she later wrote. "When they argued it was like a huge family wrangling among itself, each delighted to score at the other's expense, yet underneath bound by a strong bond of loyalty."

Loyalty was indeed the watchword in these circles, as was conformity. To fit in at Eton or Harrow or Charterhouse, one *had* to conform, *had* to abide by the customs and traditions of the public schools, handed down from the time when they were the exclusive province of the aristocracy and landed gentry. By the late nineteenth century the schools had begun to open their doors to sons of the rising professional and business classes, who, once inside the gates, had their rough edges quickly smoothed away. Middle-class boys learned to comply with patrician standards of gentlemanly behavior. They realized, as Noel Annan, a onetime Cambridge don, remarked, that "it was easier to be accepted if you adopted [upper-class] manners, dressed like them, spoke with their accent, and learnt their language and jokes." Above all, they learned the importance of abiding by what was considered the correct social code—what was "done" and "not done," "proper" and "not proper," "right" and "not right."

For any new boy, regardless of his background, there was a baffling set of rules and restrictions to master, "as unrelated to the modern world," in the words of one observer, "as the taboos of primitive man." Most of them were aimed at teaching the newcomer his lowly place in the school's pecking order. Depending on the school, junior boys were variously and arbitrarily forbidden to walk more than two abreast out-of-doors, to carry umbrellas, to roll up their umbrellas outside, to wear their boaters or top hats at a rakish angle, or to enter houses at their school other than the one in which they lived. As fags (unofficial servants) for older students they were expected to run errands and do other chores, like shining shoes or even, in winter, warming up seats for older boys in the school's outdoor lavatory. For the most part, the rules were enforced by the schools' senior students, who were in charge of monitoring their juniors' behavior. The ostensible reason for having students act as disciplinarians was to teach older boys the responsibilities of leadership. But since all this occurred when boys were at "their Lord of the Flies age," as one Eton alumnus put it, there was widespread abuse. At most schools, beatings by fellow students were a common punishment for breaking the myriad unwritten and obscure regulations.

Not surprisingly, new boys quickly realized how important it was to defer to authority, all the while waiting for the day when they would become senior boys and could do unto others what had been done unto them. The most important lessons a public-school boy learned, then, were to obey and to be part of the group. The emphasis on team sports at these schools, designed to "build character," underlined the importance attached to group harmony and cooperation. The boys who generally had the most status and prestige, the ones who were admired and looked up to, tended to be the star cricketers, rugby players, and footballers. Students who did not conform to the ideal often had a very difficult time. Boys who were shy, intellectual, inquisitive, rebellious, uninterested in sports, or otherwise different found themselves ignored, scorned, even shunned.

The idea that a boy should learn to think for himself, to question and criticize the tenets of his society, was a concept foreign to most British public schools at the time. As the historian Rupert Wilkinson has pointed out, their curricula, which emphasized Latin, Greek, and other rote subjects, "might do something for memory and logical thinking but it did little to awaken the imagination." Students who went on to Oxford and Cambridge found a much more invigorating intellectual freedom there, an opportunity, if they were so inclined, to stretch and challenge their minds. But there was the same dedication to tradition and gentlemanly standards, the same emphasis on loyalty to institutions as at their public schools. That reverence for tradition and adherence to loyalty would stay with most of them for the rest of their lives.

When some became members of Parliament years later, the pressures to defer to authority and to conform were much like the old days at Eton and Harrow. Most former public-school boys obediently yielded. It was clear that in the House of Commons, just as at school, new boys were to mind their manners, obey their superiors, and loyally advance the cause of their party if they wanted to get ahead. Undisguised ambition, open criticism, and rebellion were considered "bad form" and "not playing the game" and were dealt with appropriately. According to Jack Macnamara, a young Irishman who had served in the British army in India before coming to Parliament, most senior MPs agreed on "one matter—the suppression, completely and absolutely, of the new arrivals, who should be prepared to fag and agree, but who must never, never, in any circumstances, open their mouths, not for months and months and months."

Just as junior boys were dominated by their schools' senior students, so newcomers in Parliament were kept in line by their party's whips, MPs whose job it was to make sure their members voted the party line. The chief Tory whip and his assistants, whose party controlled the government throughout the 1930s, wielded far more power, however, than did their Labour and Liberal counterparts. They were the prime dispensers of political patronage, handing out "every amenity which makes life at Westminster tolerable," as one later Tory MP put it. Such amenities included junior ministerships, knighthoods, inclusion in parliamentary trips to exotic foreign countries, even invitations to the annual garden party at Buckingham Palace. "It is not necessary for the Whip to be so crude as to say: 'If you oppose the party policy, you need not hope for that under secretaryship, bang go your chances of a knighthood, you cannot expect to be included on any of our delegations abroad, or to serve on the committee on that subject in which you are especially interested,'" the Tory MP added. "But everyone knows that that threat is there, and it is effective." Backbenchers who defied the whips, like Cartland, Macnamara, and the other anti-appeasement Tories, did so with the sure knowledge they were endangering their political futures.

All MPs understood of course that loyalty to one's party was, and always has been, an essential prerequisite in British politics. A candidate for Parliament needs the endorsement and support of his party's local machine to be adopted, or nominated; when an election is held, voters tend to cast their ballots for the party, not the individual. And once elected, MPs who are members of the party in power must show unity in supporting the prime minister's policies to ensure, among other things, that the government does not fall.

Yet many Tory MPs in the 1930s believed that the government whips' office, under David Margesson, had carried the demand for party subservience to tyrannical extremes. "A veritable-cat-of-nine-tails," Jack Macnamara sardonically called the chief Tory whip and his deputies. Regarded as a bully and martinet by MPs who ran afoul of him, Margesson was the son of a baronet and the grandson of the Earl of Buckinghamshire. He was educated at Harrow, where he was known for his prowess at games and dislike of academics, and at Cambridge, which he left before getting a degree. Although Margesson came from an aristocratic background, his family had little money, and after Cambridge he went to the United States, where he held a variety of temporary jobs, including a short stint as a clerk at Marshall Fields department store in Chicago. When war broke out in 1914, he fought in France with the Eleventh Hussars, eventually winning the Military Cross. Elected to the House of Commons in 1922, he joined the whips' office four years later and became chief whip in 1931.

During the war Margesson had married Frances Leggett, a young American heiress who had spent much of her girlhood with his family. His wife's considerable wealth enabled Margesson to become a full-time politician, without having to worry about making a living. The marriage, however, was unhappy: she was intellectual and artistic, while he, in his wife's words, "despised culture" and was totally absorbed in politics and, in his rare free time, by fox hunting. After three children, the couple separated in 1930.

With his marriage at an end, Margesson, always a workaholic, threw himself into his parliamentary job. He once told Prime Minister Stanley Baldwin that he regarded the whips' office as his second home. "He adored the House of Commons from the first," recalled his daughter, "and was passionately interested in everything that went on there. Politics were the ruling interest of his life . . ." Often working more than twelve hours a day, Margesson ran the whips' office like the unbending army officer he once had been, keeping the troops in line for Ramsay MacDonald, Baldwin, and Neville Chamberlain, the three prime ministers he served in the 1930s. No one questioned his ability. Indeed, Lloyd George, whose tenure in Parliament spanned more than fifty years, called him the most skillful and efficient chief whip in his lifetime. Margesson's effectiveness, his daughter speculated, might have been due to his "limitations as well as his gifts. If he had had more intellectual curiosity, he might sometimes have had more doubts. As it was, he never doubted the rightness of his Party."

A popular figure in London social circles, Margesson was charming and considerate when off duty. But in the Commons he demonstrated an icy ruthlessness in bending Tory MPs to his and the government's will. "You were either for the Government or against; there was no halfway house with him," a fellow whip remarked. In the early 1930s Patrick Donner, a young Conservative MP, was summoned to Margesson's office after daring to vote against a government bill. Donner stood in front of the chief whip's desk for more than a minute, while Margesson, immaculately dressed as usual in black morning coat and black-and-white checked trousers, ignored him and continued writing. Finally Donner said, "If you are busy, I'll come back at some more convenient time." Margesson looked up. "What the hell do you mean by voting against the Government last night?" he demanded. Taken aback, Donner retorted: "What the hell do you mean by speaking to me as if I were a flunky?" As a result of this bit of impulsive effrontery, the young MP was put in parliamentary purdah. Margesson refused to speak to him for several years, and his chances for political advancement were over.

For men brought up to prize loyalty and collegiality as supreme virtues, it took great strength of will to defy their political superiors like that, especially when such defiance meant not only the loss of future political prizes but treatment as a pariah by one's colleagues. Margesson, who was addressed as Chief by his subordinates, "applies to the House of Commons Old School Tie Brigade the methods of a public school," a political commentator once wrote.

> If one of the "boys" has erred, or strayed into the wrong lobby, the rest of them will quickly be notified that the fellow is a bit of an outsider. And the friends of outsiders, in the public school code, are of course to be regarded as outsiders themselves. If the cad still won't play the game, well, he must be put in Coventry. The other chaps shun and spurn him, and shut up talking when he enters the room. It is a remarkable reflection on the frailty of humanity that even a grown man can rarely "take it."

Such ostracism was particularly wounding in an institution that considered itself the best club in town and put heavy emphasis on camaraderie and companionship. Josiah Wedgwood, scion of the famed pottery family and an anti-appeasement Labour MP, was often at odds with colleagues in both major parties, yet he loved the "extremely strong brotherhood" of the Commons, which he claimed did not exist in the U.S. House of Representatives or any other national legislature. Most MPs had no parliamentary offices of their own, so they "work (or gossip) like one family, or one club, in the writing, smoking or dining rooms," Wedgwood observed. In the U.S. House, where every member had his own suite of offices, "there is no 'family life,' nothing to discuss in common. It is not social, it is not the life of ideas, it is a business."

It stands to reason, then, that with all this togetherness in the House, peer pressure has always been one of the most potent safeguards against rebellion. Christopher Hollis, an editor of *Punch* who served as a Tory MP in the 1950s, noted years after Margesson's reign: "Nothing is more unpleasant than to sit side by side day after day with people who think that you are behaving like a traitor."

Ronald Cartland loved the camaraderie of the House, but playing the game was something that he simply could not bring himself to do. "He disdained altogether those arts by which the ambitious young politician (and Ronald was ambitious) can gain, if he wishes, the patronage of his elders," noted Richard Law, an anti-appeasement Tory who was the son of a former prime minister, Andrew Bonar Law, and one of Cartland's closest friends.

Cartland's interest in politics was sparked by his father, Bertram Cartland, the only son of a wealthy Birmingham financier. Four years before Ronald was born, his paternal grandfather went bankrupt and committed suicide. With no inheritance to count on to maintain their affluent country lifestyle, Ronald's parents were forced to give up their house, horses, gardeners, and grooms and move to a small rented farmhouse near the town of Pershore, in Worcestershire. There Bertram Cartland went to work as an organizer for the Conservative Party. In the 1910 general election he managed the parliamentary campaign of the local Tory candidate, and when his candidate was elected, Cartland became the new MP's secretary in Westminster. Encouraged by his wife, Mary, Cartland developed political ambitions of his own: he planned to stand for Parliament at the next election. But when war began in 1914, he volunteered and was sent to France, where he rose eventually to the rank of colonel. He was killed in 1918, less than five months before the armistice, in the trenches near Berry-au-Bac. Ronald, who was eleven years old when his father died, took seriously his mother's admonition: "I want you to start where your father left off."

In 1919, Mary Cartland moved her children—Ronald, eighteen-year-old Barbara, and eight-year-old Anthony—to London. The night they arrived, Barbara and Ronald went for a walk in their new South Kensington neighborhood. Enthralled with the excitement and bustle of the capital, Barbara exclaimed: "I shall get to know everybody—everybody in London." She asked her brother what he most wanted to do there. Twelve-year-old Ronald didn't hesitate. "I shall be prime minister," he said.

Wasting no time in achieving *her* goal, Barbara became one of the leading Bright Young Things of 1920s' London. At the age of twenty-three, the slender, green-eyed blonde published her first novel, *Jigsaw*, billed as "Mayfair with the lid off." The story of a young woman who falls in love with a handsome young peer after flirting with the frantic hedonism of London's smart society, *Jigsaw* was an immediate best seller, the first of more than seven hundred books that Barbara Cartland was to write in her exceedingly long and successful career as a romance novelist.

She also became a journalist of sorts, contributing regular gossip items to the *Daily Express*, owned by Lord Beaverbrook. Fond of beautiful young women, the press baron, one of the most powerful and controversial men in England, soon included Barbara in his eclectic social circle. She was invited to small dinner parties at his country house, where the guests included longtime cronies like Winston Churchill and Lord Birkenhead. "I used to listen to their stories and ask for more," she later said. "They all made a great fuss of me. I think they regarded me as something of a mascot." Churchill, she recalled, was the most loquacious. "He would begin to tell a story when the others would interrupt: 'We've heard that one before, Winston.' 'Well, Barbara hasn't,' he would answer—and continued to the end."

Ronald meanwhile was enrolled as a scholarship student at Charterhouse, where he already was voicing progressive views that seemed at odds with his ambitions as a would-be Conservative MP. As a small boy he had accompanied his mother when she did volunteer social work in the slums of Pershore. He had been deeply affected by the extreme poverty he saw there: the small, crumbling houses with rain dripping through the ceilings, the emaciated children in rags, the haggard women with despairing faces. At the age of seventeen he wrote to his mother from school of his belief that all workers should be guaranteed a decent living wage. He had been talking to laborers working on a nearby road, he said, and they "have almost convinced me that Socialism is the right policy." Ronald's progressivism was a bit worrisome to the higher-ups at Charterhouse. "If [Ronald] can curb his revolutionary tendencies," the master of his house told Mary Cartland, "I expect him to do well as head of the House next quarter."

Despite his "revolutionary tendencies," Cartland was popular with his fellow students, and he did do well, but not at the expense of tempering his beliefs. When he became head of his house, he eased some of the rules and restrictions that made the lives of the junior boys such misery. When millions of British workers staged a general strike in 1926 to support the nation's coal miners in their bitter wage dispute with mine owners, Ronald defended the miners' cause in an emotional discussion with his sister. Did she have any idea of the horrific and highly dangerous conditions under which the miners worked? To descend half a mile underground into the blackness and fumes of a coal pit was like going down into the depths of hell. For doing that seven hours every day, crouched in a cramped tunnel and inhaling fumes and coal dust, miners were paid wages that barely kept them and their families from starvation. And now the owners were demanding longer hours for less pay. Couldn't she see how wrong that was?

Barbara Cartland frankly admitted she had never given much thought to such things. Most people in her social set, dancing the nights away in the chic nightclubs of Mayfair, knew—and cared—nothing about the vast poverty and widespread unemployment that existed in industrial areas outside London—or, for that matter, in the capital's East End. As Benjamin Disraeli wrote in his novel *Sybil*, the affluent and the poor of Britain were divided by a chasm so wide that they were "two nations: between whom there is no intercourse and no sympathy, who are ignorant of each other's habits, thoughts and feelings, as if they were dwellers in different zones, or inhabitants of different planets . . ."

In spite of his passion for social justice, Cartland remained true to the Tory values that his family had embraced for generations: a staunch belief in the primacy of individual freedom and the preservation of private property and enterprise. He rejected the socialism espoused by the Labour Party: creation of full employment through public works and the eventual nationalization of industries, including railways, coal mines, and electric power. "Socialism would destroy the individual for the state," he once wrote. "Conservatism stands for . . . the continual growth of the individual, which must inevitably lead to a growth of the state. The prestige and prosperity of the one is bound up in the prestige and popularity of the other."

Cartland's mother didn't have the money to send him to Oxford or Cambridge, so after leaving Charterhouse, he went to work for the Conservative Party's Central Office in London. He wanted to stand for Parliament in 1935, but he had no money of his own to finance a campaign and was determined not to accept money from the Central Office. "I must be independent," he told his sister. "I could never be a party hack . . . with my hands tied." In the end his shoestring campaign in King's Norton was largely financed by the royalties from Barbara's novels. He was elected in the Conservative landslide that brought Stanley Baldwin to power again as prime minister, with the Tories winning 432 seats, compared with Labour's 154. The Liberal Party, which had dominated British politics in the late nineteenth century and whose leaders had included William Gladstone, H. H. Asquith, and David Lloyd George, was a pitiful shadow of its former self. Weakened by bitter internal conflicts since the turn of the century, it had secured only 21 seats.

When he entered Parliament, the twenty-eight-year-old Cartland was one of the youngest members of the Commons, and his boyish looks only accentuated his youth. He usually took a seat on the second government bench below the gangway, an area normally occupied, as

Dick Law recalled, "by the older, the sterner, and the less compromising sections of the Tory Party." The contrast between the other MPs and "Ronald, slender, elegant and boyish . . . was both comical and alarming."

During his first days in the Commons, Cartland wrote his mother: "Most of the House seem *old*! No one looks as young as I, but I shall get over that . . . I shall go slow for a bit." His resolution lasted only a few months. The first violation came when he flouted the unwritten rule that a new MP's maiden speech should limit itself to paying tribute to his predecessor, praising his constituency, and avoiding controversy at all costs. If a new member is "good and very demure," wrote the ever-cynical Jack Macnamara, the whips will "arrange that you may modestly make a few remarks . . . and, provided you spend most of those fleeting moments apologising to them for interrupting at all, they will graciously pat you on the back, after which you should return home, bursting with pride, content never to be so forward again."

Cartland's first address to the House in May 1936 was hardly in that forelock-tugging mode. It consisted of a sharp attack on the Baldwin government for its lackadaisical attitude in aiding what the government euphemistically called distressed areas, those parts of the country suffering from desperate economic depression, with unemployment rates exceeding 30 and 40 percent. Addressing the House later in the debate, Harold Macmillan, then forty-one, congratulated Cartland for his speech, noting that its spirit reminded him of the enthusiasm with which he and other young progressive Tories had made similar speeches when they first came to Parliament twelve years earlier. "I am afraid that we have made little headway," Macmillan said. He cautioned Cartland that it might be better for his political future if he curbed his courage and zeal for reform—so long as the "present control of our administration remains in hands similar to those which have controlled it in the last forty years."

Ronald Cartland was notably different from most MPs—and not just because of his outspokenness. Unlike many of his Tory colleagues, he did not come from a wellborn family, nor did he have money. A devout Anglo-Catholic, he was relatively abstemious in a place that boasted more than its share of heavy drinkers. (The Houses of Parliament were exempt from the usual restrictions on liquor sales, and alcohol was liberally consumed day and night in the Commons smoking room, as well as in other parliamentary haunts.) He did not belong to clubs—he didn't have the money to join or keep up a membership—and he disliked large parties and much of the rest of the socializing that went with being an MP. He preferred to spend his rare free time reading in his tiny flat on Petty France Street near Parliament.

Yet Cartland was hardly a loner. He enjoyed the fellowship of the House and had a large circle of friends, many of them fellow MPs. A good mimic, whose impersonations of the latest social and political celebrities were uncannily precise, Cartland was known for his charm, wit, and sense of fun. He was not conventionally handsome—his features were too sharp and his ears too big—but the magnetism of his personality was such that some people argued otherwise. Many who knew him talked about his vitality and joie de vivre. "I was always happiest when I was with him, and so, I know, were a great many of his friends," said James P. L. Thomas, a tall, convivial Welshman who was part of Cartland's parliamentary circle. His sister recalled: "No one could be indifferent to Ronald. When he joined a party, the whole tempo was accelerated, voices and spirits rose because he was there." In his diary Harold Nicolson wrote of Cartland: "When he leaves a party, it is as if the lights had grown dimmer."

The well-dressed bachelor, his black hair brushed sleekly back, was also extremely popular with the young people in his constituency, especially young women. He was regarded as "a knight in shining armour, genuinely involved in the welfare of his constituents," recalled the writer Elizabeth Longford, who in 1936 was chosen by the Labour Party to run against Cartland in the next general election.* "Every girl who did not actually belong to the Labour or Liberal parties was in love with him—and even a few who did belong to the opposition." Some constituents affectionately referred to him as Ronald Colman, a nickname (and comparison to the movie star) he hated.

---

*Longford never got the chance to run. When the war began in 1939, the government and Parliament agreed to forgo elections for the duration.

From the beginning of his parliamentary career, Cartland was seen as a possible future leader of the country. Over the next four years a number of journalists predicted that he might even attain the goal he had mentioned to his sister on that long-ago day in South Kensington. "Cartland is ambitious," wrote a *Sunday Express* correspondent in May 1936. "I should not be surprised if he hopes to be Premier himself one day. He has got a better chance than many of the other young aspirants I know . . . I think he is a first-rate Member of the House of Commons."

But to achieve high office, he was frequently warned, he would have to learn to play the game, to accept and obey the dictates of his party and prime minister. "I can't tell you the number of people who say—'You won't get on if you attack the Government like that, and so on'—as though one doesn't feel one's cause," he wrote his mother. In any event, he paid no attention to the warnings. Throughout the late 1930s he never let up in his criticism of the Baldwin and Chamberlain governments for not doing enough to help Britain's underclass. "Ronald approached life in the spirit of a continuous crusade," wrote the Tory MP Duncan Sandys, who was Winston Churchill's son-in-law. "Wherever he saw oppression, injustice or incompetence, he attacked it. What is more, he enjoyed every minute of the fight, in which he neither gave nor expected quarter." As Sandys observed, Cartland actually seemed to relish his ongoing duel with David Margesson and his deputies. Once comparing the chief whip with a character lusting for vengeance in Dickens's *A Tale of Two Cities*, Cartland dryly described Margesson as "taking on the role of [Madame] Defarge, counting heads."

In November 1936 the young renegade first earned the animosity of Neville Chamberlain, then Baldwin's chancellor of the exchequer, when he delivered a stinging assault on the Treasury for balancing the budget at the expense of the nation's poor: "If you are going to do something, you have got to spend money. If you are going to do nothing, I beg the Government to say so with complete and appalling frankness." One newspaper declared after the speech: "Mr. Cartland has burned his boats." Not for the first time, he was summoned to Margesson's office and warned that rebels were not tolerated in the Conservative Party. Soon afterward a by-election was held in a Birmingham constituency, and

Cartland was the only Tory MP from Birmingham not asked to speak for the Conservative candidate. A Birmingham newspaper speculated that the snub might foreshadow the withdrawal of official party support for Cartland at the next general election.

His growing unpopularity with the whips and the rest of the Conservative Party hierarchy was also the result of his stand on the other great issue of the 1930s, the British government's policy of placating Hitler and Mussolini. Cartland was as vehemently opposed to appeasement as he was to the government's failure to implement social reform. In August 1935, shortly before he was elected to Parliament, he and his sister visited Germany, where he was outraged by the Nazis' persecution of the Jews. Returning to Britain, he warned that Hitler was preparing to march on Austria and other Central European countries, and that sooner or later, Germany would go to war against Britain. His warnings, like those of other anti-appeasement MPs, were met with disbelief and ridicule, and he was labeled an alarmist and warmonger.

In Parliament, Cartland pushed hard for universal conscription and attacked the conciliation of Hitler, first by Baldwin and then by Chamberlain. In a letter to his constituents, he wrote that he intended to "follow his conscience" wherever it might lead him. "We must make it plain that though we hate war, we shall fight with all our strength to preserve our freedom; we must never in any way compromise our belief in democratic principles."

Although he was far more willing than most in his party to brave the whips' wrath, Cartland was not alone on the Tory benches in his fights for social justice and against appeasement. There was a core of about twenty to thirty left-leaning Tories, most of them under forty-five, who also had revolted against many of the government's economic and foreign policies. Like Cartland, a number of them had been rebelling against the strictures of their clannish upper-crust society since their public-school days. Dick Law, for example, boasted impeccable establishment credentials as the son of a Tory prime minister and an alumnus of Shrewsbury and Oxford. Yet for several years after Oxford, Law, who was described by a fellow MP as "an independent character with inconvenient ideas," worked as a newspaper reporter in the United States, including stints at the *New York Herald Tribune* and *Philadelphia Daily*

Ledger, hardly the kind of job that most affluent, well-educated young Britons sought in the 1920s. "It seems to me that there is an unbridgeable gulf between the young Members and the old die-hard Tories," Cartland wrote his sister. "The 'left' Conservatives are immeasurably nearer to the 'right' Socialists [Labour members] than they could ever be to the older Members of their own party."

Of all the progressive Tories, few were more radical in their views— or more outspoken in expressing them—than two of the MPs who had huddled with Cartland in the House lobby on August 2, 1939: Harold Macmillan and his once-close friend Robert Boothby.

CHAPTER THREE

"TROUBLESOME YOUNG MEN"

It was an odd pairing: Harold Macmillan, the inhibited, repressed publisher's son, and Bob Boothby, the warm, witty progeny of an affluent Edinburgh banker. Both had been elected to Parliament in 1924 and not long afterward joined forces in what was regarded by most of their colleagues as a quixotic battle against the government's laissez-faire social, economic, and foreign policies.

On the surface, Macmillan seemed much more suited to the life of an Oxford don than to the hurly-burly of parliamentary politics. He was bookish and shy and, by all accounts, including his own, a terrible public speaker. Even some of the Tory colleagues who agreed with his progressive views found him to be, in the words of one, "a tiresome fellow." To the journalists who covered Parliament, Macmillan was "a bit of a bore."

Yet by the late 1930s this partner in one of England's most distinguished publishing houses had become known for his increasingly vocal denunciations of appeasement and for his crusade, reminiscent of Franklin Roosevelt's New Deal, to implement radical new economic programs in Britain. "Mr. Harold," declared the old nanny who had helped raise him, "is a dangerous pink."

There was little in his background to foreshadow such a contentious future. He had grown up in the exclusive Belgravia section of London—a lonely, sensitive, anxious little boy who lived in constant terror of making a mistake or doing something wrong. "I always felt that, on the whole, the world was something alarming, and that people of all ages would be more likely to be troublesome than agreeable," he recalled. As a child he preferred to retreat to a corner and read a book; he noted years later that "I learnt books before I learnt people."

His father, Maurice, was a senior partner at Macmillan & Co., the far-flung publishing empire that Maurice's father and uncle had founded in 1843. By the time Harold came of age, Macmillan's was already an institution in the book world, with branches in the United States, Canada, India, and Australia and a stable of authors that included Lewis Carroll, Alfred Lord Tennyson, Rudyard Kipling, Thomas Hardy, Henry James, and H. G. Wells. Maurice Macmillan, a quiet and withdrawn man, had little to do with his youngest son's upbringing. He spent most of his time at his publishing house or his club, perhaps, as Harold Macmillan's biographer Alistair Horne speculates, "to escape from a domineering wife." Harold remembered his mother, Nellie, as austere and puritanical, a forceful disciplinarian with "no sympathy for the conventional feelings of English boys." There was not much fun or laughter in the Macmillan household for Harold and his two older brothers.

Nellie Macmillan, an American from Indiana, was ambitious for her sons, particularly for Harold. He had decidedly mixed feelings about her. He owed everything in his life to her "devotion and support," he once said, but he added that "if you failed at something, you felt you'd rather let her down." He remarked to a friend many years after his mother's death: "I admired her, but never really liked her . . . She dominated me, and she still dominates me."

In 1906, at the age of twelve, Harold entered Eton. Not surprisingly, this introverted child who lost himself in books and was no good at games hated the school and its hearty atmosphere. It wasn't until he arrived at Oxford that he finally came into his own. There, at Balliol College, he could indulge at last his love of learning. To Macmillan, Oxford meant freedom, an escape from "a home where discipline was severe and a mother's love almost too restraining."

When war broke out in the summer of 1914, Macmillan was commissioned a second lieutenant in the King's Royal Rifle Corps, but his mother pulled strings and arranged his transfer to the much more prestigious Grenadier Guards, many of whose officers were aristocrats. The Guards were regarded as "spoilt darlings" by other line regiments, recalled one nonguardsman. Spoiled they might have been, but they were not spared in the bloodbath in France, suffering some twelve thousand casualties before the war was over. Macmillan himself was in the thick of the slaughter for more than a year and was wounded four times. During the battle of Loos, in September 1915, which cost the British almost sixty thousand men, he was shot glancingly in the head and, more seriously, through the right hand, an injury that gave him trouble for the rest of his life. Less than a year later, at Ypres, he was wounded in the face by a grenade. Refusing medical evacuation, he moved with his battalion in July 1916 to Beaumont-Hamel, near the Somme River.

On September 15, at the height of the "wanton, pointless carnage" known as the battle of the Somme, Macmillan's battalion was ordered to attack a German machine-gun stronghold near the town of Ginchy. Advancing through heavy smoke, Macmillan and his platoon were rushing a German trench when he was hit in his left thigh and pelvis by shrapnel and machine-gun fire. He shouted to his sergeant to leave him and continue the attack. Throughout his life Macmillan carried a book with him wherever he went, even on the battlefield. This day was no different. While the battle raged around him, he lay in a muddy shell hole and read Aeschylus's *Prometheus* off and on to distract himself from the pain. Whenever German soldiers came near, he pretended to be dead.

Late in the afternoon he was rescued by fellow Guards and taken to an aid station and then to a hospital in Abbeville. By then his wounds were infected, and he was eventually sent back to London, where he underwent several operations and remained hospitalized until shortly before the armistice. Macmillan suffered lifelong pain from his various injuries, which left him with a limp right hand and a shuffling walk. Both difficulties later made him the butt of jokes, told by people unaware of the origins of the disabilities.

For the rest of his life he remained haunted by the war. Most of his closest friends had died in France, and for several years he refused to return to Oxford because to him, it was "a city of the dead. Almost every-body I knew there seemed to have been killed." Like other veterans who later entered politics, he felt guilt about having survived, as well as "an obligation to make some decent use of the life that had been spared to [me]" and "to do something for our country." Also like other veterans, he had great contempt for those "gentlemen of England now abed" who had not seen combat.

As it happened, most of the MPs who opposed appeasement in the 1930s, including Churchill, had fought in the war. (The exceptions, like Ronald Cartland, Bob Boothby, and Dick Law, had been too young.) By contrast, most of the government ministers responsible for ap-peasement had never been in the trenches. The veterans were fervent in their desire for peace; they were "dedicated," in the words of the journalist Colin Coote, "to preserving any future generation from the decimation which had shattered their own." But if it was necessary to prepare for war in order to maintain that peace, they were ready to do so, unlike many advocates of appeasement. This vast gulf in experience and understanding would play a significant role in the parliamentary battle to come.

After the armistice Macmillan, still struggling to come to grips with his wartime experiences, decided to remain in the Guards for another year before settling down to work in the family business. In March 1919 his mother came to the rescue again and helped arrange his appoint-ment as an aide-de-camp to the British governor-general of Canada, Victor Cavendish, the Duke of Devonshire. Macmillan was twenty-five years old, a serious, socially awkward young man who still found it dif-ficult to relate easily to people, especially to women, whom he tended to regard "as if they were a strange, undescribed new species." In Ot-tawa, however, for the first and only time in his life he fell deeply in love. The object of his affection was the duke's daughter Dorothy, an attractive, outgoing nineteen-year-old with a sparkling sense of humor and "extraordinary zest for life" and none of the pretensions and snob-bery so typical of the British upper classes. Wherever Lady Dorothy Cavendish was, "you knew there was going to be fun," a family friend said later. "She lit up the room." Macmillan courted Lady Dorothy with great intensity, but it took her several months to make up her mind

whether to marry him. In late December she finally said yes. The ecstatic Macmillan wrote his mother: "I love her so much I can hardly
know what to do or say or think."

Some people who knew both Harold and Dorothy were mystified
by the match. What did she see in this shy, cerebral, somewhat pedantic
captain, with his bushy, unkempt mustache, snaggle-toothed smile,
and stilted manners and walk? True, as a result of the war, there was a
shortage of eligible men, a serious problem for young British women
brought up to believe that marriage was their only future. Barbara Cartland, who was a year younger than Lady Dorothy, later noted: "A million men who had been in the right age group to be potential husbands
had been killed, and we learned with feelings of anxiety that in consequence, there were two million surplus women." But as the daughter of
a duke who also happened to be one of the wealthiest men in Britain,
Dorothy presumably would have had no trouble finding a husband. Indeed, her mother reportedly wanted her to marry the future Duke of
Buccleuch.

Then there was the speculation that Dorothy was marrying Macmillan to "escape the problems of home, a very tough mother . . ." If
anything, the Duchess of Devonshire was even more domineering than
Macmillan's mother. Described by her brother-in-law as "an unpleasant woman, accustomed to authority," Evelyn Cavendish was stingy with
money, affection, and civility. "She wouldn't speak to you unless she
wanted something, and I can't say she ever thanked you either," a longtime Cavendish servant said.

Perhaps, however, Dorothy accepted Macmillan's proposal because
she actually was in love with this young war hero, who, for all his inhi-
bitions and gaucheness, was courtly, sensitive, compassionate, and intelligent. "Uncle Harold, quoting Plato and so on, must have been
frightfully impressive," said a niece of the Macmillans'. "Probably Aunt
Dorothy was very impressed by [his] being so educated . . ." Whatever
the reasons for the match, it delighted her father. As unpretentious and
warm as his daughter, the duke was very fond of Macmillan, who quickly
became his favorite son-in-law. The duchess, however, was horrified.
Macmillan may have been a future partner of Macmillan & Co., he
may have been wealthy himself, but according to the vagaries of the

British class system, he and his family were "in trade" and therefore considered much inferior socially to the Cavendishes. But then, almost *everyone* in Britain was considered inferior to the Cavendishes, who stood at the very top of Britain's aristocratic hierarchy.

Thought to be richer than the royal family, the Duke of Devonshire and his family lived in semifeudal splendor, traveling in private trains to and from their enormous estates throughout the country. Their London mansion, Devonshire House, across the street from the Ritz Hotel in Piccadilly, featured vast gardens and two tennis courts. But the grandest of the Devonshire properties was Chatsworth, their seventeenth-century estate in the wooded hills of Derbyshire, with its 297 rooms; one hundred acres of gardens; hordes of footmen, maids, and grooms; Rembrandts, Rubenses, Van Dycks, and Gainsboroughs on the walls; and its own historian and library.

This, then, was the world that Macmillan entered when, in April 1920, he married Lady Dorothy Cavendish at St. Margaret's in Westminster, the church of choice for fashionable London weddings. It was a world to which he quickly grew attached. Of the many complexities in Macmillan's character, one of the most notable, as a longtime parliamentary colleague observed, was his "soft heart for—and the strong determination to help—the underdog, and the social habit to associate happily with the overdog."

Macmillan particularly enjoyed the weekends he spent shooting grouse on the moors of Bolton Abbey, the thirty-thousand-acre Devonshire estate in the Yorkshire Dales. After a morning of shooting, he and the other male guests would join the ladies at a cottage on the moors for a picnic luncheon, served on Devonshire china by footmen in the family's lemon yellow and dark blue livery. At Christmas, Macmillan, Lady Dorothy, and their children traveled to Chatsworth for a Devonshire family gathering that was, in his words, "almost as remote from present-day England as descriptions of Count Rostov's family in *War and Peace*." Each family arrived with its nannies, valets, nursery and ladies' maids, grooms, and chauffeurs. The duchess demanded strict adherence to the etiquette of Devonshire hierarchy. Children, for example, were served at meals in the order of their parents' ranking in the family; the offspring of Dorothy's eldest brother, Edward, the heir to the dukedom, always were fed first.

Macmillan's pleasure in joining this great ducal family was somewhat diminished, however, by the cool reception he received from a
good many of its members. While the duke continued to be cordial
toward Macmillan, most of Dorothy's six siblings and their spouses,
particularly his brother-in-law James Stuart, treated him with cool disdain. The good-looking, arrogant Stuart, son of a Scottish earl, was highly
placed in royal circles and was David Margesson's deputy in the Tory
whips' office. A languid man who talked out of the side of his mouth,
Stuart made considerable fun of Macmillan's efforts to please.

The Cavendish family as a whole mocked his serious demeanor.
They were bored by his intellectualism, and the women of the family
vied with one another not to sit next to him at dinner. "He gave the impression of being very pompous, so he needed pin-pricking all the
time," said Deborah Devonshire, one of the famed Mitford sisters, who
married Dorothy's nephew Andrew (later to become Duke of Devonshire himself). Having grown up in what he called "a simple, perhaps
narrow . . . world," where "we didn't see many people," Macmillan, for
all his enjoyment of the aristocratic lifestyle, never seemed to know the
right thing to say or do. He seemed "a rather sad figure—rather isolated
in these circles," recalled a friend who observed him at a family gathering at Chatsworth. Many years later, long after Macmillan had
served as prime minister, members of his wife's family continued to
dwell on the vast class difference between him and them. "Whereas
Uncle Harold would like to have been Trollope, he was Galsworthy,"
Andrew Devonshire remarked to one interviewer. "Trollope's political
novels were about the Duke of Omnium and the great aristocratic
grandees, whereas Galsworthy's novels are essentially about upper-
class businessmen."

Yet the snobbery that Macmillan encountered from his in-laws was
a small price to pay for the political advantages he enjoyed because of
them. He was related by marriage to at least sixteen Tory MPs, including Robert "Bobbety" Cranborne, the future Lord Salisbury and a leading member of the Cecil family. Like the Cavendishes, the Cecils had
been major players in national affairs since the sixteenth century, when
William Cecil, Lord Burghley, served as Queen Elizabeth I's most influential adviser.

Partly because of his Cavendish connections, Macmillan, who had been politically ambitious since boyhood, was given the chance in 1924 to stand for election to Parliament. His prospective constituency was the shipbuilding town of Stockton-on-Tees, a place as far removed from the world of Chatsworth and Bolton Abbey as could be imagined. Located near the northeastern coast of England, Stockton had been a thriving boomtown during the Industrial Revolution, but like many centers of Britain's old staple industries (coal, iron and steel, textiles, and shipbuilding), it had fallen on very hard times by the early 1920s. Some of the shipyards had shut down and now were industrial graveyards, full of tumbledown sheds, crumbling warehouses, rusting cranes, and empty ships moored to decaying docks. Nearly 30 percent of Stockton's male population was unemployed. Men stood idly on street corners, their caps pulled down, shoulders hunched against the knifing wind, hands in their pockets, with nothing to do but, in the words of J. B. Priestley, "wait for Doomsday."

Macmillan was greatly affected by the economic devastation he witnessed in this once proud and prosperous community, devastation he likened to the ravaged landscape of France after the Great War. Like many other young middle- and upper-class British officers, he had emerged from the conflict with an interest in improving the lot of the men from working-class backgrounds who had fought under his and others' command. In Stockton he witnessed the empty, hopeless, poverty-stricken lives that so many former British Tommies were now leading. He made numerous campaign trips to the town and grew to care deeply about its people. In the beginning, however, he had immense trouble communicating that concern. A poor and halting speaker, he hated the give-and-take of politics, "the heckling and din and having to attack and defend and all the rest of it." His native sensitivity and humor were hidden behind a stiff, formal facade. Macmillan's "manner was all wrong," observed an acquaintance. "His forays were like those of a public-school missionary to the East End."

Fortunately, his woodenness was offset by the warmth and down-to-earth nature of his wife, who showed a genuine interest in the lives of the people of Stockton. She remembered their names and problems and talked to them as if they were old friends. "She was a wizard canvasser," remarked one of her relatives. "She had a very good political sense, and in elections, she was marvelous." Lady Dorothy often stood behind Macmillan when someone approached him on the hustings and whispered in his ear who the person was and what he did. "She was the greater part of his success here," a Stockton resident declared. Another remembered: "She was very much loved."

Macmillan promised Stockton's voters that his priority in Parliament would be to help better their lives and to ease the massive unemployment afflicting their town and others in the north. When they elected him in 1924, he tried to make good his pledge, only to find that the government of Stanley Baldwin did not share his priorities. Baldwin and the Conservatives had won an impressive victory over Ramsay MacDonald's Labour Party with the vow to give Britain "a period of tranquility and prosperity in which to recuperate from war and its aftermath." But the pledge of prosperity did not include government programs to put more people back to work or to improve the wretched lot of those with low-paying jobs.

In Macmillan's fight against the government's apathy, he cooperated with a handful of other young progressive Tories, several of whom also represented dying industrial towns in the north and midlands. Among them was a gregarious twenty-four-year-old Scot named Bob Boothby.

Also educated at Eton and Oxford, the stocky, handsome Boothby, with his infectious grin and mop of unruly black hair, had an enormous appetite for life. He drove a Bentley two-seater, was passionate about jazz and opera, loved to gamble, and boasted a huge circle of friends, including Noël Coward and Sir Thomas Beecham, the founder of the London Philharmonic Orchestra.

Only two years after leaving Oxford, Boothby was elected to Parliament. Widely regarded as one of the most promising of the new Conservative MPs, he had a rich, powerful voice and, in the words of one of his Oxford dons, "a natural gift for eloquence." After Boothby's maiden speech in March 1925, Winston Churchill, then chancellor of the exchequer, rose from the Treasury bench to congratulate him. A year later Churchill asked Boothby to become his parliamentary private secretary. The job of a PPS is to help his cabinet minister in the House of Commons. He sits behind the minister and provides him with information during debates. He also serves as a conduit to other MPs and keeps the minister informed of the mood of the House. Although an unofficial and unpaid position, a PPS job is a highly sought-after prize for young MPs, since it's considered the first rung on the ladder to cabinet office. Serving as PPS to the chancellor of the exchequer, one of the top posts in the government, is, and was, regarded as a particular plum.

When Boothby joined his parliamentary circle, Winston Churchill, then fifty-two, had been one of the most notable figures in Parliament since the turn of the century. During that time he had held every important post in the cabinet except foreign secretary and prime minister. Yet when Stanley Baldwin named him chancellor in 1924, everyone, including Churchill, was astonished. For although he was supremely talented and one of the most gifted orators in the Commons, he had never followed the unwritten rules of the parliamentary game. "A natural storm center," Virginia Cowles once called him. Party loyalty had never been, to put it mildly, Churchill's strong suit.

He had entered Parliament as a Conservative in 1901, then crossed the House floor three years later to join the Liberal Party over the question of free trade. After serving as home secretary, first lord of the admiralty, war secretary, and colonial secretary in various Liberal governments, he "re-ratted," as he himself put it, and went back to the Conservatives in 1924. Stalwarts of all three parties regarded Churchill with suspicion and distrust. His party-hopping was generally seen as rank opportunism, the consequence of his intense political ambitions, rather than as the result of a sincere shift in beliefs. "Winston was very unpopular," recalled Lady Violet Bonham Carter, the daughter of the former Liberal prime minister H. H. Asquith and a close friend of Churchill's. "The Liberals regarded him as an arriviste and a thruster—and the Conservatives as a deserter, a rat and a traitor to his class."

He also had a reputation for rashness and bad judgment, based in part on his involvement, while first lord of the admiralty, in the British attack on the Dardanelles Strait in 1915, which led to the catastrophic Gallipoli campaign. And he was considered by many to be a self-absorbed egotist who cared for nothing and no one but himself. A parliamentary colleague once complained of the way Churchill "walks in, makes his speech, walks out, and leaves the whole place as if God almighty had spoken . . . He never listens to any man's speech but his own." (The comment received loud cheers from both sides of the chamber.) Even Churchill's oratory, dazzling as it often was, had frequently gotten him into trouble. He had a predilection for sarcasm and invective, and fellow MPs who had been its targets neither forgave nor forgot.

Boothby, however, didn't see any of this as a problem. Like Churchill, he was a natural rebel, taking considerable pleasure in swimming against the tide. Besides, he relished the prestige of working alongside one of the most important men in the British government. He loved, for example, the pomp and ceremony of each year's Budget Day, when clad in top hat and morning coat he jauntily followed a similarly attired Churchill from 11 Downing Street, the chancellor's official residence, to the Houses of Parliament, while flashbulbs popped and people stared. In the Commons, Churchill outlined the government's new budget as a beaming Boothby looked on.

At the age of twenty-six, Boothby was a golden boy in British politics, even touted in some quarters as a future prime minister. As he remarked later, "All doors were open to me." He was invited everywhere, to summer house parties in Venice and Capri, to glittering London soirees thrown by society hostesses like Lady Londonderry and Emerald Cunard, to less formal gatherings staged by Lady Diana Cooper (said to be the most beautiful woman in London) and other members of London's new café society. The witty Boothby more than held his own in these sophisticated circles, where style was valued far more than money and dullness was damned as a cardinal sin. "He was an adventurer—brilliant, mischievous, funny, attractive to women, and extremely dedicated to his view of doing right," recalled Marie Ridder, an American journalist who first met Boothby when she was a young girl.

As Ridder noted, Boothby was a man of substance, as well as a charming man-about-town. He was a masterful politician who worked hard for his constituency in East Aberdeenshire, a rugged, windswept agricultural and fishing area on the northeastern coast of Scotland. Like Macmillan, Boothby had grown up in well-to-do, upper-middle-class surroundings, with little or no firsthand knowledge of the poverty afflicting much of Britain. When he first arrived in East Aberdeenshire, he was shocked by the abysmal living conditions of many of his constituents, who were living, he said, "on the borderland of starvation." He became an advocate of the herring industry, his constituency's main commercial enterprise, giving frequent and heartfelt speeches in the Commons about the need for government subsidies and other support. One day the prime minister strolled into the chamber and listened for a moment to Boothby as he held forth. Shaking his head, Stanley Baldwin muttered, "Herrings again!" and walked out.

Boothby became deeply attached to East Aberdeenshire and its people, and his constituents returned the favor. He was a most unusual MP, one who actually liked spending time in his constituency, who did not regard his days there as the unpleasant but necessary price one had to pay for getting elected. Unlike Macmillan and most of his other parliamentary colleagues, he enjoyed politicking, and he particularly delighted in trading banter and barbs with hecklers. In the middle of a campaign speech one night a voter yelled at him: "Ye should've been an actor, nay a politician." Boothby shot back: "You're quite right, and I would have been a bloody good one, too!"

Boothby also enjoyed his work with Churchill, and in the early years of their acquaintance the two were close. Besides a penchant for rebellion, they shared other traits, including exuberance, impulsiveness, brash combativeness, love of the limelight, and an irrepressible sense of fun. Both were "unique, wayward, exciting," as Macmillan once said of Churchill, "with a peculiar glamour of [their] own that brought a sense of color into our rather drab political life." Indeed, for a while Churchill treated Boothby almost as a son. He was a frequent houseguest at Chartwell, where he watched Churchill lay bricks as part of his myriad building projects, all the while listening to him talk. "In the drawing-room, the dining-room, the bedroom, the bathroom, the garden, the car, the train, or in his room at the House of Commons, the flow of [Churchill's] 'private' oratory, which was in fact, great literature, never ceased," Boothby recalled. In London, Churchill and Boothby occasionally went to plays or dinner together when Churchill's wife, Clementine, was out of town.

In perhaps the most significant indication of Churchill's regard for Boothby, the younger man was invited to join The Other Club, an exclusive political dining establishment that Churchill had helped found in 1911. To be chosen, a prospective member had to be both highly accomplished and highly entertaining. The decision on whom to admit was made solely by Churchill, who regarded it as the greatest honor he could confer on a friend or associate. Members came from all three political parties, about half from the House of Commons and the rest a widely disparate group that included, at various times, the Duke of Marlborough, P. G. Wodehouse, Lord Beaverbrook, South Africa's prime minister Jan Smuts, and Frank Hodges, the head of the miners' union. Every other Thursday, Other Club members, in formal evening attire, gathered in the Savoy Hotel's Pinafore Room, and, in a haze of cigar and cigarette smoke, spent several hours eating, drinking champagne and brandy, and verbally jousting. One of the club rules stated that "nothing . . . shall interfere with the rancour or asperity of party politics," an order with which the members were only too happy to comply. "We were a very pleasant brotherhood," one member later remarked, "smugly confident that if we did not rule the world, it was the world's misfortune."

In 1928 Boothby wrote to Churchill: "I hope on some occasion to be able adequately to express my gratitude for all you have done for me. I have now been with you for over two years, & I have not the slightest doubt that I shall look back on them as by far the happiest years of my political life—and the most interesting." Yet unlike most of those in Churchill's small inner circle, the independent-minded Boothby did not see himself as a disciple. He disapproved of many of Churchill's deflationary policies and made speeches in the Commons criticizing the chancellor's decisions to return England to the gold standard and to slash defense expenditures over a ten-year period. Several of his criticisms were made while he was Churchill's PPS and were regarded by some of his colleagues as rank disloyalty. On at least three occasions Boothby offered to resign; each time Churchill refused to accept his resignation. "I loved serving him," Boothby said many years later. "As chancellor, he was a wonderful chief, marvelous, considerate, let me do pretty well anything I liked. I had endless arguments with him, but he didn't mind."

Like Harold Macmillan, Boothby rebelled against the conventional wisdom of the time that governments could, and should, do little to curb unemployment and poverty. Both men were strongly influenced by Lloyd George and his passion for social reform and by the economist John Maynard Keynes, who called for a planned economy and massive public investment to stimulate full employment. Keynes was a close friend of Macmillan's older brother, Daniel, and his books were published by the Macmillan firm, generally considered the leading publisher of economic works.

In 1927 Macmillan and Boothby, along with two other progressive Tory MPs, published a pioneering economic treatise titled *Industry and the State*, urging government intervention in the economy to stimulate economic growth and social justice. Among the book's other proposals were nationalization of the British education system and the police and provision of statutory authority for collective bargaining. The book's authors insisted they were not advocating socialism, but the Tory hierarchy had its doubts. They were roundly criticized in an article in the right-wing *Daily Mail*, which labeled them "Socialists in Conservative Disguise" and called their ideas "half-baked sentimentalism" and "crude and hasty theories characteristic of modern socialism." The young MPs' proposals were not popular with many Conservative backbenchers either. As Macmillan remarked years later, "Most Tories did not [represent] depressed areas."

Churchill was one of those who opposed the idea of government intervention—there would be no deficit spending on his watch—yet he refused to join in the general criticism of the young Tory progressives. When the chairman of the Conservative Party complained to him that Boothby's views were sounding more and more socialist, he tartly responded: "I wish you w[oul]dn't write me these sorts of letters . . . It is no use being intolerant ab[ou]t young men . . ."

In fact, Churchill's only bold move to help revive the economy during his five years at the Treasury was inspired by one of those young men—Macmillan—who had gotten to know the chancellor through Boothby. In 1927 Churchill put forward a plan, first suggested to him by Macmillan, to aid depressed British industries and agriculture by cutting local rates, or taxes, on factories and farms. Along with Boothby,

Macmillan served as an adviser to Churchill on the derating issue, providing the chancellor with nine pages of notes, which Churchill used as the basis for his arguments to the cabinet and Parliament. Despite the opposition of many in the Tory hierarchy, including Neville Chamberlain, the derating legislation was approved in early 1929.

Like Boothby, Macmillan valued his association with the ebullient Churchill. "To sit and talk to [him] was like young men at Oxford arguing with dons or even professors—and plenty of drink and cigars provided," he later said. During this period Macmillan wrote to Churchill: "I should . . . like you to know how deeply I appreciate the favour of your confidence. You have always been most kind to those of us who are ordinarily classed merely as troublesome young men."

Passage of the derating legislation was a significant achievement, and Macmillan, quite rightly, took great pride in his own key role in the process. He began to think that despite his reputation as "a troublesome young man," he might actually have a promising future in Parliament. Then, in May 1929, a general election was called, and Macmillan's hopes collapsed. At a time of continuing high unemployment and industrial unrest, Stanley Baldwin and the Conservatives had gone to the country with the slogan "Safety First." Even though he was violently opposed to Tory economic policies, Macmillan, standing as a Conservative candidate, had to defend that "feeble slogan" in Stockton. "But my unhappy constituents," he later remarked, "did not want 'Safety,' which meant hanging about the streets or haunting the factories in despair. Safety meant the 'dole.' They wanted work." Most of the rest of the country felt the same way, and the Conservatives were turned out of office, replaced once again by a Labour government under Ramsay MacDonald. Macmillan was among the many Tories who lost their seats.

He was deeply depressed by his defeat, and Bob Boothby, who had easily won back his own seat in East Aberdeenshire, decided to try to cheer up his friend and colleague and take his mind off his troubles. That summer he invited Macmillan and his wife to the annual shooting party that Boothby's father gave at Beechwood, the family estate outside Edinburgh. The Macmillans accepted. It was then that the bottom dropped out of Macmillan's world.

On the second day of the party Boothby stood on the moors, awaiting his turn to shoot. He felt the touch of a hand on his. Turning, he found Dorothy Macmillan next to him. She smiled and squeezed his hand. Her husband was nowhere in sight.

For Lady Dorothy, married life had hardly been idyllic, despite Harold's claims to the contrary. "We were young; we were happy; everything smiled on us," he recalled in his memoirs. In fact, as the years progressed, Dorothy occupied a smaller and smaller place in her husband's life. In the mornings he worked as a junior partner at Macmillan's, where he served as editor to, among others, Thomas Hardy, Rudyard Kipling, W. B. Yeats, and Sean O'Casey. In the afternoons and evenings he was busy at Parliament.

At the urging of her husband and mother-in-law, Dorothy spent much of her time at Birch Grove, a sprawling neo-Georgian mansion in Sussex owned by Macmillan's parents. For company, she had only her three small children, born in the first six years of her marriage, and her mother-in-law, a woman she found every bit as difficult as her own dreadnought of a mother. Dorothy detested Nellie Macmillan; one of the Macmillans' daughters once discovered her mother sticking pins into an effigy of her grandmother that Dorothy kept hidden in a dressing table drawer. In the frequent domestic battles between Dorothy and Nellie, Harold almost always took his mother's side.

He usually saw his family only on weekends. Even then he was distant and reserved, having grown up with the idea that it was unmanly to reveal emotion or to respond to it in others. "He could be embarrassing when he tried to show affection," his son recalled. "He couldn't cope with personal problems, his own or mine." Like many other British men who were the products of all-male schools and who had had little early contact with girls and women outside their immediate families, Macmillan seemed truly at ease only in the company of like-minded men. His was a masculine world, a "society made for men and run for men," in which women almost always felt like outsiders.

Reflecting on what it was like to be a young woman in Britain in the 1920s, Barbara Cartland wrote: "From the moment we were born, all our parents heard was: 'A girl? Never mind, better luck next time.' And we accepted resignedly that we only got the crumbs that fell from the masculine table. A boy had a better education—we were lucky to get one at all. He went to a university, he had better clothes, better food, a better time, and, of course, more money. The British looked incredulously at the American habit of dividing their money equally among their children, whatever the sex."

Dorothy Cavendish grew up knowing that as a girl she would never have the advantages of her brothers, including the opportunity to inherit the title and property of her father, the duke. She didn't seem to mind much, but others in the same situation felt quite differently. For instance, Vita Sackville-West—the wife of Harold Nicolson, who in the 1930s became a close parliamentary associate of Macmillan and Boothby's—minded a great deal. The only child of the third Baron Sackville, Sackville-West never reconciled herself to the fact that because of her gender, she could not inherit Knole, her family's fifteenth-century palace in Kent, widely considered one of the finest Tudor buildings in England. In her poetry and books, Sackville-West poured out her fury and anguish over what she considered to be the inferior status of women. In her novel *All Passion Spent*, she described how, in a typical marriage, the husband "would continue to enjoy his free, varied and masculine life with no ring upon his finger or difference in his name to indicate the change in his estate; but whenever he felt inclined to come home [his wife] must be there, ready to lay down her book, her papers or her letters . . . It would not do, in such a world of assumptions, to assume that she had equal rights."

Sackville-West refused to conform to this image of a dutiful wife. She kept her maiden name; had numerous affairs, mostly with other women; and would not campaign for her husband or appear with him at social and political functions in London. Dorothy Macmillan, on the other hand, was by all accounts, including her husband's, the perfect political wife. She charmed Macmillan's constituents, made speeches, shook hands, opened fetes and country fairs, went to endless teas and dinners. Her life was devoted to meeting the needs and demands of others—Macmillan, her children, and her mother-in-law, not to mention the people of Stockton. Yet neither Harold nor anyone else seemed much concerned about what *she* wanted or needed.

Other than their children and their mutual interest in his career, Harold and Dorothy Macmillan had very little in common. While she appreciated his intellectualism, she was not an intellectual herself and indeed, like most women of her time, was not well educated. Macmillan had an outwardly languid approach to life, while Dorothy was impetuous and emotional, simmering with energy and boasting an explosive temper. Her interests focused on the outdoors—gardening, tennis, swimming, golf. A fast driver, she was known for collecting speeding tickets and once expressed an interest in taking part in the Monte Carlo rally.

She had met Bob Boothby only once before the fateful shooting party in Scotland. He was twenty-nine, the same age as she. The emotional opposite of her husband, he liked to laugh and have fun. He was witty, flirtatious, and seductive, the kind of man whom "women would call lovely," said a journalist friend of his. According to Marie Ridder, he had "an ability that was just so devastating—of paying total attention to whoever he was talking to, especially women." When he met Dorothy, there was an immediate attraction between the two, but it was Dorothy who took the first step to turn it into something more. Not long after she clasped Boothby's hand on the moors, they became lovers.

Boothby had had many relationships—"he was forever falling in love and asking women to marry him," said one acquaintance—but this was different. Dorothy was the wife of a close friend and colleague. The situation was made worse when the casual affair turned serious. In 1930, Dorothy asked Macmillan for a divorce so she could marry Boothby. He refused. "I told her I'd never let her go," he later said. "It would have been disastrous."

Disastrous, certainly, for their social standing and for Macmillan's political future. It was one thing to have an extramarital affair; that had long been perfectly acceptable, even fashionable in upper-class British society. Indeed, Dorothy Macmillan had plenty of examples in her own family. Her famed eighteenth-century ancestor Georgianna, the Duchess of Devonshire, was notorious for her affairs and for living in a ménage à trois with her husband and her best friend, Lady Elizabeth Foster. More recently, in the late nineteenth century, Dorothy's great-uncle, the eighth Duke of Devonshire, had an affair with the wife of the Duke of Manchester that lasted for thirty years.

Yet one was expected to be discreet. When they were not alone, the

Duke of Devonshire and the Duchess of Manchester always addressed each other by their titles, even in the presence of friends who knew about their involvement. "The commandments for . . . society were very clear," Barbara Cartland pointed out. "The first was 'Thou shall not be found out,' the second, 'There shall be no scandal.'"

In top social circles, just as in politics, it was important to follow the unwritten rules. An affair might be common knowledge in London society, but it was usually kept a secret from the outside world, unmentioned in newspaper gossip columns—unless there was a whiff of public scandal. And if there were divorce proceedings, scandal usually followed, with every sordid detail revealed in the divorce courts then breathlessly repeated in the popular press. Divorce still carried a profound moral stigma in the 1920s and 1930s, and it brought severe social penalties for both husband and wife, regardless of who the guilty party was. Divorced people could not be presented at court or admitted to the Royal Enclosure at Ascot. They were struck off the invitation lists of many society hostesses. "Society used to be like a walled city, with entrances and exits," recalled Lady Violet Bonham Carter. "You needed a passport to get in, and you could be thrown out."

For an MP, divorce usually meant the end of his political career. Macmillan was ambitious; he was not about to let divorce wreck his future. He also took his Anglican faith very seriously—he had once considered becoming a Catholic—and in the words of his grandson, "it would have been a total abnegation of his faith to have thought about divorce."

There was another reason why Macmillan was opposed to ending his marriage: he still cared deeply for his wife. "I never loved anyone but her—never had a woman friend, or even knew anyone," he told his biographer. "On her side there were transient things, unimportant. What counts are the fundamentals . . . And what's physical love? She wanted everything. She had it. [Once] I said jokingly, 'Now you've had everything, husband, children, home, a lover, what more?' In the way women do, she said it was my fault . . . But what's physical love compared to things you share, interests, children?"

He may have loved her, but as this long and unusually revealing outpouring indicates, he seemed never to have understood her. For her part, Dorothy, after repeated pleas for a divorce, finally agreed to continue living with Macmillan, running his household and campaigning for him in Stockton. "[I]n spite of this great romance," said Andrew Devonshire, "politically, Aunt Dorothy was a very good wife." At the same time, in dramatic defiance of social convention, she insisted on openly leading another life with Boothby. "She was desperately in love with him," said Deborah Devonshire. "Desperately." Dorothy occasionally stayed with Boothby at a London hotel; she vacationed with him in Portugal and Paris; she wrote or telephoned him almost daily. For her, being with Boothby was like "a period in paradise," said Boothby's biographer, Sir Robert Rhodes James. "Why did you ever wake me?" she once exclaimed to her lover when they were in Portugal. "Without you, life for me is going to be nothing but one big hurt." When Dorothy's fourth and last child, a girl, was born in 1930, she told her husband that the baby was Boothby's.

The proud, extremely private Macmillan was devastated. His friendship with Boothby was shattered; his marriage, although outwardly civil, lay in ruins; all London society was gossiping about the affair, although no mention of it ever appeared in the newspapers. "The reverberations of this social earthquake were felt far and wide . . ." Janet Aitken Kidd, Lord Beaverbrook's daughter, wrote. (When he heard about the liaison, George V reportedly ordered, "Keep it quiet.") For Macmillan, a man who hated to be conspicuous, being known as a cuckold was a terrible trauma. "What [my father] minded most was being dishonored," his son later remarked.

Boothby was in emotional turmoil as well. In his political and social circles, affairs were supposed to be taken lightly. "The greatest men I have known have never been able to put up with love," the society hostess Emerald Cunard once quipped. "It's so distracting, and great men must never be disturbed at their work." But Boothby succumbed totally to the distraction. Dorothy was, and remained, the love of his life. "It has become unendurable," he wrote to a friend in 1932. "Just an interminable series of agonising 'goodbyes' with nothing to go back to. Living always for the 'next time.' Work to hell. Nerves to hell. No one can ever persuade me that a 'liaison' is anything but misery (with glorious, but oh so transitory reprieves)." To another friend, he declared:

"I am passionately in love with her . . . Sometimes I long for her so much that I feel like getting straight back and taking her off to the country and sending everything and everyone else to hell."

Boothby was known for being exceedingly loyal to his friends, but in this case passion won out over loyalty. Nonetheless, he agonized over what the affair was doing to the Macmillan marriage. He also knew that his own political future was in jeopardy. On occasion "that bloody Power Urge comes uppermost and says, 'Fool, if you [take Dorothy off], you will never forgive yourself or her,'" he wrote a friend. "'Chuck it, be ruthless . . . Romantic love is an illusion anyway. Go and do the work you can do. Get out and fulfill your destiny.'" But he was not as ambitious as Macmillan and many of his other parliamentary colleagues, and he never let his head rule his heart. He was not able to give Dorothy up.

More than a decade of social awkwardness and misery followed. In their tight, clubby little world, the Macmillans and Boothby repeatedly encountered one another at parties and dinners. The embarrassment became even more acute when Macmillan won back his parliamentary seat in the 1931 general election and once again became an associate of Boothby's in the House. In late 1930 Harold Nicolson described a dispirited weekend house party that he attended at Cliveden, Lord and Lady Astor's estate. Among the other guests were Boothby and the Macmillans. The party, Nicolson noted in his diary, "does not hang together." The guests engaged in "desultory drivel, little groups of people wishing they were alone." The diaries of other acquaintances of the threesome recounted similar uncomfortable situations. "Went down for the night to stay with Harold Macmillan [at Birch Grove]," wrote the Liberal MP Robert Bernays in 1933. "Rather trying atmosphere of coldness and restraint owing to the fact that he is not getting on with his wife." Cuthbert Headlam, a Tory colleague of Macmillan's, also visited Birch Grove, writing afterward: "The gloom of H. Macmillan is something terrible, but he is a much disappointed man quite irrespective of anything else . . . [H]e is not a cheering companion even for a weekend."

On a number of occasions Boothby tried to end the affair, even to the point of getting engaged a couple of times to other women. "It was only to break out of the web," he said later, "not because I really loved anyone but [Dorothy]." He broke off those early engagements, but in

1935 he impulsively proposed to twenty-four-year-old Diana Cavendish, Dorothy's first cousin. The daughter of the Duke of Devonshire's brother, Diana had met Boothby at a ball in 1929 and knew all about his affair with Dorothy. She had fallen in love with him anyway, and when he assured her that his relationship with Dorothy was over, she accepted his proposal, much to the dismay of her parents. They were wed on March 21, 1935, at St. Bartholomew the Great Church in London.

Like Macmillan before him, Boothby stood to gain politically by marrying into the powerful Cavendish clan. He was now related by marriage to more than a dozen members of the House of Commons, including Macmillan and Bobbety Cranborne, who soon would become undersecretary of foreign affairs. If Boothby could make a success of his marriage, he might begin to mend the damage to his reputation done by his open affair with Dorothy and help his career in the process.

But he simply could not bring himself to play by the rules. "I was a self-satisfied young man," he admitted many years later. "I became very conceited." Said a friend: "His charm and good looks certainly allowed him to get away with some outrageous undergraduate behavior. He was a born gambler in both love and money, and it clearly gave him a kick to live dangerously." Shortly after his marriage he resumed his affair with Dorothy. Diana found out and asked for a divorce. She and Boothby agreed the marriage had been a terrible mistake. "You can't have a successful marriage if you love somebody else," Boothby said years later. After the divorce in 1937 Diana remarried, but she remained friends with Boothby for the rest of his life. The Cavendish family was another matter. Many of them were furious with Boothby. He had made some powerful enemies, including the deputy Tory whip James Stuart, whose wife was one of Dorothy's sisters. In the not too distant future Stuart was to do his best to make life miserable for Boothby and the other anti-appeasement MPs.

The Cavendishes weren't the only ones offended by Boothby's chaotic and indiscreet private life; his reputation plummeted in the House of Commons as well. Many of his colleagues "drew the conclusion, not at all surprisingly, that Boothby was an unspeakable cad, who drank too deep, lived too well, gambled too heavily, and stole other men's wives," observed Robert Rhodes James. Boothby's critics now included his old mentor Winston Churchill, who chided him for the way he had treated his wife. "He was fond of Diana," Boothby later said. "He thought I had behaved badly."

For Harold Macmillan, the early 1930s were a hellish time. He tried very hard to mask his personal despair and to pretend he was above it all; he was always civil to Boothby whenever they met. "It was important to him, since he had married into that family, to accept the more rakish customs of aristocracy . . . with a kind of airy nonchalance," said Anne Glyn-Jones, a research assistant to Macmillan. "But I think those eccentricities brought him . . . enormous personal suffering." And he did not always succeed in hiding the pain. One friend was shocked to see this normally buttoned-down man, in great anguish, beating his head against the wall of a railway compartment. He told another friend, "I just can't go on." Caught in the grip of a nervous breakdown, he spent several months at a hospital in Germany. There were rumors of a suicide attempt. Finally, however, he was able to regain a certain mental equilibrium, helped by his being returned to Parliament in 1931 by the voters of Stockton.

After the Labour Party defeated the Conservatives in 1929, Ramsay MacDonald's government had proved to be no more effective in taming unemployment and reviving the economy than the Baldwin government had been. Indeed, in 1931 Britain, like the United States and much of the rest of the world, was suffering from one of the worst economic depressions in its history. Faced with a financial crisis, MacDonald defied the wishes of his own party hierarchy and formed a coalition with the Conservatives and Liberals. The election that followed was a disaster for Labour, which retained only 52 seats in the House of Commons, while the Conservatives captured 473. On paper, the government formed after the election was still a coalition National Government, with MacDonald remaining as prime minister. In reality, Baldwin and the Conservatives were calling the shots, and MacDonald was regarded as a traitor by most members of his party.

Under the guidance of Neville Chamberlain, who had become chancellor of the exchequer in November 1931, the coalition government embarked on a program of strict economy, slashing public spending, lowering interest rates, and imposing tariffs on foreign goods. Over the next few years Britain—or at least its southern half, including London—began a tentative economic recovery. The industrial north, still the country's economic black hole, remained in a depression, with unemployment figures approaching 70 percent in some areas. Millions of people went to bed hungry every night, and millions of children grew up without adequate clothing, education, or basic health care. Yet as the sociologist Richard Titmuss put it then, this "intense poverty, so considerable and so widespread," was at the same time "so veiled and hidden by British stoicism and complacency that public opinion has . . . refused to recognize it."

As one of the few MPs who had witnessed the devastation of poverty firsthand and had tried to do something about it, Harold Macmillan continued to press the government for fundamental social reforms to improve the lot of the poor. Indeed, the fight for reform had become an obsession with him. Miserable at home, he threw himself into his work—both at Macmillan's and in Parliament—with a frenetic new intensity. For a time he, Boothby, and other Tory liberals flirted with the ideas of Oswald Mosley, a wealthy young Labour MP who in 1930 espoused a radical plan for state intervention in the economy. But they backed off from association with Mosley after he quit the Labour Party, founded what he called the New Party in 1931, and then drifted into fascism.

In 1935 Macmillan and other supporters of reform pushed a plan for a "new deal" for Britain that was even more sweeping than the massive public works programs instituted in the United States by Franklin D. Roosevelt's administration. Among the British "new deal" proposals were public or semipublic control of utilities, such as gas, electricity, and transport. Three years later he wrote a book titled *The Middle Way*, a dense economic treatise in which he argued for government policies that were neither socialist nor classically capitalist, urging the introduction of, among other things, a minimum wage, the nationalization of coal mines, state planning, and deficit budget financing. Needless to say, none of these proposals had the remotest chance of being adopted by the Conservative-controlled government. Of Macmillan, a parliamentary colleague said: "I think there is something very heroic in his

persistence in being the midwife for a new world which stubbornly re-
fuses to be born."

As the 1930s advanced and Germany presented more and more of
a threat to the peace of Europe, Macmillan, although never entirely
abandoning his struggles for social justice, shifted his energies to the
anti-appeasement crusade. Once again he would be part of a small
band of progressive young Tories that would play David against the
government's Goliath. And once again the man who had cuckolded
him would be among his allies.

CHAPTER FOUR

"DICTATORS ARE VERY POPULAR THESE DAYS"

On a frosty early January day in 1932 Bob Boothby entered a large Berlin hotel room for a meeting with a German politician who had asked to make his acquaintance. The man was sitting at a table when Boothby came in. He did not glance up until the young MP reached his side. Then he rose, shot out his right arm in a Nazi salute, and barked, "Hitler."

Much of Berlin was still recovering from its frenetic New Year's Eve merrymaking, but the abstemious Adolf Hitler, wearing a brown shirt adorned with a swastika, had no time for such degenerate nonsense. His eye was fixed firmly on the future. As head of the Nazi Party, now the second largest political organization in Germany, he had just broken off negotiations with Chancellor Heinrich Brüning over possible cooperation with the government. "I am going on alone now," he told Boothby.

Already acknowledged as something of an expert on international economic issues, Boothby had come to Germany to give a series of lectures on the world economic crisis. Like most British politicians and much of the British public, the thirty-one-year-old MP strongly supported ending the punitive reparations imposed against Germany by the Versailles Treaty. In his speeches to enthusiastic, packed audiences in Hamburg and Berlin, he also called for the cancellation of German war debts, more cooperation between German and foreign banks, the stabilization of prices, and expansion of credit. But in his meeting with Boothby, Hitler curtly rejected these ideas for bringing economic stability to Germany. He declared that it was too late to save the Weimar Republic. "You have been laying far too much emphasis . . . upon the economic side," he told his guest. "This is a political crisis. Political forces will carry me to power." His eventual control of Germany, he said, was inevitable.

For much of their meeting, Hitler harangued Boothby about the injustices that he insisted had been inflicted on Germany after the Great War: the reparations, the debts, the forced demilitarization, as well as the Allied decisions to make the Baltic port of Danzig a "free city" and to award Poland a narrow strip of German territory, the so-called Polish Corridor. "How would you like it," he shouted, "if your colonies and your fleet had been taken from you, and if a corridor had been driven between England and Scotland?" Discomfited by Hitler's ranting, Boothby decided to inject a bit of levity. "You forget, Herr Hitler," he replied, "that I come from Scotland. We should have been delighted." Hitler remained stone-faced, and Boothby decided to forgo any more jokes.

That night, in considerable gloom, he made notes on his conversation with the Nazi Party chief. Boothby loved Germany and had visited it many times. Fluent in German, he came to see friends, talk politics and economics, and listen to opera (he was a regular at the Wagner festival at Bayreuth). He also sampled the decadent night life of Berlin, where "along the Kurfürstendamm," in the words of Stefan Zweig, "powdered and rouged young men sauntered, and in the dimly lit bars one might see men of the world of finance courting drunken sailors." Although Boothby's sexual relationships were primarily with women, he was known to engage in homosexual escapades. In Germany in the 1920s and 1930s, he recalled in his memoirs, "homosexuality was rampant; and, as I was very good looking [then], I was chased all over the place and rather enjoyed it."

But on that January night in 1932 Boothby's mind was far from the pleasures that Berlin had to offer. He concluded that Hitler was indeed close to his goal of seizing control of Germany and, once that was accomplished, would turn his attention, as he had pledged in *Mein Kampf*, to the domination of Central and Eastern Europe. When he returned to

England, Boothby set out his fears in an article in the *Evening Standard*: "Somehow Hitler has managed to communicate his passion to masses of desperate people. And therein lies his power. The cry 'Heil Hitler!' re-echoes through Germany today. We should not underestimate the strength of the movement of which he is the living embodiment."

Boothby was one of the first politicians in Britain to call attention to the threat posed by Hitler, but the public and government paid little attention. Returning to Germany in 1933, after Hitler had become chancellor and had taken Germany out of the League of Nations, he was appalled by the increasingly violent anti-Semitism he witnessed. When Germany began a feverish rebuilding of its army and air force in defiance of the Versailles Treaty, Boothby's warnings became more frequent and more urgent.

In November 1934 he was asked to give the annual Armistice Day address to a group of army veterans in his hometown of Edinburgh. His speech was hardly the "nice, innocuous sermon," full of platitudes about the glory of sacrifice, that the audience was expecting. "Today, tyranny has regained the upper hand in Europe, and the danger of war is as great as in 1914," Boothby declared. His eyes swept over the two thousand people in front of him, most of them wearing red poppies in memory of those who died in the Great War. "I tell you they are rearming. If we simply drift along, never taking the lead . . . then everything that makes life worth living will be swept away, and then indeed we shall have finally broken faith with those who lie in the fields of Flanders." Sitting on the platform behind him, Lady Haig, the widow of the commander of British forces in France during the war, uttered a shocked cry of "No! No!" Otherwise Boothby's fiery remarks were met with silence. Afterward he was left standing alone at the lectern; no one approached to talk to him or shake his hand.

The people in Boothby's audience, like most Britons, were in no mood to heed such warnings. How could he raise the specter of another war when the grief over those who died in the last one was still so raw? It had been only twenty years since the young men of Britain had marched off to battle, the cheers of their countrymen ringing in their ears. Only twenty years too since they had begun to fall by the thousands in the trenches of France, more than seven hundred thousand dead by the time the bloodbath ended in 1918. These were not dimly remembered warriors from a long-distant conflict. If they had lived, most of them would have been in early middle age, the prime of their lives. Many had parents still alive to mourn them. Their names, chiseled on monuments in nearly every British village and town and on the walls of schools like Eton, Harrow, Cambridge, and Oxford, were still sharp and distinct.

They had fought the war to end all wars; it was essential now that peace be maintained. Such a horror must never occur again. As Harold Nicolson, who had participated in the Paris peace negotiations, noted, "We were preparing not Peace only, but Eternal Peace. There was about us the halo of some divine mission."

But the ardent desire for peace was fueled by more than the determination to ensure that all those lives had not been sacrificed in vain. Rage, especially among the young, also played a part: rage at munition manufacturers who profited from the war, at incompetent generals and their botched battle plans, at old politicians, safe in London, who failed to stop the carnage. "We were determined never again to be fooled," recalled Noel Annan, who began his long scholarly career in the 1930s at Cambridge. "Some of us thought that there was one way certain to prevent ourselves from being so. That was to embrace pacifism."

The British public also feared that terrifying as the last war had been, the next one would be far worse. Indeed, they thought it would be Armageddon. With the advent of modern air power, soldiers on distant battlefields would no longer be the only casualties; now civilians would also be targets. Stanley Baldwin had warned the British people that "the bomber will always get through." Their top military men had told them that massive bombing attacks would decimate the country in a matter of days. In the first two months of war, the Air Ministry estimated, six hundred thousand people would lie dead, and more than a million would be injured. And what if, as in the last war, there were gas attacks too?

"Picture if you can what the results will be," a British military historian wrote in the 1920s. "London for a few days will be one vast raving Bedlam, the hospitals will be stormed, traffic will cease . . . the City will be in Pandemonium. What of the Government in Westminster? It will be swept away by an avalanche of terror. The enemy will dictate his terms which will be grasped like a straw by a drowning man." With such horrific descriptions of the cataclysm to come, it's not surprising that as Harold Macmillan wrote in the 1960s, "we thought of air warfare then as people think of nuclear warfare today."

George V undoubtedly expressed the feelings of most of his subjects when he declared: "I will not have another war. *I will not.* The last one was none of my doing and if there is another one, and we are threatened with being brought into it, I will go to Trafalgar Square and [demonstrate against war] myself sooner than allow this country to be brought in."

But it wasn't just the idea of war that was repugnant to the king; it was also the thought that Britain's enemy in the next conflict most likely would again be Germany. Staunchly pro-German, George V and his family were adamant in their belief that a strong Germany, Nazi or not, was necessary as a counterweight to the Communist Soviet Union. The king was still haunted by the murders of his first cousin, Tsar Nicholas II, and the rest of the tsar's family by the Bolsheviks after the 1917 Russian Revolution.

For the British upper class, fear of communism came much closer to home in the 1930s, when unemployed workers in the north of the country, angered at the government's inattention to their plight, decided to open Londoners' eyes to what they had been ignoring for so long. Throughout the decade, thousands of workers marched to the British capital to engage in protest demonstrations and rallies. In the most famous march, which took place in October 1936, throngs of destitute miners and shipworkers walked almost three hundred miles, from Jarrow in northeastern England to London, to protest their plight and that of the millions of other unemployed men in Britain. Prime Minister Baldwin refused to see any of the marchers, and the government paid little heed to their demands.

As the 1930s advanced, members of the upper crust nervously thought the unthinkable as they stepped around the bodies of unemployed men staging a "lie-in" in the lobby of the Savoy Hotel or watched police battling with demonstrators on Oxford Street. Was the British class system, in which everyone knew his place and stayed in it, falling apart? Would there be revolution in England too? Their fears were fueled by such incidents as a visit by the Duke of York (the future George VI) to London's East End, where he was surrounded by a mob of fist-shaking cockneys, who shouted: "Food! Give us food! We don't want royal parasites!"

In 1936, Lady Nelly Cecil, sister-in-law of the Marquess of Salisbury, noted that nearly all her blood relatives were "tender to the Nazis and idiotic about 'Communism,' which to them means everything not approved by the Conservative Central Office." Three young peers whom Harold Nicolson encountered one night at Pratt's, a London club, told him that "they would prefer to see Hitler in London than a [Labour] administration." In his diary, Nicolson wrote disgustedly: "I go to bed slowly, pondering upon the Decline and Fall of the British Empire." Later he wrote: "People of the governing classes think only of their own fortunes, which means hatred of the Reds. This creates a perfectly artificial, but at present most effective, secret bond between ourselves and Hitler."

One of the most outspoken supporters of Germany was the Prince of Wales, who told a German prince in 1933 that "it was no business of ours to interfere in Germany's internal affairs either [regarding] Jews or [regarding] anything else" and that "dictators are very popular these days and we might want one in England before long." Indeed, the prince was so vociferous in his praise of the Nazis that on one occasion even his pro-German father thought he had gone too far and told him to tone it down. The future Edward VIII "is going the dictator way . . . and is against too much slip-shod democracy," Sir Henry "Chips" Channon, a Tory pro-appeasement MP, wrote in his diary.

The prince's admiration of Germany and its government was shared by a substantial segment of the British establishment, including many prominent businessmen, politicians, former military leaders, press barons, and aristocrats. In 1935 the German Embassy in London encouraged a group of these admirers from the country's social and government elite to form the Anglo-German Fellowship to strengthen British ties with Nazi Germany. The organization touted itself as nonpolitical, but according to the historian Ian Kershaw, it "served largely as an indirect tool of Nazi propaganda in high places, a vehicle for exerting German influence in Britain." Among its founding members were fifty members of both Houses of Parliament and several retired generals and admirals, including General Ian Hamilton, the commander of British forces at Gallipoli, and Admiral Barry Domvile, former head of the Royal Naval College at Greenwich. Three directors of the Bank of England were also on the membership rolls, as were executives of such large industrial firms as Firth-Vickers, Unilever, and Dunlop.

The fellowship's first president was Lord Mount Temple, a former Tory minister of transport and the father-in-law of the future Lord Mountbatten. At one fellowship dinner, shortly before presentation of the dessert (an ice-cream confection adorned by a swastika and Union Jack), Lord Mount Temple, in his toast, expressed the hope that Britain would be fighting alongside Germany in the next war. He was joined in his pro-German sympathies by a number of fellow peers, including the Duke of Buccleuch, who had been the Duchess of Devonshire's preferred suitor for her daughter Dorothy; the Duke of Bedford; the Marquess of Lothian; Baron Allen; Baron Brocket; and Baron Redesdale, father of the Mitford sisters, two of whom, Diana and Unity, were well-known Nazi sympathizers.

Another aristocratic champion of Germany was the Duke of Westminster, believed to be the richest man in England, who owned most of Mayfair, all of Belgravia, and hundreds of thousands of acres throughout the rest of the country. Bendor Westminster (whose nickname came from the name of his grandfather's prize racehorse) was a friend and distant relative of Winston Churchill, who had been best man at Westminster's third marriage and hunted wild boar with him on his estate in France. Described as a "formidable and capricious autocrat" by his third wife, Loelia, the duke was also a staunch anti-Semite. One of his most treasured possessions, which he guarded "with elaborate secrecy," was a book called *The Jews' Who's Who*, purporting "to tell the exact quantity of Jewish blood coursing through the veins of the aristocratic families of England."

The most noted aristocratic advocate of close ties between Hitler and Britain was Lord Londonderry, another Churchill relative and head of the Air Ministry from 1931 to 1935. When Joachim von Ribbentrop, acting as Hitler's unofficial emissary, came to England in November 1933 to promote an Anglo-German alliance, he was taken up by Londonderry and his wife, a prominent London society figure known for her glittering parties and receptions at Londonderry House, the family's splendid London mansion. Ribbentrop also was fawned over by several other prominent society hostesses, including Emerald Cunard and Maggie Greville, the daughter of a millionaire Scottish brewer, who made no secret of her pro-Hitler sympathies.

By 1936 it was clear that Hitler's propaganda campaign in Britain was bearing considerable fruit. In certain upper-class circles it was considered not only politically sound but also the height of fashion to be pro-Nazi. "[T]here were a lot of quite powerful people in England who were . . . admirers of Hitler and his regime and would go out of their way to meet any Nazi socially because they were rather splendid, to their way of thinking," recalled a former debutante. Aristocrats and wealthy businessmen, she added, often sent their daughters to Germany for a summer or two before they came out in society: "Nearly all the girls I knew went to Munich when they were 16 or 17; it was the thing to do then."

The debs' parents began making the trek to Germany too. Capitalizing on his popularity, Hitler invited many of England's leading social and political figures to visit him after he became chancellor. The führer's occupation of the demilitarized Rhineland in March 1936, in flagrant violation of the Versailles and Locarno treaties, seemed to bother his British guests not at all. A host of aristocrats and MPs descended on Berlin in August for the 1936 Summer Olympics, and dozens returned to Germany in September for the annual Nazi rally at Nuremberg. Coming back from their pilgrimages bubbling over with enthusiasm, many of the visitors, "with the best intentions in the world," nonetheless "became the unpaid servants of German and Nazi foreign policy," according to the historian Donald Cameron Watt. After one of his visits, Lord Lothian wrote: "The central fact today is that Germany does not want war and is prepared to renounce it as a method of settling her disputes with her neighbors." Sir John Simon, the foreign secretary, described Hitler as "an Austrian Joan of Arc with a moustache." Returning from Nuremberg, Maggie Greville spoke affectionately of "my dear little Brown Shirts."

Even David Lloyd George, the scourge of British aristocrats, was for a time besotted with the führer. Writing in the *Daily Express* in

1936 after a visit to Germany, the former prime minister compared Hitler with George Washington and argued that he was "a born leader, a magnetic, dynamic personality with a single-minded purpose" to keep the peace. Later Lloyd George declared: "I only wish we had a man of his supreme quality at the head of affairs in our country today."

Not every politician who traveled to Germany was enthralled, however. Bob Boothby and Ronald Cartland came back with very different impressions of Hitler and his regime. So did Ronald Tree, a grandson of the Chicago department store magnate Marshall Field, who had grown up in England and had been elected as a Tory to Parliament in 1933. Tree had visited Germany in 1934 with Rob Bernays. Because Bernays had written newspaper articles critical of the Nazis, he and Tree were barred from meeting Hitler or any other officials in the German government. Instead they met clandestinely with opponents of the Nazi regime, who told them, among other things, of the concentration camps then being set up for "enemies of the state." As a result of this visit, during which Tree also witnessed considerable street violence against Jews, he "was persuaded, as my speeches bear evidence, that . . . unless Hitler could be shown early on that we would meet force with force, war on *his* terms was inevitable." When Jack Macnamara traveled to Germany a little later, he was allowed to visit a concentration camp, where he saw truncheon-swinging SS guards menacing blank-faced inmates. In all his life, Macnamara wrote later, "I have never seen human beings so cowed."

Within the small band of anti-appeasement MPs, two other members had even more extensive inside knowledge of what was happening in Germany. Before his election to Parliament in 1931, Paul Emrys-Evans, chairman of the House Foreign Affairs Committee, had served as a military attaché in the British Embassy in Washington and later worked in the Foreign Office. After entering the Commons, Emrys-Evans continued to give frequent dinners at his London town house for former Foreign Office colleagues, who shared his strong belief that the government was caving in to the dictators and "we were drifting toward disaster."

Harold Nicolson, who was vice-chairman of the committee, had served in the Foreign Office and diplomatic service for twenty years and had been counselor in the British Embassy in Berlin in the late 1920s. Aware of the secret, illegal military buildup that had begun in Germany shortly after the armistice, Nicolson had warned Whitehall, well before Hitler's takeover, of the dangers of Germany's gathering strength. "If we are weak on details," he declared, "we shall find ourselves, before we know where we are, face to face with a fully armed Germany."

The frustration felt by these men and other parliamentary rebels was enormous. They saw the growing peril to Britain and the rest of Europe but had no power to do anything about it. Most of them were under fifty; under normal circumstances, they and their contemporaries would now be moving into positions of influence and authority within the government. But there were far too few of them. Theirs was a lost generation, decimated by war. The other young men who likely would have shared their progressive views and their opposition to conciliating the dictators—their brothers, cousins, childhood friends, schoolmates— were lying in graves scattered throughout France and Belgium.

As a result, throughout the 1930s the older generation of politicians—Ramsay MacDonald, Stanley Baldwin, Neville Chamberlain, and their cohorts—continued to cling to power, as they had since the early 1920s. Of these "elderly mediocrities," as Boothby called them, MacDonald, prime minister of two short-lived Labour governments, was the least consequential. When he was nominal head of the so-called National Government from 1931 to 1936, it was Baldwin and the Conservatives who were in control.

In his early years as leader of the Conservative Party, Stanley Baldwin had been something of a hero to younger Tory progressives like Boothby, Macnamara, Emrys-Evans, and Macmillan. A bluff, stocky man, the very embodiment of decency and honesty in public life, Baldwin was a moderate, a conciliator, whose skillful handling of the 1926 General Strike was widely praised. Boothby once called Baldwin and his own father "the nicest men I have ever known."

Yet genial and decent as he was, Baldwin, who was sixty-eight when he became prime minister again in 1935, was hopelessly out of touch with the modern world. Fond of portraying himself as a simple country squire, he liked to harken back to the quiet rural values of an England that had long since vanished. The prime minister, who never served in the military and had not witnessed the bloodbath in France and Belgium, chided the younger generation for its "scorched and cynical" outlook. He urged it to accept the world "openly and joyously" as a moral place. For those who grew up in the shadow of the Great War, as Boothby wryly noted, it was "a little difficult" to follow Baldwin's advice.

In the 1930s the governments of other countries were creating revolutionary new programs and policies to cope with the Depression that had devastated their economies. The United States had the New Deal; France, the Popular Front; Germany, the Third Reich; the Soviet Union, the Five-Year Plan. The British government did not follow suit. Like Neville Chamberlain and other senior Conservatives in the government, Stanley Baldwin never comprehended how much the world had shifted. In their black coats, striped trousers, and stiff white collars, the aging men in the cabinet resembled the upright Victorians who gazed sternly out of old daguerreotypes displayed in many English parlors. Charles Ritchie, a perceptive young Canadian diplomat assigned to London before and during World War II, described England's leaders in the 1930s as "methodical, respectable, immovable men, with no understanding of this age—of its despair, its violence and its gropings—blinkered in solid comfort, shut off from poverty and risk."

Tranquillity was Baldwin's greatest desire. "Safety First" was his motto. In his stolid way he shied away from doing anything drastic to help the economy or to reduce unemployment and poverty. He had no interest in foreign affairs and was determined to avoid, at all costs, another war. His desire for peace echoed that of many of his countrymen, who, after the slaughter of World War I, wanted nothing more to do with European entanglements and yearned only to get on with their lives.

In the 1920s and early 1930s the British government, along with the public, put its faith in the League of Nations to keep world peace. But the idea of collective security, enforced by the League, was deeply flawed from the moment the international organization was created after the war. The United States refused to join the League, and Germany withdrew after Hitler came to power in 1933. Britain, the League's leading member, proclaimed itself in favor of international disarmament and began slashing its armed forces and armaments as soon as the war was over. The League was a "great and noble ideal, but no great and noble ideal can be achieved unless it is worked for," Jack Macnamara noted in 1938. "Instead, it was used as an excuse for a lack of effort . . . We in [Britain] looked to others to fight our battles for us and to take on our defence for us . . ."

From the beginning, the League proved a failure in confronting aggressors and keeping the peace. When Japan invaded the Chinese province of Manchuria in 1931, Britain, citing a lack of American support, declined to get involved, and without British leadership, the League's other members also refused to act. Hitler and Europe's other fascist dictator, Benito Mussolini of Italy, took careful note. In October 1935, after almost a year of threatening and bellicose action in the Mediterranean and North Africa, Italy invaded the eastern African country of Abyssinia, which immediately appealed to its fellow League members for protection.

Facing a general election in November, Baldwin and the Tories endorsed taking strong collective security measures against Italy's aggression. Thanks in part to their support of League-imposed sanctions, the Tories swept the election in a landslide, winning a majority of nearly 250 over the Labour and Liberal parties. Although the new government was still nominally an all-party coalition, Baldwin remained prime minister, and the Conservatives were still in control. The two Opposition parties were as impotent as the League of Nations again would prove to be.

After the election Baldwin's government and the League failed to stand up to Mussolini. Mild economic sanctions were the only punitive measures taken against Italy by the League, and they had little or no effect. Determined not to risk war with Italy and eager to keep Mussolini out of Hitler's orbit, the British government meanwhile took further steps to appease the Italian dictator. Just two weeks after the election, the foreign secretary, Samuel Hoare, and his French counterpart, Pierre Laval, secretly agreed to a plan to end the conflict by allowing Mussolini a more or less free hand in Abyssinia. When the Hoare-Laval pact leaked to the press, there was a storm of public anger. Baldwin, yielding to public pressure, forced Hoare to resign and replaced him with Anthony Eden. Yet the prime minister made no further attempt to rein Mussolini in, and the Italian campaign in Abyssinia continued. In June, a month after Italy had annexed all of Abyssinia, the economic sanctions were scrapped. Later one of the anti-appeasement Tories wrote: "The rape of Abyssinia was perhaps the turning point in the triumphant era of the dictators. Our promises to help, our failure to fulfill them, the complete cynicism and paralysis of forty nations confronted by the bombast of what we now know to have been a very feeble [Italy], constitute one of the saddest stories in European history."

Only a handful of Tories—Boothby and Macmillan among them—protested Baldwin's laissez-faire attitude to the invasion of Abyssinia. Even Winston Churchill tended to downplay Italy's attack. In a House debate, Boothby argued that turning a blind eye to the assault on Abyssinia would encourage both Hitler and Mussolini to believe that Britain would never stand up to aggression. Macmillan's opposition to the prime minister's policy was even more dramatic; on June 23, 1936, he was one of only two Tory MPs to vote against the government after it abandoned sanctions against Italy. Six days later Macmillan informed Baldwin he was resigning the whip, which meant, in effect, that he was resigning from the party, and was no longer to be "regarded as among the official supporters of the Government." In the view of *The Sunday Times*, Macmillan's rebellion had sounded the death knell to his once-promising political future and placed him in "that small group of untouchables found in every Parliament."

As Boothby had predicted, Hitler was taking careful note of Britain's failure to confront Mussolini. In March 1936 he had ordered German troops to occupy the demilitarized Rhineland, a strip of western Germany straddling the Rhine and bordering France, Luxembourg, Belgium, and the Netherlands. Under the Versailles Treaty, Germany was forbidden to install fortifications or troops in this region. This was Hitler's most flagrant violation of Germany's treaty obligations to date and his most dramatic challenge to Britain and France. It also turned out to be, as Macmillan realized, a mortal blow to Western security and power. By seizing and later fortifying the Rhineland, the Reich could make plans to attack its eastern neighbors, confident that Germany itself was protected from an attack from the West.

Yet most other British politicians were indifferent to what Macmillan called one of the turning points in history. Only a handful of MPs, including Boothby, Churchill, Emrys-Evans, and Edward Spears, urged the Baldwin government to pick up the gauntlet flung down by Hitler. Boothby told the House that the führer's Rhineland coup was an example of the "big bluff" that Hitler espoused in *Mein Kampf*, a bluff that Britain and France must call. Churchill cautioned that failure to stand up to Hitler would now leave France and the Low Countries open to German attack. But the warnings went unheeded. "The feeling in the House is 'terribly pro-German,' which means afraid of war," Harold Nicolson, one of those who spoke out, wrote in his diary.

Hitler's move had indeed been a bluff, as he himself acknowledged. "The forty-eight hours after the march into the Rhineland were the most nerve-wracking of my life," he said. "If the French had then marched into the Rhineland, we would have had to withdraw with shame and disgrace . . ." But France, despite having the largest army in the world, declared it needed Britain's help to confront Hitler. When Britain declined to help, France declined to march. Hitler's gambit had succeeded, and few in the upper reaches of British society and government seemed to mind. "After all," said Lord Lothian, a former diplomat and ex-secretary to Lloyd George, "they're only going into their own back garden."

In early 1936 about thirty-five anti-appeasement MPs, among them Macmillan, Boothby, Tree, Macnamara, Nicolson, Emrys-Evans, Spears, and the newly elected Ronald Cartland, organized what they called the December Club, named for the month in which the infamous Hoare-Laval agreement had been negotiated. Increasingly alarmed by the government's refusal to respond to Italian and German aggression, the MPs, according to Spears, wanted to show Baldwin and his men that "there were quite a number of us who are perfectly prepared in a real emergency to take action independent of the Whips, should we deem it in the national interest."

Yet for all their defiance, Spears and his backbencher colleagues knew that they did not have the numbers in the House to challenge Baldwin and the overwhelming Tory majority directly. To have an impact, the anti-appeasement forces needed to rally the country behind them, and for that, they needed a nationally recognized leader. At first glance, the choice would seem to have been obvious: Winston Churchill, the most notable opponent of appeasement and advocate of British rearmament in the House of Commons. As it happened, Churchill was sympathetic to the young Tories' frustration over not wielding more influence in the House. In 1928 he wrote to Baldwin: "You made some fine references to the wealth of young talent which the Par[liament] has produced. But v[er]y little has been done for them. They have just drummed their heels."

In melancholy fact, however, by the mid-1930s almost no one in the House, certainly not the bright young Tory progressives, wanted much to do with Churchill. Earlier in the decade he had put himself into parliamentary purdah with a vitriolic campaign against limited self-government for India, and MPs like Macmillan, who had sat at the great man's feet only a few years before, now shied away from him and what they considered his extreme right-wing views.

To Macmillan, it was an infuriating situation; following his term as chancellor of the exchequer in the late 1920s, Churchill had frittered away his influence on this India business! After the Labour Party won the 1929 election, he had remained in the Tory leadership, but in 1931 he resigned from the shadow cabinet in furious opposition to the party's support of the proposal for Indian self-government. Later that year, when a new Conservative-controlled government was formed, Neville Chamberlain, not Churchill, became chancellor of the exchequer. Churchill's resignation and his invective-filled campaign against the government over India were major factors in his future exclusion from any high posts in the Baldwin and Chamberlain administrations.

For the next four years, from his corner seat below the gangway on the government side of the House, Churchill led an acrimonious rearguard fight against the India bill. It was a deeply personal, emotional issue for him. As a junior officer in the Fourth Hussars he had spent almost a year in India in the late 1890s; nearly forty years later, still lost in dreams of empire, he had little or no knowledge of the complexities of the Indian question or of the tensions gripping the country. For Churchill, India was still the most precious jewel in the imperial crown and, as such, must remain under unquestioned British control.

In the debate over India he seemed at times "almost demented with fury," noted one government supporter. He launched bitter personal attacks against Baldwin and other government officials, and his rhetorical assaults on India and those seeking its independence were extreme, even poisonous. Hindus, he declared, were "a foul race protected by their pollution from the doom that is their due." He described as "alarming and nauseating" the sight of Mohandas Gandhi "striding half-naked up the steps of the Vice-regal palace . . . to parley on equal terms with the representative of the King-Emperor." The idea of independence for India was "a crime against civilisation" and "a catastrophe which will shake the world."

In his battle against the India bill, Churchill could claim the support of fewer than a hundred Tory MPs, almost all of them on the extreme right wing of the party. Most members, regardless of party, had little sympathy for his opposition to any kind of elective democracy in India. His attitude, in Macmillan's words, was regarded as "reactionary and unrealistic." Once again there were doubts about the soundness of Churchill's judgment. "The public looks upon him as a brilliant man, but rash, hot-headed, impulsive . . ." a political commentator named V. W. Germains noted in 1931.

Thus, when Churchill began warning in 1933 about the growing menace of a rearmed Germany, it's not surprising that few MPs rallied around him. Even for those who agreed with him on Germany, his currency as a leader had been badly devalued. Indeed, during the fight against appeasement Churchill had only three staunch supporters in Parliament: Boothby; Duncan Sandys, his son-in-law; and Brendan Bracken, a flamboyant, self-made millionaire who had been elected to the Commons in 1929. Boothby strongly disagreed with Churchill on India, and their relationship had cooled somewhat. By 1932, however, the rift had healed enough to allow Churchill to suggest to his former parliamentary secretary that they travel together to the United States to cover the Democratic and Republican political conventions for British newspapers. For some reason, the trip never took place, but Boothby, although not as personally close to Churchill as before, aligned himself with the older man in his fight to rouse the government and nation to the urgent need for rearmament. In November 1934, when Churchill offered a highly controversial amendment in Parliament declaring that Britain's armed forces, particularly the Royal Air Force, were "no longer adequate to secure the peace, safety, and freedom" of the country, Boothby was one of the amendment's five cosigners.

During a weekend stay at a friend's country house in the mid-1930s Churchill went for a walk in the woods with a fellow guest, Lady Violet Bonham Carter, who was one of his closest friends and as ardent as he in opposing appeasement. During their stroll she declared that he must alert the country to the growing peril posed by the dictators. "You must be the awakener," she said. "You must rouse public opinion. You alone can do it." He stared at her for a moment, then replied, "Yes, and the trouble is that I shall do it alone. I shan't have any press. I've got no springboard. And worst of all, I've got no following." In that case, she answered, "we must recruit a following for you, and we must create a springboard." Churchill knew better than to disagree. He had been friends with Lady Violet for almost thirty years, long enough to know that once she set her mind on something, she rarely gave up until she achieved it.

Theirs was a surprising relationship, considering that Churchill generally had very little interest in the company of women (except his wife) and believed strongly they had no place in public life. But his misogyny never extended to Violet Bonham Carter. Perhaps it was because they were so much alike. Like him, she loved the political fray; from her early twenties she had been one of the most prominent figures in the Liberal Party. She was a brilliant speaker, with an emotional force and command of language that, by many accounts, rivaled Churchill's. Tart-tongued and clever, she, like Churchill, could devastate an opponent with her wit. She relished the parry and thrust of

intellectual argument and was one of the few people who could occasionally best Churchill in a verbal duel. Lady Violet often would get so
caught up in the passion of her argument that she would lean uncom-
fortably close to the person to whom she was speaking. One acquaintance recalled "stories of a neighbour at dinner popping his fork into
[Lady Violet's] mouth, pretending that he thought it was his own." At
another social gathering her intensity drove her conversational partner—
John Colville, the young aristocrat who served as private secretary to
Chamberlain and then to Churchill—to back up against a fireplace and
badly singe his trousers. Churchill once described her as "a woman of
such *vehement* intelligence," putting heavy emphasis on the adjective.
"Had she been a man, she would have reached the top in politics," a
political commentator wrote years later.

Lady Violet and Churchill had met in 1906, when he was a thirty-
two-year-old junior minister in the government of the Liberal prime
minister Henry Campbell-Bannerman and she was the nineteen-year-
old daughter of the chancellor of the exchequer. They were seated next
to each other at a dinner party, and the elegant blonde teenager was so
dazzled by the bumptious young man's flood of talk that she ran home afterward to the chancellor's residence at 11 Downing Street, woke her
father, and told him that "for the first time in my life I've seen genius."

Their mutual love of language ignited a friendship that lasted, despite occasional storms, until Churchill's death almost sixty years later.
"Words were a kind of passport to his mind," Lady Violet once said. "In
an argument I've often battered for hours on a tight-shut door in vain.
But if one got through to him by some lucky turn of words or perhaps
some appeal to his imagination or emotions, then the door flew wide
open . . . We had a common code in a way. I don't know why."

When Asquith succeeded Campbell-Bannerman as prime minister
in 1908, Lady Violet, who was one of her father's closest confidantes,
pressured him to name Churchill to the key post of first lord of the admiralty. In 1911, he did so, after Churchill first proved his mettle as
president of the Board of Trade and home secretary. On his way to and
from cabinet meetings, Churchill often dropped by Lady Violet's sitting
room at 10 Downing Street. Many people, including her stepmother,
Margot, were convinced that Lady Violet loved and wanted to marry

him. When Lady Violet learned of his engagement to Clementine Hozier in 1908, she wrote cattily to a friend: "His wife could never be more to him than an ornamental sideboard as I have often said & she is unexacting enough not to mind not being more. Whether he will ultimately mind her being stupid as an *owl* I don't know."

As Lady Violet came to realize, Clementine Churchill was neither "an ornamental sideboard" nor "stupid as an owl," but she was certainly more willing to let her husband be the master of their world than Lady Violet would have been. Although she revered Churchill and attacked anyone who spoke ill of him, she had far too much strength of will to remain in the background and be the kind of helpmate that he needed and demanded. Instead, at the age of twenty-eight, she married Maurice Bonham Carter, her father's private secretary, who had wooed her for many years and eventually won her by promising that marriage to him would not mean a surrender of her independence and freedom. She took him at his word—perhaps more literally than he intended—and for many years carried on an affair with Oswald Toynbee Falk, a prominent merchant banker and close friend of John Maynard Keynes's.

Yet Lady Violet was traditional enough to believe that the duties of motherhood constrained her from entering the political arena and becoming a member of Parliament. For more than a decade she stayed out of politics, raising her four children, until the rise of Hitler spurred her again to political action. A passionate believer in tolerance and individual freedom, Lady Violet was never one to hold her tongue when she witnessed what she considered threats to those values. "Neutrality is not in my make-up," she once said. "I have never sat on any fence since I was born. I don't feel comfortable on fences." She viewed people and issues in stark black-and-white terms, and for her, Hitler and nazism were, from the beginning, indelibly black.

Three months after Hitler came to power in 1933, she told a Liberal Party conference: "In Germany, freedom as we conceive it seems to have perished . . . in the twinkling of an eye, almost without a struggle, and given place to a nightmare reign of force." She believed that another war was inevitable unless Britain backed the League of Nations with more than words. She and her good friend Blanche ("Baffy")

Dugdale, a niece of former prime minister Arthur Balfour and a cousin of Lord Robert Cranborne, became the confidantes and consciences of the young Tory and Liberal MPs who opposed appeasement, constantly urging them to take more resolute stands against the government. When one young rebel wavered on whether to vote against Baldwin and his men for their failure to stand up to Italy over Abyssinia, Lady Violet took him strongly to task. She asked him, as he noted gloomily in his diary, "Where are my moral principles, etc., etc. It is all very difficult."

Prompted in part by Lady Violet, Churchill became involved in a number of anti-appeasement organizations, including a group called Focus in Defence of Freedom and Peace, aimed at mobilizing people from all political parties in the fight against conciliating the dictators. Among the early Tory supporters of Focus were Boothby, Cartland, and Emrys-Evans, as well as Eleanor Rathbone, a highly respected Independent MP, and Sir Walter Citrine, general secretary of the powerful Trades Union Congress. As leader of this group Churchill made speeches and wrote articles that stressed the need for swifter rearmament and for collective security to meet the German threat. Lady Violet did the same. "Unless we, the free democracies of the world . . . are prepared to stand together and to take the same risks for justice, peace and freedom that others are prepared to take for the fruits of aggression, then our cause is lost—and the gangsters will inherit the earth," she declared to one gathering.

Gradually, the campaign gained momentum. The crowds at anti-appeasement rallies grew larger and more enthusiastic. Churchill even began to make an impression on the House of Commons. In November 1936 he managed to put the Baldwin government on the defensive, forcing it to admit that Britain's air power was still inferior to that of Germany, despite Baldwin's pledge two years earlier to build up the RAF. That acknowledgment inspired one of Churchill's most slashing and powerful attacks on the prime minister and his government: "So they go on in strange paradox, decided only to be undecided, resolved to be irresolute, adamant for drift, solid for fluidity, all-powerful to be impotent. So we go on preparing more months and years—precious, perhaps vital to the greatness of Britain—for the locusts to eat." Realizing he was on the ropes, Baldwin didn't help his cause by arguing plaintively that the Tories would have lost the 1935 election if he had "gone to the country and said that Germany was rearming and that we must rearm."

In the wake of his admission that he valued political victory over national security, Baldwin's popularity and that of his foreign policy took a steep dive. Even his staunchest advocates acknowledged he was in trouble. Churchill, Lady Violet, and their allies meanwhile detected a new spirit in the country, a growing determination on the part of Britons to force their leaders to confront the dictators. "We had the feeling that we were on the threshold of not only gaining respect for our views, but of making them dominant," Churchill wrote. Then came the uproar over Edward VIII and Mrs. Simpson, and once again, the opportunity slipped away.

It's uncanny how often, even when he didn't mean to, the king was able to aid Hitler's cause. As Prince of Wales he had been Britain's most prominent apologist for Nazi Germany. Then, less than a year after succeeding his father, George V, in January 1936, he made clear he planned to marry his paramour, a twice-married American named Wallis Simpson, plunging his country into a months-long constitutional crisis that temporarily eclipsed the issues of rearmament and standing up to Hitler. To add to the problem, one of the king's foremost champions turned out to be Churchill, whose temporizing over Edward's abdication destroyed the credibility he had so recently and painstakingly regained in his struggle against appeasement.

Churchill obviously did not approve of the king's pro-German views, but ever the romantic, he was an ardent supporter of the British monarchy—"the last believer in the divine right of kings," his wife once said. Setting himself against the conviction of the public and Parliament that the king must abdicate if he persisted in his determination to marry, Churchill urged Edward to hold on. Then, on December 7, 1936, "filled with emotion and brandy," he begged the Commons not to rush to judgment, only to be shouted down by an overwhelmingly hostile House. "It was," wrote *The Times* the next day, "the most striking rebuff in modern parliamentary history." Bob Boothby saw it in a different context. "In five fatal minutes," he said, Churchill's Focus crusade against appeasement "crashed into ruin."

Like Violet Bonham Carter and Churchill's other allies, Boothby was appalled by this latest Churchillian error in judgment. As *The Spectator* put it, "No one will deny Mr. Churchill's gifts, but a flair for doing the right thing at the right moment—or not doing the wrong thing at the wrong moment—is no part of them." Most of Churchill's supporters were able to contain themselves; a furious Boothby was not. Immediately after the Commons adjourned on December 7, he wrote Churchill a scathing letter that said in part: "What happened this afternoon makes me feel that it is almost impossible for those who are most devoted to you personally to follow you blindly (as they w[oul]d like to do) in politics. Because they cannot be sure where the hell they are going to be landed next."

After he calmed down a few days later, Boothby regretted his impulsiveness in sending the letter. "It was frightfully silly of me," he said years later, "because [Churchill] knew very well that he'd made a very great mistake and I shouldn't have rubbed it in." He apologized to Churchill for his diatribe, explaining that his bitterness sprang from his passionate belief that "you are the only man who can save this country, and the world, during the next two years." Churchill, who acknowledged later that he had badly misjudged the mood of the country, assured Boothby that there were no hard feelings. Yet as Boothby later saw it, his relationship with his old mentor suffered a major blow over this incident, with serious repercussions to come in the future.

While the abdication crisis, in Harold Macmillan's words, "undermined the reputation and political stature of the greatest and most prescient statesman then living," it restored the prestige of Stanley Baldwin, whose skillful, moderate handling of the controversy was widely praised. When Baldwin handed over the premiership to Neville Chamberlain the following May and retired to his country house in Worcestershire, Harold Nicolson remarked that "no man ever left in such a blaze of affection." Meanwhile Churchill, painfully aware that Britain's rearmament was falling "ever more into arrears" but with no political capital to do anything about it, was out of the spotlight for much of 1937, devoting himself to writing newspaper and magazine articles and finishing a four-volume biography of his illustrious ancestor the first Duke of Marlborough.

With Churchill again in the political wilderness, the Tory foes of appeasement looked to another parliamentary colleague for leadership of their cause. He was forty-year-old Anthony Eden, the foreign secretary and one of the very few young Tories to be given high office. An advocate of the League of Nations and collective security, Eden was seen by many in his political generation as the only stalwart champion of rearmament and resistance in a cabinet filled with irresolute conciliators. Surely, his supporters believed, he would realize the urgency of the situation and step forward to rally the anti-appeasement forces. Surely, they thought, they could count on him for that.

CHAPTER FIVE

"I LACK THE 'SPUNK'"

—⁀—

Anthony Eden was to Britons in the 1930s what John F. Kennedy was to Americans in the early 1960s: a handsome, glamorous war hero who seemed the embodiment of hope and idealism in a troubled time. The youngest foreign secretary in almost 150 years, a figure of international stature before he turned thirty-five, Eden was the shining star of his generation.

A man of dash and style, he was noted for the soft, silk-brimmed black homburg he wore, always at a jaunty angle. The hat underscored his youth and emphasized the gulf that separated him from the much older men with whom he served in the cabinet. Eden's homburg set the style in men's headgear; as late as 1977 a salesman at Locke's, the exclusive hatters in St. James's, remarked, "We are still asked for the Anthony Eden."

Eden's political rise was effortless. From the start of his parliamentary career, he was seen as a future prime minister. He was, said the director of the National Gallery Kenneth Clark, "the darling of the gods." Years later Violet Bonham Carter observed: "Paradoxically as it may seem today, [in the late 1930s] he possessed a following incomparably greater than any which Winston could command. He had no enemies. He was admired and trusted both by the Liberal and Labour parties. To supporters of the League, he was the Knight of the Covenant (and he looked the part). To that vast floating mass who have no politics or ideologies, he was a matinee idol. I believe that . . . he and he alone could have brought Chamberlain down."

Yet notwithstanding his appeal to the public and to a number of his fellow MPs, Eden was uncomfortable with the idea of being a leader. All his life he had been something of a loner. Growing up on an eight-thousand-acre estate in northern England, a middle son of a baronet, he was quiet and bookish, not much interested in the horseplay and games of his three brothers. At Eton he had few friends. He was high-strung, sensitive, and prone to sudden gusts of anger and bad temper, traits that stayed with him all his life.

Like many other young Britons, Eden was barely out of childhood when he went to war. From Eton, he joined the Yeoman Rifles and was sent to France in May 1916. A year later he was awarded the Military Cross for rescuing his wounded platoon sergeant from no-man's-land during the battle of the Somme. Affectionately called "the Boy" by the men he commanded, he was promoted to brigade major in 1918 at the age of twenty, the youngest in the army.

Eden was among the few young officers serving more than a year at the front to return home physically unscathed. Yet he bore invisible scars from the carnage. Two of his brothers were killed, one near Ypres and the other, only sixteen years old, at the battle of Jutland. His mother noted how Eden's experiences in the trenches of France had "deprived him of all youthful ideas and thoughts and made him prematurely old." When he went up to Oxford in 1919, he devoted himself to his studies, declining to get involved with the Oxford Union, the university's famed debating society, and other popular student organizations and having no time for the carousing of younger fellow students like Bob Boothby. He did, however, indulge his lifelong passion for art and began to amass a collection of paintings that in time included works by Corot, Monet, Derain, Degas, Picasso, and Braque. In 1922 he received a first-class degree in Persian and Arabic, and a year later, at the age of twenty-six, he was elected to the House of Commons.

Eden spent more than thirty years in the Commons, but he never felt at home there. A man who valued civility and tolerance, he hated the partisanship of the place, the constant intrigues and infighting. Although he could be gregarious and charming on the hustings and at

London dinner parties, where he was a prize guest, Eden was at heart an "unclubbable" man. In contrast with most of his parliamentary colleagues, he was uncomfortable with the hearty bonhomie and camaraderie of London men's clubs. To Churchill's great indignation, he even refused an invitation to join The Other Club. He was rarely seen in the Commons smoking room, which, to his mind, was even worse than clubs like the Beefsteak, Pratt's, or White's. Although it boasted brown leather chairs and sofas and had a panoramic view of the Thames, the smoking room often seemed more like a pub than a club. MPs could get a drink there any time they liked. When Parliament was in session, it was an exceedingly noisy place, filled with shouts, boisterous laughter, and occasional intense arguments.

No, Eden decided, this was not his idea of a congenial refuge. He much preferred the genteel, patrician world of the Foreign Office. Within a few years of his arrival in Parliament, he had carved out a niche in foreign affairs, and in 1931 he was named the Foreign Office's parliamentary undersecretary, which made him the foreign secretary's representative in the Commons. The following year he was sent to Geneva as Britain's chief delegate to the World Disarmament Conference, sponsored by the League of Nations. After two years of work the conference ended in failure. Germany withdrew its representatives and stepped up its rearmament campaign. The League, not for the first time, was shown to be well-meaning but unable to halt the rapidly growing threat of war. Yet despite its collapse, the disarmament conference made Anthony Eden a star.

At Geneva, Eden had won the respect of his fellow delegates; he was hardworking, well versed in the arcane complexities of disarmament issues, a skilled negotiator. But the British newspapers turned him into something more. They touted him as the "outstanding success" of the conference, a survivor of Britain's lost generation who was trying to make a better world, determined to ensure that the deaths of all those other young men were not in vain.

In a government crowded with drab, stiff old men, Eden shone. Newspaper stories enthused over his movie-idol looks and his impeccably tailored Savile Row suits. Women swooned over him. In the United States a poll proclaimed him "the fourth best dressed man in

Europe." Photographs showed him with his beautiful wife, Beatrice, the daughter of a Yorkshire squire, and their two equally photogenic sons.

Yet not everyone was smitten. Some of Eden's colleagues, no doubt driven in part by envy, muttered that his success was a triumph of image over substance. They saw vanity in the care he took with his hair and clothes and his refusal to wear glasses in public, although he almost always wore them in private. His speeches were derided by his critics as dull and full of platitudes. "Anthony Eden was brought in to tell us about foreign affairs and made a little speech, telling us nothing that we didn't know before," a fellow MP once snorted. It was "a very commonplace effort, but of course it was treated as if it was delivered to us by an oracle." After another Eden speech, Churchill was said to have quipped: "My God, the boy managed to use every known cliché except 'May the blessing of God be upon you' and 'Gentlemen will please adjust their dress before leaving.'"

None of his perceived failings, however, put a brake on Eden's meteoric rise. In June 1935 he entered the cabinet as minister for League of Nations affairs. Six months later he was named foreign secretary, after Hoare's resignation in the wake of the Hoare-Laval fiasco. Churchill, to whom Eden would be closely allied in the future, worried at the time that the younger man did not have sufficient gravitas for the job. "Eden's appointment does not inspire me with confidence," Churchill wrote to his wife. "I expect the greatness of his office will find him out." He added, "I think you will now see what a lightweight Eden is."

Throughout most of his two-year tenure at the Foreign Office, Eden differed little from the prime minister and his cabinet colleagues in his views regarding the overall direction of British foreign policy. He was more hostile to Mussolini than were most other British officials, but he agreed with the general consensus that it was not only possible but necessary to reach an agreement with Germany. In 1934 he had gone to Berlin to meet Hitler and, after the session, had reported back to London that he didn't think the führer wanted war. "Dare I confess it?" he wrote to his wife. "I rather liked him." To Ramsay MacDonald, Eden wrote: "I think we can trust the Chancellor not to go back on his word."

When Hitler marched into the Rhineland in 1936, Eden began to change his mind about Hitler's trustworthiness, expressing unease to the cabinet about the growing threat of war. Yet in public he sounded no such warning. In a speech to Parliament, he declared there was no reason to "suppose that the present German action implies a threat of hostilities." When the French foreign minister argued for military and economic intervention against Germany, Eden refused to do anything to help France throw the Germans out.* In the months after the Rhineland crisis, he continued to support the idea of negotiations with Hitler while at the same time arguing for intensified British rearmament. To friends and subordinates, he revealed increasing frustration with the lackadaisical, vacillating drift of Stanley Baldwin's approach to the dictators.

When Neville Chamberlain succeeded Baldwin in May 1937, Eden's relief was shared by many other Tories, regardless of their stand on appeasement. Harold Macmillan, having resigned the whip in June 1936, once again was a Tory in good standing; it was his hope and belief that Chamberlain would give a much-needed jump start to national policy. Here at last was a prime minister with energy and purpose, two qualities that had been absent at 10 Downing Street for well over a decade. As chancellor of the exchequer the hard-charging Chamberlain had been the most effective minister in the MacDonald and Baldwin cabinets. He had been instrumental in reviving the economy after the 1931 collapse, although progressives like Macmillan, Boothby, and Cartland faulted him for his unwillingness to do more to solve the problems of unemployment and poverty.

At the same time, they acknowledged his sterling record as a social reformer in the cabinet post he had held before becoming chancellor. As secretary of health in the 1920s Chamberlain had been responsible for legislation reforming the Poor Laws, reorganizing local governments, and providing for widows' and orphans' pensions, slum clearance, better health care, and more housing. "There are many homes in England that would be motherless today but for the impetus which . . . Chamberlain gave to the campaign against maternal mortality,"

---

*Years later Eden had second thoughts about his actions during the Rhineland crisis. "I should have been more responsive to what the French appeared to want to do, and stiffer to Hitler," he declared. Intervention, he added, "would have been the right thing to do, and many millions of lives would have been saved."

Churchill wrote in the mid-1930s. He quoted Chamberlain as saying: "My own mother died in childbirth. And I know how great is the injury to the family when the mother is taken away." Many years later Macmillan declared that if Chamberlain had not become prime minister, "he would have been remembered . . . [as] one of the most progressive and effective social reformers of his own or almost any time."

Neville Chamberlain was the younger son of Joseph Chamberlain, one of Britain's leading political figures in the late nineteenth and early twentieth centuries, who was known for his devotion to empire and to social reform. A wealthy industrialist and former mayor of Birmingham, the elder Chamberlain had created a family machine that dominated the political life of that midlands city for almost fifty years. Neville followed in his father's footsteps, also serving as a reformist mayor of Birmingham before his election to Parliament in 1918. As mayor he guided the creation of the Birmingham Symphony Orchestra and the University of Birmingham.

Chamberlain, who was sixty-eight when he became prime minister, was very much a product of the Victorian age—he was in his thirties when Queen Victoria died—and was always uncomfortable with modern inventions and ideas. He had never been in a plane before his dramatic visits to Hitler in September 1938, didn't like cars and phones, and never took to the fountain pen, preferring to write his letters and speeches with a plain steel nib.

Unlike his father and elder half brother, Austen, Neville was not a natural politician. Shy, self-conscious, and aloof, he had few friends. His speeches, clear and logical as they were, were also dry and colorless, with no spark of eloquence to stir the imagination. For much of his life he lived in the shadows of his father, who possessed an intimidatingly forceful personality, and his half brother, an eminent foreign affairs expert who served as foreign secretary under Baldwin. While Joseph Chamberlain groomed Austen for stardom in politics, he pushed his younger son toward a career in business, a path Neville obediently took for twenty years before veering off to enter politics in Birmingham. He was forty-nine when first elected to Parliament.

Winston Churchill speculated that the death of Chamberlain's mother when he was five "led to the creation of that cloak of icy reserve in which, at times, the man appears to be wrapped." His favorite forms of recreation—fishing, bird-watching, gardening, reading Shakespeare and Conrad, listening to Beethoven—were solitary pastimes. With his family and close friends, he could be sensitive, affectionate, charming, even playful on occasion. But not many people saw that side of Neville Chamberlain. "Only a few of us, who knew him best, could appreciate his finer qualities, even when we differed profoundly with him over policy," said Leo Amery, a onetime close friend and political ally.

To the dismay of those, like Eden and Macmillan, who applauded Chamberlain's becoming prime minister, those finer qualities were not on display when he moved into Downing Street. The only Chamberlain to reach the premiership, he seemed determined from the beginning to prove he could outdo his father in toughness and outshine his half brother in formulating foreign policy, despite his lack of expertise in that area. While Baldwin may have been too much of a conciliator, Chamberlain showed no interest at all in getting along with anybody who disagreed with him. "His face seemed to wear a perpetual sneer, even when, as must have sometimes been the case, no sneer was intended," recalled Francis Williams, editor of the *Daily Herald*, a Labour newspaper. "His manner was frigid and condescending . . . He was the most charmless of men."

Chamberlain did not subscribe to the idea that civility should guide political discourse. Unlike Baldwin, he did not frequent the Commons smoking room to have an occasional whiskey and chat with backbenchers. When he did visit, Harold Nicolson remarked, an awkward hush would fall over the room, as if the headmaster, "with unconvincing conviviality," had intruded on "the sixth-form tea." In the House itself Chamberlain introduced a new sense of divisiveness, a feeling of "us" against "them." He brought an edge of harshness and confrontation to debates, using "my sharp tongue" and "my nasty sarcastic way," as he put it, to score points off opponents, be they Labourites, Liberals, or Tory rebels. One Tory MP said: "He was always able to arouse cheers from his supporters by some snide remark, as much as to say, 'What do you know about this subject? I, with the full facts behind me, am alone capable of arriving at the right decision.'" Yet at the same time, Chamberlain was very sensitive about attacks against *him*. "[His] vanity takes the form of resenting any kind of criticism or mockery," noted John Colville. "There is no surer way of gratifying him than to make some allusion to the exceptional importance of his position. In other words, he likes to be set on a pedestal and adored, with suitable humility, by unquestioning admirers."

Among Conservatives, Chamberlain insisted on total loyalty to himself and his beliefs. He once heard rumors that Frank Pakenham, a young worker in the Tory Party's research department, was about to jump ship to the Labour Party. When Pakenham married a young woman named Elizabeth Harman, Chamberlain refused to attend the wedding, even though Harman was his cousin and Chamberlain's own daughter was a bridesmaid. He also instructed Pakenham's Tory coworkers not to attend the reception.*

Determined to save England and the rest of the world from another conflagration, Chamberlain would listen to no one who disagreed with him about how that was to be done. His two closest government associates—Sir John Simon, chancellor of the exchequer, and Sir Samuel Hoare, resurrected after the Hoare-Laval debacle and now home secretary—both were champions of appeasement. Chamberlain's resolution to avoid war stemmed in part from a fundamental fear and hatred of combat and its consequences. "I am myself a man of peace to the depths of my soul," he later declared. "Armed conflict between nations is a nightmare to me." But peace, in Chamberlain's view, also made good economic sense. Haunted by the economic depression from which Britain had so recently emerged, he refused to risk his country's still-fragile recovery by going all out for rearmament, as Churchill and the other Tory rebels demanded. Even though Baldwin had begun to bolster the nation's meager defenses in 1934, the effort was halfhearted, in part because of the determination of Chamberlain, as chancellor of the exchequer, to put strict limits on the military

---

*Pakenham, who succeeded his brother as Earl of Longford in 1961, did indeed join the Labour Party and was a minister in postwar Labour governments. His wife, Elizabeth Longford, also a strong Labourite, gained prominence as a biographer of Elizabeth I and Queen Victoria. The Pakenhams were the parents of eight children, among them the writers Antonia Fraser, Thomas Pakenham, and Rachel Billington.

budget. Chamberlain believed there were too many demands on the nation's economic resources, prominently including maintaining its far-flung empire, to allow sharp increases in defense spending. Once he became prime minister, he continued to limit rearmament. "A boxer cannot work himself into a proper psychological and physical condition for a fight that he seriously believes will never come off. It was the same with England," John F. Kennedy wrote in *Why England Slept*, his 1940 study of British appeasement.

Most of the budget increases sanctioned by Baldwin and Chamberlain went to the development and production of fighter planes to counter the long-feared specter of German aerial attack. There was little emphasis on bomber production, and the army was even more badly neglected. In early 1937 Robert Bruce Lockhart, a former British diplomat and intelligence agent, noted in his diary "a very depressing" conversation he had with a high-ranking army officer about rearmament. "Very little is being done," the officer told Lockhart, who wrote: "He thinks our decline is at the flood and that we shall deserve all we get. Inertia in high quarters is complete. The tragedy is that there are always so many plausible reasons for doing nothing."

In truth, Neville Chamberlain thought *he* was Britain's most effective weapon against the dictators. He was adamant in his belief that he could bargain with them and bring them to heel. Despite abundant evidence to the contrary and despite the fact that he did not meet either Hitler or Mussolini until 1938 and did not know much about them or their countries, Chamberlain could never bring himself to believe that they wanted to go to war. Clinging to the security of his ignorance, he created a peace-loving image of them that defied reality. "He thought you could do business with Hitler and Mussolini like you do business between businessmen, both of whom trust each other and know the other to be a man of complete integrity," said Harold Macmillan. "He didn't believe people existed [who would] say one thing and do another . . . It was pathetic, really."

While Chamberlain's steadfast belief in negotiation probably did stem from his background as a businessman, it also was an intrinsic part of the public-school values espoused by him and the rest of the British establishment. (Chamberlain was a Rugby man while Simon

and Hoare were Etonians.) The prime minister and his supporters held
to the idea of fair play and to the notion that gentlemanly behavior was
universal. In late 1937 Chamberlain wrote a letter on Downing Street
stationery to Ivy Chamberlain, his brother's widow, who was then acting as the prime minister's unofficial emissary to Mussolini. Eden was
appalled when he learned that the letter had been sent by regular mail
to Rome. "Prime Minister, your letter will be opened and read by the
Italian government!" the foreign secretary exclaimed. Chamberlain
snorted. "What a nasty mind you have," he snapped. "Gentlemen don't
do that." Eden later discovered that the letter was on Il Duce's desk the
following day.

Alfred Duff Cooper, who served as first lord of the admiralty under
Chamberlain, once remarked: "A man who is both so confident of himself and so confiding in others has as little chance in a Europe dominated by [the dictators] as Little Lord Fauntleroy would have of
concluding a satisfactory deal with Al Capone." Nonetheless, from the
first days of his premiership Chamberlain made clear he planned to
play a far more dominant role in foreign affairs than his more easygo-
ing predecessor had. That decision put him on a collision course with
his young foreign secretary.

In the spring of 1937, just as Chamberlain was about to move into
10 Downing Street, a shadowy government figure named Sir Horace
Wilson paid a call on James P. L. "Jim" Thomas, Eden's new parliamentary private secretary. On paper, Wilson was the government's chief industrial adviser, an expert on labor negotiations. In reality, he was to
become Chamberlain's closest and most trusted counselor. The prime
minister installed Wilson in an office adjoining his own at Downing
Street, went for daily walks with him, and consulted him on issues for
which the civil servant had no expertise, prominently including foreign
affairs. "He is the most remarkable man in England," Chamberlain
once told Kenneth Clark. "I couldn't live a day without him."

In his visit to Jim Thomas, Wilson brought with him Warren Fisher,
head of the British Civil Service. The two men indicated to Thomas
their disapproval of what they perceived as the Foreign Office's bias

against appeasement, and they urged him to help "build a bridge" between the Foreign Office and Downing Street. Thomas met with the two officials several times in the summer and fall of 1937. Aware that they wanted him to spy on Eden and other Foreign Office staffers, he finally made clear he had no intention of "work[ing] behind the back of my own chief."

At about the same time, Thomas was told by acquaintances in the government that several of Eden's cabinet colleagues, including Simon and Hoare, were intriguing against the foreign secretary. At a dinner party, Lord Swinton, the air minister, reportedly declared that "foreign policy was now to be transferred from the Foreign Office to No. 10" and would be dictated by Chamberlain, Simon, and Hoare. The situation, Thomas remarked, "was becoming intolerable."

Chamberlain's appeasement of Mussolini was the breaking point. The prime minister believed he could keep Italy out of Hitler's orbit by reaching an agreement with Mussolini that would formally recognize Italy's annexation of Abyssinia. When Eden argued that Mussolini must make certain concessions before negotiations began, Chamberlain bypassed him and met with the Italian ambassador to discuss the possibility of an agreement. Then, in January 1938, again without consulting Eden, he rejected an offer by President Roosevelt to help in defusing international tensions. Already irritated by Chamberlain's one-man approach to diplomacy, Eden was angered by his cold-shouldering of Roosevelt and his deference to Mussolini. His fury was stoked by his closest associates at the Foreign Office. Chief among them was Lord Bobbety Cranborne, Eden's undersecretary and best friend.

Bobbety Cranborne's nickname, which he acknowledged was "ridiculous . . . but the one by which I am known to my friends," was the only thing foolish about him. He was a Cecil. If there was any family that could claim to have been born to govern England, it was his. Cecils had held high offices of state since the reign of Elizabeth I. Cranborne's grandfather the third Marquess of Salisbury had been prime minister, as had his cousin Arthur Balfour. In the 1930s the Cecils had the added distinction of being one of the few great aristocratic families in Britain whose members were strongly opposed to appeasement. For generations they had been known for their independence of thought and their determination to champion unpopular causes. "The Cecils are deaf to the howling of the mob," declared one nineteenth-century admirer. In the newest political generation of Cecils, it was Bobbety Cranborne who led the way.

A product of Eton and Oxford, the thin, balding Cranborne, who had fought with the Grenadier Guards in the war, was an anomaly in the hushed, well-mannered world of the Foreign Office, just as he was in the more raucous milieu of the Commons. He was a man of unshakable moral conviction who, like Ronald Cartland, never hesitated to say what he believed, regardless of the consequences. "He saw so clearly the rights and wrongs of [a situation]," said Jim Thomas. "He was completely untrammeled by the worldly considerations of the average politician."

Cranborne was certain that appeasement would lead to catastrophe for Britain. Jim Thomas and Oliver Harvey, a career diplomat who was Eden's departmental private secretary, agreed with him. If Eden had not had the counsel of these three men, it is questionable whether he would have responded to Chamberlain in the way that he ultimately did. The very qualities that made Eden successful in diplomacy—caution, a penchant for conciliation and compromise—made him considerably less effective as a political leader. Cranborne, Thomas, and Harvey helped him by bolstering his self-confidence and courage. They urged Eden to capitalize on the growing public uneasiness over appeasement and to confront the prime minister. Eden was the most popular figure in the cabinet. If he withdrew his support, his advisers said, the Chamberlain government would surely fall. "The Government is living on your popularity and your reputation," Harvey wrote Eden in late 1937. "You are not only entitled to, but you are able to, impose your terms." Echoing that sentiment, Hamilton Kerr, who was Duff Cooper's parliamentary private secretary, told Cooper in February 1938 that if Eden left the government, "the situation in the House would be hopeless, that more than a hundred of our supporters would vote against us," including, Cooper suspected, Kerr himself.

The clash between Chamberlain and Eden came to a head on February 19, when Chamberlain announced to the cabinet that he intended to open direct negotiations with Mussolini despite Eden's opposition.

The foreign secretary told Chamberlain that he now had no option but to resign. Yet Eden still seemed unsure. Other cabinet members, fearful of the country's reaction to the news, pressed him hard over the next twenty-four hours to reconsider, and Eden wavered, thinking perhaps there was some compromise that could keep him in the government. If he resigned, would he lose all chance of becoming prime minister? His conscience was at war with his ambition, and Cranborne and Thomas did everything in their power to see that his conscience won. In between his meetings with cabinet members, they acted like a prizefighter's seconds between rounds, sitting him down, bucking him up, assuring him he was doing the right thing. He would not be alone in leaving, they said; they too would resign. And together, they would tell the House of Commons why they had done so. Finally Eden agreed. On the evening of February 20 he made his resignation official.

The news electrified London. "The newspapers blaze with Eden's resignation," Harold Nicolson wrote in his diary. "Telephone messages all morning—everybody not knowing what to do. I tell them to keep calm . . ." In Germany, newspapers crowed that Eden's resignation was a sign of Chamberlain's capitulation to Hitler. The führer had made a speech attacking the foreign minister on the day he resigned; the following day, a headline in Berlin blared: "Hitler Speaks, Eden Goes." Arthur Mann, the editor of the *Yorkshire Post*, gloomily told a friend that Hitler and Mussolini "doubtless think they have got Chamberlain on the run."

Mann was one of the few newspaper editors in Britain to endorse Eden's action; most of the national papers, based in London, strongly supported Chamberlain and his government. Even so, Eden's resignation alarmed many Britons. In a nationwide opinion poll, 71 percent of those surveyed said they thought Eden had been right to resign. Only 26 percent said they approved of Chamberlain's foreign policy; 58 percent said they did not.

A full-blown political crisis seemed to be at hand. "The whole country is in a ferment," Chips Channon, an ardent Chamberlain supporter, noted worriedly. "[N]o one knows yet which way the cat will jump." Tory dissidents, along with appeasement foes outside Parliament, were delighted. They were sure that Eden would capitalize on the burgeoning public opposition to Chamberlain's policies, that he would take full advantage of this opportunity to rally Parliament and the nation against the prime minister and his men. Along with the rest of the country, they awaited his resignation speech with anticipation.

At times of national crisis and controversy, large crowds have traditionally gathered outside Parliament and 10 Downing Street. Early in the morning on February 21, Parliament Square began filling up with people. As Eden and Cranborne entered the grand neo-Gothic building in midafternoon, they were greeted with wild cheers by the hundreds outside. The chamber itself was crowded to capacity and charged with tension. When Chamberlain took his place on the government bench, he was loudly cheered by the Tories behind him. Half an hour later Eden and Cranborne came in and took seats below the gangway, the traditional spot for ministers who have resigned. Pale and nervous, Eden seemed oblivious to the shouts of encouragement he received from the Opposition benches and from Tory supporters, who included Churchill, Macmillan, Cartland, Harold Nicolson, Edward Spears, Ronald Tree, Paul Emrys-Evans, and Jack Macnamara. The rest of the Conservatives sat in silence, waiting to hear what he had to say.

Just hours before the debate, Churchill sent a note to Eden urging him not to shrink from taking Chamberlain on. His was the cause of England, Churchill declared. But when Eden stood up to speak, he offered no call to battle, no ringing denunciation of appeasement. The excitement and anticipation in the chamber turned to bewilderment. His convoluted remarks, touching only on his and Chamberlain's disagreement about launching talks with Italy, were as polite and gentlemanly as he himself. They were so bland and diplomatic, in fact, that many of his colleagues were not sure why he had resigned.

It was up to Bobbety Cranborne to make the case that Eden failed to make. Looking more like an accountant than a politician, the bespectacled Cranborne rose as soon as Eden finished. The issue at stake was not just a disagreement over the fine points of a diplomatic negotiation, he declared. It was a question of fundamental principle. Should Britain negotiate with a country that had repeatedly violated treaties and agreements? Lord Cranborne thought not. Chamberlain's determination to pursue talks with Italy, he said, was nothing but a "surrender to blackmail." According to *The Daily Telegraph*, Cranborne, not known for his eloquence, "took the House by surprise with the vigour of his language" and stole "Mr. Eden's thunder."

As effective as Cranborne was that day, however, it was Eden to whom appeasement foes looked for leadership. Even after his equivocal speech, they continued to hope that he would take up the challenge. In the days to come, he received hundreds of letters from all over the country imploring him to do exactly that. Anthony Eden "is at this hour the most powerful man in Great Britain," a Canadian newspaper declared six days after his resignation. "He can split the Conservative party in the House and in the country. In the general election which he might make inescapable, he [could] emerge as leader of the government with a more extensive, more varied, and more passionate support than has been given to any prime minister of our time in Britain." Although Chamberlain still had a huge majority in the House, "[t]here is another soul in Britain which has found little opportunity for expression," which is sick of the "expediency and timidity which has spread like a poison gas over that once gallant land . . ." It was up to Anthony Eden, the paper said, to answer the call.

Ten years later, after the end of World War II, Winston Churchill wrote in his memoirs about the sleepless night he spent after learning that Eden had resigned as foreign secretary. Churchill described Eden as "the one strong young figure standing up against long, dismal, drawling tides of drift and surrender" in 1938. It was a generous, romanticized view of the man who became Churchill's chief wartime lieutenant, and it reinforced for future generations the earlier popular image of Eden. The trouble was, the image did not square with reality. In their yearning for leadership in the battle over appeasement, Eden's supporters invested him with a spirit of defiance that he never possessed. "We assumed," said the journalist Douglas Jay, that Eden was protesting "against the general drift of Chamberlain's policies." In fact, although he had resigned over negotiations with Italy, he did not differ radically with Chamberlain over the prime minister's appeasement of Germany.

Moreover, Anthony Eden had no desire to bring the government down. Rebellion was not in his blood. Years later he wrote in his diary: "I truly hate the game of politics, not because I am better than [other politicians], God forbid, but because I lack the 'spunk.'" Before his resignation, he had made no attempt to rally to his side Duff Cooper and other cabinet colleagues who had voiced increasing concern about the direction of Chamberlain's foreign policy. Perhaps he hoped that without any major effort on his part, the government would collapse and the House would rally around him. But that did not happen, and to make sure it did not, members of the cabinet and the government whips' office started a whispering campaign claiming that Eden had resigned because of physical and mental problems.

Despite the slander, Eden made clear he had no intention of cutting himself off from the Conservative leadership. Indeed, before giving a postresignation speech in his constituency, he submitted his remarks to the secretary of the cabinet for approval—hardly, as his biographer D. R. Thorpe notes, "the move of a rebel out to cause trouble." He then took his wife to the south of France for a vacation that lasted almost two months. Eden is "too shrewd a statesman to burn his boats irretrievably," Chips Channon wrote in his diary in late February. "Already there is talk of him coming back" to the government.

On March 12, less than a month after Eden's resignation, Hitler's troops goose-stepped into Austria, while the former foreign secretary remained on the Côte d'Azur. Those who had looked to him for leadership were thunderstruck. If there was ever a time to draw the line over appeasement, the moment when Germany took over a sovereign nation surely was it. After militarizing the Rhineland, Hitler had pledged that "Germany neither intends . . . to annex Austria or to conclude an Anschluss." How many more broken promises would there have to be before Chamberlain and his men recognized the führer's rapacity for what it was?

On London street corners, newsboys yelled, "Germany on the march again!" while outside 10 Downing Street, tense crowds watched ministers hurry in and out. The British capital was gripped by fear of war, a fear that "hung in the air like poison gas," Virginia Cowles recalled. Young men rushed to volunteer for the Territorial Army, and women and older men signed up to work in ambulance services and air-raid precaution organizations. A few days after the Anschluss, thousands marched through Hyde Park, shouting and carrying signs declaring CHAMBERLAIN MUST GO!

Lord Halifax, the tall, stork-like former viceroy of India who had replaced Eden as foreign secretary, told the cabinet that "public opinion was moving fast in the direction of placing the defences of the country more nearly on a war footing." The House of Commons "has been in almost continuous uproar since you left," Ronald Cartland wrote Jim Thomas, who had accompanied the Edens to France. "The P.M.'s refusal to [do anything about Austria] has produced a lot of whispering and hatching of plots in the lobbies and smoking room . . . Austria has shaken people."

Chamberlain hastened to put an end to the warlike mood, assuring the cabinet and his countrymen that Britain would not become involved in this latest international furor. As further assurance, *The Times*, which usually reflected the government's views, ran photographs of throngs of wildly enthusiastic Austrians welcoming Hitler to Vienna. There were no photos of the hundreds of Austrians, many of them Jews, who were shot in those first days of Nazi rule or of the tens of thousands who were arrested and sent to concentration camps. Likewise, there were no pictures of the wholesale looting of Jewish shops and homes by storm troopers or of Nazis forcing Jewish doctors, lawyers, and professors to clean toilets and scrub streets on their hands and knees. A shaken Douglas Reed, *The Times* correspondent in Vienna who had witnessed firsthand such scenes of humiliation and terror, was not as complaisant as his paper. "In my wildest nightmares I had not foreseen anything so perfectly organized, so brutal, so ruthless, so strong," Reed wrote to *The Times'* editor, Geoffrey Dawson. "When this machine goes into action, it will blight everything it encounters like a swarm of locusts. The destruction of life will make the World War look like the Boer War." CBS correspondent William Shirer, another witness to the Nazi brutalities in Austria, declared that "the behavior of the Vienna Nazis was worse than anything I had seen in Germany. There was an orgy of sadism."

At Cap Ferrat, meanwhile, Anthony Eden kept tabs on the situation by reading French newspapers and listening to broadcasts from Vienna. In a letter to Paul Emrys-Evans, Jim Thomas reported that

Eden was "at the top of his form. Six sets of tennis per day and scarlet in the face with sun. My feet are blistered, my wind has gone, but A[nthony] is ruthless." A ruthlessness, Eden's supporters noted unhappily, that he failed to apply to politics back home.

In Britain the sense of crisis over Austria soon dissipated, and in Virginia Cowles's words, the "public settled back in the comfortable illusion of peace." But the foreign secretary's departure from government did have an impact that slowly gathered strength in the coming months. Tory anti-appeasement MPs began to join forces, speaking out in support of Eden and refusing to back the government in its opposition to a Labour-sponsored vote of censure of the prime minister. There weren't many Tory abstainers in the vote, only about twenty—a group that, in addition to Churchill, included Macmillan, Cartland, Boothby, Thomas, Nicolson, Emrys-Evans, Macnamara, Spears, and Tree. And their decision had no real effect; the Tory majority resoundingly defeated Labour's censure resolution. But their actions marked the first green shoot of open rebellion, and Chamberlain and the Tory Party hierarchy were determined to stamp it out.

Emrys-Evans and Nicolson, the two former diplomats and Foreign Office veterans, were the first to feel the consequences.

Paul Emrys-Evans, then forty-eight, was chairman of the House Foreign Affairs Committee, which oversaw the work of the Foreign Office. Emrys-Evans had grown up in South Africa, the son of a British banker who had emigrated there. An alumnus of Harrow and Cambridge, he, like many of his colleagues, was a war veteran; his left arm had been shattered on the first day of the battle of the Somme. After six years in the diplomatic service and Foreign Office, he was elected to Parliament in 1931 and joined the small group of progressive Tory MPs who urged social reform, although he was, as he later put it, "certainly nothing like as far left as Macmillan."

But his consuming interest remained foreign affairs. "After Hitler seized power in Germany I felt strongly that a revolution had taken place," he recalled, "and that we should . . . do everything in our power to contain Germany and resist Hitler." Following Hitler's march into the Rhineland, Emrys-Evans sent David Margesson a scathing letter about the government's refusal to respond to Germany's remilitarization. "The events of this year have been little short of disastrous," he declared. "A lead simply must be given if the rot is to be stopped. There is far too much defeatism in the Government."

Emrys-Evans, whom one acquaintance described as "blazingly honest," was particularly irate at the failure of British leaders to let the public know what was really going on. He believed that the British people, in their support of the Tory call for sanctions against Italy in the 1935 election and their subsequent fury over the Hoare-Laval pact, had sent an unmistakable signal that they would back a more assertive foreign policy and intensified British rearmament, a signal that Baldwin and his men ignored. "It is fashionable to say that public opinion was so pacifist that we could not have rearmed or adopted a strong foreign policy," Emrys-Evans wrote years later. Such a belief, in his opinion, was "a libel on the people by incompetent and timid leaders. The country was never told the truth, and those who endeavoured to explain what was going on in the world and gave a warning of what was likely to happen if we didn't act, were written off by the Government, the Party Machine, and the Press as a small body of alarmists."

With Baldwin as prime minister, Emrys-Evans's letter did not create much of a stir in the government. But when Chamberlain succeeded Baldwin and the number of dissidents began to swell, such tolerance came to an abrupt halt. In early 1938 Margesson intervened to tone down a communiqué from the Foreign Affairs Committee urging Chamberlain to adopt a tougher line with Hitler. The statement would only "provoke" the führer, he declared. Emrys-Evans reluctantly agreed to soften the communiqué's language (despite protests from Churchill), because he didn't want to add to Eden's difficulties in his struggle with Chamberlain. "It was a humiliating episode," Emrys-Evans later recalled in a letter to Eden, "and [it shows] what pressure the Whips were already trying to apply to the backbenchers."

The committee chairman's willingness to compromise ended when Eden resigned. He was disappointed that Eden hadn't quit over the issue of rearmament, which the foreign secretary had been "pressing on an unsympathetic and reluctant Cabinet without success." Nonetheless, Emrys-Evans gave an outspoken speech supporting Eden in the House. He called the resignation "a calamity" for the country and accused the government of adopting "undignified and panicky methods" of appeasing both Mussolini and Hitler.

Joining him in the attack was Harold Nicolson, who was Emrys-Evans's deputy on the Foreign Affairs Committee. Nicolson echoed Bobbety Cranborne's assertion that Chamberlain, in agreeing to negotiate with Italy, had succumbed to blackmail. Was it right, he asked the House, that a "country which has continuously, consistently, deliberately and without apology, violated every engagement into which she has ever entered" be "taken back into the fold with a smile"? "However weak we might be, however divided, however muddle-headed, we never defended wrong with cool and planned deliberation as we are doing now," Nicolson declared. "I regret that those great principles of our policy should now lie tattered at our feet."

Like Ronald Cartland, Nicolson was a relative "new boy" in Parliament—he had been an MP for slightly more than two years—but his expertise in foreign affairs was far greater than that of Emrys-Evans or, for that matter, virtually any other backbencher. The son of Sir Arthur Nicolson, an eminent British ambassador who ended his career as permanent undersecretary of the Foreign Office, Harold had spent much of his boyhood in British embassies in the Balkans, the Middle East, Spain, and Russia. After attending Wellington and Oxford, he joined the Foreign Office, and his knowledge of the Middle East and the Balkans quickly made him indispensable to the foreign secretaries he served. As an adviser to Arthur Balfour he helped draft the Balfour Declaration, which in 1917 gave British support to the establishment of a Jewish homeland in Palestine. At the Paris Peace Conference in 1919 he aided Balfour with the drafting of postwar peace terms and was involved too in the drawing of borders for the newly independent country of Czechoslovakia. Later Nicolson wrote several books on the art of diplomacy, based on his experiences in Paris. *Peacemaking, 1919* (1933) and *Diplomacy* (1939) became classics.

In the 1920s Nicolson was counselor in the British legation in Tehran and then in the embassy in Berlin. After his stint in Germany, he was to go to the embassy in Washington as the ambassador's deputy.

"He seemed marked out for a dazzling career," a fellow diplomat remarked. As the decade ended, there was little doubt in Whitehall that
Nicolson, like his father, would eventually wind up as an ambassador
himself.

But in January 1930, at the age of forty-three, he abruptly resigned
from the Foreign Office and joined the staff of the *Evening Standard*,
one of the newspapers owned by Lord Beaverbrook, to help write a daily
column of political and social gossip titled "Londoner's Diary." It was an
astonishing end to a brilliant diplomatic career, and speculation about
why he had quit was rife in London social circles. As it happened, he
had done it, in large part, because of his wife, Vita Sackville-West. Devoted to her writing career and her independence, Sackville-West
hated the duties of a diplomatic wife and made clear to her husband
she would not accompany him to Washington, just as she had not been
with him in Tehran and Berlin. Her absence was barely acceptable at
his first two posts, but it certainly would not do for the number two
man in Washington to have a missing spouse.

It was also true, however, that Nicolson had been miserable without his wife in Iran and Germany. Theirs was a most unusual marriage.
Both of them had been involved in numerous homosexual affairs,
Sackville-West most notably with Violet Trefusis and Virginia Woolf.
But they were emotionally dependent on each other, and both were to
feel an intense attachment to Sissinghurst Castle, a decrepit old manor
in Kent that Sackville-West bought in 1930, several months after her
husband left the Foreign Office. There Nicolson and Sackville-West
would plant the beautiful gardens that were to make Sissinghurst famous throughout the world.

The journalistic job offered by Lord Beaverbrook afforded Nicolson
good money and the chance to spend more time with Sackville-West
and their two sons. To the *Standard* editors, the gregarious, urbane
Nicolson seemed perfect for the position. He was a brilliant raconteur
with a lively sense of irony and humor, who was very much at home in
social London. A member of several of the capital's best clubs, he loved
attending the endless dinner parties and other social gatherings to
which he was invited. Even when the parties were dull, he still had
fun. "It is so odd. I enjoyed it," he wrote in his diary after one such

party. "I always enjoy everything. That is dreadful. I must pull myself together and be bored for once."

Yet Nicolson also was a deeply literate and cultured man—while at the Foreign Office, he wrote biographies of Tennyson, Swinburne, Byron, and Verlaine—and not surprisingly, he found his work on "Londoner's Diary" trivial and degrading. After eighteen months he quit the *Standard* and went back to writing books and making occasional radio broadcasts. As the threats to European peace mounted in the mid-1930s, he missed being "in the center of things" at the Foreign Office and concluded that his life had been a failure. "I have lost all serious employment, sacrificed my hopes of power, and am up against the anxiety of not having one penny in the world beyond what I earn," he wrote.

Then came the chance to stand for Parliament in 1935 as a National Labour Party candidate. The National Labour Party was a tiny Labour splinter group that supported the Conservative-controlled coalition government and hewed to the Tory Party line. When he was adopted as the National Labour candidate for West Leicester, Nicolson asked a party organizer if he could ever say what he thought, rather than just mouth the party's position. The man was shocked. "Most certainly not, Mr. Nicolson!" he exclaimed. "Very dangerous, indeed!"

Sackville-West refused to campaign for him, but despite the lack of a supportive wife by his side, Nicolson narrowly won the seat. In his initial days in the House he felt tentative and uncertain, very much a new boy. When he first visited the smoking room, full of "shouts and laughter and an almost complete absence of decorum," he walked quickly through, with "that far-away look which signifies, 'I am not in the very least bit shy. I am merely looking urgently for someone of immense importance.'" Then he heard someone shouting his name. Turning, he saw Winston Churchill approaching him with outstretched arms. "Welcome!" Churchill boomed, and drew him into the circle of MPs to whom he had been holding forth. "Nothing," Nicolson wrote to his wife, "could possibly have been so delightful as they were."

Yet although he came to love serving in Parliament, Nicolson, like Anthony Eden, did not feel completely at home there. Like Eden, he was a man of moderation and civility who never had much lust for battle. "I do not possess sufficient combative instincts to impose my personality upon the House of Commons . . ." Nicolson wrote in his diary at the end of 1937. "1938 will decide. At present, I am still, for the majority of the House, an open question. This time next year, that question will have been answered one way or the other."

Like the outlines of a photo in a chemical bath, the answer began to emerge in February 1938, when Nicolson made his speech supporting Eden, then abstained in the vote of censure against Chamberlain, the only member of his small party to do so. The National Labourites all but disowned his conduct, and he was summoned to a meeting of his constituency association to explain himself. When his party agent told him it would be better to say nothing at the meeting, Nicolson refused to heed the advice: "I have come up here to explain my action to my constituents, and explain it I shall." He did, and they gave him a unanimous vote of confidence.

But his Tory colleagues in the House, prompted by the whips, were not so tolerant. The 1922 Committee, a group to which all Conservative backbenchers belonged, condemned Nicolson's and Emrys-Evans's responses to Eden's resignation and called for them to resign from their leadership positions on the Foreign Affairs Committee. After weeks of discussion, both of them did so in April. At about the same time, Emrys-Evans received a stern letter from the chairman of his South Derbyshire constituency association: "I wish to be very frank and to say that we do not expect you to harass the Government . . . To oppose [the prime minister] is definitely a headlong rush to war."

For both men, the first warning shots had been fired in what would turn out to be a long and nasty fight. Neither had backed off. And despite his disclaimer, Nicolson discovered that he possessed a combative streak after all. After he was booed by Tory hard-liners at a public meeting in May 1938, he wrote with delight to his wife: "Why is it that when I face a yelling audience of 2,000 hostile people, I feel absolutely elated? I *loved* it. Why is that? I who loathe rows to the point of real cowardice."

CHAPTER SIX

"QUITE SIMPLY, HE TOLD LIES"

It was after midnight. The oak-paneled House of Commons library was almost deserted. Yet Ronald Cartland was still talking. He had been at it for several hours now, spilling out his anger over Britain's slide toward disaster and the seeming inability of anybody to do anything to stop it. If during the evening of April 7, 1938, any Chamberlain supporter had caught sight of Cartland and his listener, sequestered in a corner in green leather armchairs, the word undoubtedly would have reached David Margesson by morning. The result, in all probability, would have been another of Margesson's scalding lectures, for the young Tory was talking to a Labour MP named Hugh Dalton, one of the few Opposition leaders who had recognized early on the threat posed by Hitler and the need for British rearmament. Along with a few other Labourites, Dalton, who had been foreign affairs undersecretary in the first of Ramsay MacDonald's two governments, had been responsible for nudging his party away from pacifism toward opposition to appeasement.

A former professor at the London School of Economics, Dalton made no secret of his loathing for the landed aristocracy and was noted for his biting, sarcastic attacks on wealth and privilege, which included calls for stiffer death duties and a steeply progressive income tax. His exceptional talent for goading Tory colleagues stemmed from the fact that he shared a similar background with many of them. His father, an Anglican clergyman, had been tutor to the future George V and to his brother the Duke of Clarence. The duke was Dalton's godfather. Dalton himself had attended Eton and Cambridge, where one of his fellow students was John Maynard Keynes. Of Dalton, Ellen Wilkinson, a fellow Labour MP, noted: "Nothing delights him more as an old Etonian than to face a group of his ex-schoolfellows on the warpath at question time . . ."

Cartland, however, didn't care about possible repercussions from his conversation with a man whom the Tory leadership considered an archenemy. He was already in trouble with the whips' office and his own constituency association for his outspoken speeches against appeasement. One more misdeed, he told Dalton, wouldn't matter much. The prime minister and his men, he said, were out to crush all Tory opposition. Anybody who doubted that fact should consider the whispering campaign denigrating Eden after his resignation and the forced resignations of Paul Emrys-Evans and Harold Nicolson. The Conservative Party now had its own führer, Cartland continued; Chamberlain was becoming more and more dictatorial. It was astonishing how blindly most Tories followed him, amazing that so many were "still terrified of the Communist bogy" and so few recognized the imminent danger to the country posed by Hitler and the Nazis.

Other than provide a sympathetic ear, there was little that Dalton could do for Cartland. He suggested that the young MP might be happier in the Labour Party and offered to help if Cartland decided to switch. That, however, was not going to happen. Cartland still believed strongly in traditional Conservative values. Besides, he would have even less of an impact on policy as a member of the weak and divided Labour Party. Although Labour now demanded firm action against the dictators, it had greatly undermined its position by espousing pacifism for most of the 1930s. Most Labour MPs had bitterly opposed rearmament and had voted against every defense appropriation. Even in mid-1938 there still was a strong pacifist wing within the party.

No, Cartland would remain a Tory, and he and the other dissidents would have to find a leader to energize and inspire the others. There was plenty of potential support in the House, he told Dalton. After Hitler's annexation of Austria, some forty Tory MPs, twice the number that abstained after Eden's resignation, had been so angered by Chamberlain's failure to respond that they were prepared to vote to bring the government down. But no leader appeared to seize the moment and encourage further disaffection, and the opportunity vanished. The number of rebels soon dwindled, returning to its original twenty.

For Cartland and the other rebels, it was particularly maddening that Anthony Eden was sticking to his refusal to answer the call. In late March, Eden, still in his self-imposed exile in the south of France, received an urgent letter from Ronald Tree, warning that this extended stay on the Riviera was now being questioned even by some of Eden's anti-appeasement colleagues. It was vital that he return to London to speak out against Hitler's march on Austria and the führer's obvious designs on Czechoslovakia. A few weeks later Duncan Sandys wrote to Eden: "I, for one, and many others will follow you wherever you choose to lead. What we want more than anything else is for someone like yourself to give us some cohesion. Most of us are heartily sick of fighting little independent guerilla engagements all over the place . . . You alone can provide the leadership which will make these elements in the party united and effective."

But Eden did not return to England until later in the spring, and when he did, he made clear he had no intention of challenging Chamberlain. "While I wish to point to the dangers of Germany's armaments, I do not want to take up the role of the irreconcilable opponent of the Dictators," he wrote to Bobbety Cranborne.

Churchill, the only other possible leader of the rebels, continued to denounce Chamberlain's failure to confront Hitler, but he was still tarred with a reputation for recklessness and lack of judgment. Even if the anti-appeasement backbenchers had been inclined to follow him, he too was absent from Westminster for long periods during the spring and summer of 1938. Hard pressed financially, he had retreated a bit from the political fray and closeted himself at Chartwell, writing a succession of magazine pieces, finishing up *Marlborough*, and beginning what became his four-volume work, *A History of the English-Speaking Peoples*.

The vacuum of leadership was particularly damaging at a time when the threat posed by Hitler was rapidly increasing. By April 1938 there was no doubt that Germany had settled on Czechoslovakia as its next target. Hitler was encouraging the residents of the Sudetenland, a mountainous industrial area inhabited in large part by ethnic Germans, to rise up against Czechoslovakia. The Czech government held firm against Hitler's threats and bullying, confident of the might of its well-trained, well-equipped forces, thirty to forty divisions when fully mobilized. In addition, the French Army, under the terms of the mutual defense treaty signed in 1924 between Czechoslovakia and France, would be obliged to come to Czechoslovakia's aid in the event of a confrontation with Germany.

A German invasion of Czechoslovakia, which was Hitler's real intent, would have far more dire consequences for England and the Continent than the Reich's absorption of Austria. For one thing, Czechoslovakia was the only democracy in Eastern Europe. It was also the region's most highly industrialized country, with one of the world's greatest armament works. If Germany crushed Czechoslovakia, it would control Czech munitions, industrial capacity, and natural resources. Moreover, a German conquest of Czechoslovakia would pose a serious threat to the rest of Eastern and Central Europe; it would mean the encirclement of Poland on three sides and would threaten Hungary and oil-rich Romania.

But to Neville Chamberlain, still determined to avoid military confrontation, the strategic importance of Czechoslovakia counted for nothing. He refused to give Czech leaders a pledge of support in the event of a threat to their country's independence. Instead, throughout the spring and summer of 1938, he and Lord Halifax played a guessing game with the Czechs and the French, to whom Britain was bound by treaty. Although he would not promise to aid Czechoslovakia if it were attacked, Chamberlain announced in late March he would not rule out the possibility of such help either.

During this critical period, another prominent senior Tory, who in his long parliamentary career had held several key cabinet positions, began to take the dissidents' side in the increasingly rancorous appeasement debate. Initially, Leo Amery's participation, welcome as it was to the rebels, did not seem significant. That would soon change.

At first glance, Amery's decision to ally himself with a group of mostly liberal Tories seemed odd. Widely thought of as a right-wing Conservative, the short, stocky, bespectacled MP had been a friend and supporter of Chamberlain's for almost thirty years and a rival of Churchill's since their days together at Harrow. Like Churchill, Amery had long urged an intensification of British rearmament; he had been as outspoken on the necessity of a larger army as Churchill had been on the importance of an expanded RAF. For years Amery had preached the need for "an army to match the foreign policy to which we were committed," a well-trained, well-equipped large force of professional troops. Yet he also held firm to the view that Britain should focus on protecting and strengthening its empire and should remain detached from Continental disputes. A believer in realpolitik, Amery was convinced that nothing could prevent Germany from rearming and that it was vital, therefore, to stay on good terms with Hitler and to accept Germany's economic domination of Eastern and Central Europe. He was an advocate of friendly relations with Mussolini as well; he opposed the imposition of sanctions after Italy's invasion of Abyssinia and created a furor in the House when he declared he was "not prepared to send a single Birmingham lad to his death for the sake of Abyssinia."

The catalyst for his conversion was Hitler's march into Austria. The sixty-four-year-old Amery was a man of unquestioned integrity and honor—Churchill once called him "the straightest man in public life"—and what he saw happening in Austria, particularly the Nazis' brutal persecution of the nation's Jews, sickened him. In a letter to *The Times*, he said there could be no more discussion of a "settlement" with Germany. "The best hope of peace," he added, "now lies in telling Germany that if she touches Czechoslovakia we are in it too."

What Amery did not tell his colleagues in the Commons, and what he kept secret from virtually everyone else he knew, was that he himself was half Jewish. His mother was a Hungarian Jew who had grown up in Constantinople and settled later in England; his father was a low-level British forestry official who spent much of his career in India, where Amery was born. Charles Amery abandoned his family when Leo was still a child, and his mother moved back to England, where she scrimped, living in boardinghouses and cheap hotels, to save enough money to give her son the education of a proper English gentleman.

From the day he entered Harrow, Amery threw himself into his studies, determined to live up to his mother's expectations. A brilliant student, he captured prize after prize and was the top boy at school by the end of his second year. In the summer term of 1889 fifteen-year-old Leo Amery, now in the upper reaches of the sixth form, was a VIP at Harrow, a fact that fourteen-year-old Winston Churchill discovered to his chagrin when they first encountered each other at the school's swimming pool. Churchill, who had entered Harrow a short time before, was already gaining a reputation as a "troublesome boy." He heartily disliked the traditions of Harrow, not to mention its emphasis on learning Latin and Greek. "He consistently broke almost every rule made by masters or boys, was quite incorrigible, and had an unlimited vocabulary of 'back chat,'" recalled a former classmate.

One of Winston's few pleasures during that summer term was swimming in Ducker, the school's large, curving pool at the base of a grassy hill. On sunny days he and the other boys spent as much time as possible at Ducker, sunbathing on its concrete deck between dips. The mischievous Churchill was fond of enlivening those lazy hours by sneaking up behind unsuspecting schoolmates, preferably those smaller than him, and pushing them into the pool.

One hot afternoon he spied a likely target, a small red-haired boy with a towel around his middle, who was standing at the pool's edge. Churchill, also a redhead, stealthily crept up behind his victim, snatched the towel, and shoved him in. To his surprise and dismay, the boy sputtered to the surface, an outraged look on his face, and swam vigorously to the side of the pool, obviously determined to retaliate. Churchill ran, but his pursuer easily caught up with him and hurled him into Ducker's deep end. When he scrambled out, he was surrounded by several lower-form boys. "Now you're in for it!" one exclaimed. "Do you know what you have done? [That's] Amery. He is in the Sixth Form. He is Head of his House; he is champion at Gym; he has got his football colours." On and on went the list of Amery's achievements, along with a recitation of the various awful retributions that Churchill might expect for assaulting a senior boy.

Overwhelmed with terror and the "guilt of sacrilege," Churchill nervously approached Amery. "I am very sorry," he said. "I mistook you for a Fourth Form boy. You are so small." Amery's expression grew stormier, and Churchill, realizing he was digging himself in even deeper, quickly added: "My father, who is a great man, is also small." (Actually, both boys were very short and remained so; as an adult, Amery was five feet, four inches tall, and Churchill, only two inches taller.) To Churchill's relief, Amery laughed at his cheeky remark and told the younger boy to be more careful in the future. Yet while Amery let Churchill off easily that time, the encounter set the tone for the competitive, often testy relationship that existed between them for the rest of their lives.

While Amery continued to shine at Harrow, Churchill never achieved distinction there. He never became part of what he called the school's aristocracy. Indeed, he did not make it officially out of the lower school and thus did not have a fag of his own. More than thirty years after attending Harrow, Churchill told Amery that he "always had the greatest sympathy for convicts . . . as I myself have undergone eleven years of penal servitude in the private and public schools of Britain."

After Harrow, Churchill headed to Sandhurst, the academy for infantry and cavalry officers, while Amery went to Oxford to continue his seemingly effortless academic ascent. There he took a first-class degree and, already fluent in German, Italian, and French, learned to speak several new languages, including Serbo-Croat and Magyar. At the age of twenty-four he was elected a fellow of Oxford's All Souls College, one of the most prestigious honors in British intellectual life. All Souls, a college without undergraduates, was made up of approximately fifty fellows, among them renowned scholars and prominent men in the arts and public life, including judges, government ministers, journalists, and businessmen. When Amery was selected for membership, the All Souls fellows included the prime minister, Lord Salisbury, and George Curzon, a future viceroy of India and foreign secretary. The idea behind this curious institution was to bridge the gulf between academia and the outside world, with scholars associating on a regular basis with men involved in public affairs. Years later the *Birmingham Post* called Amery "one of the finest classical scholars of his day."

For all his academic prowess, however, he was no ivory tower intellectual. An ebullient and gregarious man, he loved sports and adventure. He was an enthusiastic lifelong skier and mountain climber; he scaled the Matterhorn several times, and in 1929, while serving as secretary of state for the dominions and colonies, he climbed an eleven-thousand-foot peak in the Canadian Rockies, named Mount Amery in his honor. When he left Oxford, he turned to journalism. His years as a correspondent for *The Times* turned out to be almost as colorful as Churchill's early career.

On the eve of the Boer War *The Times* sent Amery to South Africa to organize the newspaper's coverage of the conflict. The venturesome young reporter, who was in charge of more than twenty other *Times* correspondents and stringers, managed to persuade the head of the Boer forces to let him cover the war from the enemy side, although when the fighting actually began, his accreditation to the Boers was quickly revoked. A few weeks later, at the front at Natal, Amery crossed paths with Churchill, who was writing for the *Morning Post*. The two shared a tent near the railway station at Estcourt, from which a small British force, nervously expecting a Boer attack, occasionally sent out an armored British train to Ladysmith on reconnaissance missions. For lack of anything better to do, Amery and Churchill decided to accompany the train on its next journey.

But when the day came, it was pouring rain, and Amery, sure that the train would never leave on time, stayed in his sleeping bag, while Churchill dragged himself to the station to find out what was going on. Not long afterward Amery was roused from sleep by the sound of gunfire in the distance. Jumping out of bed, he and another British correspondent ran along the tracks in the direction of the sound. Soon they saw the train's engine coming toward them, with British soldiers clinging to its sides. The soldiers told the journalists what had happened: the train had left on schedule, with Churchill aboard, and had been ambushed by Boers about five miles away. They described how Churchill, waving his pistol, cried, "Keep cool, men," and "This will be interesting for my paper." He had helped clear derailed cars from the tracks and had loaded injured British troops onto the tender of the engine, which somehow managed to escape. After returning to the scene of the ambush to assist the remaining wounded, Churchill was captured by the Boers. His exploits during the attack and his subsequent daring escape from a Boer prison created headlines around the world and made him a celebrity in England.

Many years later Churchill and Amery, in one of their frequent verbal duels, debated the merits and demerits of getting up early in the morning. Their experience with the train in South Africa proved that "the early worm was apt to get caught," Amery said. Churchill's comeback was swift: "If I had not been early, I should not have been caught. But if I had not been caught, I could not have escaped, and my imprisonment and escape provided me with materials for lectures and a book, which brought me in enough money to get into Parliament in 1900— ten years before you!"

Actually, Amery was not elected to Parliament until 1911, turning down an offer to become editor of *The Times* in order to enter politics. His constituency was in Neville Chamberlain's hometown of Birmingham, and Chamberlain's support was crucial to his victory. "I owe it nearly all to Neville . . . who saw and persuaded a number of people . . ." Amery wrote in his diary. For the next twenty-five years he allied himself politically with the Chamberlain family, particularly with Neville's father, Joseph. Indeed, Amery soon became the House's most outspoken advocate of imperial preference, a protectionist scheme advanced by Joseph Chamberlain that would bind Britain and its empire together in an economic common market and would impose stiff tariffs on imported goods from nonempire countries. "Winston Churchill once remarked that my father seemed to think that the British Empire was his private property," observed Amery's son, Julian. "There was a grain of truth in the criticism. The unity and strength of the Commonwealth and Empire were the central themes of my father's life." His stand on imperial preference put Amery on a collision course with Churchill, whose support of free trade had prompted him to defect from the protectionist-minded Conservative Party in 1904. In the years to come, the two repeatedly crossed swords in House debates on the issue.

Amery proved to be just as pugnacious as Churchill. "All through life, a masterful energy struggled in him against the handicaps of an insignificant appearance and unimpressive voice," observed the *Manchester*

Guardian. "By physical instinct a born fighter, he was of too pygmy a stature to give the instinct free rein." Nonetheless, on at least two occasions Amery knocked down men who insulted him, one a heckler on the hustings and the other a fellow MP.

Although Churchill and Amery had considerable respect for each other, their competitiveness was always the hallmark of their relationship. According to Roy Jenkins, Churchill considered Amery a "semi-enemy." Amery undoubtedly felt the same way. As first lord of the admiralty in 1924 he opposed Churchill's appointment as chancellor of the exchequer, calling it disastrous. Churchill, he once declared, was "a brilliant talker and military strategist who is frankly incapable of understanding finance." On that point he never changed his mind. In his next cabinet posts, as colonial secretary and then as minister in charge of all British colonies and dominions, Amery was at constant logger-heads with Churchill on various issues, including the chancellor's plans to cut Amery's budget for improving living standards in the empire. "My diary is an almost continuous story of our day-to-day differences in Cabinet and in the conduct of inter-departmental business," Amery wrote. Stanley Baldwin "once jestingly said that more than half the time of the Cabinet was taken up by Churchill's speeches and my [Amery's] rejoinders."

In the early 1930s the two also collided over the future of India, with Amery supporting Indian self-government and Churchill opposing any loss of British control. Amery strongly believed that colonial peoples could not be held in the British Empire against their will. "I had been brought up from childhood with an interest in Indian affairs and a just pride in the story of the British raj," he remarked. "But my contact with Dominion problems also convinced me that it was far wiser to meet the demand for self-government halfway than to keep the safety valve screwed down—and that, sooner or later, the time would come when India could only be kept in the commonwealth as an equal partner."

The exchanges between Churchill and Amery over India revealed a considerable amount of one-upmanship, and Amery was delighted when he was able to score rhetorical points off the more oratorically gifted Churchill. One such occasion occurred in June 1933, in the wake of an accusation by Churchill that Sir Samuel Hoare, then secretary of state for India and the man in charge of the government's India bill, had committed a serious breach of parliamentary privilege. The accusation was referred to the House of Commons Committee of Privileges, which found in Hoare's favor. Refusing to surrender, Churchill launched another vitriolic attack on Hoare in the House, to which Amery replied, accusing his old schoolmate of trying to cripple the government. Knowing that Churchill detested Latin and had done everything in his power to avoid learning it at Harrow, Amery inserted a Latin phrase in the last sentence of his speech, declaring that, "at all costs," Churchill "had to be faithful to his chosen motto, *Fiat justitia, ruat caelum* (Let justice be done though the heavens may fall)." Seated on the bench in front of him, Churchill turned around and asked bluntly: "Translation?" Amery was elated: "I had hardly expected my fish to swallow the fly so greedily." With a broad smile, he replied with an unquestionably loose translation: "If I can trip up Sam, the Government is bust." MPs on both sides of the House erupted in boisterous laughter, and Churchill sat back, glowering, in his seat. That night an exuberant Amery wrote in his diary: "And so to bed, having given Winston the best ducking he has had since he first pushed me into Ducker . . ."

But such triumphs were unusual for this bantam rooster of an intellectual. Public speaking was one of the areas in which Churchill almost always outshone him. "If only I had any power of parliamentary oratory comparable to Winston's, I could do things single-handed," he wistfully wrote. Amery was a man of great energy and vision, who loved the give-and-take of politics and the sense of getting things done. But he was greatly hampered by his reputation as a dull, droning, long-winded speaker, who never could develop a knack for the memorable phrase. If he were only half a head taller and his speeches half an hour shorter, one parliamentary colleague quipped, he might have become prime minister.

Amery's party agent, a straightforward Scot named Geordie Buchanan, once listed for him the reasons that "ye haven't got a greater reputation." First, said Buchanan, "ye're small. Second, ye aren't a Douglas Fairbanks. Third, what ye say is verra good, but ye say it too straightforwardly. Ye say two and two make four, but if ye would only go on to say

2.5 plus 1.5 also make four, they'd all say what a wonderfully clever fellow ye were."

Leo Amery's time had not yet come. Even if he had been an orator of heroic proportions, it seems unlikely that he would have been any more successful than Churchill in persuading the government to confront Hitler. As the spring of 1938 yielded to summer, everything seemed stacked against the anti-appeasement Tories. They were stymied in the House of Commons, and since Chamberlain and his men dominated not only Parliament but also most of the national press, the rebels found it impossible to go over the heads of the party leaders to convince the public of the growing threat of Germany. The minds of the British people "had not been prepared either by the Government or by the press to accept the idea that any immediate danger existed," Duff Cooper wrote later. "To talk as if it did seemed to them unwise, rash and almost indecent."

Margery Allingham, a noted British mystery novelist, echoed Cooper's assessment. Allingham, who lived with her husband in Tolleshunt D'Arcy, a small village in Essex, recalled that neither Chamberlain nor the press gave the British public, including the residents of her village, any idea that there was imminent peril. "After the Anschluss, which startled us considerably, we cocked an anxious eye at the Government, but received no warning dig in the ribs from it," she wrote. "There was none of the time-honoured rumbling on the drums, no sudden and gratuitous reminder that the army was a man's life; nothing, only an insistence on social improvements at home, which as everybody knows, indicates an all-clear abroad . . . Even as late as July 1938, although no one [in Tolleshunt D'Arcy] could help realising that something was going to happen, the general impression was that it could hardly be war because none of the signs were right."

At a time when British newspapers were enjoying a golden age, when more papers were reaching more people than ever before, the British people were starved of real news about the growing international crisis. They were told little or nothing about the deplorable state of British rearmament or the divisions within the government over Chamberlain's appeasement policy. In the months leading up to Munich, no alternatives to that policy were ever seriously broached in the British press. The BBC and most newspapers (with the notable exceptions of *The Daily Telegraph* and *Manchester Guardian*) consistently supported the prime minister's efforts to negotiate with Germany and Italy, as well as his refusal to oppose their aggressions. At most of the major papers, letters to the editor that were critical of the papers' and government's proappeasement policy simply were not printed. When it came to news coverage, the "real power rests with the government," said Lord Lothian, who was to become Chamberlain's ambassador to Washington in 1939. "We decide what to do, and then send for the newspapers and tell them to sell it to the public."

James Margach, a veteran political correspondent for *The Sunday Times*, remarked years later: "From the moment [Chamberlain] entered No. 10 in 1937, he sought to manipulate the press into supporting his policy of appeasing the dictators . . . In order to cling to power, Chamberlain was prepared to abuse truth itself. He made the most misleading and inaccurate statements, which he was determined to see published so as to make his policies appear credible and successful. Quite simply, he told lies."

The government did not directly censor the press, although Chamberlain made clear he envied Hitler and Mussolini their power to do so. What he and his government could, and did, do was prod the press to censor itself. During a meeting with Joseph Goebbels in 1937, Lord Halifax agreed with the Nazi head of propaganda about the need to keep "the press in either country from making mischief." Shortly after his trip to Germany, Halifax wrote to the British ambassador in Berlin: "If only we can get the press in both countries tame." In Britain that was not a difficult undertaking. The BBC, for example, agreed docilely to its muzzling. The only source of radio news for most Britons, the BBC received government funding and was ultimately answerable to Parliament, yet it was supposed to have editorial independence. Its director general, John Reith, saw his charter differently, however. "Assuming that the BBC is for the people, and the Government is for the people, it follows that the BBC must be for the Government," Reith declared. As a result of that reasoning, the government was given an important role in deciding which politicians were allowed to make BBC broadcasts. In the middle and late 1930s Winston Churchill was effectively banned from the air, and Harold Nicolson, a popular radio speaker, was restricted to giving talks on noncontroversial subjects.

While Chamberlain may have been old-fashioned in his manners and style of dress, he proved to be well ahead of his time in the manipulation and massaging of the press. He and the head of his press office, George Steward, were masters of what came to be known a half century later as spin. From the day he took over as prime minister, Chamberlain cultivated the press, particularly the newspapers' lobby correspondents, who were influential political journalists with special access to Parliament and its members. The prime minister invited the lobby correspondents to chat with him—off the record—at a series of luncheons at St. Stephen's Club, a popular hangout for MPs and government officials near Parliament.

Steward, meanwhile, moved to restrict journalists' access to other government offices besides that of the prime minister. He was particularly concerned in stopping leaks from the Foreign Office, many of whose officials were known to be strongly anti-appeasement. All government press briefings soon were centralized at Downing Street, meaning that the prime minister and his men were the primary sources for government news. According to the briefings' ground rules, the sources of information were never to be revealed in a newspaper story; that meant officials could not be held responsible for any information they released or stories they inspired.

James Margach, who, as the longtime lobby correspondent for *The Sunday Times*, had known and covered Chamberlain long before he became prime minister, noted a dramatic change in his personality as the furor over appeasement escalated. Before ascending to the country's highest office, Chamberlain was "the most shy, kindly, generous-minded and warm-hearted of men, always friendly and understanding, although by nature cold, indrawn and lonely," Margach recalled. Within two years of becoming prime minister, however, he turned into "the most authoritarian, intolerant and arrogant of all the Premiers I have known."

Hypersensitive to any criticism, Chamberlain deeply resented questions from journalists that he regarded as implying criticism of himself or his policies. Sometimes, after being asked such a question at a briefing, he would pause and, in an icy tone, ask the offending journalist which newspaper he represented. Everyone present recognized the query for the intimidation it was meant to be. The prime minister was implying that a complaint from Downing Street over such effrontery would get the reporter in trouble with his paper's editor and owner. On other occasions, when confronted with a question he didn't like, Chamberlain would stare contemptuously at the responsible journalist for what seemed an eternity, then look away and bark, "Next question, please!" Inquiries about Hitler's persecution of the Jews or other examples of Nazi tyranny would be met with an acid expression of surprise that such an experienced reporter could be so naive as to believe "Jewish-Communist propaganda."

Chamberlain was particularly incensed by allegations that he was becoming authoritarian. Once, trembling and pale with fury, he summoned Margach and a few other top political reporters to Downing Street to complain about some such attack. "I tell you that I'm not dictatorial, I'm not intolerant, I'm not overpowering!" the prime minister shouted as he repeatedly pounded the table. "You're all wrong, wrong, wrong, I tell you! I'm the most relaxed and understanding of people! None of you, I insist, must ever say I'm dictatorial again!"

Many journalists, particularly lobby correspondents, who considered themselves, in Margach's words, "honorary members of a power establishment and ex-officio members of the political system," went along with the government's line on appeasement. But many others, including foreign correspondents who had witnessed firsthand the results of Hitler's aggression, did not. The Chamberlain government responded to the journalistic dissidents' skepticism and criticism by courting their bosses, the owners and editors of the country's national newspapers, most of whom were members of the political and social establishment themselves.

Since most newspapers in Britain were closely linked with one or another of the country's political parties, there was not the same separation between government and press that existed in the United States. For British papers, party allegiance was often equated with the national interest. But the cozy relationship between the government and the press also was reinforced by the strong personal and social links between government officials and the newspapers' owners—the old boy network in action again. The country's leading press barons in the 1920s and 1930s—Lord Beaverbrook, Lord Rothermere, Lord Camrose, Lord Kemsley, among them—were not exactly to the manor born. They received their peerages, with all the social status and benefits accompanying such lofty titles, from prime ministers grateful for the services rendered by their newspapers and themselves to the government and the party then in power. With few exceptions, newspaper proprietors and their top editors, who were in the habit of lunching, dining, and spending country weekends with those in political power, had little sympathy with the idea of the press as governmental watchdog.

One of the closest government-press relationships was between Lord Halifax and Geoffrey Dawson, editor of the country's most influential newspaper, *The Times*. Halifax and Dawson were longtime friends linked by common backgrounds: they had attended Eton; were, like Leo Amery, fellows of All Souls College, Oxford; and lived near each other in North Yorkshire, where they often shot and hunted together. When Halifax became foreign secretary, the two met almost daily, and Dawson was known as the Chamberlain government's chief mouthpiece, particularly regarding appeasement.

"I do my utmost, night after night, to keep out of the paper anything that might hurt [Nazi] susceptibilities," Dawson wrote to a *Times* correspondent in April 1937. "I can really think of nothing that has been printed now for many months to which they could possibly take exception as unfair comment." In addition to suppressing critical editorials and stories, *The Times* often omitted or quoted out of context debates in the House of Commons. On occasion, Dawson also inserted into articles comments of his own that were favorable to Hitler's regime. "I spend my nights," he told Lord Lothian, "dropping in little things which are intended to soothe them." When Basil Liddell Hart, the paper's noted military correspondent, wrote a series of articles about the inadequacy of Britain's air defense system, Dawson refused to print them. "I urged that the readers of *The Times* ought at least to be given a clear idea of the situation and the developing menace, but my requests were always turned down on one excuse or the other," Liddell Hart recalled. It wasn't the first time, he added. "I had been repeatedly gagged when I had tried to say anything in *The Times* from a military angle that ran contrary to the prevailing editorial line on foreign policy."

While *The Times* was a strong advocate of appeasement, only one major British newspaper, the *Daily Mail*, was an out-and-out supporter of Hitler's regime. Its owner, Lord Rothermere, who was almost unbalanced in his hatred and fear of communism, was a frequent guest of Nazi officials in Berlin. Rothermere used his paper to promulgate the importance of giving Hitler a free hand in Eastern Europe, so that he could attack and destroy bolshevism. If Hitler did not exist, the *Daily Mail* once declared, "all Western Europe might soon be clamouring for such a champion."

Another noted proponent of Chamberlain's conciliation of Germany was Lord Beaverbrook, whose three newspapers, the *Daily Express*, *Sunday Express*, and *Evening Standard*, boasted a combined circulation of more than four million. When Hitler appointed Ribbentrop foreign minister shortly before the Anschluss, Beaverbrook assured Ribbentrop that he would have the "loyal support" of all the Beaverbrook papers. In June 1938 the press lord sent a note to the acting editor of the *Evening Standard*: "Frank, be careful of your attacks on Ribbentrop. If you [continue], you are going to disturb the immense efforts that are now being made for an accommodation with Germany." Although Beaverbrook was a longtime friend of Winston Churchill's, his newspapers regularly attacked Churchill as a warmonger, and in the spring of 1938 Beaverbrook himself ordered the cancellation of Churchill's two-year-old contract to write a biweekly article for the *Evening Standard*, at a time when Churchill desperately needed the income. The country's best-known foe of appeasement was told by the paper's editor that "your views on foreign affairs and the part this country should play are entirely opposed to those held by us."

The Times, the *Daily Mail*, and the Beaverbrook papers all were regarded as Tory publications and were expected to back government policies. But even newspapers that supported the Labour or Liberal Party caved in to government pressure on occasion, usually for business reasons. A prime example was the *News Chronicle*, a financially ailing Liberal newspaper whose editors and journalists generally opposed appeasement but whose publisher and staff were inclined to shy away from questioning the government's policy for fear of financial repercussions from advertisers. In general, newspaper proprietors were concerned that unsettling news from the continent meant bad news for the British economy and thus for their newspapers and themselves. Douglas Jay, an editor on the Labour-supporting *Daily Herald*, wrote: "I was acutely conscious of the insistent pressure from the [business] establishment and the . . . advertising interests in favor of appeasement, and above all against any suggestion in the press that we perhaps ought to prepare for war."

The press lords' support of appeasement created tremendous friction within their newspapers. Many reporters and subeditors were strongly opposed. "Most of the office is against Dawson and me," confessed Robert Barrington-Ward, deputy editor of *The Times*. The ultimate futility of that opposition, however, proved that while freedom of the press continued to exist in Britain, there was little freedom *within* the press. As a character in a popular British television series noted more than forty years later, "It is hard to censor the press when it wants to be free, but easy if it gives up its freedom voluntarily."

Fleet Street's "habit of suppressing or 'playing down' unpalatable news" was a constant source of amazement to American journalists based in London in the mid and late 1930s. American correspondents were also confounded by how readily the British seemed to accept the soothing promises of their prime minister and the press that there would be no war, not taking into account how little truth about the situation the public was actually receiving.

In June 1938, Martha Gellhorn, a correspondent for *Collier's* magazine, traveled throughout England with her good friend Virginia Cowles to get a sense of what the public thought about the increasingly troubled international situation. Gellhorn, who, with her lover Ernest Hemingway, had recently covered the civil war in Spain and seen German planes bombing Spanish civilians, was infuriated by what she regarded as British complacency in the face of growing German aggression.

When the two young women stopped for tea one afternoon at the Yorkshire estate of the Earl of Feversham, Gellhorn became even more indignant when the young lord, who was the son-in-law of Lord Halifax and a junior government minister himself, made fun of their fact-finding trip. "Fancy going round to the pubs and asking people what they think," Feversham drawled. "You two are a couple of warmongers.

Just trying to upset the country and stir up trouble." Gellhorn replied that she intended to stir up even more trouble by talking to Feversham's own "peasants." Arching an eyebrow, he said, "In England, we call them farmers." Gellhorn retorted, "I know that's what *you* call them."

Accompanied by Feversham, Gellhorn and Cowles tramped across the fields to interview the earl's tenants. Introducing the women to one old man, Feversham told him: "These two girls have been driving around England, warmongering. They think there's going to be a war. Now, you don't think there's going to be a war, do you, Geoff?"

The old man, clutching his cap with both hands, shook his head. "Oh, no, m'lord. No, m'lord."

"You think things are all right, don't you, Geoff?"

"Yes, m'lord. Yes, m'lord."

"You don't think Hitler wants a war with England, do you, Geoff?"

"No, m'lord."

"In fact, you think this talk is rather silly, don't you, Geoff?"

"Yes, m'lord."

Enraged by Feversham's lighthearted superciliousness, Gellhorn turned on her heel and stamped back across the fields. Three months later *Collier's* ran the story of her trip, entitled "The Lord Will Provide for England." The world's horror is "kept quiet" in England, she wrote, "and you forget that across that choppy and uncomfortable channel lies Europe, and you just think: 'I am in England, a fine green island, and everybody outside is a foreigner and very likely nasty, and here we'll tend to our own affairs, which means: Business as Usual.'"

CHAPTER SEVEN

"OUR OWN SOUL IS AT STAKE"

In late August 1938 Bob Boothby settled back in his seat in Bayreuth's red-brick Festival House as the curtain rose on the opera *Tristan und Isolde*. For the next four hours he sat transfixed as Wagner's passionate music crashed over him in what he later said was "the greatest performance of *Tristan* it has ever been my good fortune to hear." He was told that Hitler had attended the opera two nights before and had left in a "highly emotional state," refusing to talk to anyone.

Boothby had been attending the annual Wagner festival in this small Bavarian town for almost as long as he could remember. As he left the swastika-bedecked festival hall that night, he thought about the two music-loving leaders who were now at the center of the world stage: Neville Chamberlain, with his devotion to Beethoven, and Adolf Hitler, with his passion for Wagner. It occurred to Boothby that for Chamberlain to understand Hitler, he would have to understand what drew the führer and his countrymen to the fevered operas of Wagner, with their gods and mythic heroes, their vision of a triumphant Germany. To know this Germany, Boothby later remarked, "you had to feel Wagner in your blood and bones," with all the music's "sentimentality, brutality, passion [and] fanaticism." That was something, he was sure, that the British prime minister would never be able to do.

Boothby had stopped off in Bayreuth on his way home from a short stay in the spa town of Marienbad, in Czechoslovakia's Sudetenland.

Visiting a village a few miles from Marienbad, he had witnessed a Nazi-inspired demonstration of Sudeten Germans against the Czech government, one of many erupting that summer throughout the region. There was no question that Europe was lurching toward war. The furor over the Sudetenland had reached a crisis point, with the anti-Czech riots and demonstrations and the announcement of German troop maneuvers near the Czech border. In a desperate attempt to tamp down the crisis, the Chamberlain government urged Czechoslovakia to accede to the Sudeten Germans' demands for local autonomy, hoping that such a move would appease Hitler. Of Chamberlain and his men, Theodor Kordt, the German chargé d'affaires in London, wrote to Berlin on August 23: "They are undoubtedly prepared to do everything they can to meet our wishes, although at a price: they want to avoid a military solution . . ." Under intense pressure, the Czechs finally agreed to give the Sudeten Germans almost everything they asked for. But a peaceful solution was not what Hitler had in mind. Prodded by the führer, the Sudeten Germans stepped up their demands. Now they wanted full independence, including control of Czechoslovakia's border fortifications.

Kordt was right. The Chamberlain government, convinced that Britain was in no shape to go to war, *was* determined to find a peaceful way to end this dispute. After four years of halfhearted rearmament, the country still had no army worthy of the name, and the air force wasn't ready for combat either. Those were the conclusions of a report to the prime minister by the British chiefs of staff that had been prepared immediately after the Anschluss. The regular British Army amounted to only about 180,000 men; the weekend soldiers of the Territorial Army added another 130,000. The regular German Army, by contrast, numbered slightly more than 500,000 soldiers, with another 500,000 in reserve. If Britain went to war with Germany, the chiefs' report declared, it could send to the Continent no more than two regular army divisions, both of them "seriously deficient of modern equipment." The dispatch of even this tiny force would mean that troops could not be sent to reinforce British forces elsewhere. "In the circumstances," warned Lord Gort, the new chief of the Imperial General Staff, "it would be murder to send our forces overseas to fight against a first-class power."

Reports of the two countries' comparative strengths in the air were equally gloomy. The RAF's first-line strength was about sixteen hundred aircraft, while the Luftwaffe had about thirty-three hundred planes fit for action. According to the British Air Ministry, a minimum of fifty fighter squadrons were needed for the air defense of the country, yet despite the fact that much of the British rearmament budget had gone to Fighter Command, only twenty-seven squadrons were operational at that point. Of those, only five had been equipped with new Hurricane fighters; the even newer Spitfire was still being developed. As the result of the government's emphasis on air defenses, Bomber Command had received little of the money given to the RAF; of forty-two bomber squadrons, only ten were equipped with heavy bombers, most of them obsolescent. No modern bombers were currently in production. The RAF "cannot at the present time be said to be in any way fit to undertake operations on a major war scale," the Air Ministry concluded.

The Royal Navy, long the pride of Britain and still the most powerful navy in the world, provided the only good news. In far better shape than its sister services, it was greatly superior to its German counterpart, boasting 15 large battleships, 15 heavy cruisers, 7 aircraft carriers, some 50 submarines, and about 180 destroyers. Germany meanwhile had no heavy battleships (modern warships like the *Bismarck* were still in production), no heavy cruisers or aircraft carriers, 7 destroyers, and 12 deepwater submarines.

But the Royal Navy, strong as it was, could not fight a war by itself. The dispiriting facts about the nation's other services helped spawn a mood of defeatism in the British government and press. By 1938 there was a feeling that "things had gone so far that to plan armed resistance to the dictators was now useless," noted Kingsley Martin, editor of the *New Statesman*. "We should, therefore, seek the most peaceful way of letting them gradually get all they wanted."

But a few members of Chamberlain's cabinet, Duff Cooper prominent among them, argued that Germany, despite its intensified rearmament, was not yet ready for a prolonged war itself. According to British intelligence, the German economy was in trouble, and the country's current supplies of fuel, rubber, and other important raw materials would not last six months. Hitler's own generals opposed war, declaring that

their forces did not possess the striking or staying power for a long conflict. The Luftwaffe, despite its numerical superiority, was not yet in a
position to launch air attacks against the British; few of its bombers at
that point possessed the range or bomb-carrying capacity to reach London from Germany. Cooper argued that Britain would be far better off
joining France and going to war with Germany now, regardless of British
weaknesses. Another cabinet dissident—Oliver Stanley, president of the
Board of Trade—warned that in "a year or so, Germany would be in an
immeasurably stronger position for fighting a long war than at the present time." Neville Chamberlain ignored them both.

The British people meanwhile knew almost nothing of the gravity of
the situation, thanks to the Chamberlain government's efforts to keep
it quiet. Urged by the government to downplay what was happening in
Czechoslovakia, the press, for the most part, minimized both Britain's
unpreparedness and the threat facing the Czechs. The news that Hitler
was holding army maneuvers near the Czech border was "written down . . .
as much as possible so as not to create a sudden panic." There also was
little in the papers about the fact that Britain was pressuring Czechoslovakia to give in to Hitler's demands and virtually nothing about opposition within the government to such arm-twisting. Tory dissidents
had no forum in which to voice any protests, since Parliament was on
its two-month summer holiday and Chamberlain had no intention of
calling it back.

Not everyone, however, was willing to keep the lid on. When
Harold Nicolson was warned by the BBC not to alarm the public un-
duly in his regular radio broadcasts, he replied: "I feel strongly that the
public has got to be alarmed." His script for a September 5, 1938,
broadcast was turned down by the Foreign Office because it urged
British support of Czechoslovakia. In its place, a "very angry" Nicolson
was forced to deliver an "innocuous" talk, but even then a radio engineer was standing by, ready to interrupt the broadcast if Nicolson so
much as mentioned Czechoslovakia. In another encounter with the
censor that month, Nicolson delivered a speech, recorded by newsreel
cameras, that condemned Hitler's threats against Czechoslovakia. "We
must warn Hitler that if he invades, we shall fight," he declared. "If he
says, 'But surely you won't fight for Czechoslovakia,' we will answer,

'Yes, we shall.'" The newsreels containing footage of his speech were not released to theaters.

Two days after Nicolson's BBC broadcast, *The Times* published a leading editorial advocating the dismemberment of Czechoslovakia—specifically, the severing of the Sudeten German areas from the rest of the country—which was exactly what the Sudeten Nazis wanted. Because it appeared in a newspaper widely considered to be the unofficial voice of the government, the editorial touched off a furor in London political circles. It went far beyond anything Whitehall and Downing Street had officially proposed. The widespread outrage over this clearly pro-German stand caused the Foreign Office to deny that the government had anything to do with it. Yet according to Geoffrey Dawson, Lord Halifax "did not seem to dissent from it himself." There was no dissent because *The Times'* proposal was in fact what Halifax and Chamberlain had in mind.

Incredibly, the two leaders, by Halifax's own account, failed to understand the dire strategic implications of the idea, not realizing until later in September that Czechoslovakia's formidable defense fortifications, its own version of the Maginot Line, were primarily located in Sudeten areas. As Winston Churchill wrote at the time, the proposal "would have the effect of handing over to the German Nazis the whole of the mountain defence line which marks the ancient boundaries of Bohemia, and was specially preserved to the Czechoslovak state as a vital safeguard of its national existence."

Yet even if he had known about the fortifications earlier, Chamberlain probably would not have cared. He had no interest in what might happen to Czechoslovakia in the future as the result of losing some of its territory. He wanted to save the peace *now*. Still clinging to the belief that he was Britain's most effective weapon against the dictators, he now seized personal control of the government's handling of the crisis. His chief adviser during this period was Sir Horace Wilson. Accustomed to working behind the scenes, Wilson was a key figure in putting pressure on newspapers and the BBC to support appeasement and in launching secret talks with the German Embassy about a possible agreement to settle the Czech crisis. In a meeting with Theodor Kordt on September 1, Wilson told the chargé d'affaires that if their two countries could reach a settlement, "we shall simply brush aside the resistance that France or Czechoslovakia herself may offer to the decision."

As the crisis escalated, Prague declared martial law on September 13, and Chamberlain came to the conclusion that only he and Hitler together could resolve the situation. Consulting only Wilson, Halifax, and a few other officials, the prime minister fired off a cable to the führer, suggesting that he come to Germany for face-to-face negotiations. On September 14 he informed the cabinet what he had done. "We were being told, not consulted," recalled Duff Cooper. In his pursuit of personal diplomacy, Chamberlain was flouting the recognized conventions of the British system of government, which entrusts the cabinet with the responsibility for making policy. He had not received the cabinet's consent to consult Hitler, and he had failed to tell the king, who by tradition must give his approval for the prime minister to leave the country. Nonetheless, the idea of this sixty-nine-year-old man, who had never traveled on an airplane before, setting out alone on a desperate mission of peace, captured the imagination of Britain. "British press receives news of P.M.'s visit with marked approval," Oliver Harvey wrote in his diary. "[The business establishment] is much relieved."

Accompanied only by Wilson and a mid-level Foreign Office staffer, Chamberlain flew to Berchtesgaden, the führer's retreat in the Bavarian Alps, on September 15. When the two leaders met, Hitler demanded self-determination for the Sudeten areas and their annexation to Germany. Chamberlain replied that he would have to consult his cabinet and the leaders of France. But he left Hitler with the clear understanding that he would get what he wanted. The führer promised Chamberlain he would not launch an attack on Czechoslovakia before the two held another summit meeting, again in Germany, within the next few days. Pleased by what he regarded as Hitler's tractability, Chamberlain wrote to his sister: "I got the impression that here was a man who could be relied upon when he had given his word."

Several members of his cabinet did not share that view. When Chamberlain returned to London and reported on his trip, Duff Cooper, Oliver Stanley, and a handful of other ministers found the results "frightful." As Cooper noted, "From beginning to end Hitler had not shown the slightest sign of yielding on a single point." He and Stanley, backed by the lord privy seal, Lord De la Warr, and the health minister, Walter Elliot, refused to endorse the ceding of the Sudetenland to Germany without further discussion. Stanley argued that Britain should go to war rather than give in to Hitler's demands.

A number of other prominent figures joined in criticizing the Berchtesgaden deal. In Washington, President Franklin D. Roosevelt summoned the British ambassador to tell him that the plan to dismember Czechoslovakia was "the most terrible, remorseless sacrifice that has ever been demanded of a state" and that "it would provoke a highly unfavorable reaction in America." Churchill declared that if Czechoslovakia were neutralized, at least twenty-five German divisions would be freed to threaten France and the Low Countries. It was "not Czechoslovakia alone which is menaced," Churchill said, "but also the freedom and democracy of all nations." Clement Attlee, leader of the Labour Party, told Chamberlain: "You have abandoned these people completely. You have made an absolute surrender. All eastern Europe will now fall under Hitler's sway."

Since the House of Commons was in recess, anti-appeasement MPs had no organized way to voice their opposition to what Chamberlain was doing. As the custodian of democracy Parliament was supposed to hold the prime minister to account. His failure to consult its members was a violation of the principle of representative government; he was treating Parliament like a cipher. Frustrated and infuriated by their impotence, Tory dissidents worked feverishly to come up with a plan to stop the sellout. "More telephone messages," Harold Nicolson wrote in his diary. "Everybody is in hysteria." Once again pressure was put on Anthony Eden to take the lead, and once again he declined. He told Nicolson he would "not lead a revolt or secure any resignations from the Cabinet." When Nicolson suggested he was losing support in the country as a result of his inaction, Eden disagreed. But even if that was true, he said, he was still young—only forty-one—and could afford to wait "until popular favor returns to him." Nicolson refrained from asking: *What about the country? Can it afford to wait too?*

When Neville Chamberlain returned to Germany on September 22 for his second meeting with Hitler, he carried with him the agreement of France and Czechoslovakia to German annexation of the Sudetenland. The Czechs' approval had been obtained by blackmail; the country's leaders, who strongly resisted at first, were told by Britain and France that if they did not acquiesce, neither Western ally would come to Czechoslovakia's defense in the event of a German invasion. The Czechs were stunned. Their nation was the only democracy east of the Rhine, and here were two sister democracies agreeing to its dismemberment and consigning it to what the Czechs knew would be eventual control by Germany.

Before this second meeting with Hitler—at Godesberg, a small town on the Rhine—Chamberlain had been instructed by the cabinet to insist on a "fair and orderly" secession of the Sudetenland, including supervision of the transfer by an international commission and a German guarantee of the new Czech borders. But Hitler, giving him no chance to outline those conditions, suddenly raised the stakes. He declared that all Czechs must leave the Sudetenland by October 1, when it would be occupied by German troops. He set Wednesday, September 28, as a deadline for a response to this ultimatum. Hitler's demands, Duff Cooper later wrote, "were such as a victorious and brutal enemy would impose upon a conquered people after a long and bitter war."

When those terms were transmitted back to London, they were greeted by a torrent of criticism. Lord Halifax, who received protesting letters and phone calls from Churchill, Eden, Boothby, Macmillan, and many other MPs, sent Chamberlain an urgent cable warning that "the great mass of public opinion seems to be hardening in the sense of feeling that we have gone to the limit of concession and that it is up to [Hitler] to make some contribution." Leo Amery was one of the most forceful naysayers. In a letter to the prime minister, Amery declared: "As I understand it, the demand is that the Czechs . . . should abandon their only defensive line before they have time to construct even the rudiments of a new one, as well as abandon all their own friends in the ceded districts to the tender mercies of their political opponents . . . How can anyone expect them to commit such an act of folly and cowardice? . . . Are we not bound to tell Hitler that the demand is in our opinion unreasonable, that we cannot blame the Czechs for rejecting it?" He was even more outspoken in a letter to *The Times*: "The issue has become very simple. Are we to surrender to ruthless brutality a free people whose cause we have espoused but are now to throw to the wolves to save our own skins, or are we still able to stand up to a bully? It is not Czechoslovakia but our own soul that is at stake."

When Chamberlain returned to London, he tried to put out the fire, telling the cabinet he was confident that he had achieved considerable influence over Hitler, that "the latter trusted him and was willing to work with him." His assurances went nowhere. Supported by several colleagues, Duff Cooper demanded that Chamberlain make clear to Hitler there would be war if he attacked Czechoslovakia. If Britain deserted the Czechs "or even advised them to surrender," Cooper added, "we should be guilty of one of the basest betrayals in history." Lord Halifax, who at first had endorsed the results of the Godesberg meeting, changed his mind and joined the dissenters. At the same time, Jan Masaryk, Czechoslovakia's ambassador in London and son of the country's first president, Tomáš Masaryk, formally rejected Hitler's latest demands, declaring that his country would not be "a nation of slaves." Faced with the Czech refusal and the specter of a possible cabinet revolt, Chamberlain backed down. The Foreign Office informed Germany that Britain would stand by Czechoslovakia.

Suddenly, in the time it took to transmit that cable to Berlin, Britain stood on the very edge of war. Having been told repeatedly there would be no conflict and knowing little about the seriousness of the crisis building up in Czechoslovakia for months, the British people were in a profound state of shock. Armageddon, they were now informed, was just around the corner. The wireless, Margery Allingham remarked, "became frankly hysterical, bursting into news bulletins every forty-five minutes or so . . . It was all very alarming, but, perilous though the situation looked, we still could not believe that it was actually war. We were still blinded by the absence of any hint whatever sent direct to us from the Government. It was that which kept us thinking that there must be a catch in it somewhere. The notion that for twenty years our politicians might have been inefficient, to put it mildly . . . never came into our heads for a moment." It wasn't until she and her fellow villagers were fitted with gas masks ("obscene, elephant-foetus" things, she called them) and observed how "startled and helpless" her friends' and neighbors' eyes appeared behind the masks' small mica windows that the reality of the situation truly set in.

Throughout the country, as in Allingham's village, "the sense of impending tragedy was suffocating . . . To some of us, war seemed then to mean quite literally a sentence of death on everyone and everything we most loved." The funereal gloom was especially pronounced in London, which was widely expected to be devastated within weeks of the outbreak of war. The British capital "is like a nightmare in a film," Rob Bernays, an anti-appeasement junior minister, wrote to his sister. "Laughter and even smiles have gone from it. We are like a people waiting for the day of judgement." At one solemn dinner party, when Bernays tried to lessen the tension by telling a joke, a fellow guest shouted hysterically: "Damn you! [Don't] you realize that we may be dead next week?"

Sandbags were frantically piled up in front of government buildings, stores, and clubs, while searchlights were mounted and hospitals were cleared for air-raid casualties. Slit trenches were dug in the capital's major parks, and cellars and basements were requisitioned for air-raid shelters. Duff Cooper, on his own initiative, mobilized the British fleet.

The next several days were a nightmare. As the minutes and hours ticked away toward Hitler's deadline, the Tory dissidents held a series of clandestine meetings to decide what to do. Some of the younger firebrands—Macmillan, Boothby, Cartland, and a few others—wanted to topple Neville Chamberlain there and then. At a meeting on September 27 they were "very wild, clamouring for an immediate pogrom to get rid of Neville," Leo Amery wrote in his diary. Earlier Boothby had told a friend that "this Cabinet must be hurled from power . . . being unfit to conduct either a peace or a war." Although Amery had joined the anti-appeasement camp, he had not yet lost all faith in Chamberlain, and he certainly was not in favor of a coup against the prime minister. "I poured cold water on that sort of talk . . ." he noted.

The evening before, Amery, Macmillan, Nicolson, Boothby, Spears, and Law gathered at Winston Churchill's top-floor flat at Morpeth Mansions, overlooking Westminster Cathedral. Also present were Archibald

Sinclair, the Liberal Party leader and an old friend of Churchill's, and several anti-appeasement members of the House of Lords. With war looming, Parliament had been summoned to an emergency session, its first meeting since early August. The time had come to take a stand, the dissidents decided. "If Chamberlain rats again," Nicolson said, "we shall form a united block against him."

The men meeting in Churchill's flat were not reassured by Chamberlain's broadcast to the nation on September 27. In it, there was no mention of honor or drawing a line in the sand, no expression of sympathy or support for the beleaguered Czechs. Chamberlain, his voice flat and dry, had an entirely different message: "How horrible, fantastic, incredible it is that we should be digging trenches and trying on gas masks here because of a quarrel in a faraway country between people of whom we know nothing."

On the morning of September 28, vast, silent crowds jammed Parliament Square and nearby streets, watching MPs entering the Palace of Westminster for the emergency session. But if emotions were high outside, in the packed Commons chamber and galleries, the tension was almost unbearable. Shortly before 3:00 p.m. the prime minister, looking totally exhausted, rose slowly from the government bench and placed his notes on the dispatch box in front of him. The chamber fell silent. As Chamberlain launched wearily into a recounting of his meetings with Hitler, a *Times* reporter, Arthur Baker, thought that never had he listened to a "speech more devoid of hope . . ."

Chamberlain had been speaking for more than an hour when, in the Peers Gallery, Lord Halifax was handed a piece of paper by Alexander Cadogan, the permanent undersecretary at the Foreign Office. After scanning it, the foreign secretary rose from his seat and hurried downstairs to an area behind the Speaker's chair, where he passed the paper to Lord Dunglass, Chamberlain's parliamentary private secretary. Dunglass in turn gave it to Sir John Simon, who rose and handed it to the prime minister. Having read it, Chamberlain turned to Simon and said, "Shall I tell them now?" Simon smiled and nodded. Gazing around the hushed chamber, Chamberlain, his voice considerably stronger now, announced that Hitler had agreed to postpone German mobilization for twenty-four hours and had invited the leaders of Britain, France, and Italy for more talks in Munich.

At first there was silence. Then somebody yelled, "Thank God for the prime minister!" and bedlam broke out. With a roar, members on both sides of the chamber shot to their feet. Because the Tory majority in the House was so large, there wasn't enough room for all Conservative MPs to sit on the government side of the chamber, so Harold Macmillan and other Tories often took their places on the Opposition side. Although he was one of the most adamant of the anti-appeasement rebels, Macmillan joined his colleagues in their jubilant shouts and cheers. Some MPs were crying. There would be no war, at least not now. Macmillan's son could go to Oxford, rather than into battle, the following month. His home and family would be spared.

Looking across at the Tory benches that afternoon, Macmillan saw that not everyone shared the same feeling of "incredible, almost stunning relief." Churchill half rose, as if to respond to Chamberlain, then sat back down with a grim, set expression. In a surprising public display of dissent, Eden got up and walked out of the chamber. Amery remained seated, glowering and silent. Nicolson sat too, ignoring an MP behind him who hissed, "Stand up, you brute!" Others yelled, "Get up! Get up!"

As members from all three parties crowded around the Treasury bench to shake Chamberlain's hand, nobody noticed that Ambassador Masaryk had risen from his seat in the gallery and left the chamber. Czechoslovakia's leaders had not been invited to Munich. Later that evening Masaryk told Halifax and Chamberlain: "If you have sacrificed my nation to preserve the peace of the world, I will be the first to applaud you. But if not, gentlemen, God help your souls."

After the session Violet Bonham Carter, who also had observed the chaotic scene from the gallery, confronted Archie Sinclair over his failure to say anything to rebut Chamberlain. The Liberal leader protested that it would have been physically impossible to do so, but Lady Violet was "hard as steel," noted her friend Baffy Dugdale, who witnessed the scene. "Parliament, on which we had set such hopes, had failed her." She even refused to sign a resolution critical of the prime minister's Munich trip because it began: "While sharing the universal relief . . ." She did not share that relief, she wrote years later. "The betrayal had already taken place."

The following day, as Chamberlain headed to Munich, Lady Violet and Churchill presided at a luncheon of the Focus group. Also invited to the gathering in the Savoy Hotel's Pinafore Room were several anti-appeasement MPs, including Harold Nicolson. For months now, Lady Violet had been urging her friends in Parliament to take a more resolute stand against Chamberlain. Still seething from the night before, she enthusiastically agreed to Churchill's suggestion that they draft a telegram to the prime minister urging him not to make any more concessions to Hitler and warning him that if he did so, "he would have to fight the House of Commons on his return." They worked on the wording of the cable, and ultimately the threat of a floor fight was left out. They decided to have it signed by half a dozen or so prominent parliamentary figures, including Churchill himself, Eden, Sinclair, and Attlee.

The phrasing of the cable was hardly incendiary, but when Churchill read it to Eden over the telephone early that evening, he refused to attach his name to it, saying Chamberlain would view the message as hostile. Attlee wouldn't sign either, because, he said, he needed the permission of his party first. Stunned by their refusal, Churchill sat, frozen, in his chair, "like a man of stone." When Lady Violet spoke scathingly of Eden and Attlee for refusing to put their names behind their principles, Churchill looked at her, tears in his eyes. "What are they made of?" he said. "The day is not far off when it won't be signatures we'll have to give but lives. Can we survive? Do we deserve to do so when there's no courage anywhere?" Trying to raise his spirits, Lady Violet remarked, "There is your courage still. Your day will come." Besides, "however fast we run away, we shall be caught at last."

"Yes, caught at last—alone—without an ally or a friend," he replied. "We shall have betrayed them all by then." The two old friends sat together silently for a moment. Then she asked him where he was dining. "Here, at The Other Club, in a few minutes," he said. "I don't look forward to this evening."

Teary-eyed herself, Lady Violet left for home. On her way out of the Savoy, she met a jaunty Edward Marsh, a friend of Churchill's and a member of The Other Club. "Isn't it glorious?" he said. "We are not going to be bombed after all." Lady Violet stared at him through narrowed eyes. "Glorious?" she retorted, biting off the word with contempt. "Where do you see the glory? You think of nothing but your own skin!" Head high, she swept on, leaving poor Eddie Marsh to wonder what on earth he had said that was so wrong.

Notwithstanding their formal attire and the gentility of the Pinafore Room in which they regularly dined, the members of The Other Club always took great pride in abiding by the club's chief rule: that "nothing . . . shall interfere with the rancour or asperity of party politics." But on the night of September 29 the acrimony reached new heights, thanks largely to the group's cofounder.

Still smarting from the afternoon's events, Churchill was furious, and he let everybody know it. The twenty or so members in attendance, including Boothby, Brendan Bracken, Lloyd George, and Dick Law, were exposed to the Churchillian rage from the moment they had their first drinks of the evening in hand. But Churchill reserved the brunt of his fury for the two cabinet ministers in the room, the minister of health, Walter Elliot, and the first lord of the admiralty, Duff Cooper. How could these two honorable men, with their fine war records and their extensive government experience, condone Chamberlain's cowardly policy over Czechoslovakia? Churchill thundered. Didn't they realize how "sordid, subhuman and suicidal" it was? Didn't they see that it was "the grossest act of bullying treachery since Benedict Arnold"? Didn't they understand that the sellout of Czechoslovakia would mean not just the sacrifice of honor but the "sacrifice of lives—our people's lives"?

The forty-eight-year-old Cooper, a good friend of Churchill's, had an explosive temper too, and he used it in full measure to counter what another member termed Churchill's "savage" attack. Cooper regarded the accusations as egregiously unfair. He, after all, had been leading an antiappeasement charge within the cabinet, trying to persuade Chamberlain to hold firm against Hitler, to be prepared to go to war if necessary. At the same time, as an important member of the government he felt obliged in public to defend its actions, even when he violently disagreed with them.

Next to Anthony Eden, Cooper had achieved the most political success of the young liberal Tories who had entered Parliament in the

1920s and 1930s. Like Eden, he was a product of Eton and Oxford and also a war hero; he had won the Distinguished Service Order in August 1918 for capturing eighteen Germans single-handed in the Allied advance near the Albert Canal in Belgium. Elected to Parliament in 1924, he became war secretary under Stanley Baldwin in 1935 and first lord of the admiralty under Chamberlain in 1937.

Yet for all Duff Cooper's achievements, there was a general feeling in London's political circles that he had not lived up to his potential, that he could have done so much more with his many talents. He was a powerful orator, a brilliant conversationalist, a talented writer. He wrote poetry in his spare time and had published a critically acclaimed biography of the French statesman Talleyrand. But he was also a dedicated hedonist, who valued his pleasures more than slaving away at his Admiralty desk. Well known for ducking out of boring government meetings, he spent hours drinking and playing backgammon with friends at White's and his other clubs.

The adjective invariably used by *Time* magazine to describe Cooper was "swank." He had a taste for well-cut clothes, fine wines, good food, and beautiful women. He was married to Lady Diana Manners, one of the most celebrated society beauties in England, who seemed to make news wherever she went. Lady Diana, the daughter of the Duchess of Rutland and her lover Harry Cust, had been one of the leaders of a group of raffish young scions of aristocratic families who made headlines before and during World War I with their wild parties, nightclub-hopping, and heavy use of alcohol and drugs. Although still flamboyant, Lady Diana had settled down to become (more or less) a proper politician's wife. But the couple's hectic social life contributed to Cooper's reputation for idleness and frivolity, and he was written off by many of the sedate denizens of Whitehall as a political dilettante. At a luncheon party early in Cooper's career, the foreign secretary, Lord Curzon, leaned over the table to ask him: "And Mr. Cooper, in the intervals between entertaining your beautiful wife, how do you occupy yourself?"

In the mid and late 1930s Cooper's preoccupation was the growing might of Germany. He considered himself a patriot as well as a pursuer of pleasure, and he was alarmed by the threat to England posed by Hitler. In the summer of 1933 he visited Germany as a junior minister and, when he returned home, delivered a speech on the dangers of nazism, only to be denounced as a warmonger by Lord Beaverbrook's newspapers. As war secretary he repeatedly clashed with Neville Chamberlain, then chancellor of the exchequer, over Chamberlain's refusal to fund a large, well-equipped army that could be sent to the Continent in the event of a German attack. "I was sure that war was approaching," Cooper recalled. "I believed that there was only one way of preventing it, and that was to convince the Germans that if they fought they would be beaten." Chamberlain, as usual, won the argument. As first lord of the admiralty Cooper continued his fight for accelerated rearmament, demanding a faster buildup of the Royal Navy and denouncing the spending limits imposed by Chamberlain and the Treasury on the budgets of all the armed services. As the Munich crisis escalated, he argued that the time for bargaining with dictators was over.

When Cooper lost his temper, as he had done repeatedly with Chamberlain, the sight was awesome to behold. "Veiners," his family and friends called these explosions of anger. A vein in Cooper's forehead would enlarge and pulsate, his face would grow purple, and his voice could be heard for blocks. That evening at the Savoy he engaged in a full-blown veiner, shouting at Churchill and at Professor Frederick A. Lindemann, a close associate of Churchill's. As the evening wore on and more wine and brandy were consumed, more members took part in the shouting.

Cooper and Boothby hurled so many insults at J. L. Garvin, the pro-appeasement editor of the Sunday paper *The Observer*, that Garvin left in a rage. (When he got home, he wrote a letter resigning from the club.) Then, as Cooper remembered it, "everybody insulted everybody else, and Winston ended by saying that at the next general election he would speak on every [Labour] platform against the Germans." The invective flying back and forth across the table was so extreme, one participant told Violet Bonham Carter, that if these had been the days when "honour demanded vindication by single combat," at least three duels would have been fought at dawn.

At about 1:00 a.m. someone looked at his watch and remarked that the newspapers' early editions must already be on the streets, with news of what had happened in Munich. Another member left and returned with a paper a few minutes later. Snatching it from him, Cooper studied its front page silently for a moment, then read the story aloud with "obvious anger and disgust." The details were sketchy but left no doubt that Chamberlain and the French prime minister, Édouard Daladier, had given in completely to Hitler, handing him everything he had demanded at Godesberg. Czechoslovakia would be forced to surrender the Sudetenland immediately, along with its vital fortifications and major centers of industry. Czech representatives were not consulted about the British and French decision. Chamberlain and Daladier informed them about it afterward and said it would be useless to argue.

When he finished reading the article, Cooper threw the newspaper on the table and stalked out of the room without a word. Behind him, there was shocked silence. In the Pinafore Room on that early autumn morning, "humiliation," as one member put it, "took almost material shape."

CHAPTER EIGHT

"'TERRIBLE, UNMITIGATED, UNPARALLELED DISHONOR'"

The Other Club members were a distinct minority in their despondency over Munich. Most Britons greeted the news with an almost hysterical outpouring of relief and thanksgiving. The newspaper coverage, lavish in its praise of Chamberlain, helped orchestrate the jubilant mood. In two-inch type, the single word "PEACE!" was emblazoned across the front page of the *Daily Express*. Of the prime minister, *The Times* declared: "No conqueror returning from a victory on the battlefield had come adorned with nobler laurels." Lord Castlerosse, the portly socialite gossip columnist for the *Sunday Express*, exulted: "Thanks to Chamberlain, thousands of young men will live. I shall live."

Journalists who tried to inject a note of caution into their stories were rewarded with heavy editing or worse. An article headlined "From Madrid to Munich," outlining the history of Hitler's conquests, was yanked from the *News Chronicle* by the paper's chairman, who said that since Chamberlain had "received a great national welcome, we must be careful." Also spiked was a story by Vernon Bartlett, the *News Chronicle* correspondent covering the Munich Conference, who wrote that the results of the meeting were an almost complete capitulation to Hitler. Bartlett's story, said the *News Chronicle* chairman, was too depressing.

Even many who believed that Chamberlain had betrayed Czechoslovakia couldn't help sharing in the general feeling of joy. Among them was Francis Williams, the anti-appeasement editor of the Labour news-paper the *Daily Herald*. "One knew intellectually that trying to appease Hitler was not going to get us anywhere except into a worse mess," Williams later wrote. "One could feel with one's will that, even if stopping appeasement meant war, this was preferable to constant retreat . . . But at the same time, emotion refused to accept this logic as final. It . . . demanded that one stop thinking of war in the abstract and think of its effect on human beings, one's own children and those of millions of others." Picturing in his mind his small daughter doing handstands and his son riding a bicycle, Williams concluded that "such things—and a hundred others—came between intellect and will and cried out that it was worth doing anything to avoid war."

When Chamberlain's plane returned from Munich on the afternoon of September 30, a delirious crowd of several thousand people stood in a driving rainstorm at Heston Airport, waving newspapers and Union Jacks, waiting to greet the man they considered the savior of the world. The crowd went wild when the prime minister, carrying his signature umbrella, emerged from the plane. The dozens of policemen on horse-back had a difficult time holding back the surging mass; everyone, it seemed, wanted to shake Chamberlain's hand.

From Heston, Chamberlain was whisked away by car to Buckingham Palace, where King George and Queen Elizabeth waited to offer their congratulations. Through the car's rain-streaked windows, Chamber-lain looked out at thousands of cheering, flag-waving Britons lining the streets, some of whom, in their exuberance, leaped onto the running boards of the car and banged on the windows. At the palace another huge throng waited, and when Chamberlain and his wife stepped out onto the palace balcony with the smiling king and queen, there was an earsplitting ovation. It was an unprecedented event, the first time a ruling monarch had allowed a commoner to be acknowledged from the balcony of Buckingham Palace. According to Tory MP Edward Grigg, it was also "the biggest constitutional blunder that has ever been made by any sovereign this century." By appearing on the balcony with Chamberlain, George VI was publicly associating himself with the prime minister's policy, a violation of the political impartiality required of a sovereign in a constitutional monarchy.

But few people were thinking of such issues that day. Continuing his triumphal procession, Chamberlain returned at last to Downing Street, which was jammed by hundreds of people who had been waiting in the rain for hours. Across the street from the prime minister's residence, Orme Sargent, an assistant foreign affairs undersecretary and a strong opponent of appeasement, watched the crowd from a first-floor balcony of the Foreign Office. Turning to a colleague, he acidly observed: "You might think that we had won a major victory instead of betraying a minor country."

Duff Cooper, who was looking out at the throng from the hall of 10 Downing Street, was thinking much the same thing. He had walked the short distance from Admiralty House to the prime minister's residence, pushing his way through the dense mass of people and "feeling very lonely in the midst of so much happiness that I could not share." He had spent a troubled night, debating what to do. He loved being first lord of the admiralty. "Of the various posts that I have occupied in the Government," he later said, "it was the one in which I was happiest." The job paid a substantial salary, which, since he had little money of his own, Cooper greatly appreciated. And it had two wonderful fringe benefits: living at Admiralty House, one of London's most splendid residences, and use of the beautiful Admiralty yacht *Enchantress*, with its crew of more than a hundred. If he resigned, he would lose all that. He would be guilty, moreover, of committing the cardinal sin in his tight-knit world: disloyalty to his party and prime minister.

Acknowledging the cheers of the crowd and its singing of "For He's a Jolly Good Fellow," Chamberlain disappeared inside 10 Downing Street. When the shouts, applause, and singing showed no sign of stopping, he appeared at an open upper-floor window, holding a piece of paper in his hand. Watching from his office balcony, Orme Sargent said to his colleague: "I can bear almost anything, provided he doesn't say 'peace with honor.'"

During Chamberlain's last meeting with Hitler, he had asked the führer to sign a document that expressed "the desire of our two peoples never to go to war with one another again." Now he waved the paper, inscribed with his and Hitler's signatures, and declared to the cheering crowd that he had brought "peace with honor" back from Germany.

"I believe," Chamberlain added, "it is peace in our time." As the crowd roared, Sargent spun on his heel and strode back into his office, slamming the French doors behind him.

Duff Cooper's mind was finally made up. "It was 'peace with honor' that I couldn't stomach," he later told friends. "If he'd come back from Munich saying 'peace with terrible, unmitigated, unparalleled dishonor,' perhaps I would have stayed. But peace with honor!" A few minutes later, at a cabinet meeting to discuss the Munich agreement, Cooper resigned. Chamberlain, he said, was "as glad to be rid of me as I was determined to go."

When he heard the news, an acquaintance of Cooper's remarked: "Most honourable conduct. *She* won't like it. She won't like giving up Admiralty House and the yacht." He was right. Lady Diana didn't like it. She had enjoyed her frequent trips on the *Enchantress*, and she loved Admiralty House as much as her husband did. In fact, she had presided over an extensive redecoration of its interior. But Lady Diana's first allegiance was, as it had always been, to her husband. Theirs was a close, if complicated, marriage. Exasperated as she often was by Cooper's peccadilloes, including his compulsive womanizing and gambling, Lady Diana never lost faith in him. She supported him in his resignation, as she supported him in most things he did.

Over the next few days Cooper received thousands of letters applauding his courage. The wife of Oliver Stanley declared: "I think you are grand!" She added: "My lips have been ordered to be sealed . . . but I can't find anything strong enough to do it with!" When Bob Boothby found out about Cooper's resignation, he wrote, "my heart leapt—for the first time in months . . . [You have] brought a gleam of hope to thousands who have hitherto believed in the fundamental decency of British public life, and who were beginning to despair." Rob Bernays told Cooper that he had been tempted to stand outside Admiralty House and shout, "We want Duff Cooper!" and "God bless you, sir!" He didn't do it, Bernays said, only because "it would have been thought that the crisis has disturbed the balance of my mind."

The praise that Cooper valued most, however, came from naval officers under his command. "May I say how sorry I am that you have found it necessary to resign, and how much I admire you for doing so," wrote Admiral Lord Cork and Orrery, commander in chief of the Royal Navy base at Plymouth. "I find myself in complete agreement with your views and regret I am not in a position to say so publicly." Prince Louis Mountbatten, a close relative of the British royal family's and a future first sea lord, declared: "I expect that it is highly irregular of me, a serving naval officer, writing to you . . . but I cannot stand by and see someone whom I admire, behave in exactly the way I hope I should have had the courage to behave, without saying 'Well Done.' . . . Your behavior has been an inspiration to me."

With Cooper's resignation, it became obvious that a sharp clash between Chamberlain and the opponents of appeasement would be the key feature of the upcoming House of Commons debate over Munich. For the next few days the hottest topic of discussion at London luncheons and dinner parties was whether any other cabinet members who had spoken out in private against the prime minister's actions would leave the government with Cooper. Some people, like Harold Macmillan, argued that the government could be brought down if this were to occur. Others said that nothing could shake the government now, that the nation's overwhelming support of Chamberlain had made him invulnerable.

Much of the speculation over possible defections focused on health minister Walter Elliot, who, along with Cooper, had been the target of Churchill's anger at The Other Club dinner. A physician, Elliot was an up-and-coming progressive Tory, liberal on social issues and a strong supporter of rearmament. Like Cooper, he had urged Chamberlain to stand up to Hitler. Many of his anti-appeasement friends now urged him to quit, declaring it was time to take sides. No one was more vehement on that score than Baffy Dugdale, who was perhaps Elliot's closest friend. The aristocratic Dugdale was as unwavering in her opposition to appeasement as was her friend Violet Bonham Carter. Dugdale talked to Elliot virtually every day, and he confided in her as he did in no other person, including his wife. There were those who thought that Dugdale was in love with Elliot. Whatever her feelings toward him, she made clear after Munich that she expected him to resign. He would "count for nothing" if he stayed.

After much agonizing, Elliot chose not to leave. "The Munich terms stick in my throat as much as ever they stuck in Duff's," he wrote Dugdale. "Of course, it is true that Neville had no authority to sign such terms," which were "a great crime and scandal." But in a bit of tortured logic, he insisted that because he had not resigned over the government's response to earlier events—the Rhineland, Eden's resignation, the Anschluss—he had to stay in the cabinet now or be accused of hypocrisy. Dugdale's response was unyielding: she informed Elliot that "for both our sakes, and for the sake of our past and our future," it would be better if they stayed away from each other for a while.

Elliot's parliamentary colleagues, even those most ardently opposed to appeasement, were far more sympathetic than Dugdale to his and the other ministers' dilemma. They knew how difficult it was for a politician to choose conscience over ambition and loyalty, how hard it was to defy the norms of their society. Years later Macmillan wrote: "All these men were friends of mine . . . I realize now the great stress under which they had to make their decision and the divided loyalties by which they were distracted. At the time, so great was Chamberlain's dominance that resignation in protest against [his] policy may well have seemed illogical and useless."

Whatever the reasons, there were no more resignations—not from Elliot, Oliver Stanley, Lord De la Warr, or war secretary Leslie Hore-Belisha, all of whom had expressed opposition to Munich. When the House debate began on October 3, Duff Cooper sat alone on the bench traditionally reserved for retiring or resigning cabinet ministers. It was the place where Anthony Eden and Bobbety Cranborne had sat less than eight months before. Before Neville Chamberlain could stand to receive the plaudits of the House, he had to wait on the Treasury bench while the spotlight shone first on his critic.

Cooper spoke without notes for nearly an hour as his wife watched from the gallery. If he had concurred in forcing Czechoslovakia to accept the Munich decision, "I should never be able to hold up my head again," he declared. "I have forfeited a great deal. I have given up an office that I loved, work in which I was deeply interested and a staff of which any man might be proud . . . I have ruined, perhaps, my political career. But that is a little matter. I have retained something which is to me of great value. I can still walk about the world with my head erect."

Cooper's eloquence had a noticable effect on the House* and when Chamberlain rose to speak, he was cheered, but without the hysterical enthusiasm of the previous Wednesday, when he had announced his trip to Munich. When he talked of his "profound feeling of sympathy" for Czechoslovakia, several Labour MPs shouted, "Shame!" The prime minister was "obviously tired and irritable and the speech does not go down well," Harold Nicolson observed. Chips Channon noted glumly that "Wednesday's glow had gone."

In the three days of debate that followed, Chamberlain was supported by many members of his party. But as had been expected, there also was intense criticism from a number of Tories, despite pressure from David Margesson and the other Tory whips to toe the line. It took considerable courage for the rebels to stand up and assail the actions of a man lauded throughout the country for preventing another world war. Already under attack in the press and their own party, the dissidents were labeled as unpatriotic warmongers, traitors to the national interest. At this point, "to question [Chamberlain's] authority was treason: to deny his inspiration, almost blasphemy," Macmillan observed. Yet, one by one, the rebels rose to denounce Munich.

Richard Law, who, until the Munich debate, had not been particularly outspoken in his opposition to appeasement, now emerged as one of the most unyielding of the Tory rebels. When Chamberlain entered the House chamber to begin the debate, the thirty-seven-year-old Law remained in his seat while those around him rose to cheer the prime minister. MPs on adjacent benches shouted abuse at him, and a few tried to pull him to his feet, but he "clung like a limpet" to the rail in front of him and refused to move. The fact that one of those manhandling him was a close acquaintance, "normally a most friendly and comfortable person," underscored the intensity of the bitterness and hostility on both sides of the chamber that day.

---

*When Anthony Winn, the young lobby correspondent for *The Times*, wrote that Cooper's speech had been well received by fellow MPs, Geoffrey Dawson rewrote the story. Winn promptly resigned, informing Dawson of his "distaste for what I frankly regard as a silly and dangerous policy" of manipulating news coverage in favor of the government. Almost four years later he was killed in action at El Alamein.

One of the first rebels to address the House, Law "spoke with the burning sincerity of the converted," Anthony Eden later remarked. Thanks to Chamberlain's capitulation to Hitler, Law said, Britain had become a "junior partner" of Germany, "the most cruel, the most inhuman tyranny that the world has ever known." He added that the ideals for which Britain had always stood—"decency and fairness and liberty"—had been abandoned at Munich.

In another slashing attack, Bobbety Cranborne said that despite Chamberlain's claim of achieving "peace with honor," there was no honor in the Munich agreement; indeed, it was a "wicked mockery" to give it "so noble a name." "The peace of Europe," Cranborne said, "has in fact been saved . . . by throwing to the wolves a little country whose courage and dignity in the face of almost intolerable provocation has been an inspiration to us all."

Leo Amery rose to say he felt nothing but "shame and humiliation" at Britain's role in the "fate which has befallen a gallant and freedom-loving nation." Munich, Amery added, was "the greatest and the cheapest victory ever won by aggressive terrorism . . . the triumph of sheer, naked force, exercised in the most blatant and brutal fashion." Harold Macmillan argued that "the situation with which we are faced today in this country is . . . more dangerous and more formidable, more terrible than at any time since the beginning of Christian civilization."

By the third day of the debate, emotions were boiling over in the chamber. When Winston Churchill stood to declare that "we have sustained a total and unmitigated defeat," jeers and catcalls erupted from the Tory benches, and Lady Astor shouted, "Nonsense!" Whirling around, Churchill snapped: "When the noble lady cries 'Nonsense' she could not have heard . . . that the utmost [the prime minister] has been able to gain for Czechoslovakia . . . has been that the German dictator, instead of snatching his victuals from the table, has been content to have them served to him course by course." Ignoring the continuing din, Churchill declared: "All is over. Silent, mournful, abandoned, broken, Czechoslovakia recedes into the darkness. She has suffered in every respect by her association with the Western democracies." Churchill's assault was, in the words of Baffy Dugdale, "a great and *terrible* speech."

But there still was one more powerful denunciation of Munich to come. Throughout the three days of debate, Harold Nicolson, like Ronald Cartland and Paul Emrys-Evans, had leaped repeatedly to his feet to be recognized, but the Speaker had not called on him. Neither Cartland nor Emrys-Evans was given the chance to speak, but finally, late on the last evening of the debate, Nicolson got the nod from the chair. As a former diplomat who had helped draw the frontiers of Czechoslovakia at the Paris Peace Conference in 1919, he was infuriated by what he regarded as Chamberlain's amateurish meddling in diplomacy and his willingness to betray Britain's honor. Fueled by that anger, he delivered the most compelling speech of his political career. Calling Munich "one of the most disastrous episodes . . . in our history," Nicolson declared: "We have given away not merely Czechoslovakia, not merely the Sudeten Germans, but we have given away the whole key to Europe." He and the other rebels who opposed Munich, he said, were now being accused of disloyalty to party and country. "The actual expression used to me was 'You must not bat against your own side'—as if it were a game of cricket that was being played in this most revered assembly."

Nicolson continued: "I know that in these days of realism, principles are considered as rather eccentric and ideals are identified with hysteria. I know that those of us who believe . . . that one great function of this country is to maintain moral standards in Europe [and] not to make friends with people whose conduct is demonstrably evil . . . are accused of possessing the Foreign Office mind." He paused for a moment and looked around the chamber. "I thank God," he said, "that I possess the Foreign Office mind."

The intensity of the rebels' speeches led to a flurry of speculation and rumor in London's political and social circles about what they would do next. Having spoken out against Chamberlain, would the opponents of Munich have the nerve to mount an actual revolt against the prime minister? As whispers circulated of plots and counterplots, Chamberlain's men moved to squelch any rebellion before it began. On October 4, a shaken Bob Boothby told Baffy Dugdale that "threats were used" against him and the others. If they voted against the government, he was told, "the Whip will be withdrawn and candidates run against them.".

The rebels believed that Chamberlain planned to capitalize on his popularity and call for an immediate general election, expecting another Tory landslide and the defeat of his opponents. Under British law, general elections must be held at least every five years. In October 1938 the deadline for the next one was two years away. But the government could call an election anytime it liked, and some of the prime minister's closest advisers were urging him to do so now. The prospect was clearly tempting to Chamberlain, who saw it as a way of silencing the critics in his party.

Late on the night of October 3, just after the end of the Munich debate's first day, Harold Macmillan pulled Hugh Dalton aside. The two found a dark corner in the Palace of Westminster for a quiet chat. They knew each other quite well, having worked together in previous years on proposals for economic and social reform. The left-leaning MP from Stockton was one of the few Tories whom the tall, balding Dalton could abide.

At their meeting, Macmillan told Dalton about the rebels' fear that Chamberlain would call a snap election. He also mentioned their anxiety that anyone who abstained or voted against the government over Munich "would be marked down for destruction and official Tory candidates run against them." He then made a startling proposition: that Dalton meet with Tory dissidents to discuss a possible cross-party alliance. The idea of direct cooperation with Conservatives, regardless of their political stripe, had long been anathema to Labour stalwarts like Dalton. Indeed, only a few weeks before the Czech crisis broke, he had declared that Labour must reject "all proposals for coalition with other party organizations, Liberal, Communist or Tories." But the shock of Munich had made him think differently about such collaboration, and the idea of conspiracy appealed to his love of machination and intrigue. He agreed to accompany Macmillan to a midnight conclave of Winston Churchill and other Tory insurgents at Brendan Bracken's house on Lord North Street.

There Dalton was asked whether his party would consider backing the rebels in their constituencies if an election were indeed called. He said he would find out. He was also urged to stop his Labour colleagues from calling for a vote of censure against the government, for fear it would frighten away Tories who might be thinking of allying themselves with the insurgents. Dalton and the Tories agreed to hold more discussions in the near future. He left the clandestine meeting with the intriguing thought that "a large-scale Tory revolt against Chamberlain" might indeed be on the horizon.

That was the decision that the rebels now had to make. At the end of the debate the Commons would be faced with a vote of confidence, "in which this House approves the policy of His Majesty's Government by which war was averted in the previous crisis, and supports their efforts to secure a lasting peace." The resolution was skillfully worded: a vote against it, or even an abstention, might well result in further charges of disloyalty, warmongering, and lack of patriotism. The dissidents had already been branded as renegades; if they went further and actually voted against the prime minister, if they joined the Labourites and Liberals in the opposition lobby, their political careers almost certainly would be over. For the most part, these were ambitious men, some of whom had dreams of becoming prime minister themselves. Yet when they met again at Bracken's house to decide what to do, Macmillan, Law, and Cartland wanted to take the risk and vote their consciences. Churchill felt the same way. Abstaining, the method they always had used before to show disapproval of Chamberlain's policies, was a weak compromise, he argued. It signified that the insurgents "half-agreed with the government's policy."

Whatever they did, the rebels knew they had to act together, and Anthony Eden and Leo Amery, the two other leading members of the group, were arguing for abstention. Although Eden had spoken against Munich in the debate (in his first major speech in the Commons since his resignation), his effort was widely regarded as being too timid and cautious. He appeared to have repented of his rashness in walking out of the chamber after Chamberlain's September 28 speech; now he praised the prime minister for his efforts to preserve peace, though he made it clear he could not support the results of those efforts. In its account of the debate, *The Times* said of Eden: "He seemed willing to scratch but not to kill." Those who looked to Eden for leadership, wrote Oliver Harvey, "were disappointed, not to say shocked," by the mildness of his oratory.

Amery too could not bring himself to break completely with the Tory hierarchy and his old friend Chamberlain. Although he was firmly now in the dissident camp, Amery still bore lingering traces of a top boy at Harrow, imbued with public-school views of loyalty and conformity to tradition. "Neville's performance" over Munich was "ignominious," he acknowledged, but it was important to keep open the lines of communication with other Tories and not "separate ourselves from the main body." Amery's arguments swayed most of the others, and on October 6, shortly before the division in the House, they all agreed to abstain.

Even then Amery had doubts whether he should go that far, especially after Chamberlain's speech wrapping up the debate. It was far better than his first one; the prime minister acknowledged the necessity of more rapid rearmament and promised that the government would give its full attention to speeding up the process. On hearing that, both Amery and Eden wavered, believing that Chamberlain may finally have seen the light and wondering if they shouldn't support him. In the members' lobby, just before the vote, they told some of the younger rebels that they were thinking of voting for the government. The others vigorously disagreed. It was essential, they said, that they register their opposition to Chamberlain's action at Munich. "None of them wished to go back on the decision," Amery later wrote, "and in view of that, neither Anthony nor I felt we could very well . . . change our minds."

With its huge majority in the Commons, the Chamberlain government easily won the vote of confidence. But most of the attention went to the thirty or so Tory MPs who abstained. Several of them, including Churchill, Cartland, Nicolson, Law, and Duncan Sandys, remained ostentatiously in their seats during the vote, the targets of angry mutters and disdainful glances from the Tory faithful. The abstentions "must enrage the Government, since it is not our numbers that matter but our reputation," Nicolson wrote in his diary. "It was clear that the Government were rattled by this." Although, in retrospect, the rebels' action seems a mild enough protest, it was not regarded as such by Chamberlain and his men or by the rest of London's political world. Nicolson was right: it did infuriate the government, and repercussions were soon to follow.

For the moment, though, Chamberlain just wanted a rest from carping MPs. Despite his sizable victory in the House, he complained to his sister: "All the world seemed to be full of my praises except the House of Commons." Following the vote, Chamberlain moved that the House adjourn for four more weeks—until November 1. The motion carried, despite heated opposition from Labour and Liberal MPs and a number of the Tory rebels.

The Labour Party's parliamentary leaders now came up with their own initiative for a cross-party coalition. Hugh Dalton met with Macmillan again and told him that Clement Attlee and other key party figures were interested in pursuing the idea of an alliance of Labour, Liberals, and Tory rebels to oppose Chamberlain's appeasement policies and work for intensified rearmament. Macmillan responded shamefacedly that "there was some difficulty within their group." Eden, it seemed, had announced he wouldn't go along with any such coalition, and since many of the dissidents were followers of Eden, "they would not move further and faster than he." In any event, much of the urgency for an alliance had vanished, since the prime minister had decided not to call an immediate general election after all. (Chamberlain very much wanted to "get rid of this uneasy and dispirited House of Commons," he wrote to his sister, but David Margesson and others had told him that several months of careful preparation were needed before "we could win an Election handsomely.")

Unlike Eden, Churchill *was* interested in continuing the coalition talks, as were Macmillan, Cartland, Boothby, Law, and Bracken. Dalton applauded Churchill's aggressiveness ("He is much more attractive than the Edens and other gentlemanly wishy-washies. He is a real tough and at the moment is talking our language"), but "in view of the refusals of the others, we on our side decided to call a halt." For now the cross-party conspiracy was dead. Before he took his leave of Macmillan, Dalton gave the younger man a bit of advice to pass on to his dissident Tory colleagues. Abstaining against the government was all very well, he said, but if they truly wanted to change the course of events, they would have to summon up their courage and "be prepared to vote against the Government . . . Otherwise the buds of rebellion would never break."

After Munich, Neville Chamberlain was spoiling for a fight—but not against Germany. Despite his pledge to the House to accelerate re-armament, he told the cabinet that while Britain should continue to strengthen its defenses, he still believed it was possible to reach an agreement with the dictators to ward off war. "A good deal of false emphasis had been placed on rearmament," he said, adding he had no intention of beginning a new arms race. Instead, he was to turn his combative instincts to the destruction of those who dared to oppose him over Munich.

In Czechoslovakia, meanwhile, the Germans marched into the Sudetenland and took control of its frontier fortifications, munitions factories, other heavy industry, and raw materials. In Prague a leading Czech industrialist outlined for Martha Gellhorn just how much the country had lost. "Forty per cent of the metallurgical industry [is] gone," he said. "Sixty per cent of soft coal, sixty-three per cent of the textile industry, fifty-seven per cent of the glass industry, forty per cent of the chemical industry, sixty-three per cent of the paper industry." He said all this and more in a "gray, matter-of-fact voice," Gellhorn wrote. At a Prague coffeehouse she watched a group of young people at a nearby table, who were bent over a map of their country and similarly toting up its losses from Munich. Suddenly one of them stood up and shouted, for everyone in the room to hear: "If we had fought alone and been defeated, it could not have been worse!"

Other small countries in Europe, realizing they could no longer count on Britain and France to defend them against Germany, took the hint and vowed not to do anything to upset the Reich. Although the Netherlands and Belgium both took steps to protect themselves against German attack, they refused to join France and Britain in talks about a possible alliance. "What possible advantage could there be in military talks at a time when England is not ready for war, France is in chaos, and the Germans are rearmed?" the Dutch foreign minister asked in a letter to *The Times*. In a speech to his constituents defending his abstention in the Munich vote, Eden's former parliamentary private secretary, Jim Thomas, declared: "A month ago, we had friends in Europe who, in the event of an emergency, would have stood by our side. Tomorrow—except for France—we shall have to face this new and powerful Germany alone. We have lost our friends."

In the United States, where radio programs for at least a month had been interrupted every half hour with bulletins on the Czech situation, the news from Munich was greeted with shock and outrage. The refusal of Britain and France to stand up to Hitler alienated Americans, both in and outside the government, who favored a greater U.S. involvement in the growing European crisis. At the same time, the sellout of Czechoslovakia strengthened the hand of isolationists in Congress and elsewhere, who were pressing the Roosevelt administration to stay clear of European wars. "Certainly His Majesty's Government have contrived to lose American sympathy utterly," Anthony Eden remarked after a trip to New York in December. "[W]hile I was there, most of my time was spent in asserting that Neville was not a Fascist." Eden noted in his diary that many Americans believed "we are giving ground because our nerve has gone—Nothing could be more dangerous than that."

For his part, Hitler, convinced that Britain would never try to stop him, made plans for new conquests. In his encounters with Chamberlain, he had taken the measure of the prime minister: not as a strong, respected, influential negotiator, as Chamberlain believed, but as a weak and deluded man who would do anything to avoid going to war. "Poor worms," the German leader later called his British and French counterparts. Returning to Berlin after Munich, Hitler contemptuously told his associates, "I said the word 'war' and [Chamberlain] trembled."

CHAPTER NINE

RETRIBUTION

For weeks after Munich, it was impossible to escape from Neville Chamberlain. Everywhere one went in Britain, it seemed, there were reminders of the prime minister and his historic journey. Toy shops featured booted Chamberlain dolls, holding a rod and reel in one hand and a little sign saying PEACEMAKER in the other. Candy stores sold sugar umbrellas, while florists displayed Chamberlain's picture framed by flowers and bearing the inscription WE ARE PROUD OF YOU. Companies took out large newspaper advertisements lauding the prime minister, and the poet laureate, John Masefield, wrote a poem comparing him to the tragic Greek hero Priam and declaring that he had been "divinely led."

Ten Downing Street meanwhile was flooded with letters, telegrams, flowers, umbrellas, toys, trinkets, and other items celebrating Chamberlain's achievement. He put many of these articles on display in a large showcase, which he loved to show off to visitors. When Kenneth Clark and his wife came to lunch one day, Chamberlain proudly led them to the showcase, explaining that the articles "were sent to me in gratitude for the Munich agreement."

As John Colville noted in his diary, Munich fed the prime minister's vanity as well as his arrogance. With Chamberlain "almost canonized" because of Munich, it was "small wonder," Violet Bonham Carter dryly remarked, "that he began to see himself as a Messiah sent down from heaven . . ." Bolstered by his immense popularity, Chamberlain and his men came to regard any opposition as a lack of patriotism approaching treason, and they dealt with it accordingly. Geoffrey Cox, a foreign correspondent for the *Daily Express* who returned to England in late 1938, was stunned to find such intense intolerance for any criticism of the Munich accord: "If you argued that it was an illusion, that Munich had bought merely a respite, at huge cost, and that war would assuredly come, you were deemed to want war to come." Eventually, Cox added, the government's intolerance developed "undertones of totalitarianism."

Above all, Chamberlain was determined to punish his critics, particularly the Tory abstainers in the vote of confidence over Munich, whom he disdainfully likened to "birds fouling their own nests." Lord Rothermere, the pro-German owner of the *Daily Mail*, warned soon after the vote that "Neville Chamberlain's reputation will not be undermined so long as he is prime minister, and any member of his Party who challenges that fact may suffer a complete eclipse." Several newspapers, including those that Rothermere owned, reviled and ridiculed the Tory rebels, labeling them as "jitterbugs." The few papers that occasionally had been sympathetic to the rebels and their point of view came under attack as well. A pro-Chamberlain MP lambasted the *Evening Standard*, which had printed several articles by Duff Cooper, for publishing Cooper's "vaporous effusions" that keep "his fellow countrymen in a constant state of jittery anticipation and endlessly fan the flames of prejudice and hatred."

Lord Beaverbrook, Geoffrey Cox's employer, had promised Lord Halifax after Munich that he and his newspapers "will do anything to help you." As partial fulfillment of that pledge, Beaverbrook encouraged his papers to attack the Tory rebels. "The jitterbugs asked in quavering voices if Hitler would attack us . . ." the *Daily Express* thundered in early 1939. "The Daily Express said 'No!' Now we know that Hitler agrees with the Daily Express. He says that he expects there will be peace for a long time . . . We have got the confirmation straight from Hitler's mouth. There will be no war involving Britain in 1939."

The retribution against the rebels went far beyond press attacks. As soon as the Munich debate was over, the Conservative Party's Central Office, joined by David Margesson, James Stuart, and the other Tory

whips, embarked on a relentless campaign to force them into political
oblivion. The Central Office, which ran the party's day-to-day operations
under Chamberlain's personal command, was a political machine so
powerful that it "would make Tammany green with envy," observed Helen
Kirkpatrick. In early 1939, Leslie Hore-Belisha, the secretary of war,
told a *Times* correspondent that the "Conservative party machine is even
stronger than the Nazi party machine. It may have a different aim, but
it is similarly callous and ruthless. It suppresses anyone who does not
toe the line." Hore-Belisha, who was fast growing disenchanted with
Chamberlain, may have been guilty of a bit of hyperbole, but there was
no question that under the prime minister, the Tory hierarchy had developed a sophisticated network to spy on political opponents and to
quell dissent.

The Central Office and the whips put intense pressure on local constituency associations to punish their wayward MPs. A local association
had no power to force its member of Parliament to resign, but it could
select a new candidate for the next election, which, in most cases,
would end an MP's parliamentary career.

As the rebel most in the spotlight, Duff Cooper was given an especially difficult time. His constituency was in the Westminster section
of London, a pro-Chamberlain stronghold, and he was questioned harshly
by the Tory association there for well over an hour before it handed
down its verdict. Acknowledging that Cooper had the right to resign from
the cabinet, the association nonetheless declared it was "in complete
agreement with the actions of the Prime Minister" and that Cooper was
obliged to support the government and to work for party unity. It also
reserved the right to choose a new candidate for the next election. The
warning was unmistakable. If Cooper stepped out of line again, he would
lose his seat.

In his Epping constituency, Winston Churchill, who deplored "the
mood of intolerance" in the Conservative Party, narrowly survived several attempts to unseat him, instigated by James Stuart and led by local party members who previously had been among Churchill's most
vigorous supporters. In Bobbety Cranborne's constituency in South
Dorset, the local Tories were "breathing fire and slaughter," Cranborne
told Jim Thomas, "and I am quite expecting to be stoned next week."

The hostility he faced for his lacerating criticism of the Munich agreement "shows how wise you were to be more moderate," Cranborne wrote to Anthony Eden. (Eden was one of the few Tory abstainers to suffer no repercussions in his constituency. His mild speech in the House, as Cranborne noted, was probably a major reason.)

Bob Boothby, meanwhile, received a telegram from his association's executive committee expressing great concern over "your non-support of the Government" and ordering him to appear before the association to explain himself. He did so but made it clear that he had come in "no white sheet of repentance." Munich, he declared, was "the greatest diplomatic defeat this country has suffered" in more than two hundred years. Boothby was extremely popular in his constituency, and to the dismay of the association leaders, the group's rank and file gave him their support. Dick Law, summoned by his "infuriated" association in the Yorkshire town of Hull, similarly defended his vote and told the group that if they "did not there and then give me a vote of confidence I would resign my seat and fight a by-election." Like Boothby, Law won the vote, although it was far from unanimous.

Among others who faced strong constituency challenges were Ronald Cartland and Paul Emrys-Evans, neither of whom had been called upon, despite their best efforts, in the Munich debate. Having been thwarted in speaking to the House, Cartland, outspoken as always, made sure that no one had any doubt about where he stood on Munich. Chamberlain's failure to consult the cabinet or Parliament before his final acquiescence to Hitler was "unconstitutionalism run mad," Cartland declared. "Power is passing from the hands of Parliament into the hands of the executive and of the Civil Service, with the assistance of the party machine." In a letter published by Birmingham newspapers, the young MP wrote: "Quite recently the Prime Minister said that 'Democracy can afford to make mistakes.' Every responsible citizen must ask himself now, if we are to survive, whether we can afford to make any more."

Like Cartland, Emrys-Evans decried what he saw as Tory assaults on parliamentary authority and freedom of speech. To his constituency in South Derbyshire, he declared that his role, as he saw it, was to be its representative, free to make his own judgments and decisions. He was not, in short, his constituency's slave. Told that an MP should pay "the greatest attention" to the views of his constituents, Emrys-Evans replied: "I do so and have done so, but . . . a Member also owes his knowledge and his judgment to his constituents . . . If I am fettered in any action I take in matters I consider to be vital to the safety of the country, I should become a mere delegate—the mouthpiece of an outside organization." To underscore the point, he read aloud to his constituency association a famous speech delivered by Edmund Burke in 1780 on the rightful role of a member of Parliament. "If the people choose their servants on the principle of mere obsequiousness and flexibility, and total vacancy or indifference on opinion on all public matters," Burke argued, "the State will cease to be sound, and it will be in vain to think of saving it."

Burke's and Emrys-Evans's philosophy did not go down well with several members of the South Derbyshire Tory association, including its chairman, Sir Robert Doncaster. From then on, Doncaster did everything he could to drive Emrys-Evans from office, including barring him from speaking at party meetings. The affair came to a head early the next year, when Emrys-Evans confronted Doncaster at his office and the two engaged in a nasty shouting match. Doncaster angrily ordered Emrys-Evans to leave. When he refused, the association chairman called the police. Before they arrived, however, Doncaster announced that "he would have nothing to do with South Derbyshire" as long as Emrys-Evans represented it and therefore was resigning. With his chief enemy gone, the campaign against Emrys-Evans died down. For the moment, at least, he was safe.

In the end none of the men who abstained in the Munich vote lost his official standing as a Tory candidate in the next election. But most were put on notice by their constituency associations that from then on, their speeches and actions would be closely watched, and any future party disloyalty would be severely dealt with. Any doubts about that were quickly dispelled by the punishment meted out to the dissidents' parliamentary colleague, the Duchess of Atholl.

Nothing in Katharine Atholl's background or temperament suggested her emergence, in the aftermath of Munich, as the boldest Tory rebel of all. Her marriage to the Duke of Atholl made her a ranking member of Britain's aristocracy. Her husband was one of Britain's biggest landowners, and the couple lived in a white stone castle in the Scottish Highlands. A Canadian cruise ship, the *Duchess of Atholl*, was named after her. Before her marriage, she had studied at the Royal College of Music in London and was widely acknowledged as a gifted pianist and composer. A diminutive woman with large, expressive blue eyes, Kitty Atholl was cultured, diffident, and unworldly, with little interest in calling attention to herself.

In 1921, Prime Minister David Lloyd George, noting her extensive work with local and national charities, suggested she stand for Parliament. For the duchess, it was a startling idea. She had opposed the British suffragette movement and had no interest in a political career. But at that time not many women in Britain had envisioned a future in politics; it had been only three years since they had won a limited right to vote and to stand for Parliament. With the backing of her husband, Kitty finally gave in to Lloyd George's urging, and in 1924, she won election as a Conservative from the rural Scottish constituency of Kinross and West Perthshire.

Only the third woman to win election to the House of Commons, Kitty Atholl found herself in an institution considered "the best [men's] club in London," where many, if not most, of her male colleagues regarded the advent of women members with horror. In a very real sense, women had been invisible in the House until their admittance as MPs; as late as 1917 women visitors were forced to sit, like cloistered nuns, behind a grille in the Ladies' Gallery. Lady Astor recalled that when she became the first woman in Parliament, "men whom I had known for years would not speak to me if they passed me in the corridors." One of them was Winston Churchill, whom she and her husband had often entertained at Cliveden, their country estate in Berkshire. When she asked Churchill why he was so rude to her, he retorted: "Because I find a woman's intrusion into the House of Commons as embarrassing as if she burst into my bathroom, when I had nothing with which to defend myself, not even a sponge."

By the late 1930s the number of women in the House had increased only slightly—to nine—and chauvinism was still rampant, even among the anti-appeasement rebels, most of whom considered themselves liberal-minded. "There is no place in the [House of Commons] for women," Duff Cooper declared, "and women cannot excel there any more than they can on the football field." Although women MPs were entitled to use all the facilities of the Commons, there remained an unwritten rule that they were to stay out of Parliament's most exclusive male bastion, the members' smoking room, where whiskey was drunk, cigars puffed, and deals cut.

Kitty Atholl would never have dreamed of invading that sanctum, nor would she ever challenge any other parliamentary convention to keep women in their place. When she was told after her election that many male Tory MPs had not yet reconciled themselves to having women as colleagues, she replied that "if I could do anything towards smoothing over matters, I felt it my duty to try." Unlike the iconoclastic, sharp-tongued Lady Astor, the duchess was regarded as unthreatening by the Tory leadership and rank and file. Her usual attire—long tweed skirt, wool jacket, and single string of pearls—reflected her personality: modest, decorous, and highly conventional.

Ironically, in light of what happened later, it was Neville Chamberlain who emphasized Kitty's dependability when he suggested to Prime Minister Baldwin in 1924 that she be given a junior minister's post, as parliamentary secretary to the Board of Education. The appointment, it was hoped, would help the Tories with women voters, and Kitty, unlike Lady Astor, could be counted on never to rock the boat. Baldwin agreed that the party loyalty of the Duchess of Atholl was unquestioned. Thus it was that Kitty Atholl became the first woman Tory MP to hold ministerial office.

A decade later, however, she was showing distinct signs of rebellion. She joined Churchill and other Tory hard-liners in opposing the government's bill to grant India limited self-rule because in her view, the Hindu majority would victimize the Muslim and untouchable minorities. Then, in late 1935, she picked up a copy of *Mein Kampf* in the original German. As she read Hitler's outline of his political philosophy, she was appalled by its hatred and bigotry but, most of all, by its explicit blueprint for German aggression against much of the rest of Europe. "Never can a modern statesman have made so startlingly clear to his reader his ambitions . . ." she later wrote.

An English translation of *Mein Kampf*, entitled *My Struggle*, had been published in the autumn of 1933 by Hurst & Blackett, a small subsidiary of Hutchinson, one of Britain's most prominent publishing houses. The translation had been done by Edgar Dugdale, a wealthy gentleman scholar and translator who was married to Baffy Dugdale. A few months before the book's publication in Britain, Dr. Hans Wilhelm Thost, a London correspondent for the official Nazi newspaper *Völkische Beobachter*, informed Hurst & Blackett that Dugdale's translation would have to be approved by the German government before it could be published. Concerned that it might lose the rights to the book if it didn't agree to the demand, Hurst & Blackett reluctantly agreed to the vetting by Berlin. The result was a watered-down, bowdlerized version of the führer's manifesto, totaling only 297 pages (compared with 781 in the German original) and omitting a number of Hitler's most inflammatory statements, particularly his expressions of hatred for Jews.

Kitty Atholl sent to Churchill both the German edition and the English translation, along with copies of passages that had been left out of the English version. "Sometimes the warlike character of the original is concealed by mistranslating," she said in an accompanying note. She also sent Churchill some "extreme" passages from Hitler's speeches that "had not been circulated to the foreign press." Churchill read *Mein Kampf* with great attention, writing in his memoirs that "no book . . . deserved more careful study."

For Kitty Atholl, *Mein Kampf* served as a call to battle. No longer the docile backbencher who wanted to "smooth matters over," she became an outspoken foe of appeasement. She again joined forces with Churchill, this time in his campaign to awaken Britain to the dangers posed by Hitler and the need for rearmament. Like Churchill, she received confidential information from knowledgeable sources about the rapid pace and size of German rearmament, which she passed on to him and to officials in the Foreign Office. But she parted company with Churchill and other anti-appeasement Tories in her fervent opposition to *all* fascism, not just nazism. She did not, for example, share the realpolitik view that Mussolini must be placated so that he would not ally himself with Hitler. When the Spanish civil war erupted in 1936, neither Churchill nor the other Tory rebels expressed much concern about the fascist general Francisco Franco's revolt against the democratically elected Republican government in Spain. Nor did they speak out when both Hitler and Mussolini sent troops, planes, and other aid to Franco. Indeed, most of the Tory dissidents backed Chamberlain's policy of nonintervention in Spain, on the grounds that it was a sideshow to the main event in Germany. Kitty Atholl did not share that view either.

On a fact-finding mission to Spain, she had seen the damage done by German bombers: whole neighborhoods destroyed, hundreds of civilians maimed and killed. Along with several other women MPs, she launched a campaign to help Spanish refugees, and she criticized Chamberlain and his ministers for refusing to sell arms to the Spanish government. The fact that the Spanish Republicans were backed by the Soviet Union did not bother her. She had long opposed communism—she condemned all forms of totalitarianism—but she regarded fascism as the worst of the perils facing Europe at the time. To the duchess, "cruelty was cruelty by whoever committed it, and was an evil not to be tolerated."

In supporting aid for the Republican government, however, she was allying herself with British Communists, socialists, trade union leaders, and other groups considered anathema by the Conservative Party. Many Tories in her constituency, which contained more than its share of aristocrats, landed gentry, and retired military officers, were outraged. A duchess, of all people, sharing rally platforms with Communists! Regarded as a traitor to her class, she was openly referred to by some of her constituents as "the Red Duchess."

The prime minister and the Tory whips were equally furious with her. In April 1938 she wrote to Chamberlain, suggesting she might have to withdraw her support from the government because of its stand on Spain. In a preemptive strike, Chamberlain wrote back that he was withdrawing the whip from her, meaning that he was expelling her from the party. She would remain an MP, but unless her party membership was restored, she would not have official Tory support at the next election. No other Tory rebel had received such severe punishment.

At the time of the Munich Conference, Kitty Atholl was in the United States on a lecture tour. She was not present for the Commons debate or vote. When she returned home in October, her husband, worried that she would get into even more political trouble, urged her to support the agreement. But when she was summoned to appear before the officers of her constituency association, she told them she strongly opposed what Chamberlain had done. To make sure there was no doubt about her views, she also published them in a pamphlet, which she distributed widely in her constituency.

That was all the Tory whips needed. For months James Stuart, the whip who handled Tory affairs in Scotland, had been urging the duchess's constituency association to adopt a new candidate for the next election. He pressed even harder now, and in November the association did as he asked. It selected a wealthy local farmer, William McNair Snadden, to stand in the duchess's place. With that, she resigned her seat and declared she would stand as an Independent candidate in the by-election to follow. Several people close to her, including Churchill and her husband, pleaded with her not to take such a drastic step. To the duchess, however, it was a matter of honor and conscience. She meant to make the by-election a referendum on the government's appeasement of the dictators, hoping to awaken public opinion to the dangers facing the country.

For their part, Chamberlain and his men, who also saw the by-election in Scotland as a referendum on their policy, were determined to do everything in their power to defeat the duchess and to send an unmistakable message to the other rebels about the dangers of dissent. Thus began one of the shabbiest, most disreputable electoral campaigns in modern British history. Night after night cabinet ministers and other pro-appeasement Tory MPs came to Kitty's constituency to speak against her, while pamphlets denouncing her and praising Chamberlain were sent to every voter. Tory canvassers warned residents that if they voted for the duchess, "there will be a war and your sons will be killed." Rumors circulated that she was getting money from the Communist Party, and she was sent fake telegrams signed "Stalin," with the message "Greetings from Moscow." Shortly before the December 21 election, workers on a number of estates in the area reportedly found unexpected bonuses in their pay envelopes, along with notes from the estates' owners urging a vote for the duchess's Tory opponent. Some landowners who opposed her notified their tenants of reductions in their rent, accompanied by cards that read "Vote for Snadden." The word went around local pubs and other gathering places that workers who supported Kitty might find themselves out of their jobs.

To combat such tactics, Kitty appealed to other Tory rebels to come to her aid. None of them did. When Violet Bonham Carter, one of her staunchest supporters, asked Anthony Eden when he was going to Scotland to speak for her, he replied that he was not planning to campaign for her at all. Lady Violet, whose Liberal Party had ordered its candidate in the by-election to withdraw in favor of the duchess, was astonished. If ever Eden was going to show courage, she wrote later, "it surely should have been that election in which a member of his own party was risking her political existence for the course for which he stood."

In response to Kitty's appeal for aid, Harold Macmillan wrote that he was too busy and was sorry that he couldn't help. Bob Boothby, who at first did volunteer to come to speak on her behalf, later shame-facedly retracted his offer. He wrote Kitty that James Stuart had threat-ened to withdraw the whip from him if he actively campaigned for her, and his own association chairman, who had earlier helped save him from Tory wrath over Munich, had threatened to resign. Boothby would be happy, he said, to send her a public letter of support instead. The duchess tartly declined the offer, saying Boothby's resignation of the whip would have been far more helpful.

Churchill, who, of all the Tory rebels, was closest to the duchess, also considered campaigning for her when the by-election was announced, telling the chairman of his constituency association that he felt he ought to support her if she wished it." But he too came under in-tense pressure from Stuart and from Tory stalwarts in his own con-stituency, and in the end he decided not to speak. He did send a letter of endorsement, which the duchess's supporters circulated throughout the constituency. "You are no doubt opposed by many Conservatives as loyal and patriotic as yourself, but the fact remains that outside our is-land, your defeat at this moment would be relished by the enemies of Britain and of freedom in every part of the world," Churchill wrote. "It would be widely accepted as another sign that Great Britain . . . no longer has the spirit and willpower to confront the tyrannies and cruel persecutions which have darkened this age."

The lack of active support for the duchess was obviously not one of the rebels' finest moments. When they came to write their memoirs, few mentioned their reluctance to brave the wrath of the whips and their own constituency associations to go to her aid. But their decision likely was affected by factors other than party pressure: Macmillan, for example, campaigned hard for an anti-Munich Independent candidate in an Oxford by-election held at about the same time. Kitty Atholl's real problem was her gender. As a woman she had never been part of the parliamentary old boy network. She was not invited to join the circles of anti-appeasement MPs coalescing around Eden and Churchill. To put it simply, they did not regard her as one of their own.

On the day of the by-election more than twenty-two thousand voters in Kinross and West Perthshire braved a heavy snowfall to cast their ballots. While those voting for the duchess had to find their own way to the polls, a fleet of cars dispatched by the Tory Central Office ferried Snadden supporters to vote. In the end Kitty was defeated, but by fewer than fourteen hundred votes. Considering the resources and effort expended by the Tory Party, the closeness of the election could hardly be regarded as a ringing endorsement of Chamberlain's policy. Nonetheless, the prime minister and his supporters were ecstatic. Chamberlain wrote David Margesson that he was "overjoyed" by the news of the duchess's defeat. Ivor Cobbold, a local landowner and a relative by marriage to Macmillan and James Stuart, sent a jeering telegram to Kitty: "Am delighted you are out. Hope my . . . people voted against you." Stuart himself needled Churchill, suggesting that he would be the next to fall. "I naturally told him," Churchill wrote his wife, "to go to hell or Epping."

For her part, the Duchess of Atholl retired from politics and spent the last year of peacetime, and the next six years of war, working to help refugees throughout Europe.

The mastermind behind the Tories' smear campaign against the duchess was a short, fleshy bureaucrat named Sir Joseph Ball. Having served as director of investigations for MI5, the British domestic intelligence agency, before heading the Tory Central Office's research department,

Ball was an acknowledged specialist "in the seamy side of life." He also was Neville Chamberlain's fishing companion and closest political adviser. Ball considered one of his chief duties to be the undermining of those whom he and Chamberlain considered the prime minister's enemies; he secretly controlled a weekly publication called *Truth*, which regularly savaged Churchill and other anti-appeasement Tories.

But Ball's real specialty was spying. Early in his tenure he placed Tory agents in Labour Party headquarters and on the staffs of left-leaning newspapers. In the late 1930s he collected information about the Tory rebels, working with Margesson and the other government whips. The whips' office had traditionally gathered intelligence about the private and public behavior of MPs, but under Margesson's tenure the practice had been taken to new heights—or depths. In his diary, Chips Channon noted the role of Thomas Dugdale, an assistant whip, as "the government spy. He reports every conversation to the PM or to David, and it is his role to pump people . . . [He is] the arch-informer. He listens, offends no one, and reports all."

In his surveillance, Ball used methods akin to the "dirty tricks" employed more than thirty years later by President Richard Nixon and his men in Watergate. One of Ball's main targets was the wealthy American Ronald Tree, whose four-story town house in Queen Anne's Gate had become the favored meeting place for the rebels. The house's location, a couple of blocks from Parliament, made it perfect for their clandestine get-togethers. Tree had installed a division bell, which rang whenever a vote in the Commons was imminent.

Directly across the street from Tree's home was the office of the *Whitehall Letter*, a weekly foreign affairs newsletter critical of appeasement, which was edited by Helen Kirkpatrick and Victor Gordon-Lennox, the *Daily Telegraph*'s diplomatic correspondent. The *Whitehall Letter* was one of several private newsletters created in the 1930s as an alternative to the national press and its unquestioning support of Chamberlain's policy. Most of the new publications were edited by newspaper correspondents frustrated by the press's failure to function as a watchdog. "We pointed out what was in *Mein Kampf* and what the Germans were doing in . . . Europe," said Kirkpatrick, who was to become a correspondent for the *Chicago Daily News* in the spring of 1939. "It was clear to us that Britain was headed for a war with Germany."

Gordon-Lennox and Kirkpatrick had excellent sources in foreign embassies and in the Foreign Office, several of whom leaked information to them about British military weaknesses and Germany's rapidly growing strength. The newsletter's publication of such material was an irritation to the prime minister and to Ball, and both Gordon-Lennox and Kirkpatrick were aware that their office was under surveillance. The same was true of Tree's house; Kirkpatrick had occasionally seen men loitering on corners, keeping an eye on it. Then, in early 1939, she and Gordon-Lennox were given a tip that the surveillance of Tree went far beyond the odd stakeout. Kirkpatrick, who was a good friend of the MP and his wife, Nancy, immediately called him. Did he know that his phone was being tapped? she asked. Tree was stunned. For the past few weeks he had noticed odd clicking sounds when he picked up the receiver, but he had no idea what they were. He couldn't believe that "the Government thought us to be so dangerous." Kirkpatrick cautioned him that from then on, he should not discuss any anti-appeasement activity over the phone or give the names of contacts or sources.*

Tree's was hardly the only name on Chamberlain's "enemies list." The phones of other rebels, including Churchill's, were also tapped, as were those of several government staffers and journalists considered anti-Chamberlain. The prime minister's critics, "of course, are totally unaware of my knowledge of their proceedings," Chamberlain wrote to his sister a few days after the Munich debate. "I [have] continual knowledge of their doings & sayings which for the nth time demonstrates how completely Winston can deceive himself when he wants to."

The prime minister's ruthless tactics against his opponents were just one aspect of the deep stresses and fractures in British government and society caused by the dispute over the government's policies toward Hitler and Mussolini. Munich, in particular, created unparalleled feuds, many so venomous that they went unhealed for years. "Among Conservatives, families and friends in intimate contact were divided to a degree the like of which I have never seen," Churchill observed. "Men

---

*Years later, during the war, Joseph Ball "had the gall to tell me that he himself had been responsible for having my phone tapped," Tree reported.

and women, long bound by party ties, social amenities, and family connections, glared upon one another in scorn and anger." Diana Cooper recalled that "husbands and wives stopped speaking to one another, fathers and sons said unforgivable things to one another." She and her husband knew at least twelve married couples who were bitterly divided over Munich. "In every case," Duff Cooper said, "it was the husband who supported and the wife who opposed Chamberlain." That was certainly true of Dorothy Macmillan's brother, the new Duke of Devonshire, and his wife, Mary, who was Bobbety Cranborne's sister. Edward Cavendish was a member of Chamberlain's government and an ardent supporter of the prime minister's; Mary Cavendish just as fervently opposed him. In their family, however, there were no raging arguments because as the couple's son, Andrew, recalled, "my mother was prepared to subjugate her feelings and—on the surface at least— appear loyal to my father."

They were exceptions. Overall, traditional British politeness and civility became rare commodities during this poisonous time, as Duff and Diana Cooper learned to their chagrin. After he resigned as first lord of the admiralty, Cooper was shunned by friends and acquaintances; one old friend in his constituency went so far as to cancel a political meeting at his house because he didn't want Cooper crossing his threshold. On the night of Cooper's resignation, Lady Willingdon, whose husband had been viceroy in India, snapped, "I should like to crush his head to a jelly." Lord Maugham, the lord chancellor and brother of the novelist Somerset Maugham, declared in a speech that Tory rebel "war-mongers" like Winston Churchill and Duff Cooper should be "shot or hanged." When Lady Diana defended her husband at a party, several of the other guests, among them friends she had known from childhood, listened in "hostile silence," noted one of the guests. "They think Duff mad or inexplicably silly." Actually, where Munich was concerned, Cooper had no interest, either, in civility or politeness. He told Leo Amery's son, Julian, that he was having made a special walking stick in which he could hide a furled umbrella. Chamberlain's umbrella, he said, "had become such a symbol of appeasement that he would not be seen dead with one."

During this period, attending a dinner party, luncheon, or tea could be perilous; such gatherings often turned into minefields, exploding in bitter disputes. A debate over appeasement at the home of Kenneth Clark became so rancorous that one dinner guest, an eminent Oxford don, roared at another guest: "I look forward to using your skull as an inkpot!" Clark expelled both men from his house. At a London luncheon a society matron, echoing Lord Maugham's feelings, hissed to Barbara Cartland that "those traitors—Winston Churchill, your brother, and his like—should be shot." Violet Bonham Carter's stepmother, Margot Asquith, refused to come to lunch with Lady Violet and her family, saying, "I know you would say something wicked about dear Neville, and I should burst into tears."

Lady Astor, another strong Chamberlain supporter, quarreled so violently over Munich with her niece Nancy Tree and Nancy's husband, Ronald, that Nancy Tree refused from then on to see her aunt or allow her to come to Ditchley Park, the Trees' grand country estate in Oxfordshire. She did not change her mind until after the war began. The Trees also parted company with friends who had been so close to Tree that they had designated him as guardian of their children in the event of their deaths, Euan Wallace, the financial secretary to the treasury, and his wife, Barbara. The Wallaces, Nancy Tree said, wouldn't speak to her husband after Munich.

Churchill's wife, Clementine, was also caught up in the fray. In January 1939 she was cruising off Barbados aboard a yacht owned by Lord Moyne, a good friend of the Churchills, when she and Moyne's other guests heard a shortwave radio broadcast from Britain denouncing the anti-appeasement MPs, including her husband. When several of the other guests gleefully echoed the sentiments of the broadcast, Clementine, who had been subjected to pro-Munich rhetoric for much of the voyage, could take no more. She stormed out of the cabin, took a launch ashore, and booked passage on a ship leaving for England the next day.

As the story of Duff Cooper and the walking stick suggests, the acrimony and vitriol were not one-sided. A number of the Tory rebels went on the offensive themselves, labeling Chamberlain "the umbrella man" and the "coroner" and lashing out at their critics in other ways. Harold Macmillan was perhaps the most defiant. Some of his associates thought that his standing up to Chamberlain after Munich went beyond bravery, that an element of recklessness was involved. They were probably right. Macmillan was still suffering from the humiliation of his wife's continuing affair with Bob Boothby, and the passion with which he threw himself into the anti-appeasement fight following Munich seemed, in the minds of some, an attempt to assuage the pain.

On one occasion, he invited Violet Bonham Carter and her teenage daughter, Cressida, to accompany him and his son, Maurice, to a benefit screening in London of a new film version of Gilbert and Sullivan's *Mikado*. A newsreel, shown before the movie, featured footage of a recent visit of Chamberlain and Lord Halifax to Mussolini in Italy. When the umbrella-carrying Chamberlain appeared on the screen, Macmillan shouted, "Ombrello! Ombrello!" at the top of his voice. Hardly a shrinking violet, Lady Violet was astonished at Macmillan's audacity, considering that they were sitting in the midst of a black-tie, mostly pro-Munich crowd. The memories of that evening were still vivid in her mind some twenty-five years later, when she wrote to Macmillan, reminding him of the event. "Some of our neighbours shuddered," she recalled, "but I glowed with admiration at your courage."

Macmillan went even further in November 1938, vigorously campaigning in Oxford for an anti-appeasement Independent candidate who stood against the official Conservative nominee in a parliamentary by-election. This election campaign was as much a cause célèbre as the Duchess of Atholl's contest, involving as it did well-known candidates associated with the most prestigious university in the country. The Conservative nominee was Quintin Hogg, a brilliant young pro-Munich barrister who was an Oxford graduate and the son of Lord Hailsham, a former lord chancellor. Hogg's anti-Munich challenger was Alexander Lindsay, the master (or dean) of Balliol College, Macmillan's alma mater.

As in the Kinross and West Perthshire election, the Tory Party sent in a throng of Conservative MPs to speak for Hogg. They were countered by a sizable number of anti-appeasement students at Oxford, including Maurice Macmillan and Julian Amery, who campaigned hard for Lindsay. While not as nasty as the contest involving the duchess, the Oxford election did have some colorful instances of vilification, such as the slogan "A vote for Hogg is a vote for Hitler," which was painted on walls all over Oxford. (Hogg responded with: "Vote for Hogg and save your bacon.")

Macmillan was the only anti-appeasement Tory MP to appear on Lindsay's behalf. The Independent candidate had also asked Churchill and Eden for their public support, but both declined. After the election, which Hogg won by a narrow margin, Macmillan felt the wrath of Chamberlain's men. He was threatened with withdrawal of the whip, the possibility of another candidate chosen in his place at the next general election, and ejection from London's Carlton Club, a Conservative Party stronghold.

Undismayed, Macmillan continued to thumb his nose at the prime minister. Another striking demonstration of that disdain occurred during his family's 1938 observance of Guy Fawkes Day, the commemoration of the foiling of a plot by Fawkes and other conspirators in 1605 to blow up Parliament and kill James I. Every year the anniversary of the Gunpowder Plot is celebrated throughout Britain with fireworks and bonfires on which effigies of Guy Fawkes are thrown.

At Birch Grove, Macmillan's country house in Sussex, he and his family were joined for the celebration by other members of the Macmillan and Cavendish clans, as well as by several dozen Jewish refugees who had fled Czechoslovakia after Munich and had been given shelter by Macmillan and some of his neighbors. On that chilly November night Macmillan and his children built the traditional Guy Fawkes bonfire into an impressive blaze. As flames leaped into the night air, casting lurid shadows on the faces of those gathered around it, Macmillan held high that year's Guy and threw the straw figure onto the fire. Several of Macmillan and Lady Dorothy's relatives gasped in disapproval at the sight of the effigy, dressed in a frock coat, striped pants, a black homburg—and sporting a furled umbrella. They were not amused by this mocking of the prime minister, and the incident, in Macmillan's words, caused a "deep feud" that lasted for years.

CHAPTER TEN

"WAITING FOR A STIRRING LEAD"

On a summer day in 1939, Dick Law, son of a former Tory prime minister, sat down with an American acquaintance to talk about how to topple the current Tory prime minister from power. Law had met Felix Frankfurter five years earlier, when the Harvard Law School professor and longtime adviser to President Franklin Roosevelt had been the visiting Eastman professor at Balliol College. Now the fifty-seven-year-old Frankfurter was a U.S. Supreme Court justice.

Over lunch at a London club, the tall blond Law poured out to Frankfurter the deep frustration and discouragement that he and the other Tory rebels felt. More than six months after Munich, Europe was again on the verge of war. Yet despite the obvious failure of his policies, Chamberlain maintained his firm grip on office, while Britain remained unprepared for the conflagration that Law and the other dissidents were sure was coming. As Ronald Cartland later declared, "Time can seldom have been purchased more dearly—and never have been more wantonly wasted afterwards."

Yet in those months the Conservative rebels still had not mounted a serious challenge to the government. They signed resolutions and made speeches attacking Chamberlain's policies and, in return, were denounced as warmongers by the progovernment press and David Margesson and his deputies. But they refrained from any attempt to bring the government down. How could they possibly hope for success? Their numbers had grown slightly since Munich, but they still numbered only a few more than thirty, a tiny minority with no power in a ruthlessly controlled House.

After a while Frankfurter had heard enough. "My dear Dick," he said, "the trouble with you people is that your acts don't line up with your convictions. You know that this is one of the turning points in history. Yet you act as if the issue were Welsh disestablishment or perhaps Home Rule. Thirty resolute men in your House of Commons could save the world. You won't convince the House by argument nor even by facts—only by the strength of your own conviction."

Frankfurter was right, and Law knew it. He, Cartland, Macmillan, Boothby, and a few other rebels were resolute in their conviction that Chamberlain must go. But a number of the others favored less extreme measures. The Tory Party's retaliatory campaign against them had had its intended effect; they were anxious to avoid further retribution. In a letter to *The Spectator*, the Independent MP Eleanor Rathbone, a staunch foe of appeasement, acidly noted how after attacking the Munich agreement, several of the Tory insurgents "sat mute for a few months . . . [until] the wrath of the Party Whips subsided." The more cautious rebels also were concerned about creating disunity in the country at a time of national peril. They still hoped that Chamberlain could be induced to step up rearmament and broaden his government.

The problem was, as it always had been, a lack of leadership. Who was there with the ability to convince wavering MPs that Britain's survival depended on getting rid of Chamberlain? And who could take them into battle in the Commons and in the country? Law continued to hope that Anthony Eden, despite all signs to the contrary, would accept the challenge. Ever since Munich, most of Chamberlain's Tory opponents, who had come to be known as the Eden group (or the "glamour boys," as Chamberlain's men derisively called them), had met regularly at Ronald Tree's town house. Among the most active were Amery, Law, Cartland, Macmillan, Nicolson, Tree, Bobbety Cranborne, Jim Thomas, Paul Emrys-Evans, Edward Spears, and Duff Cooper, who joined the rebel group after Munich. Eden usually attended but did little leading.

The most prominent rebel of all was not invited to these clandestine meetings. If Eden was thought to be too cautious, Winston Churchill was still regarded as too rash, too prone to mistakes in judgment, qualities that were particularly undesirable at a time of international crisis. Churchill meanwhile was leading a much smaller band, comprised only of Boothby, Duncan Sandys, and Brendan Bracken. The two groups had little to do with each other.

For his part, Eden was reluctant to associate with Churchill not only because of his perceived recklessness but also because he saw the older man as a potential rival. When Ronald and Nancy Tree invited the Edens and the Churchills, among others, to spend a weekend at Ditchley Park during the autumn of 1938, Eden had been upset that Churchill was included. "I'm rather annoyed with Ronnie for asking Winston," he told Nancy Tree during a Saturday stroll in the woods. "I think Winston wants to get in on my bandwagon." Others in the Eden group were concerned that Churchill "would dominate our proceedings and associate us with courses we did not want to follow," Paul Emrys-Evans later recalled.

Boothby also was unwelcome. He still was openly carrying on his affair with Dorothy Macmillan, and although he and Harold Macmillan were civil to each other in public, Macmillan tried to avoid his cuckolder's company as much as possible. Yet it wasn't just the possibility of embarrassing encounters that made the Eden group shy away from Boothby. His reputation had not recovered from the affair with Dorothy and his failed marriage to her cousin. Moreover, he, like Churchill, was considered too rash and impulsive. "The general feeling was that [Boothby] was far too unreliable in private conversation and in his public actions," Emrys-Evans remembered.

Whatever the reasons for his and his little group's exclusion, Churchill was upset by it. "Several of my friends [were wondering] whether there was not some . . . desire to isolate me as much as possible from the other Conservatives who disagree with the Government," he had written bitterly to Duff Cooper in late November 1938. More than a decade later Emrys-Evans noted to Amery, "Winston greatly resented his exclusion from our Group and has never forgotten it."

By the summer of 1939, with Europe about to burst into flames, Dick Law believed that such rivalries and divisions were inexcusable. He said as much to Eden in an impassioned letter written the day after his lunch with Frankfurter. It was time, Law wrote, for Eden to forget about his ambitions and caution and to join forces with Churchill, "to put yourselves at the head of a movement to turn the Government out, and offer an alternative Government." The only reason Chamberlain was able to hang on, Law added, was that there was no alternative. "You and Winston can provide an alternative, and you [two] alone. It means attacking the Prime Minister, and that, you will say, will only rally the party to him. This is what will happen. But it's only a stage. You've got to pass through that stage, and you will pass through it very quickly. Opinion in the country would force you through it, if you were resolute. The country is crying out for leadership . . . [but] so far, there is no leader to evoke a response."

In truth, a large part of Great Britain had been crying out for new leaders since shortly after Munich. Once the initial euphoria had evaporated, there lingered in the minds of many people a sense of shame over Czechoslovakia's fate, along with a belief and fear that Hitler undoubtedly would strike again. In late October 1938 a Gallup poll had revealed that almost 40 percent of the British public was dissatisfied with Chamberlain and his policies, and 72 percent wanted faster rearmament. Those figures were published in the *News Chronicle*, which owned exclusive rights to print Gallup poll results, but another finding, showing that 86 percent of the public believed that Hitler was lying when he said he had no more territorial ambitions, was not printed. The *News Chronicle*'s publisher had censored that figure, not because he believed it inaccurate but because, as he wrote to Chamberlain, "I fear that so blunt an advertisement of the state of British opinion on this matter would exacerbate feelings in Germany."

The anti-Semitic madness of *Kristallnacht*, which occurred just a few days later, only intensified the British public's growing antipathy toward Germany and its leader. On the night of November 9, Nazi thugs, under orders from the Gestapo, launched a pogrom against German Jews, torching synagogues, ransacking and looting Jewish businesses, vandalizing hospitals, homes, schools, and cemeteries, and killing dozens of people. More than thirty thousand Jews were arrested; most were later sent to concentration camps. The Nazi atrocities during this "night of broken glass" and in the days to come caused widespread dismay and anger in Britain, and even some of Chamberlain's strongest supporters began to question the prime minister's certainty that Hitler was a reasonable man with whom he could "do business." Lady Willingdon, who in October had wanted Duff Cooper's brains turned into jelly, told fellow guests at a luncheon in November that it would be "madness" for the Conservatives to call a general election in early 1939 because the country "was turning anti-Chamberlain."

At the same time, there was increasing talk of forming a new all-party coalition of anti-appeasement MPs like the one that Hugh Dalton had discussed with Macmillan. In the October Gallup poll, 40 percent of the public said it would favor such a coalition under Eden's leadership, while only 39 percent said it would not. It was a significant finding, indicating, as the *News Chronicle* noted, that "if Mr. Eden chose to assume the leadership of such a group he could command a considerable following in the country." Neville Chamberlain, *The New York Times* reported, was facing "a slow crumbling of confidence in his leadership." The newspaper estimated that at least half of all British voters were now opposed to Chamberlain and his policies.

In a letter to the editor of the *Manchester Guardian*, A. L. Rowse, a young scholar at All Souls College (in later years a noted expert on Shakespeare and Elizabethan England), said he believed that at least three-quarters of the nation opposed the "unrepresentative junta around Mr. Chamberlain" and would rally behind Eden and a "truly National Government." Three professors at St. Andrews University in Scotland used the same venue, a letter to the *Guardian*, to plead with anti-appeasement MPs to heed the people and mount a direct challenge to the government before it was too late. The prime minister "is plunging us farther and farther into a chaos" that can end only with surrender to "German hegemony [and the] abandonment of our civil and political liberties," the professors declared. It was essential that the Tory MPs who abstained on Munich "give a strong lead to Parliament and to the nation" and join the Labour Party to create an all-party government and "save the national soul."

Eden was deluged with hundreds of letters, many of them from Labour and Liberal members, making the same appeal. But he was as unswayed by this national outpouring as he was by the urging of parliamentary colleagues to shed his caution and demonstrate bold leadership. "It seemed as if the nation—or a large part of it—was determined to have Eden as their leader and he was equally determined not to lead them," noted *Picture Post*, a popular photo-oriented weekly magazine. When Eden received an impassioned seven-page letter from Lady Juliet Rhys-Williams, a noted Liberal economist and social reformer, declaring that "the destiny of England is in your hands" and outlining in great detail how he could organize a new all-party group, this was his reply in full: "Thank you so much for your letter, which I was most interested to read. I know that you will not expect me to comment at length upon what you write, but only say that I do, I think, appreciate the political difficulties and confusion of the present time."

It had been a year since he had resigned as foreign secretary, and in that time Eden, while making vague speeches throughout the country about the need for national unity, was no closer to breaking with the Tory Party and the government than he had been in February 1938. At a time when such great issues were at stake, his reluctance to become a party maverick, in part because he feared the fate of the Duchess of Atholl, drove many people wild, prominently including Sir Timothy Eden, his elder brother. "It is ridiculous that you, who are an expert in Foreign Affairs, may not vote as you please on questions on which the fate of the world depends because some rich old woman or some ga-ga old colonel in Warwickshire . . . would be annoyed if you voted otherwise," Timothy Eden wrote. "It is not only ridiculous. It is immoral—and it is wrong. If a man may not vote according to his conscience, liberty is *already* dead in England." Incensed that Anthony had declared himself "in effect a Government supporter," his brother asked: "In what do you support [Chamberlain]?—Not in Foreign Policy and not in rearmament . . . You are *not* a Government supporter." In order to maintain his position "as leader on foreign affairs in this country," Anthony must propose "something positive and definite for the future" as soon as possible.

Other Eden supporters seconded that point of view. "The whole youth of the country is waiting for a stirring lead," Harold Nicolson complained to Bobbety Cranborne, "and all Anthony is [doing] is to repeat flabby formulas." Cranborne in turn wrote to Jim Thomas: "I agree that Anthony must go further now than he has up to the present . . ."

In late November 1938, when Eden accepted an invitation to deliver the main address at a huge anti-appeasement rally at Queen's Hall in London, there had been a brief flicker of hope that he finally would steel himself to do what his supporters wanted. The military correspondent of *The Times*, Basil Liddell Hart, had helped Eden prepare a tough speech attacking the government's foreign policy, and the thousands who packed the hall buzzed with anticipation as they stood to give him a resounding ovation. Once he launched into his speech, however, their enthusiasm turned to puzzlement and then to anger. Eden had dropped every criticism that Liddell Hart had prepared; there was no mention of the sellout of Czechoslovakia or the folly of placating Hitler. Instead, he delivered "rather timid generalizations" about the need for national unity. The audience grew more and more restive, and Liddell Hart, seated on the platform next to Eden's wife, feared that the mutters and whispers heard throughout the hall would soon turn to booing.

Violet Bonham Carter moved swiftly to rescue the evening. She had been assigned to give a short speech thanking Eden for his address, but she used the opportunity to do what Eden was supposed to do: deliver an indictment of Chamberlain's foreign policy. Her searing extemporaneous address "saved the day," Liddell Hart later wrote. "It was one of the most brilliant speeches to which I ever listened, and roused the apathetic audience to an enthusiastic response." (After hearing another of her anti-appeasement speeches, Leo Amery wrote in his diary: "With such gifts of eloquence I might easily have been Prime Minister long ago.") But Eden, who was "visibly disconcerted" by Lady Violet's speech, did not join in the praise. He later wrote to a friend: "I think that Violet Bonham Carter rather spoilt the effect of [my speech] by her vehement attack on the Prime Minister. It was brilliant of course as rhetoric, but unwise as politics. It even made me feel a little resentful."

Lady Violet herself thought about the irony of fate as she left Queen's Hall that evening. "Here was Anthony Eden—a leader widely trusted and respected, [with] large sections of 'the public' offering him a sword he would not draw. And on the other side was Winston, armed with unflinching courage and matchless eloquence, [who] for some reason failed to inspire their trust. Even among critics of the government, Anthony was regarded as 'respectable' and Winston was not." She wondered if Eden's "tepid impartiality" might not reflect his desire to get back into Chamberlain's good graces and the cabinet.

She was, in fact, right. Eden *was* angling for a job. A week after the vote of confidence over Munich he had told Lord Halifax that he "agreed with 90 percent of Chamberlain's position" on Munich, boosting the figure to 100 percent when Halifax told him that the prime minister had found Hitler to be an unattractive figure. At the same time, Eden was anxious to maintain his credentials as a critic of appeasement, so that if Chamberlain's government fell, he would be, in the words of Victor Gordon-Lennox, "lying pretty for the leadership of the Party." It was a difficult juggling act and one that Chamberlain was well aware of. "Our Anthony," he wrote sarcastically to his sister, "is in a dilemma from which he would very much like me to extract him." But he had no intention of taking Eden back into the fold, despite urgings from Halifax that the time had come for a government of national unity. "I have had trouble enough with my present Cabinet," he said, "and I feel that what I want is more support for my policy and not more strengthening of those who don't believe in it or at any rate are harassed by constant doubts. I don't think therefore that you will see any drastic revision or reconstruction of the Cabinet."

Even though some opponents of the government still regarded Winston Churchill with suspicion, he too began receiving a flood of letters after Munich, many of them from young people who begged him to lead a campaign to form a new national party and government. Thomas Horabin, a Cornwall businessman and Churchill supporter, wrote to him that when he told a large public meeting at Penzance that Churchill was the only possible future prime minister, the crowd of more than five hundred people leaped up and applauded. "There is an intense anxiety on the part of the ordinary people of this country for decisive leadership—and an earnest desire to be told the true facts of the situation and to face up to them," Horabin declared. Echoing that view,

Eleanor Rathbone wrote to Churchill: "There is a great longing for leadership, and even those who are far apart from you in general politics realize that you are the one man who has combined a full realization of the dangers of our military position with a belief in collective international action against aggression. Excuse my butting in. But as an admirer and an outsider to political parties . . . I cannot help fearing that your silence and Mr. Eden's may be misunderstood."

Alastair Forbes, a Cambridge student and a friend of Churchill's son Randolph, was far less polite in a ten-page letter urging Churchill to lead the fight against Chamberlain. "Do you claim the right of the politician to swallow down your convictions and your ideals until such a time when it will be more expedient to raise them?" wrote the twenty-year-old Forbes.* "Why should you have to stoop to such an action? . . . To dismiss the prickings of your political conscience at this time would be treasonable." If Chamberlain remained in office and appeasement continued, "what sort of hope will there be for the young of the country? What to believe in, what indeed to fight for?"

But Churchill, like Eden, refused to accept the baton. Prone all his life to bouts of depression, he was sunk in deep gloom over Munich. "At Chartwell, there were occasions . . . alone with him when the despondency was overwhelming," his nephew recalled. When the magazine editor R. J. Minney urged him to launch another national speaking tour to rouse public opinion, Churchill replied that giving speeches "did not seem to produce the slightest result." In his response to a young lawyer who had written to him that "the inarticulate mass of the electorate is crying out for new leaders and a new party," Churchill declared that "the same views have been put to me literally by hundreds of people in the last two months" but that the "difficulties of organizing and forming a new Party have often proved insuperable." Harold Macmillan, one of the few members of the Eden group to keep in close touch with the older man, was concerned that Churchill was "in danger of relapsing into a complacent Cassandra." To Hugh Dalton, he worried that Churchill now took the view: " 'Well, I have done my best.

---

*Forbes, an American by birth, was a cousin of President Franklin Roosevelt's and also an uncle of Senator John Kerry, the 2004 Democratic nominee for president.

I have made all these speeches. Nobody has paid any attention. All my prophecies have turned out to be true. I have been publicly snubbed by the Government. What more can I do?'"

There was still another reason for Churchill's reluctance to mount a campaign against Chamberlain: he, again like Eden, hoped that the prime minister would ask him to join the cabinet. Although Churchill never wavered in his opposition to appeasement, there had been times in the previous four years when it appeared that Baldwin or Chamberlain might bring him into their administrations; during those periods he tended to tamp down his criticism of the government. This was one of those times. "Winston found no pleasure in playing the independent critic," Violet Bonham Carter observed. "His imagination, his energy, and his capacities could be best expressed only when he occupied a seat of power." So, while continuing to make ringing anti-appeasement speeches in the House of Commons, Churchill turned down almost all requests for public appearances in the months after Munich and spent most of his time at Chartwell working on his *History of the English-Speaking Peoples*.

Near the end of his long life Alexander Cadogan, permanent undersecretary of the Foreign Office under Chamberlain and Halifax, examined his diary for the first three months of 1939. He was appalled by what he found. His entries left the "impression of a number of amateurs fumbling about with insoluble problems . . . Our own military capabilities were deplorably inadequate. We were being swept along on a rapid series of surprises sprung upon us by Hitler with a speed that took one's breath away."

In a front-page article on Britain's defenses in January 1939, *The New York Times* concluded there was little evidence that "Britain is better prepared for her potential enemies than at the time of Munich. Crowded centers of population remain dangerously undefended against air attack; the civilian population does not yet know what to do or where to scurry for shelter if a German bombing fleet should roar over London." While hundreds of thousands of small steel shelters were being produced for use in the gardens of private houses, millions of

Britons did not have gardens or access to them, and no deep bomb-proof shelters were being built. The gas masks distributed during the Munich crisis were gathering dust in people's closets, and the trenches hurriedly dug in parks and other public places were full of rainwater; guards had to be hired to prevent passersby from tumbling in and drowning.

"There is a total lack of drive," Churchill wrote his wife, "and Chamberlain does not know a tithe of the neglects for which he is responsible." Janet Flanner observed in *The New Yorker* that the British people desperately wanted to know what to do if war broke out next spring or fall, "when, judging by the present lack of organization, the Englishman's umbrella is going to be his best bomb protection . . ." The Chamberlain government, she added, "seems to be in that state, awake, in which individuals find themselves in dreams—a nightmare of running without arrival."

From the beginning of its relatively modest rearmament campaign in 1934, the government had spent most of the money on the Royal Air Force. By early 1939 a number of vitally important radar stations had been built, and the production of planes, particularly fighters, had greatly increased. But their numbers still fell far short of the quantity of aircraft being turned out by Germany, and the RAF continued to have a difficult time getting sufficient equipment and men. Basil Liddell Hart, whose own newspaper would not publish his criticism of Britain's defense deficiencies, turned to the *Evening Standard* to write that the RAF expansion program, inadequate in the first place, was not being carried out on schedule. Shortly after Munich, Horace Wilson explained to air minister Kingsley Wood that the RAF would not be allowed to increase its production "to a level equal to the estimated German capacity" because Germany would "take it as a signal that we have decided at once to sabotage the Munich agreement."

As for the most neglected service, the army, Chamberlain continued for several critical months after Munich to spurn appeals from Leslie Hore-Belisha and Leo Amery, among others, to beef up the pitifully small troop levels, so that at least six regular and twenty-six Territorial divisions could be properly equipped and, if need be, sent to the Continent within eight months of the breakout of war. By early 1939, after four years of a military draft, the German Army boasted fifty-two active and fifty-one reserve divisions, totaling more than 3,000,000 men. The regular British Army, which, alone of all the armies of European powers, had no conscription, still numbered only about 180,000 men, with another 130,000 in the Territorials. Even these relatively minuscule numbers were starved for adequate equipment, arms, and training.

Chamberlain argued that there was no need for an expanded army because in his view, it would never be required. In a February 21 debate in the House the prime minister had restated his belief that Germany had "no more intention of aggression than we have" and that "we are now piling these ruinous armaments under a misunderstanding." Not long afterward, however, he finally capitulated to cabinet pressure and agreed to a scaled-down plan that would send four regular divisions to the Continent at the outbreak of war, with more to follow in the coming months.

In Britain's economic sector, meanwhile, there had been virtually no stockpiling of essential supplies and raw materials. In January 1939, for example, only a four-month supply of wheat and sugar was on hand, a month's more than the normal reserve. When Amery, Hore-Belisha, Churchill, and others demanded the creation of a ministry of supply to mobilize British industry and accelerate production of war matériel, Chamberlain rejected the idea. Putting industry under government control, he declared, would interfere with business as usual. A former government official confided to the Eden group that the real reason for the prime minister's opposition to a ministry of supply was that he thought it "would arouse the anger of Germany." With no one to urge them on, British factories continued to plod along. In late December 1938 a *New York Times* reporter, Ferdinand Kuhn, asked the manager of a large armaments factory when he thought the country would be prepared for war. "Give us three years, and we will be ready for them," the man replied. In a *Times* article, Kuhn noted dryly: "If Chancellor Hitler waits three years, all will be well."

Neville Chamberlain was so convinced there would be no war that on March 9, 1939, he summoned several political journalists to Downing

Street to tell them he hoped to call a disarmament conference by the end of the year. The journalists were incredulous. Wasn't Chamberlain receiving the same reports that their newspapers were getting: that Hitler's army was, even now, mobilizing to take over all of Czechoslovakia? In fact, the government did know about the reports, but the prime minister and his men simply didn't believe them. The following day Sir Samuel Hoare rhapsodized that the world was entering a new "golden age" of peace and prosperity, one that would be created through the cooperation of Chamberlain, Hitler, Mussolini, and Premier Daladier. Five days later, on March 15, German troops marched into Prague.

With the German seizure of Czechoslovakia, Chamberlain's "whole policy of appeasement [fell into] ruins," a morose Chips Channon wrote in his diary. Once and for all the führer had proved himself a liar. The idea of further conciliation was anathema to the shocked British public, even to the dwindling number of people who had supported the government's appeasement policy only days before. "A chap like myself, only too happy to be left alone, begins to notice indignation rising within himself," mused a young novelist named George Beardmore. "This must mean that the rest of the country is noticing the same indignation in themselves, perhaps even more so. Here, I tell myself, is the point where a tyrant must be stopped."

Still clinging to the belief that Hitler would eventually listen to reason, Chamberlain at first had no clue to the sea change in national opinion. He argued to the cabinet that Germany's occupation of Czechoslovakia was largely "symbolic" and that the government's basic policy toward the Reich should remain unchanged. That was no longer an option, Lord Halifax told him. The foreign secretary convinced Chamberlain that he must condemn Hitler's action, that the country would stand for nothing less. Even the newspapers that had earlier supported his policy were now saying that appeasement was over. Finally, in a speech in Birmingham on March 17, the prime minister denounced the occupation, although he seemed much more upset about the humiliating personal affront that he had suffered than about the destruction of a semisovereign country. "Surely," he snapped, "as a joint signatory of the Munich agreement, I was entitled, if Herr Hitler thought it ought to be undone, to that consultation which is provided for in the . . . declaration."

Speeches, however, were no longer enough. The public was demanding action, and so were Chamberlain's critics in the House of Commons. On March 29 the Tory rebels mounted what *The New York Times* called an "open challenge" to the prime minister, their first serious opposition to the government since the Munich debate. A group that now totaled more than thirty MPs, including Churchill, Amery, Macmillan, Boothby, Cartland, Eden, Law, Nicolson, and Cranborne, introduced a resolution calling for the formation of a new national all-party government to mobilize the country for possible war. "The feeling in the lobbies is that Chamberlain will either have to go or completely reverse his policy," Nicolson wrote. Halifax and other Chamberlain advisers feared that the Tory insurgents were on the verge of igniting a rebellion that would spread throughout the country. The foreign secretary warned Chamberlain that his government might be in danger if it did not take immediate action to show it "meant business" in opposing Germany's aggression.

The prime minister's response to Halifax's warning astonished the nation. On March 31 he appeared before the House to announce one of the most dramatic reversals of foreign policy in modern British history. Britain, he declared, would go to the aid of Poland, next on Germany's hit list, if it were invaded. "In the event of any action which clearly threatened Polish independence and which the Polish Government . . . considered it vital to resist with their national forces," he said, "His Majesty's Government would feel themselves bound at once to lend the Polish Government all the support in their power." France, the prime minister added, had authorized him to make the same guarantee on its behalf.

This pledge would have been remarkable for any British prime minister—all the more so for one who had been so ardently in favor of appeasement. No British government in history had ever promised military support to a nation in Central or Eastern Europe. Even more startling, Chamberlain's new policy in effect yielded to Poland, which was considered far more vulnerable militarily than Czechoslovakia, the power to decide whether or not Britain would go to war. Unlike Czechoslovakia, with its formidable mountain fortifications and mighty munitions arsenal, Poland was in effect naked to its enemies, with almost no natural protection to its east or west. Even worse, Germany, thanks to its seizure of Czechoslovakia, now threatened Poland on its northern, western, and southern borders.

Chamberlain had made the commitment against the advice of Britain's top military leaders, who were astounded by the pledge and vehemently insisted that the country did not have the means to fulfill it. When Hore-Belisha asked him if a paper expressing the armed force's view could be circulated to other members of the cabinet, Chamberlain refused, saying that would be "tantamount to a criticism of his policy."

Casting around for additional measures to show he "meant business," the prime minister made another spur-of-the-moment decision that turned existing policy on its ear. Two days before the guarantee to Poland, Hore-Belisha had announced that the Territorial Army would be more than doubled, with the addition of another 210,000 men to its ranks. Chamberlain's decision to expand the Territorials came after a brief conversation with Hore-Belisha, but he had not consulted army officers about the practical implications of such a sweeping proposal. Where would the equipment, arms, training camps, and instructors be found for hundreds of thousands of new volunteers when there weren't nearly enough for the current Territorials?

Leo Amery, who had been pressing for an expansion of the British Army for more than a decade, was appalled. He knew that time and careful planning were required to repair the defects of a neglected army and make it grow. Convinced that this kind of seat-of-the-pants approach would only lead to chaos, he denounced the plan as "eyewash" in a House debate on April 6.

Undeterred by his critics, the prime minister had one more surprise in store. On April 26 he proposed in the House a limited program of mandatory military training, the first peacetime conscription measure in Britain since the days of Oliver Cromwell. Under the bill, every twenty-year-old man in the country—a total of two hundred thousand—would be called up for six months' training. The pace would hardly be feverish; as Janet Flanner pointed out in *The New Yorker*, the last of the conscripts would not finish the program until July 1940, "if Herr Hitler doesn't mind waiting for the enemy until then." Flanner added that "the Nazis may operate with lightning speed," but the "English are still moving with all their traditional majesty."

Modest as it was, the conscription program put further strain on an army infrastructure that was struggling to cope with the swelling flood of new Territorial volunteers. Having served as a Territorial officer for two years, Ronald Cartland, whose men trained with World War I–vintage rifles, was already well aware of the critical shortages that plagued the volunteer force. Several other MPs discovered the deficiencies for themselves when they volunteered for military training that spring. Anthony Eden joined a battalion of the King's Royal Rifle Corps, which had no rifles and no proper hall in which to train; he and the other men in his unit drilled in the aisles of a posh Oxford Street shop after the clerks had gone home for the day. Ronald Tree, who trained with the Ninth Lancers on the Salisbury Plain, was horrified to learn that the armored cars assigned to his unit could travel for only a few hundred feet before breaking down. Even worse, the cars' machine guns could not be mounted because the mountings had not yet been manufactured.

Having suddenly been called to arms by their government, the young men of Britain were now being denied the weapons they needed to face the mighty military machine of Germany. If war did break out, British soldiers, poorly trained and badly equipped, would be the ones to suffer the consequences of the government's sluggishness in rearming. "Those old men ruined the world for my father," one youth told Ronald Cartland. "Now they are ruining it for me."

CHAPTER ELEVEN

"HERE IS THE TESTING"

With his guarantee of Poland and the introduction of conscription, Neville Chamberlain took much of the steam out of his critics' campaign. He had not broadened his government, as they had demanded, but he had finally taken a stand against appeasement, ordering his government to prepare—if not full throttle, then at least half throttle—for war. Even Winston Churchill said he now supported the prime minister's policy.

But Chamberlain's dramatic about-face was not what it seemed. He had no plans to live up to his pledge of going to war if Poland was attacked. Indeed, he had not given up on his hopes of keeping the peace by reaching an agreement with Germany. A disheartened Leslie Hore-Belisha told an acquaintance that the prime minister "seemed to think that an occasional bold speech was enough in itself" and that "he had no real intention of doing anything." According to the war secretary, "Neville still believes he can control Hitler and Mussolini and that they heed him."

Chamberlain's promise was made to assuage angry public opinion and to warn Hitler of the consequences that would result from a failure to negotiate. Yet the German leader never paid attention to the warning. Why should he? Almost immediately after the British guarantee of Poland, there were unmistakable signs that Chamberlain's show of firmness was just that, a show. On April 4, less than a week after Chamberlain's speech about Poland, *The Times* published a leader (an editorial), declaring that the prime minister's guarantee did not "bind Great Britain to defend every inch of the present frontiers of Poland." The leader, like the one on the Sudetenland the previous year, caused a storm of controversy. The government's critics saw it as an indication that Chamberlain was backing away from his commitment to Poland. The Foreign Office denied that the government had prompted the newspaper, but Chamberlain privately acknowledged that it reflected his point of view. "It is we who will judge whether [Poland's] independence is threatened or not," he wrote to his sister.

The government meanwhile continued to press the newspapers and the BBC to go easy on Hitler and Germany. "The public are not being informed of the extent or the imminence of our immediate danger," Harold Nicolson wrote in *The Spectator* in May. "I believe that at this moment the country *ought* to be alarmed, and *ought* to be disquieted." That same month Horace Wilson, who had been promoted to head the British Civil Service earlier in the year but who still was acting as the prime minister's right-hand man, urged top BBC executives not to broadcast reports on Hitler's speeches, declaring that such stories create "a war mentality." Another Chamberlain staffer informed the BBC that "it is definitely undesirable that, at times like the present, issues of foreign policy should be discussed in a controversial spirit on the air."

German officials carefully noted such attempts to avoid riling Hitler. In early summer, Herbert von Dirksen, the German ambassador in London, cabled Berlin that while "hostility toward Germany is growing [and] the readiness to fight has become more pronounced" among the British people, the prime minister and his cabinet favored "a constructive policy vis-à-vis Germany." Dirksen assured his superiors that "Chamberlain's personality is a certain guarantee that British policy will not be placed in the hands of unscrupulous adventurers."

When Hitler escalated his demands over Poland, the British government advised Polish officials to negotiate. Hitler insisted that the Baltic port of Danzig, which the Versailles Treaty had declared a free city, be returned to Germany. He also demanded that Germany be allowed to build a highway and railway across the Polish Corridor, a narrow strip of formerly German territory that had been awarded to Poland at the Paris Peace Conference in 1919. Bolstered by promises of help from

Britain and France, the Polish government refused all of Hitler's claims. "We in Poland do not recognize the concept of peace at any price," declared Polish foreign minister Józef Beck. Unlike Czechoslovakia, Beck said Poland "will fight."

Although British officials privately warned the Poles that they must be more accommodating, they never said that Britain had no intention of coming to Poland's rescue in the event of a German invasion. As a result, the Poles continued to trust in the promises of their allies, even as negotiations with Britain over loans and credits to buy arms and ammunition dragged on through the summer without resolution. "Surely the whole purpose of these negotiations is to arm Poland, and to arm her quickly," Hugh Dalton declared in a House of Commons debate in late July. "Is it, perhaps, feared that if the Poles get too many arms too quickly, they will get above themselves? . . . [Is there] some sinister and unrevealed purpose to try to keep Poland weak and irresolute?" In his diary, Dalton wrote of his concern that the government was getting ready to "sell the Poles down the river, as they sold the Czechs last year."

As it happened, other negotiations were going on in London that summer that, if successful, would indeed "enable Britain," in the words of Horace Wilson, "to rid herself of her commitments vis-à-vis Poland." These talks, unlike the ones with Polish military officials, were top secret. "If anything about them were to leak out," Ambassador Dirksen cautioned the German Foreign Ministry, "there would be a grand scandal, and Chamberlain would probably be forced to resign." The subject under discussion was undeniably explosive: behind the backs of the British people and Parliament, Wilson had been delegated to sound out Germany on the possibility of concluding an Anglo-German pact that would involve, among other things, wide-ranging economic cooperation between the two countries, including massive loans for German industries. In effect, it was a bribe to Hitler, to try to persuade him to behave himself and not to precipitate a war with Poland.

The German official involved in these negotiations was Dr. Helmut Wohlthat, a high-ranking government expert on foreign trade. Wilson presented Wohlthat with a cornucopia of offers: a nonaggression treaty, under which both Britain and Germany would renounce unilateral aggressive action; a disarmament agreement; settlement of Germany's demands for the return of its former colonies in Africa, taken away by the Versailles Treaty; and acknowledgment of Germany's economic sphere of interest in Central and Eastern Europe. In a conversation with Dirksen, Wilson made clear that the conclusion of such an Anglo-German entente would, in the view of the British government, invalidate Britain's guarantee of Poland. The proposed agreement, however, failed to get very far. Word of the talks did in fact leak to the British press, and in the furor that followed, Chamberlain's government quietly ended them while denying that any such negotiations were under way. Yet the aborted discussions did have one major result: they hardened Hitler's belief that Chamberlain had no intention of going to war over Poland.

With rumors and speculation swirling in London about Chamberlain's latest appeasement moves, a number of the Tory rebels became convinced that the prime minister was preparing to betray Poland. The firebrands among them, particularly Macmillan, Boothby, Cartland, and Law, were furious over what they considered the timidity of their more moderate colleagues. As the crisis over Poland deepened in early summer, divisions among the dissidents widened, and tensions occasionally erupted into fierce arguments. "Dick Law wants us to start fighting at once," even if it meant that "we may all lose our seats," Harold Nicolson noted. He added that Macmillan, who had advocated getting rid of Chamberlain for months, "thinks that all we Edenites have been too soft and gentlemanlike. That we should have clamoured for Chamberlain's removal. That no man in history has made such persistent and bone-headed mistakes, and that we all go on pretending that all is well." At one meeting of the Eden group, Macmillan scornfully declared: "If Chamberlain says that black is white, the Tories applaud his brilliance. If a week later he says that black is after all black, they applaud his realism. Never has there been such servility."

Nicolson himself was the recipient of a scalding letter from Bob Boothby, attacking him for faintheartedness. In a touching reply, Nicolson, who had shown considerable courage at the time of Munich but had backed off from direct criticism of the government since then, acknowledged that a combative spirit did not come naturally to him. "The

real fact is that old queens like myself are capable of hysterical hero-
ism but are not good at the constant fight," he wrote Boothby. "I lack
(as do many of my kind—those of what we may call a literary temperament) a lust for battle . . . Anyhow your letter has given me a shake."
As so often happened with the impulsive Boothby, he had regretted the
vehemence of his letter as soon as he sent it. "I have never doubted your
sincerity," he now replied to Nicolson. "But I have always taken you
much more seriously than you have taken yourself . . . Anything I know
about the conduct of foreign affairs you have taught me. In short, I admire you no end . . . But don't forget that these people will betray us
unless they are watched with vigilant suspicion . . ."

Ronald Cartland meanwhile indicted *all* parliamentary critics of
Munich, including himself, for not expressing their opposition suffi-
ciently loudly or often enough. What he wanted, he wrote in a liberal current affairs magazine titled *Headway*, was "a revolution. For nothing else
is needed." In Cartland's mind, the only man who could save Britain
from the disaster which he was sure was looming was Winston Churchill.
Although still a member of the Eden group, Cartland had long since
given up on the former foreign secretary. He had witnessed in his own
constituency a growing enthusiasm for Churchill; when the older man
visited the Austin aircraft factory in Birmingham at Cartland's invitation,
the workers greeted him with thunderous applause and cheers. "The
men were thrilled to see him," Cartland told his sister. "The man in the
street realizes that he has been right in everything he has said since
1933. Those in high places say he's finished—I don't believe it. He has
a following in the country far bigger than those in Westminster think."
Macmillan and others in the Eden group had also switched their allegiance to Churchill. And, as Cartland pointed out, so had much of the
country. Anthony Eden, having repeatedly refused to lead the charge
against the government's appeasement policy, had lost his chance.

In April the *Sunday Pictorial*, one of the few newspapers that consistently opposed appeasement, ran a front-page article headlined "Why
Isn't Winston Churchill in the Cabinet?" The paper received more than
twenty-four hundred letters in response, almost all of them agreeing
with the view that Churchill should be included in the government.
The paper's editor, Hugh Cudlipp, told Churchill that the overwhelm-

ing sentiment of the letters was "No more bootlicking to Hitler" and "We want a strong man who is not afraid."

Noting the *Sunday Pictorial* story, several members of the Eden group decided to ask other national newspapers to mount a campaign calling for the inclusion of Churchill, Eden, Amery, and Cooper in the cabinet. The rebels were eager to exploit the fact that a number of previously pro-Chamberlain papers had become much more critical of the government after Hitler's takeover of Czechoslovakia. At the end of June, Macmillan, Eden, Nicolson, and several other dissidents paid a call on Lord Camrose, owner of *The Daily Telegraph*, to ask him to kick off the campaign. As they entered the *Telegraph* building, Nicolson noted with amusement that "Anthony is terrified of being recognized and keeps his head bowed under a big black hat."

Camrose agreed to the rebels' request, although he had significant doubts about Eden. As a result, when the *Telegraph* ran a leading editorial pressing for a broadening of the cabinet, only Churchill was mentioned. "The plain fact is that when people speak of a reconstruction of the Cabinet, they are thinking first and foremost of the inclusion of Churchill," the *Telegraph* leader declared. "[I]t is quite certain that no step would more profoundly impress the Axis powers with the conviction that this country means business."

The Telegraph was now joined by a number of other newspapers in the country, including *The Observer, Manchester Guardian, Evening News, Daily Mirror, Daily Mail*, and *News Chronicle*, in urging Chamberlain to bring Churchill into the government. It was a remarkable outpouring of dissatisfaction with the current administration by a previously subservient press. Only the Beaverbrook papers and *The Times* refused to participate in the campaign.

At the same time, several of the publications also called for the inclusion of Eden and Amery. "Mr. Amery possesses a vast fund of knowledge and is a dynamo of energy when many of our ministers are tired," *Picture Post* noted. Echoing that view, the *Manchester Guardian* remarked: "Both in ability and experience of office, Mr. Amery could claim to supplant a tired member of this cabinet. Why he has been so constantly passed over, first by Lord Baldwin and then by Mr. Chamberlain, is one of the minor mysteries of politics."

The central figure of the campaign meanwhile did nothing to stoke the fire that it created. Churchill remained sequestered at Chartwell, refusing to make any statements or give any speeches that might be interpreted as putting pressure on Chamberlain. Two months earlier Churchill had, in effect, asked for a job in the cabinet. He had informed David Margesson of his "strong desire to join the government," said he could work "amicably" with Chamberlain, and assured the chief whip that he agreed completely with the prime minister's new anti-appeasement policy. Still waiting to hear from Chamberlain, Churchill had no intention of doing anything to antagonize him now.

At one point in early July, Churchill went so far as to write a statement disassociating himself from the press campaign on his behalf. "I have taken no part in the movement in favour of broadening His Majesty's Government, in which my name has been mentioned," he declared. "I feel it is my duty to place on record that I am willing to serve under Mr. Chamberlain on the basis of the policy declared by him and by Lord Halifax." He had second thoughts about the statement, however, and decided not to publish it.

But even if he had made it public, it almost certainly would have done no good. Infuriated by the pro-Churchill drive, Chamberlain was convinced that a conspiracy had been hatched by the press lords, in league with the Tory rebels. Of the prime minister, *Time* magazine observed: "Nothing could be calculated to go against the grain more than to have to ask Mr. Churchill to join the cabinet . . . There is perhaps no man in Parliament whom Mr. Chamberlain likes less than Mr. Churchill." Chamberlain believed he had given in enough to his opponents by guaranteeing Poland. Telling colleagues that Churchill's presence in the cabinet would be "a message of open warfare to Berlin," he spurned the newspapers' appeals, just as he paid no heed to a recent opinion poll showing that 60 percent of the British public wanted Churchill in the cabinet. With his huge majority in the House of Commons to protect him, why should he worry about public opinion where Churchill was concerned?

In *The New Yorker*, Janet Flanner wrote: "It's common talk that never before in modern parliamentary times have the government and the country been so separated, with so little chance either of getting together or of getting rid of each other." *Contemporary Review*, an influential British opinion journal, declared: "Chamberlain has resisted and will resist any [broadening of the cabinet] for he knows that it would mean the end of his personal dictatorship . . . It is remarkable that he continues to hold the Conservative forces as well as he does, but [his] grim imperviousness to events and narrow partisan determination neither to see nor to admit that anything has ever been wrong under his guidance . . . seems to have hypnotised a certain number of people into believing that it really must be so."

In the face of Chamberlain's stubborn resistance, the press drive on behalf of Churchill faded away. But the prime minister's fury at his critics remained unabated. "The Prime Minister cannot stand the slightest criticism . . ." Harold Nicolson noted in his diary at the end of July. "He keeps on contending that the slightest enquiry is an insult to himself." When the British ambassador in Paris told Chamberlain that Daladier wanted to suspend the French legislature for two years, the prime minister replied that the idea of suspending Parliament "makes my mouth water." He didn't have the power to put the House of Commons out of commission for two years, but on August 2 he did ram through the traditional two-month summer break, prompting Ronald Cartland's headline-making denunciation of Chamberlain as a dictator. Realizing by then that Chamberlain had no intention of including him in the cabinet, Churchill shed his reticence and mounted his own angry assault against the prime minister's determination to close down Parliament for the summer.

Once the Commons was out of the way, Chamberlain headed for Scotland for a bit of fishing while Halifax adjourned to his native Yorkshire. Other members of the government scattered to their favorite vacation spots. The commander of the British Expeditionary Force's Third Division, which was to proceed to France if war broke out, spent the entire summer trolling for salmon in Ireland rather than preparing for combat. Churchill meanwhile traveled with Edward Spears to inspect France's Maginot Line. While both men were impressed with the French defenses, Spears, a former brigadier general who had headed the British military mission in Paris at the end of the Great War, noted with concern the German fortifications being built across the border. A year ago Germany "had no defences facing France," he wrote. "Now they have the Western Wall, a formidable obstacle."

On the Salisbury Plain, meanwhile, Ronald Cartland trained with the Worcestershire and Oxfordshire Yeomanry. Knowing no doctor would approve him for military service, he had pulled strings two years before to wangle his way into the Territorials without undergoing the required physical examination. When Cartland was eighteen, a friend accidentally shot him in the leg during a partridge hunt; the wound failed to heal properly and still gave him considerable trouble. But when Cartland's mother expressed concern about whether he was fit enough to serve, he replied that sooner or later Britain would be at war and "he couldn't ask other young men to go and fight for him."

As the Territorials drilled and other Britons embarked on their summer holidays, Hitler's diatribes against Poland became more shrill. It was the Poles who were disturbing the peace of Europe, he ranted, the Poles who were threatening Germany with invasion. Then, on August 23, German and Soviet leaders detonated a diplomatic bombshell, announcing a nonaggression pact between their two nations. News of this extraordinary treaty came as a shock to governments around the world, but to the British, it was an especially stunning blow. For months they had been engaged in desultory talks with the Soviet Union about a possible alliance for the protection of Poland. Britain's guarantee of Poland, however, had put Stalin in an excellent bargaining position, and, of the two countries bidding for his services, Germany had considerably more to offer. The most the British could give him was almost certain war with Germany in defense of Poland, an ancient enemy. Hitler, by contrast, offered him the chance to stay out of the conflict; the Soviets and Germans agreed that each would remain neutral if the other went to war against a third party. Even better, Hitler secretly offered Stalin control of the eastern half of Poland, as well as Finland, Estonia, and Latvia, in exchange for Soviet neutrality.

When news of this nonaggression treaty was made public, no one, not even Neville Chamberlain, could now deny that Europe was close to being pitchforked into war. The prime minister made a number of panicky, last-ditch attempts to avert it. Joseph P. Kennedy, the U.S. ambassador to Britain, informed the State Department in late August that the British government wanted the Roosevelt administration to "put pressure on the Poles" to make concessions to Hitler. Chamberlain and his men "felt that they could not, given their obligations, do anything of the sort, but we could," Kennedy reported to undersecretary of state Sumner Welles. Roosevelt rejected the idea out of hand. "As we saw it here, it merely meant that [the British] wanted us to assume the responsibility of a new Munich and to do their dirty work for them," Jay Pierrepont Moffat, chief of the State Department's division of European affairs, wrote contemptuously in his diary.

The House of Commons was recalled, as were all military officers and Foreign Office staff. The fleet was ordered to its battle stations, and naval, army, and air force reservists were called up. Construction of basement air-raid shelters was accelerated, and more trenches were dug in the parks. Outside Buckingham Palace the sentries' little wooden shelters were replaced by conical steel structures, looking like giant bells with doorways. Sandbags were piled up around the palace and other government buildings.

When the Commons met on August 24, it hurriedly passed legislation giving the government unprecedented emergency powers, and approved a number of other war-related bills. The MPs listened gravely to the matter-of-fact debate, exhibiting none of the emotion of the August 2 session. "Somehow, when one thought of the future, the scene was unreal," Cartland later wrote. "The words one listened to did not register the horrors of war. The speeches seemed out of focus to the picture that one's imagination so easily, so terribly conjured up."

As Cartland returned home that night, he saw hundreds of reservists on their way to join their units. In a matter of days, he knew, he might well be among them. For the young MP, that knowledge was a source of exhilaration rather than anxiety. "Here is the testing," he told his sister. "Here is the moment" when he and his generation must prove themselves, just as their fathers had done in the trenches of France. Having felt so frustrated, so powerless, in Parliament, he could now "begin to live fully." As his mother had once instructed him, Cartland would "start where [his] father left off."

CHAPTER TWELVE

"SPEAK FOR ENGLAND"

———◆———

Throughout the south of England, September 1 dawned unusually warm, with barely a breath of wind. After breakfast at Sissinghurst, Harold Nicolson took a deck chair outside to sit and enjoy the sun, but he placed it by the door so he could hear the phone if it rang. He had been there only a few minutes when Vita Sackville-West, who had been listening to the wireless, emerged from her study and walked quickly toward him. "It has begun!" she exclaimed.

Near his seaside home at Bognor, Duff Cooper played a morning round of golf to try to get his mind off the drumbeat of war. It didn't work; Cooper later said the round was the worst golf he'd ever played. When he went into the clubhouse afterward, he joined two acquaintances at the bar for a drink. After they had chatted about horse racing for a while, one of the men turned to Cooper and casually said: "Hitler started on Poland this morning." Then he turned back to his other companion and resumed the conversation about racing. "That," Cooper wrote later, "was how I heard that the Second World War had begun."

Ronald Cartland was spending the weekend with his mother at Littlewood, her sixteenth-century cottage near the Malvern Hills in Worcestershire. She came to him after breakfast with the news that the Wehrmacht had moved into Poland. She'd also heard over the wireless that Parliament would be called into session at six o'clock that evening. Cartland hurriedly changed his clothes, jumped in his secondhand Austin Cooper, and headed for London.

As MPs made their way back to the capital, the children of London were flooding out of the city. Thousands of youngsters, along with their parents and teachers, jammed the platforms of London's railway stations, waiting for trains to take them to the country and presumed safety. An evacuation on September 1 had been planned by the government for months—it was supposed to be a trial run—but by the time the children reached the stations, the placards on newspaper stands were screaming the words POLAND INVADED! and the parents knew this was no game. The small evacuees wore name tags pinned to their clothing or tied around their necks, and all of them carried gas masks. Some, thinking it was a grand adventure, ran around the platform, shouting excitedly. Others fearfully clutched their mothers' hands. When the trains pulled out, they leaned out the windows, waving good-bye to their weeping parents. The adults were not told where their youngsters were going or when they would see them again.

By midafternoon huge silver barrage balloons were floating lazily above London's skyline as a defense against low-flying enemy aircraft. Army trucks rumbled along the streets, decanting soldiers in front of government buildings. The narrow cul-de-sac that is Downing Street was jammed with hundreds of people. Kept back by policemen wearing tin helmets, the throng watched as ministers rushed in and out of No. 10 to consult with the prime minister. There was a rustle of excitement and the pop of news photographers' flashbulbs when a car carrying George VI pulled up. The same occurred when Winston Churchill arrived in late afternoon. He had been summoned by Chamberlain, who realized that if he wanted to survive in office, he finally would have to bow to pressure and include his most prominent political bête noire in the government. Churchill readily accepted Chamberlain's offer of a ministership without portfolio in the new War Cabinet.

As the shadows lengthened, huge crowds gathered too in Parliament Square, to watch MPs hurrying into the Palace of Westminster, now barricaded by sandbags. In the houses of Parliament, a blackout already had been imposed, and the only illumination in the lobbies and corridors came from small electric lamps that cast a bluish light on the mosaic floors. Entering the Commons from the darkened members' lobby, Harold Nicolson found the chamber, which usually reminded him of a "dim aquarium," to be "quite garish by comparison."

By 6:00 p.m. the benches and galleries were packed, the buzz of excited conversation filling the chamber. The Polish ambassador, who sat in the front row of the Distinguished Strangers Gallery, had, just a few hours before, transmitted to the Foreign Office a message from Warsaw: "The Polish Government is determined to defend its independence and honour to the last, and is convinced that in accordance with the treaties in force, it will receive immediate assistance from its Allies in this struggle." Like almost everyone else in the small, stuffy hall, Count Edward Raczyński was sure that, in a matter of minutes, Chamberlain would announce a state of war between Britain and Germany. After all, the terms of the Anglo-Polish treaty could hardly be clearer: Britain would go to the aid of a besieged Poland "at once," with "all the support in its power."

Shortly after six o'clock a loud cheer went up when Chamberlain and Arthur Greenwood, deputy leader of the Labour Party, entered the chamber together. The prime minister took his seat on the government front bench, then rose almost immediately to speak. In an emotion-choked voice, he told the House that it was time for action, not for making speeches, that unless he received assurances from Germany that it had halted its invasion and had begun withdrawing from Poland, Britain would fulfill its obligations to that unhappy country. Another, more muted cheer greeted his declaration. MPs looked at one another with puzzlement. Where was the action that Chamberlain had just promised? He had offered only a speech after all—"fine words," in Edward Spears's opinion, "but the plain fact was that, by the terms of our treaty with Poland, we should now have come to her help." Some MPs glanced over at Churchill, wondering if he would respond. But he remained seated, glum and silent. He had just accepted a cabinet post, and in his view that meant he could no longer question or criticize Chamberlain's government in public.

With no rejoinder made to the prime minister, the House adjourned for the evening. Still engaged in informal debate about what in God's name was going on, MPs scattered to nearby clubs and restaurants. Churchill dined at the Savoy Grill with Duff and Diana Cooper and a few others, all agreeing on the necessity of a declaration of war the following day. When the party broke up, the Coopers walked out into the unfamiliar darkness of a newly blacked-out London. The Duke of Westminster, who was leaving the Savoy at the same time, offered them a ride. The moment they stepped into his Rolls-Royce, the duke launched into a virulent anti-Semitic harangue, ranting about how the Savoy was infested with Jews. For a few moments Cooper held his tongue. But when Westminster declared how happy he was that Britain was not yet at war and that Hitler must know "after all, that we were his best friends," Cooper could keep silent no longer. "I hope," he snapped back, "that by tomorrow he will know that we are his most implacable and remorseless enemies." A glacial silence prevailed for the rest of the short ride. The next day, Cooper was told, the duke was passing the word around London that "if there was a war, it would be entirely due to the Jews and Duff Cooper."

Saturday, September 2, proved even warmer than the day before. It was sultry and airless in London, with dark clouds piling up on the horizon. A storm clearly was going to break before the day was over. Throughout the city there was an uneasy sense of waiting—for the storm and for the war.

The streets and parks were quiet, without the usual shouts and laughter of children playing on a late-summer weekend day. The children were gone, as were other London treasures. The Coronation Chair and Liber Regalis, a prized fourteenth-century manuscript, had been evacuated from Westminster Abbey. Eros, the famed statue of the god of love hovering over the fountain at Piccadilly Circus, no longer aimed his arrow at the traffic hurtling around the circle. He had been removed to safety, as had the precious cricket memorabilia in the Long Room at Lord's. That afternoon Harold Nicolson paid a visit to the National Gallery, only to find the paintings there had vanished as well. "It is an odd effect," he mused. "Great frames hanging, still with their labels but without any pictures. All the canvases have been taken out," removed for safekeeping to museums and country houses in Wales.

When Nicolson arrived at the Commons for a rare Saturday session, he was directed to Room 14, where he found House employees earnestly giving instructions to a group of MPs about *their* possible evacuation in the event of heavy air raids on London. An elaborate plan had been devised; there were printed hand baggage and personal baggage labels and a collecting station for members' luggage. The House staffers refused to divulge where the new seat of Parliament would be, but the rumored destination was Stratford-on-Avon. As Nicolson entered the room, he was handed a traveling pass, stamped by the sergeant at arms. Duff Cooper, who also had just come into the room, snorted and tore his pass to pieces. He was damned if he was going to take part in a scheme to turn tail and leave London, bombs falling or not.

In Poland, bombs had been raining down for more than twenty-four hours. Luftwaffe dive-bombers and fighters were blasting and strafing airfields, cities, towns, bridges, and roads choked with Polish reserve soldiers on their way to join their units. Nearly two million German troops meanwhile had smashed into the country from the north, south, and west, and hundreds of armored panzer tanks were slicing through the Polish countryside. The Poles, whose resistance was valiant but whose army and air force were woefully undermanned and badly equipped, had lost all their frontier battles. Chaos was spreading—and still no sign of help from their two Western allies.

The appeals from Warsaw for aid grew increasingly desperate. At the Foreign Office, however, Lord Halifax told Count Raczyński that no decision had yet been made about what to do. The Polish Senate had been meeting all day, and its members made brave speeches, Raczyński later told Hugh Dalton. "But there has been one thing missing. No speaker has felt able to make any reference to our friends."

In his top-floor flat near Westminster, Winston Churchill paced the floor "like a lion in a cage," awaiting a call from 10 Downing Street that would nail down his cabinet job. It never came. At one point he phoned Raczyński, who told him that Britain and France, despite their treaty obligations, still had not made up their minds about what action to take. Churchill replied slowly: "I hope . . . I hope that Britain will keep . . . will keep its . . . ." At that point, his voice caught, and he began to cry. "He sounded both anxious and deeply humiliated," the Polish ambassador later recalled.

Churchill was also deeply angry. After his conversation with Raczyński, he placed a call to the French ambassador, Charles Corbin. If France ratted on the Poles as it had ratted on the Czechs, Churchill told him, he, who had always been a close friend of France, would be completely indifferent to its fate. Corbin claimed that the delay in helping Poland was due to "technical difficulties," to which Churchill exclaimed: "Technical difficulties be damned! I suppose you would call it a technical difficulty for a Pole if a German bomb fell on his head!"

Having received no call from Chamberlain by midafternoon, Churchill joined his colleagues at the House. For hours, debate over a series of war-related bills dragged on, while members anxiously awaited word from the prime minister. Some gathered around the news ticker in the members' lobby, examining the latest reports of civilian casualties in Poland. Others clustered in the smoking room, downing drink after drink. ("The amount of alcohol being consumed was incredible!" declared a cabinet secretary who visited the smoking room that day.) The buzz of conversation grew louder. What was causing the delay? Was Chamberlain trying to arrange a last-minute peace? That was impossible. Britain could not back down now. "In their own minds," a *New York Times* correspondent wrote that day, members of Parliament and the rest of the British people "are already at war."

Baffy Dugdale, who had been given a ticket to the Members' Gallery by Walter Elliot, was watching the desultory afternoon debate when Bob Boothby beckoned her out for a drink. Churchill had been invited to join the cabinet, Boothby told her, but unless other Tory rebels were brought in too, it would be folly for him to accept. "Bob said [Churchill] could never prevail under those circumstances and would only ruin his value later by defending the Government," Dugdale wrote in her diary. She and Boothby agreed that the "honour of Britain [is] vanishing before our eyes. Thirty-six hours now since Germany invaded Poland, and we have not yet honoured our pledges!"

They were hardly the only ones to feel anger and despair over what they considered the slipping away of their nation's integrity. "I had never seen the Commons so stirred, so profoundly moved, as it was that afternoon," Edward Spears later noted. "It was dawning upon even the most uncritical of the Government's supporters that Great Britain's honour, of which we were the collective guardians, was in danger."

The whips passed the word that Chamberlain would speak at 6:00 p.m. Members crowded into the chamber, cabinet ministers took their places on the front bench, and the galleries rapidly filled up. Then, just before 6:00, the Speaker rose from his chair and declared there would be another short delay. The ministers filed out, the chamber emptied, and the smoking room became crowded once more. In the haze of cigar and cigarette smoke, the conversations grew more heated; occasional angry bellows could be heard above the tumult. Finally, at 7:30, bells rang throughout the House, and members, some of them fueled by several whiskeys over the course of the afternoon and evening, rushed back into the chamber, anticipating the prime minister's declaration of war, in the words of Harold Nicolson, "exactly like a court awaiting the verdict of the jury." Tension hung heavy in the air. When Chamberlain and Greenwood strode in at 7:42, the chamber rang with shouts and cheers. The prime minister took his place at the dispatch box, his voice sounding thick and hoarse, as if he were coming down with a cold. He began by recounting the events of the day: the talks with French leaders, the stiff note Britain had sent Germany demanding withdrawal from Poland, the lack of a German response.

As Chamberlain droned on, however, it became increasingly clear to MPs that no ultimatum had yet been given to Germany. In fact— could they really be hearing this?—the prime minister was talking of the possibility of further negotiations with the Reich, with Mussolini acting as intermediary. Germany's delay in responding to the British note, Chamberlain declared, might be caused by its "consideration of a proposal which had been put forward by the Italian Government." Having clung to the idea of peace for so long, the prime minister seemed to hope that it still could be produced, like a rabbit out of a hat. As he continued his dry recital of facts, he made no mention of the death and destruction that continued to descend on Poland as he spoke.

When Chamberlain finished his statement and sat down, there was dead silence. Even his staunchest supporters could not bring themselves to utter a single "Hear, hear!" Two Tory backbenchers abruptly left their seats and raced to the members' lavatory to be sick. The faces of others, like Duff Cooper and Leo Amery, were flushed with fury. "For two whole days the wretched Poles had been bombed and massacred, and we were still considering within what time limit Hitler should be invited to tell us whether he felt like relinquishing his prey!" Amery later wrote. "Was all this havering the prelude to another Munich?" Sensing the mounting outrage, David Margesson signaled to his deputies to prepare for possible violence.

Then Arthur Greenwood rose to his feet to reply for the Opposition. As deputy head of the Labour Party in the House, the tall, lanky Greenwood was to speak in place of Clement Attlee, who was recuperating from prostate surgery. At the best of times Greenwood, with his bland, monotonous north-country voice and his cliché-ridden speeches, was not known for his oratory. And these clearly were not the best of times. Greenwood had come into the chamber ready to applaud the prime minister for at last declaring war. Now, with this unexpected turn of events, he had no prepared speech to fall back on. He was also known for his heavy drinking, and like a number of his colleagues, he had had several whiskeys in the smoking room before the prime minister appeared. When he stood up, he seemed to sway a little as he put his hands on the dispatch box in front of him and peered through his spectacles at Chamberlain.

As he faced the prime minister, the Labour benches behind him exploded with cheering, followed, astonishingly, by a second volley of cheers from the Conservative side. Greenwood glanced at the Tories in surprise. Then, slowly and hesitantly, he began. "I am speaking under very difficult circumstances," he said, "with no opportunity to think about what I should say, and I speak what is in my heart at this moment."

In his corner seat on the government side, Leo Amery was apoplectic. Neville Chamberlain was tearing to shreds every principle that the country and its people held dear, and Parliament, supposed to be the protector of those principles, was doing nothing to stop him! To hell with Greenwood's speaking only for himself and the Labour Party! Amery shot to his feet. "Speak for England, Arthur!" he shouted.

Amery's outburst stunned the House. Chamberlain's head whipped around, and he stared hard at his erstwhile ally and friend. Greenwood meanwhile did what Amery demanded. "I am gravely disturbed," he declared. "An act of aggression took place thirty-eight hours ago. The moment that act took place, one of the most important treaties of modern times automatically came into operation . . . I wonder how long we are prepared to vacillate at a time when Britain and all that Britain stands for—and human civilization—are in peril. Every minute's delay now means the loss of life, imperiling our national interests . . ."

210 TROUBLESOME YOUNG MEN

On the other side of the House, Bob Boothby did not approve of that choice of words; more than national interests were at stake. "And our honour!" he shouted at Greenwood. The deputy Labour leader glared at Boothby. "Let me finish my sentence," he said sharply. "I was about to say—imperiling the very foundations of our national honour."

Although there was little eloquence that night from Greenwood, he managed to put into words what was in his colleagues' hearts. Everyone agreed it was the greatest speech of his life, "a speech that would illuminate a career and justify a whole existence," as Edward Spears put it. "It wasn't dramatic, although the drama was there, we were all living it, we and millions more whose fate depended on the decisions taken in that small Chamber." When Greenwood sat down, both sides of the House showed their appreciation in an explosion of shouts and cheers. "The tension became acute," noted Harold Nicolson, "since here were the P.M.'s most ardent supporters cheering his opponent with all their lungs. The front bench looked as if they had been struck in the face . . . The P.M. must know by now that the whole House is against him."

At that moment, having alienated virtually everyone in the chamber, Neville Chamberlain and his government might well have been toppled. His appeasement policy was in ruins, and it appeared that he might be about to renege on the treaty with Poland. Conceivably, condemnation by prominent members of his own party could have prompted a call for a vote of confidence. If that had happened, in the view of Hugh Dalton, among others, "Chamberlain . . . would have been overthrown."

Once again many of those on the benches and in the galleries, among them Violet Bonham Carter, looked expectantly at Churchill. "Winston . . . could have spoken for England with the tongues of men and angels," Lady Violet said. "Surely this was his moment." But Churchill did not stir. He desperately wanted to address the House, he told friends later, but he still felt shackled by his acceptance of a cabinet post, even though Chamberlain had ignored him since the offer of a job first was made. Anthony Eden also remained in his seat, despite an earlier appeal by Duff Cooper and several other Tory dissidents that he speak. No one else stood up, and the moment and opportunity were gone. Margesson quickly moved "that this House do now adjourn." As Baffy Dugdale noted, "The familiar voice and figure saying the same thing he had said every night for the past five years worked by force of habit."

At 8:09 p.m., some twenty-five minutes after the session began, Margesson's motion carried, and the members spilled out into the lobbies, their pent-up anger and frustration now boiling over. "All the old Munich rage, all the resentment against Chamberlain was again on display," observed Chips Channon, still a Chamberlain loyalist. But rage was no longer the exclusive property of the Tory rebels. It had, as Nicolson pointed out, infected even some of the prime minister's strongest advocates. When Channon later approached Margesson and begged him to do something, the chief whip shrugged his shoulders. "It must be war, Chips, old boy," he drawled. "There's no other way out." In the prime minister's parliamentary hideaway, Margesson, in "the strongest possible language," told Chamberlain the same thing. Unless he declared war the next day, Parliament would rise up against him. Even now his own cabinet was on the verge of mutiny.

As they left Parliament, MPs were confronted by driving rain and the sharp crack of thunder. A tempest had broken outside as well as in. Late that night, as the storm continued to rage, Boothby, Cooper, Eden, Duncan Sandys, and Brendan Bracken gathered at Churchill's flat at Morpeth Mansions, its windows swathed in blackout curtains. Many years later Diana Cooper offered this florid but accurate account of the meeting: "Conspiracy was in the air . . . the heavens themselves were blazing forth the death of something, while Brutus and the rest plotted through the night." Boothby was the leading conspirator. Chamberlain's defeatist government had betrayed Britain and its honor, he argued. How could it be allowed to continue? Most Tories were ready to revolt. It was in Winston's power to go to the House tomorrow, oust Chamberlain, and take his place. Under no circumstances should Churchill now accept a seat in the cabinet. If he did, he would save the prime minister.

But to the dismay of his colleagues, Churchill steadfastly refused to follow Boothby's advice. He had given his word to Chamberlain, he felt himself to be a member of the government already, and he would do nothing to bring it down. In the midst of the heated argument, Churchill received a phone call from Whitehall. He came back and told the group that by the time the House convened at noon the following day, Britain would be at war. Chamberlain would make a broadcast to the nation just before the parliamentary session. It turned out that the cabinet, which had voted for war earlier that day, met with Chamberlain and Halifax after the debacle in the House and demanded immediate action. The prime minister and foreign secretary finally gave in.

With that news, the discussion came to an end, and the exhausted would-be conspirators left for home. But they were not taking any chances. Sandys stopped off at the Polish Embassy to see Count Raczyński. He told the ambassador that "he, Churchill, and their friends would not give way and that they could count not only on moral support from the Labour Party, but on a large section of the Conservatives. All were resolved not to capitulate, and if Chamberlain were to weaken once again, he would be overthrown."

Shortly after 11:00 a.m. on Sunday, September 3, Robert Dunbar, the portly head of the Foreign Office treaty department, left his office, descended the stairs, and walked out the side entrance of the building, a stiff white document in his hand. He crossed the Horse Guards parade ground and headed for the German Embassy, a few blocks away in Carlton Terrace.

It was a beautiful morning. The storm had blown itself out, and the air was now crystal clear. As he walked along the Mall, Dunbar saw few other Londoners out on the streets enjoying the late summer sun. Most were at church or at home, waiting to hear the news that they knew would turn their lives upside down. In minutes Dunbar arrived at the embassy, housed in three Regency town houses at the edge of St. James's Park. Standing guard outside were two tin-hatted British policemen, gas masks slung over their shoulders.

Once inside, Dunbar paid little attention to the embassy's grandiose neoclassical interior, designed a few years earlier by Hitler's favorite architect, Albert Speer. He proceeded immediately to Theodor Kordt's office. The two men exchanged greetings; then Dunbar handed Kordt the document in his hand. Signed by Lord Halifax, it contained a simple message: as of 11:00 a.m., Great Britain was at war with Germany. The two diplomats shook hands, and Dunbar told Kordt goodbye. He had to remind himself not to add, "Good luck."

Earlier that morning, just across St. James's Park, most of the Tory rebels had gathered at Ronald Tree's house to hear Chamberlain's

Lady Dorothy Macmillan (National Portrait Gallery, London)

Harold Macmillan (Getty Images)

Harold Macmillan and Lady Dorothy Macmillan on their wedding day in April 1920 (British Pathe/ITN)

Robert Boothby (National Portrait Gallery, London)

Lady Violet Bonham Carter (Library of Congress)

Chancellor of the Exchequer Winston Churchill and his parliamentary private secretary, Robert Boothby, on their way to Parliament for the chancellor's annual Budget Day address in 1928 (Getty Images)

Prime Minister Neville Chamberlain and his wife wave to cheering crowds at 10 Downing Street after Chamberlain's return from the Munich Conference on September 30, 1938. (Getty Images)

David Lloyd George and
Leo Amery (Getty Images)

Ronald Cartland (CORBIS)

Anthony Eden and his wife (Topham/The ImageWorks)

Lord Robert "Bobbety" Cranborne and his wife at a society wedding (Getty Images)

Harold Nicolson (National Portrait Gallery, London)

Alfred Duff Cooper (National Portrait Gallery, London)

Richard Law, as British minister of state for foreign affairs in 1945 (Getty Images)

The Duchess of Atholl, who lost her seat in the House of Commons over her bold anti-appeasement stance (Library of Congress)

David Margesson, the chief government whip, who made life difficult for anti-appeasement Tories (Getty Images)

Winston Churchill and Anthony Eden on their way to Parliament on September 3, 1939, the day Britain declared war on Germany (British Pathe/ITN)

Lady Violet Bonham Carter in a characteristically intense conversation—in this case, with MP Tom Driberg (Getty Images)

Prime Minister Harold Macmillan and Lady Dorothy Macmillan (Getty Images)

broadcast. For the first time two of Churchill's adherents, Boothby and Sandys, joined the Eden group. While still awkward, the relationship between Boothby and Macmillan had thawed somewhat, and in the last couple of months the two had begun to work together in trying to oust Chamberlain. The rebels engaged in desultory conversation as they stood in the long, flower-scented drawing room, with sunlight pouring through the tall windows and glinting off the crystal pendants of the chandeliers. One of them pointed out that *The Sunday Times* had made no mention of the previous night's turbulence in the House. Clearly the Tory hierarchy wanted to act as if it had never occurred. Someone else had seen Chamberlain and Margesson together shortly after the session ended. Margesson, he said, was "purple in the face," and Chamberlain "as white as a sheet."

Standing at the window, Edward Spears paid no attention to the talk as he stared out at the lushness of the park, determined to absorb all he could of London's beauty before the onset of war. "I felt no regrets for what we had done," he later recalled, "but in that moment I wanted to miss no glint of sunshine or of colour . . . I was too greedy of the trees and the lovely day to turn and look back into the room about which my friends were scattered."

One of the MPs opened his large gold pocket watch and placed it on the table. As the watch ticked away the minutes, Tree suddenly remembered there was no wireless in the house, and there was a mad scramble to find one. Hearing the commotion, one of the Trees' housemaids said she had one in her room, and she was asked to fetch it. It was set up and turned on just as the prime minister began his speech, precisely at 11:15.

"I am speaking to you from the Cabinet Room at 10 Downing Street," Chamberlain began. Then came the stark announcement that had just been handed to Kordt: Germany had failed to respond to a British ultimatum to withdraw its troops from Poland, and "consequently, this country is at war with Germany."

Like the MPs at Tree's house, millions of other Britons had clustered around their wirelesses on that brilliant September morning, listening in hushed silence to the prime minister's declaration of war. When she heard the fateful words, a young woman in Leeds collapsed against her husband and "went quite dead for minute or two." In London the writer Vera Brittain sobbed while listening to the broadcast, thinking all the while of her fiancé and brother, both killed in the Great War. Margery Allingham received the news with "a breathless feeling of mingled relief and intolerable grief." "Well, it's come," she thought. "This is where our philosophy led . . . This is what comes of not interfering when you see something horrible happening, even if it isn't your business. This was our portion after all."

A BBC announcer who sat with the prime minister during the broadcast thought that he looked "crumpled, despondent, and old." Chamberlain's trembling voice conveyed that dispiritedness, as he told his countrymen of his profound distress that war could not be averted after all. "You can imagine what a bitter blow it is to me that all my long struggle to win peace has failed," he said. At Ronald Tree's house the Tory rebels glanced at one another. Chamberlain was supposed to be calling the nation to battle, not wallowing in self-pity. Surely there were more important things to think about right now than his own defeat. Chamberlain's "personal note . . . shocks us," Harold Nicolson noted in his diary. "We feel that . . . he cannot possibly lead us into a great war."

Thirty minutes after the prime minister finished his broadcast, he was scheduled to address the House of Commons. Several MPs at Tree's house decided to take advantage of the beautiful weather and stroll the short distance to Parliament. Almost as soon as they left, however, the stillness of the morning was shattered by a long, ear-piercing wail. "They ought not to do that after what we have heard on the wireless. People will think it is an air raid warning," Leo Amery grumbled to Harold Nicolson, who was walking beside him. Amery had barely finished his last sentence when another wail was heard. "My God!" Nicolson shouted. "It *is* an air raid warning!" The men picked up their pace, all the while trying to pretend that nothing untoward was happening, as they attempted to continue their casual conversations over the scream of the sirens. Just then Spears drove up alongside them, his car containing several of their colleagues. "Get in!" he yelled. By that time anxiety had triumphed over dignity, and the strollers swiftly piled into the car, with Nicolson perched on Amery's knee and Anthony Eden sitting on Nicolson's.

As Spears turned into Great George Street leading into Parliament Square, his passengers saw scores of people, part of the crowd that had already gathered in front of Parliament, running for cover, many of them carrying small children in their arms. The car drove slowly into Palace Yard, threading its way through a mass of people; when it stopped, the MPs disentangled themselves and got out, looking for all the world like clowns in a circus act. They hurried into the House lobby, where a policeman directed them to Parliament's newly improvised air-raid shelter, a room adjacent to the terrace.

All over the city people were seeking safe haven. Policemen stopped traffic and herded motorists and pedestrians into the nearest air-raid shelters, many of them as makeshift as the House refuge: basements and other areas in railway stations, shops, offices, and government buildings. Strollers in the parks rushed into the trenches dug after the Munich crisis. As one young woman hurried into a newly built public shelter in North London, an air-raid warden shouted, "Mind those electric wires," and she realized that the shelter was still under construction. "I wondered," she wrote, "how many more, up and down the country, weren't ready yet . . ."

When the siren first shrilled, Winston Churchill, who was dressing to go to Parliament, went onto the roof of his apartment building to search for enemy planes. Finally succumbing to his wife's pleas to take cover, he grabbed a bottle of brandy, and the couple headed for their designated shelter, the basement of a nearby building where most of their neighbors had already gathered. From the doorway Churchill looked out onto the empty street, imagining "vast explosions shaking the ground, of buildings clattering down in dust and rubble." Having been warned for years that war would bring Armageddon, other Londoners were envisioning the same horrific scenes. "We were absolutely terrified," a woman later remarked. "We knew what it would be like. Bombs raining down, fires everywhere, gas, hundreds of thousands dead."

Violet Bonham Carter heard the sirens while in a vast, bare shed at Paddington Station, the ad hoc headquarters of a volunteer nursing unit to which she was attached. She hoped her unit would not be called upon to take care of casualties that morning since the shed did not contain a single bandage, basin, table, or water tap. She and her fellow nurses could not even carry injured persons to safety; they had no stretchers. When the warning sounded, Lady Violet refused to go to a shelter. All she could think of was her husband, who was an air-raid warden, out on the street now with no protection at all. She ran out of the shed, frantically searching nearby streets and squares until she found him on patrol. Her sense of relief was mixed with a "strange exhilaration and peace of mind." Britain, thank God, was now at war. The nation's honor had been saved. Watching the barrage balloons dance above her in the bright sky, she thought, *We no longer need to feel ashamed.*

At Westminster, meanwhile, a single MP sat in the Commons chamber throughout the alarm. Josiah Wedgwood had come early that morning, as had several other members, to claim a good seat for the prime minister's speech. When the sirens went off, Wedgwood's colleagues quickly vanished, but the Labour MP, a staunch foe of appeasement, remained, "feeling like the Roman senators when the Gauls stormed the Capitol" and ignoring the pleas of a warden to take cover. He, at least, "would perish at my post." But when the raid did not come, he decided to give up what he wryly described later as his "play acting" and joined his fellow MPs in the shelter, along with a number of journalists and House staffers, all of them marveling at Hitler's swift response to Chamberlain's declaration of war.

Moments later the sirens sounded again, but this time with a long, steady note, the all clear signal. The whole thing had been a false alarm. Whiling away the few minutes before Chamberlain's address, some of the members drifted out onto the terrace to enjoy the sunshine and observe with disapproval the efforts of a barrage balloon crew across the Thames, struggling vainly to raise their rain-sodden balloon from its moorings.

The prime minister's speech to the House turned out to be no more inspiring than his broadcast to the country. "Everything that I have worked for, everything that I have believed in during my public life, has crashed into ruins," he declared. Chamberlain's declaration of war, Anthony Eden wrote, seemed more the "lament of a man deploring his own failure rather than the call of a nation to arms." His audience, emotionally exhausted after the drama-filled session the night before, responded with cheers that could only be described as tepid.

Then Churchill rose to speak. Still in the dark about his future, he put into words what Chamberlain was unable to express: why Britain felt compelled to go to war. "We are fighting," Churchill declared, "to save the whole world from the pestilence of Nazi tyranny and in defence of all that is most sacred to man. This is no war of domination or imperial aggrandizement or material gain; no war to shut any country out of the sunlight and means of progress. It is a war . . . to establish, on impregnable rocks, the rights of the individual, and it is a war to establish and revive the stature of man."

Listening to Chamberlain and Churchill that day, a number of the Tory rebels were struck by the same thought. "It would perhaps have better if, at this moment of failure and disappointment, [Chamberlain] had passed the burden into other and stronger hands," Harold Macmillan believed. In Amery's view, Chamberlain's statement was hardly "the speech of a war leader" and "I think I see Winston emerging as P.M. out of it all by the end of the year." Boothby, still determined that Churchill take Chamberlain's place as soon as possible, wrote to his former mentor: "Your immediate task seems to have been made much easier by the P.M. today. His was not the speech of a man who intends to lead us *through* the struggle."

Shortly after the session concluded, Chamberlain summoned Churchill to his office in the Commons and offered him his old job of first lord of the admiralty, with a seat in the War Cabinet. At Churchill's urging, Eden was brought back into the government too, but as dominions secretary, a post that would have no responsibility for running the war. In Chamberlain's belated effort to create a coalition, he asked Labour and Liberal leaders to join the government, but neither party would do so.

Meanwhile the crowds that had regrouped outside Parliament, jamming the nearby streets, left no doubt about where their feelings lay. They lustily cheered well-known MPs as they emerged from the building, but their loudest cheers were saved for Churchill and some of the other Tory dissidents. One of them was Macmillan, who, leaving the clamor behind, walked to his nearby home, thinking of that long-ago day in 1914 when as a twenty-year-old Oxford student he had first learned that England had entered the war against Germany. A time when he and other young men were filled with gaiety and confidence, "setting out on something like a crusade . . ." Having experienced the horrors of that war firsthand, still suffering from the wounds he received in France, he had no such feeling of buoyancy at the outbreak of this conflict. Now he was the father of an eighteen-year-old Oxford student, who undoubtedly would go off to fight just as he had done. As Macmillan strolled along the streets of London on that lovely day, one question occupied his mind: Would Maurice still be alive when the war came to an end?

In the midlands, meanwhile, one MP was already preparing for battle. Lt. Ronald Cartland had joined his regiment at King's Heath on the morning of September 2. The constituency meeting to decide his future would have to wait.

CHAPTER THIRTEEN

PLAYING AT WAR

When word came to Poland that Britain had declared war on Germany, there was unrestrained euphoria. Residents of bomb-battered Warsaw rushed out of their homes, weeping, shouting, and dancing in streets littered with rubble. They marched to the British Embassy, tens of thousands of them, waving improvised Union Jacks, singing the Polish national anthem, and trying to sing "God Save the King." A Warsaw resident later remarked: "Of course, no one knew it, but we all tried our best." When the British ambassador, Sir Howard Kennard, appeared on the embassy's balcony, a roar erupted from the huge crowd. The tumult grew after Kennard shouted: "Long live Poland! We will fight side by side against aggression and injustice!" When news of the French declaration of war reached Warsaw a few hours later, throngs of Varsovians celebrated at the French Embassy as well.

It had taken three long days for Britain and France to make up their minds. Many people had died. But now, the Poles were sure, their allies would save them.

In London the trappings of war were everywhere. Sandbags and barbed-wire barricades shielded government buildings, while barrage balloons, tethered on their cables, floated high above the city. Soldiers and policemen stood guard at bridges and tunnels, keeping a sharp eye out for saboteurs. Store windows were boarded up or taped with strips of brown paper to prevent shattering after bomb blasts. Tailor shop windows that had displayed dinner jackets only days before were full of officers' uniforms.

Now that Britain had been hurled into war, its citizens steeled themselves for the massive bombing attacks they were sure would follow. At the same time, they nervously awaited the first reports of battle skirmishes with the enemy. "Within a day or two," *The New York Times* predicted, British and French troops would be locked in combat with German forces. Yet nothing happened. Serious military action remained the farthest thing from Neville Chamberlain's mind. "Loathing war passionately, he was determined to wage as little of it as possible," Leo Amery later wrote. While Hitler ordered his military commanders in Poland to "close your hearts to pity" and "act brutally," the British and French governments declared their "firm desire" to spare Germany's civilian population and historical monuments and ordered their armed forces to attack only "military objectives in the narrowest sense of the word."

After destroying most of Poland's air force, German planes roamed freely over the landscape, machine-gunning women and girls picking potatoes in a field, bombing churches and hospitals, and strafing toddlers being herded to safety after the bombing of their nursery school. During one raid German aircraft dived low over a Warsaw cemetery and machine-gunned mourners attending funerals for victims of previous raids. "It is like a shooting party," a distraught Edward Raczyński told Hugh Dalton. "We are the partridges and they are the guns."

In one of several urgent cables he dispatched to the Foreign Office urging immediate British military action, Ambassador Kennard wrote that the "machine gunning of civilians is a daily occurrence." A young officer with the British military mission in Poland returned to London to plead with his superiors to help the Poles. The government turned a deaf ear to all such entreaties, and R. A. Butler, undersecretary of foreign affairs, told the House there was no conclusive proof that the Germans were bombing nonmilitary targets in Poland.

At a meeting of the War Cabinet on September 4, Sir Cyril Newall, the British air chief of staff, opposed any proposal to have the RAF as-

sist Poland. British planes, he declared, must be held in reserve to protect against attacks on France or Britain. His comment caused the new
first lord of the admiralty, Winston Churchill, to wonder aloud if the
cabinet shouldn't be more concerned about the attack of the moment.
Churchill urged that the French Army and the RAF immediately assault
the Siegfried Line, the string of German fortifications facing France. His
recommendations were ignored.

Other than a couple of failed attempts to bomb German warships,
the sum total of Britain's defense of Poland in the first few months of
the conflict was the dropping of millions of propaganda leaflets over
Germany, informing the German people that they did "not have the
means to sustain protracted warfare" and were "on the verge of bankruptcy." According to a *Daily Telegraph* story, a pilot flying one of the
leaflet planes returned to his base two hours ahead of schedule, reporting that he had flown over enemy territory as ordered and dumped the
leaflets out. "Do you mean you threw them out still roped in bundles?"
his commanding officer asked. When the pilot said yes, the senior officer bellowed: "Good God, man, you might have killed somebody!" True
or not, the story reflected the derisory attitude of most Britons to the
leaflet campaign. Mollie Panter-Downes referred to it in *The New Yorker*
as "the Leaflet-of-the-Month Club for the Third Reich."

In the House of Commons many members were stunned by the
government action. The leaflet dropping was "ignominious," nothing but
a "confetti war against an utterly ruthless enemy who [is] destroying a
whole nation," Edward Spears stormed to air minister Kingsley Wood.
Britain was "covering itself with ridicule by organizing this kind of car-
nival." Such a gesture would have as much impact on Hitler as "reading a lesson on deportment to a homicidal maniac at the height of his
frenzy."

Spears, to whom Raczyński had given a list of Polish towns and villages bombed by the Germans, told Wood he planned to speak out in
the House about the lack of British support for the Poles. Wood urged
him to reconsider, saying he was touching on a question of military strategy and, thus, of national security; British commanders believed that
air strikes would not help the Poles and would only provoke retaliation.
Spears replied he wasn't suggesting that the RAF fly to Poland. But it did

seem obvious that attacking German airfields and communications might relieve some of the pressure on Poland. In any case, Spears snapped, "How can we justify the Prime Minister's pledge that we would go to the support of the Poles immediately with all our forces, when we [are] not even bombing Germany?"

Swayed, nonetheless, by Wood's national security argument, Spears decided not to speak in the House. Even though he didn't accept the reasons for the inaction, he didn't want to run the risk, however slight, of endangering Britain's security. "Today I regret that I kept silence," he later wrote. "Not that it would have mattered either way, but it would have helped the Poles to feel there were some who favored running risks to help them."

When Spears told Leo Amery about his conversation with Wood, Amery recounted his own encounter with the air minister. It was widely known that Germany's famed Black Forest contained munitions works and military installations, and Amery urged Wood to drop incendiary bombs on the area. Wood looked at him in horror. "Are you aware it is private property?" he exclaimed. "Why, you will be asking me to bomb Essen [an industrial city in the Ruhr] next!" Amery "went away very angry." At the very least, he declared, "we could . . . have made the German people realize that they were at war, and not merely undisturbed spectators of a Hitler triumph."

At about the same time, Hitler sent a directive to his generals declaring that the "greatest danger" to the German war effort was "the vulnerability of the Ruhr. If this heart of German industrial production were hit, it would lead to the collapse of the German war economy and thus of the capacity to resist." Yet as long as Chamberlain continued in power, the Ruhr was to remain untouched by British bombs.

Left to fight alone, the Poles, pounded by the Luftwaffe and beset by panzers, struggled to resist the German blitzkrieg, fighting on as best they could against a form of unrelenting warfare no one had ever seen before. On September 10, eight Polish Army divisions launched a counterattack across the Bzura River, west of Warsaw. For three days they drove the German Eighth Army back and captured more than fifteen hundred prisoners from one division alone. The Poles were trying hard to hold out until September 17, when France's treaty obligations required a retaliatory assault against Germany. That day came, and the Soviet Union invaded Poland from the east. France did nothing. Knowing the country was now doomed, Poland's armed forces headed for its borders, determined to reorganize and carry on the fight from outside. Ringed by thirteen German infantry divisions and pounded day and night by bombs and artillery shells, Warsaw continued to resist.

In Britain, meanwhile, the government and press paid windy tribute to Poland's suffering. "In the agony of their martyred land," *The Times* declared, "the Poles will perhaps in some degree be consoled by the knowledge that they have the sympathy, and indeed the reverence, not only of their allies in western Europe but of all civilized people throughout the globe." On September 20 the BBC broadcast a message to the people of Warsaw: "All the world is admiring your courage . . . We, your allies, intend to continue the struggle for the restoration of your liberty. Please reply, if you can, to this message." Stefan Starzynski, Warsaw's indomitable mayor, made clear that the city wanted action, not words of encouragement. "When will the effective help of Great Britain and France come to relieve us from this terrible situation?" he asked. "We are waiting for it."

On September 28 Warsaw fell to the Germans, and by October 5 Hitler was in control of all of Poland. His Majesty's Government meanwhile declared that it had every intention of restoring freedom to Poland—but not until Germany was finally defeated. In a cable to British embassies and legations in foreign capitals, the government explained: "To have devoted hundreds of British planes to bombing raids in Germany would have meant spectacular successes but [it also would have meant] the inevitable loss of machines which will be used more effectively on the Western Front." For many Britons, that was an unacceptable rationale. "This is a terrible episode in our history," the *Manchester Guardian* editorialized, "whatever the explanation may be."

For the men of the British Expeditionary Force, which had been dispatched to France on September 10, it was also turning out to be a phantom conflict. The two BEF corps, made up of four regular infantry divisions, were dug in on the French-Belgian border, north of the Maginot Line and more than 100 miles from the nearest German troops. British commanders had no plans for any sort of offensive against Germany. Neither did the French, who counted on the Maginot Line, a 280-mile-long fortified zone of underground forts, barbed wire, pillboxes, and tank traps, to keep the enemy at bay.

"What kind of war, what kind of game is this?" the CBS correspondent William L. Shirer demanded in a broadcast from a peaceful Germany. There were various answers to Shirer's question: to British troops, it was the "bore war"; to the French, the *drôle de guerre*; in the United States, the "phony war." Everywhere one looked on the so-called western front, there were scenes of bucolic peace, with cattle grazing in the fields and French farmhands bringing in the harvest. In the view of Maj. Gen. Roger Evans, who commanded Britain's First Armoured Division, it was a disgraceful way to conduct a war, "an ignoble contrast to the great battle on the eastern front, where the last desperate resistance of Poland was beaten down by the mighty torrent of German arms."

For Generals Alan Brooke and John Dill, the two British corps commanders, the lack of action was a godsend, since in their opinion British troops were totally unfit for combat. The British Army, which had held no major maneuvers since 1930, was, in the words of one observer, "a mere parade-ground army." In addition to their insufficient training, the troops were faced with a desperate shortage of almost everything they needed: trucks, field artillery, radios, heavy gun tractors, antiaircraft guns and ammunition, antitank guns, mortars, machine guns and their carriers, and, above all, tanks. While the Germans were slicing through Poland with their tanks and mechanized infantry, the British had no effective medium or heavy tanks and wouldn't have them in any great numbers until 1941. As Maj. Gen. Bernard Law Montgomery noted, the scarcity of modern tanks was particularly infuriating since the tank was a British invention and had been used against the Germans in the Great War.

Early in October, General Brooke, who was given command of the entire British Army later in the war, wrote in his diary that he and Dill were "in the depths of gloom" over the lack of arms, equipment, and training. Britain, Brooke added, is "facing this war in a halfhearted way."

He concluded that the government had sent the BEF to France not to fight but as a public relations gesture, to show that some action, however minimal, was being taken. "The most depressing part of the business is the apparent failure on the part of GHQ to realize how serious these difficulties are!"

Montgomery, who took over command of the army's Third Division in France, used much stronger language to describe what he considered the government's ineptitude, calling it "scandalous" and "shameful." Later he wrote: "My soul revolted at what was happening. France and Britain stood still while Germany swallowed Poland; we stood still while the German armies moved over to the West, obviously to attack us; we waited patiently to be attacked; and during all this time we occasionally bombed Germany with *leaflets*. If this was war, I did not understand it."

With the British Army and the RAF missing from action, the only service to see real combat in the early months of the war was the Royal Navy. Fittingly, the cabinet minister in charge of its operations was the sole British official to reorganize his ministry on a war footing and to call for prompt and vigorous action against the enemy.

From the moment he accepted the job of first lord of the admiralty, Winston Churchill showed a singular sense of urgency, in sharp contrast with the Foreign Office, which still began its day at 11:00 a.m., and 10 Downing Street, where John Colville grumbled at having to start work at the "disgustingly early hour" of 9:30 a.m. Chamberlain's office operated much as it did in peacetime, Colville remarked. "There was no unseemly hurrying. Everything was done . . . in accordance with established routine."

That was not Churchill's style. Observing that "the opening hours of war may be vital with navies," he took charge of his post the night that war was declared. The Admiralty library was immediately transformed into a twenty-four-hour-a-day War Room, with maps and charts showing the current position of all British and Allied warships and merchant ships. Working up to sixteen hours a day, Churchill was a tornado of energy, burying his staff and military commanders in a blizzard of memoranda demanding ACTION THIS DAY. Three days into the war he ordered naval vessels to escort merchant ships in convoys, to protect them from German raiders. When he discovered that no navy ship had been fitted with radar, he ordered it done immediately. He pushed hard to speed up the slow pace of ship construction, declaring that the present schedule "cannot possibly be accepted" and ordering penalties levied against sluggish contractors.

Yet while Churchill prepared the navy to defend itself, his overall outlook was hardly a defensive one. From the first days of the war he wanted the British government to hit hard at Germany and to use the navy to do it. In the war's first week, for example, he proposed a naval attack on German ships in the Baltic, which he called "the supreme naval offensive open to the Royal Navy." Not long after that, he proposed that every possible effort be made to stop the shipping of iron ore from Sweden to Germany down the coast of Norway. If the movement of the ore, which was desperately needed by Germany's war machine, could not be halted by diplomatic means, Churchill suggested the laying of mines inside Norwegian territorial waters, among other things. Such a maneuver would force German ore ships onto the high seas, where they could be attacked by British vessels.

Anxious not to antagonize Germany or neutral countries like Norway, Chamberlain and the rest of the cabinet decided the time was not yet ripe to launch an offensive operation. Over the next few months an exasperated Churchill repeatedly urged the prime minister and the other ministers to go on the attack, only to be met by more dithering. The intensity of his frustration could be seen in his scribbled comments on an Air Staff note that disapproved of one of his proposed offensives. After the words "The conclusion thus appears to be . . ." Churchill inserted, "Based on false premises & carefully designed to hamper British action, while leaving the enemy free." Over a sentence concluding that retaliation against the Germans would be "unprofitable," the first lord wrote sarcastically, "Don't irritate them, dear!" In his memoirs he wrote: "This idea of not irritating the enemy did not commend itself to me . . . Good, decent, civilized people, it appeared, must never strike till after they had been struck dead."

Thus, in the first months of the war, the most offense-minded minister in the government, despite all his best efforts, was forced to pre-

side over a service forced largely on the defensive. The German Navy
had no such compunctions about attacking, and the resulting British
losses at sea were substantial. On September 18 a German submarine
sank the *Courageous,* one of Britain's first aircraft carriers, in the Bris-
tol Channel off South Wales, killing more than six hundred men. Less
than a month later a German U-boat slipped past sunken ships and
chains used as antisubmarine nets and entered the sheltered lagoon of
Scapa Flow, the sea anchorage of Britain's Home Fleet, off northern Scotland. In the spring of 1939 senior officers at Scapa Flow had warned
that the base's defenses were grossly inadequate, but the Admiralty
had ignored the report. After taking office, Churchill ordered immediate
defensive measures, but they couldn't be adopted in time to prevent the
submarine from penetrating a basin that should have been impregnable. The U-boat's second torpedo charge struck and sank the battleship
Royal Oak, sending to their deaths more than eight hundred men, including the rear admiral commanding the Second Battle Squadron.

   Although the sinking of these two ships were serious blows, the
loss of merchant shipping at the hands of Germany was far more critical to the fate of Britain. At a time when the British government insisted on attacking only German military objectives (and not doing much
of that), German U-boats and raiders were having a field day picking
off British and neutral merchant ships despite Churchill's convoy system. In the first week of the war, eleven ships, containing sixty-five thousand tons of cargo, were sunk. Two weeks later the total was twenty-six
ships, and growing fast. At various times the English Channel and the
Thames and Tyne rivers were closed temporarily to shipping, thanks to
the success of the German predators. When Germany added magnetic
mines to the mix, dropping them by parachute into British channels
and harbors and wreaking even greater havoc with shipping, Churchill
wanted to retaliate by dropping mines into the Rhine. That plan was
also dropped, after the French government declared that such "aggressive action" would only "draw reprisals upon France."

There was no British military offensive during the initial months of the
war for one simple reason: the prime minister saw no need for one. In

November, his government imposed a naval blockade against Germany; Royal Navy ships stopped ships carrying food, raw materials, and other goods to and from Germany. Chamberlain was convinced the blockade would be enough to "bring Hitler to his knees" and thus end the conflict without much bloodshed. He had a "hunch," he wrote, that the war would be over by the spring of 1940. "It won't be by defeat in the field," he said, "but by German realization that they can't win, and that it isn't worth their while to go on getting thinner and poorer when they might have instant relief." His hunch had little basis in reality. While the blockade did considerable damage to the German economy, it in itself was not enough to vanquish the enemy. For one thing, the Soviet Union, as part of its nonaggression pact with Hitler, was making up some of the shortfall by supplying Germany with food and raw materials.

In the Reich the economy had been placed on a clear war footing. The Nazis were rationing food and other consumer goods (leading Chamberlain to the mistaken conclusion that they were in dire economic straits), while speeding up production of munitions, planes, tanks, and other war equipment. In Britain, in response to calls from Leo Amery and other MPs for the appointment of an economic czar to mobilize the country's industry and coordinate its economy, Chamberlain named Lord Stamp, director of a major railway company, as his economic adviser. It was only a half-time position, however, since Lord Stamp felt obliged to run his railway at the same time.

Within the British government there was little enthusiasm for diverting workers, factories, and raw materials from the production of consumer goods to weapons, planes, and other war matériel. According to Sir John Simon, the chancellor of the exchequer, it was important to keep British industry on a peacetime footing, so that the country could return to normal economic conditions as quickly as possible after the war was over. Still, not all of Chamberlain's men were as complaisant about the future as the prime minister and Simon. John Colville wrote in his diary: "I am alarmed to read in Cabinet papers how long it will be before our production of armaments, and particularly aeroplanes, is satisfactory . . . I am not impressed by our efficiency or ability to get a move on."

Wary of running up massive budget deficits, Chamberlain and his advisers were also nervous about provoking trade unions and angering the British public with rationing and other belt-tightening measures. Despite German depredations on British merchant shipping, no rationing of food was instituted in Britain until January 1940; indeed, the Chamberlain government ridiculed the Germans for their rationing policy. When the government, in its first wartime budget, raised the standard income tax rate from five shillings sixpence per pound to seven shillings, the British upper class gasped ("Father is sunk in depression," wrote John Colville). It was hardly a confiscatory increase, however, and did not reflect in any sense a state of national emergency. Nor did the news that Britain's unemployment rate had actually risen since the war began; in December 1939 more than 1.3 million Britons were still out of work, despite the introduction of conscription.

During this twilight period "a sense of great urgency and bold decisive action were utterly lacking" in the councils of Chamberlain and his men, wrote Leland Stowe, a foreign correspondent for the *Chicago Daily News*. "Downing Street was playing for time and counting on everything working out in the end, and this mental attitude cast a palsy upon all sorts of wartime preparations and adjustments." Stowe, who arrived in London two weeks after the war began, was shocked at the "extraordinary number" of military-age men in the capital who were still in civilian clothes. When he asked one official why all available men hadn't been summoned to arms, he was told: "They really aren't needed now . . . Besides, they say we haven't got enough equipment to supply another 300,000 men even if they were called up. Obviously you can't make soldiers out of men if you can't give them uniforms."

In the first weeks of the war Chamberlain had reluctantly agreed to a proposal, pushed in the cabinet by Churchill and Leslie Hore-Belisha, to have eleven army divisions ready for battle within six months and twenty within a year. But little was being done to translate the plan into reality. Indeed, the army still did not have the infrastructure necessary to take care of the troops it already had. Men who had rushed to enlist during the first days of the war were turned away; there weren't enough training camps, instructors or equipment for them and no indication that the situation would improve anytime soon. As a result of an act passed by Parliament on the first day of the war, men aged eighteen to forty-one were liable for conscription, but even the mere act of registering them for the draft turned out to be a tortuous process, progressing, as one commentator quipped, "with the speed of an elephant trying to compete in the Derby." When war finally erupted in Western Europe in the spring of 1940, men in their late twenties still had not been called up, and forty-year-olds were not summoned until July 1941.

In the final analysis, Neville Chamberlain was as loath to call for a full-scale military and economic mobilization of the country as he was to launch any sort of offensive against Germany because he had no intention at all, as Bob Boothby had said, of leading the nation "*through the struggle.*" Gen. Hastings "Pug" Ismay, who, as secretary to the Committee of Imperial Defence, was privy to Chamberlain's private discussions and consultations about the war, told John Colville that he was convinced the prime minister was determined to avoid war entirely, not just postpone it until Britain was better prepared.

Shortly before the war Chamberlain told his sister that if it broke out, he probably should resign because he knew "what agony of mind it would mean for me to give directions that would bring death and mutilation and misery to so many." But as it turned out, he later wrote, "the war was so different from what I expected that I found the situation bearable . . ." What he failed to mention was his determined efforts to make sure it stayed that way. "I was never meant to be a War Minister," he confessed to his sister. When he visited the BEF in France in December, he remarked how "sickened" he was to "see the barbed wire and pill boxes and guns and anti-tank obstacles, remembering what they meant in the last war." Following his inspection of General Montgomery's troops near the Belgian frontier, the prime minister drew Montgomery aside and whispered: "I don't think the Germans have any intention of attacking us. Do you?"

Astounded by Chamberlain's obtuseness and wishful thinking, especially in light of British intelligence reporting Germany's mounting preparations for an assault on the West, Montgomery retorted that an attack was surely coming and that "we must get ready for trouble to begin when the cold weather was over."

———

As the government continued to shrink from confronting Germany, the MPs who had forced Neville Chamberlain into war could only look on in frustrated impotence. Although Parliament had won the first skirmish with Chamberlain by making him declare war over Poland, it followed that victory by bestowing breathtaking powers on the prime minister and his government and, in the process, losing much of its own authority. Caught up in the surge of patriotism and loyalty that swept the country when war was declared, the House of Commons quickly passed a series of emergency bills giving the government a blank check to do anything it wanted to ensure public safety and to wage war.

Precious British liberties like habeas corpus were swept away for the duration. The government was given the authority to jail indefinitely without trial any person judged to be a danger to public safety. It could prevent the holding of demonstrations or putting out of flags; requisition without payment any building or other property, from a horse to a railway; tell farmers what to plant and what to do with their crops; enter anyone's home without warning or a warrant. "It is probable," wrote a British law journal, "that no such interference with [individual] rights . . . has ever taken place without adequate discussion and criticism in Parliament." The British people, Helen Kirkpatrick argued, "have voluntarily accepted a dictatorship as all-embracing as that against which they are fighting."

While Kirkpatrick was certainly exaggerating, there was no question that the Chamberlain government had been given a license to be as authoritarian as it pleased. The three major political parties had agreed that no general election would be held for the duration; as a result, the prime minister did not even have to worry about being held accountable by the British public. "A lot of my politically minded . . . friends came to believe that the House of Commons could have no major part to play in the struggle, if the Government was to be made strong enough to conduct the war efficiently," wrote J. E. Sewell, *The Daily Telegraph*'s parliamentary correspondent. "At question time, [MPs] might be able to keep some sort of check on the behavior of the bureaucrats. Beyond that, they were no longer important."

Chamberlain, in any event, wanted them around as little as possible. "I secretly feel he hates the House of Commons," wrote Chips

Channon. "Certainly he has a deep contempt for Parliamentary interference." After war broke out, the prime minister wanted Parliament to
take another long recess. Fierce opposition from MPs put an end to that
idea, although a compromise proposal, calling for Parliament to meet
only three days a week, was accepted. Another Chamberlain plan—to
evacuate the House of Commons from London to someplace in the
hinterlands—came under even stronger attack from members. When
he received a notice about the evacuation, an outraged Josiah Wedgwood told David Margesson he wouldn't go. Furthermore, he said, once
he found out where Parliament's new home was supposed to be, "I would
tell Hitler at once." Margesson, who already had received a flood of
protests about the notice, replied wearily that there would be no evacuation until and unless Buckingham Palace was bombed. In the view
of Wedgwood and many other MPs, there should be no evacuation at
all. "If there is danger, our duty is to be at the post of danger, especially
since it is against democracy that Hitler wages war," Wedgwood wrote
in a letter that appeared in several British newspapers. "I personally do
not believe that the danger amounts to much; but I fear that the suggestion to go elsewhere comes from those in high places who dislike and
despise Parliament."

For the Tory rebels who had battled so hard against appeasement,
there was an especially profound sense of uselessness. Now that their
country was at war, they wanted to serve it, but no one, it seemed, had
anything for them to do. Certainly not Chamberlain, who, having been
pressed to bring the two most prominent dissidents, Churchill and
Eden, into the cabinet, made very clear he wanted nothing to do with
the rest. When Eden passed him a note at a cabinet meeting suggesting
he give Amery a job, the prime minister pushed it away with what Eden
called "an irritated snort." He was not about to reward his former friend
for being a turncoat.

While Ronald Cartland and some of the other rebels were young
enough to fight in the war, most were now in their forties, too old to
be taken back into the forces. It was a severe blow for a number of
them, especially those who had fought in the Great War and wanted to
do the same now. Duff Cooper, for one, had his old uniform altered,
tried on his puttees and Sam Browne belt, and tried to get back in the

Grenadiers. But he was told there was no room for a forty-nine-year-old second lieutenant. "At the beginning of the first war, I had too much to do, now I had too little," he observed. When a friend noted that Hitler often denounced Cooper in his speeches, he replied: "Hitler is the only man in Europe today who remembers that I exist." An amateur poet, he described in verse his unhappiness and resentment at being idle:

> As autumn fades and winter comes
> With menace deep and dire,
> We sit and twiddle useless thumbs
> And chatter round the fire.

For lack of anything better to do to support Britain, Cooper decided to go to the United States with his wife and give a series of lectures to plead his country's cause at a time when anti-British and anti-Chamberlain feeling was strong there. Cooper knew some people were pointing fingers at him, accusing him of running away from the war. But it was a phony war, for God's sake! What was there to run away *from*?

Harold Macmillan, on the other hand, was staying put. So was his family's publishing firm. During one of Macmillan's hurried trips to the office during the first weeks of war, Lovat Dickson, a Macmillan editor, asked him if the company should run an advertisement announcing its evacuation from London, as many other publishers were doing. Macmillan said nothing for a moment, then took out a pad of paper and wrote for a minute or two. He handed the pad to Dickson and remarked, "Say something like that." The announcement ran in the newspapers exactly as Macmillan wrote it: "Macmillan & Company Limited, in response to numerous enquiries from authors, booksellers, and members of the public, wish to state emphatically that they propose to carry on their business at St. Martin's Street, London, WC2, until they are either taxed, insured . . . or bombed out of existence."

As a partner in a prestigious publishing house Macmillan, at least, had a high-level position to retreat to. But the last thing he wanted to do was to confine himself to publishing for the duration. His son, Maurice, had left Oxford in the first days of the war and joined the army. Macmillan wanted to do the same. Like Duff Cooper, however, he was rejected when he tried to get back into his old Grenadiers regiment. Not even the Grenadiers reserve units would take him. He was too old at forty-five and still suffered from his earlier war injuries.

For Macmillan, the future looked depressingly bleak. His marriage was in tatters. During the rare times he and Dorothy were together, they acted like polite strangers toward each other; she spent much of her time with Boothby, as she had for years. His political career wasn't in much better shape. He had been in Parliament for fifteen years and, unlike several of his contemporaries, had precious little to show for it. Cooper, for all his current frustration, had at least held two high-ranking cabinet positions before he was fifty. Eden had been foreign secretary in his thirties. Even Boothby, with his "don't-give-a-damn" attitude, had been parliamentary private secretary to the chancellor of the exchequer. Macmillan had done none of those things, and it did not appear likely he ever would.

In his search for some meaningful job, he had gone so far as to ask Boothby to intercede with Churchill on his behalf. Boothby complied, writing the new first lord: "I have in the past had personal differences and difficulties with Harold Macmillan, but we have always worked closely together in politics . . . Surely he should be used in the new Ministry of Economic Warfare, which calls for constructive ability of the highest order in the economic field." The letter bore no fruit, however; no one in government seemed to want Macmillan now, not even in a low-ranking post. And what was there to look forward to in Parliament, since it "did not seem likely to play a great role in the drama that was unfolding"? Perhaps, Macmillan thought glumly, he could volunteer to drive a lorry for the Cuckfield Rural District Council, near his country house in Sussex.

Considerably older and more experienced than the other rebels, Leo Amery found himself reading Proust at the outbreak of the war, having nothing better to do. As a former senior cabinet minister he had a particularly acute sense of frustration in having no role to play. "It is absurd that I should not be made use of today," he wrote Geoffrey Dawson. "After all, next to Winston . . . I know more about the conduct of war than any of them [in the cabinet], not to speak of my greater knowledge of European affairs and my authority with the Dominions. And if I am just senior to Winston in actual years, I am, I think, a good deal junior in body . . ."

Having finally joined forces with his old rival in the fight against appeasement, the sixty-five-year-old Amery was eager to work with Churchill now. The first lord of the admiralty was the only member of the War Cabinet with any "offensive fighting spirit," Amery thought, and should be put in charge of "coordinating the whole sphere of defence, if not the whole conduct of the war." Putting aside the decades-old competitiveness he felt toward Churchill, Amery wrote to him that "if I can be of any service to you, in the way of working up memoranda on general policy outside the purely naval sphere, or in any other way, please command me. I shall be only too happy to work for you." Churchill replied that he doubted Chamberlain would approve of such a plan but that he would try to think of a possible slot for Amery. Nothing, however, came of it.

It was just as well. Amery's greatest contribution to the war effort was to come in opposing the government, not in helping one of its ministers. After Munich, he had wanted to believe Chamberlain's promises that the country would be readied for war as soon as possible. But it soon became clear that the pledges were not being fulfilled, and from the first day of the war he was convinced that the prime minister was the wrong man to lead Britain at such a critical time. Amery didn't think Chamberlain was a villain, as a number of his colleagues did. In his view, his old friend was simply "a civilian to the very marrow, hating war, obsessed by the sufferings it would cause and determined to avoid them if it were humanly possible . . . He had no conception . . . of the demonic drive behind the enemy, or of the heights of sacrifice and achievement to which our own people were ready to rise if rightly led."

As the governmental muddle and inertia grew worse, Amery stopped reading Proust, shook off his lethargy, and became the pugnacious scrapper of old. He reentered the fray with a fierce determination not to let Chamberlain run roughshod over Parliament. Having taken a back-seat to Churchill and Eden in the anti-appeasement battle, he now emerged as the unquestioned leader of the Tory rebels. In the House of Commons he assumed Churchill's mantle as senior Conservative critic of the government, mounting attack after attack on its failure to gear up for war on both military and economic fronts. Amery was adamant that Chamberlain and his men be called to account for what he saw as their chaotic, amateurish fumbling of the war effort and the danger facing Britain as a result.

In a flurry of speeches and newspaper articles, he demanded a crash mobilization of manpower and the economy. "I am for taking every volunteer that comes forward and somehow or other giving him some sort of training and equipment," he wrote. "The idea that we should have men able-bodied and on the dole in a life-and-death struggle is preposterous." Like Churchill, he called for halting the shipments of iron ore from Sweden to Germany and for dropping mines in the Rhine. He also urged air strikes against German military and industrial targets. The failure of Britain and France to mount any offensive of this sort, Amery said, was allowing Hitler to stockpile the petrol, oil, rubber, and other raw materials essential for his own future attacks.

A front-page *Daily Mirror* story about one of his speeches was head-lined "MAKE THEM FIGHT!" His speech, eloquent and urgent, put one in mind of some of Churchill's prewar addresses. Declaring that Britain was fighting for "our own existence," Amery warned his London audience against what he considered the government's over-optimism. "Don't let us underestimate the terrible power of our enemies or their staying power," he declared. "I am not one of those who would try to cheer you up by saying Germany is going to collapse through internal discontent or hunger . . . Nothing short of sheer defeat is going to bring Germany down."

By the end of 1939, *Picture Post* reported, Amery's repeated assaults on the government were creating a "great stir," and his "agitation has given rise to a wave of criticism, in Parliament and in the country, of the shortcomings of the Government's policy." According to the *Western Mail*, "Mr. L. S. Amery is the most talked-of man in British politics at the moment." The *Manchester Guardian, Daily Mail,* and other major

British newspapers again pressed Chamberlain to bring Amery into the cabinet. "Amery remains the most powerful Conservative outside the [government]," the *Daily Mail* remarked. "Why has he been excluded in all the years of the National Government? . . . He is more able than many raised to office, both in intellect and energy." Again Chamberlain paid no attention to the newspapers' appeals.

As important as his articles and speeches were in rousing resistance to the phony war, Amery was to play an even more vital role in the drama to come. He took control of the Eden group, infusing its members, whom he called "my young men," with a vigor and combativeness that its previous leader lacked. As government ministers Churchill and Eden now owed their loyalty to Chamberlain, and neither took part in the plotting that was to follow. Eden did come to one of the group's meetings, which were held weekly over dinner in a private dining room at the Carlton Hotel. That particular dinner was "rather flat," one rebel wrote to a friend. "Anthony is so fair-minded (or senselessly loyal) about his [government] colleagues that his presence seems to deaden any constructive criticism."

But there was criticism aplenty at the group's other sessions. Amery's pugnacity and outspokenness helped stiffen the backbone of some of the moderate rebels, like Harold Nicolson, who previously were reluctant to consider any sort of uprising against Chamberlain and his men. Under Amery's leadership, the dissidents decided that their function, for the moment, was to "harass the government until it conducted the war as though it meant it." If it failed to respond to pressure, more drastic action would be taken. Nicolson summed up the attitude of his colleagues when he wrote in his diary: "Let Chamberlain remain [for the time being]. But let him know, and his satellites know, that he remains on sufferance and under the very sharpest observation."

As it happened, the Amery faction wasn't the only group tracking the government's conduct of the war. Bob Boothby had helped form a new cross-party organization, which, along with the Amery group, was to become a focal point for disaffection with Chamberlain in the months to come. Churchill had left Boothby behind when he went to the Admiralty; he had taken Brendan Bracken with him as his parliamentary private secretary. That was fine with the independent-minded Boothby.

He was not much suited to the role of devoted disciple, which is what Churchill wanted and what Bracken was. Boothby had always been much better at rebellion.

By November 1939 the new all-party group, which came to be dubbed the Vigilantes, had acquired as members more than fifty MPs who spanned the political spectrum: twenty-five Tories, sixteen Labourites, eight Liberals, and four Independents. Besides Boothby, the group's other guiding lights were Clement Davies, an Independent MP from Wales, and Eleanor Rathbone, the Independent from Liverpool. Until the war Davies, a prosperous lawyer and businessman, had been a Chamberlain supporter and member of the tiny National Liberal Party, a splinter Liberal group that, like Nicolson's National Labour Party, supported the government. But the prime minister's refusal to go to the aid of Poland and to preside over a vigorous prosecution of the war had disillusioned and angered Davies, who quit the National Liberals and became an Independent. Rathbone, a noted feminist and social reformer, was widely regarded as the most effective woman in Parliament. She had focused chiefly on domestic issues until the mid 1930s, when she emerged as an ardent opponent of appeasement, joining the Duchess of Atholl in pressing for change in the government's nonintervention policy in the Spanish civil war.

Although all three founding members of the Vigilantes were critics of Chamberlain's handling of the war, the purpose of the group, at least as it was announced, was to monitor the war's progress, not plot against the government. Indeed, the Vigilantes invited the prime minister to meet with them and discuss the government's war policy in secret session. When he refused, they began asking economic and military experts, both inside and outside the government, to brief them on what was going on. Among those who accepted the invitation was Boothby's friend John Maynard Keynes, who was highly critical of the government's wartime economic policy, declaring that the government departments "are at sixes and sevens, and the home front is a real mess."

While the Amery group and the Vigilantes operated independently of each other, there was considerable communication and cooperation between the two, unlike the relationship between the earlier Eden and Churchill groups. Amery, Macmillan, and Nicolson, for example, attended

Vigilante meetings, and Amery occasionally met with the group's leaders to compare notes. Unlike Eden, he was not averse to working with
Labour and Liberal critics of the government, and his increasing contacts with Clement Attlee, Hugh Dalton, Archibald Sinclair, and other
leading Opposition figures were to affect future events significantly.

The rebels' stepped-up activities meanwhile were not going unnoticed by the government. Thanks to its sophisticated spying network,
Chamberlain and his men were well aware of what the two groups
were up to. "Today I noticed signs of the 'glamour boys' beginning to intrigue again," Chips Channon observed sourly in his diary. "We must
watch out." A little later David Margesson sent a scorching letter to
Boothby, blasting him for getting involved with the Vigilantes. Defiant as
ever, Boothby shot back an equally scalding reply: "Dear David . . .
I ask you to believe that I have not attacked the Government for the
last twelve months simply for the fun of the thing, but out of very genuine conviction. The inescapable truth . . . is that, within a miraculously
short period of five years, your Government reduced this country from
a position of world supremacy and absolute security to one of mortal
peril. It took the Roman Empire a hundred years of the most enjoyable
decadence to achieve the same result."

CHAPTER FOURTEEN

"THE MISERY
OF DOING NOTHING"

~

The government may have been playing at war, but the enormous up-
heaval of people's lives that resulted from its declaration was all too
real. Millions of city dwellers, many of them children, left their homes
in September 1939, marking the largest migration in Britain since the
Great Plague of 1665. Houses were shut up, families separated, careers
abandoned, schools and businesses closed.

For much of the country it was a time of trauma. Parents felt bereft
without their children, and the children, trying to adjust to strangers
and alien surroundings in the countryside, desperately missed their
families and homes. Much-loved pets were put down by distraught
owners who were being evacuated or who feared the animals would be
destroyed by bombs; the bodies of dead dogs and cats were heaped high
outside veterinarians' offices. Hospital patients, including more than
eight thousand tuberculosis sufferers, were sent home to make room
for nonexistent air-raid casualties. Guests in seaside hotels were evicted
by government agents, who then confiscated the establishments for
government use. Although Parliament managed to avoid evacuation, a
number of government ministries were not so fortunate. Thousands of
civil servants were forced to leave their families behind in London
when their agencies were relocated elsewhere.

The psychological dislocation was acute even for those whose own
lives had not been turned upside down. "One's friends join up, or go to

the country, sail to America, or evacuate school children," observed the Canadian diplomat Charles Ritchie. "If you see a friend, you cling to him. For when he is gone, he is swept away, and God knows when you will see him again." A *New York Times* correspondent, Frederick Birchall, found it depressing to be in a London empty of children and dogs. "You have to live for a while in a childless, petless town to realize how much that changes the landscape," he wrote. "It becomes the dreariest sort of place, even to a childless male." Another journalist, watching a long line of children trooping off to a train station, mused: "One feels that the future goes with them, into hibernation."

Yet painful as these disruptions were, there was a general feeling in the first days of the war that they were worthwhile, that Britain had reclaimed its honor, had stood up—at long last—to Hitler. Though it didn't want war, the country had steeled itself to accept its necessity, believing that defending Poland was the right and honorable thing to do. As Harold Nicolson put it, fear "changed into determination, the gloom of anticipation melted into the gaiety of courage." Faced with the challenge they had dreaded for so long, the British allowed their reserve to thaw a bit, and class distinctions faded. The idea that "we're all in this together" took fragile root. "The spirit of cooperation is really wonderful," wrote Oswald Garrison Villard, owner and editor of *The Nation* magazine, who was in London during the early weeks of the war. "Everyone wants to do his or her share, and everyone is so courteous that it seems quite unnecessary to post signs telling what constitutes good manners in an air raid shelter."

Such unity, however, did not last much longer than the gloriously sunny days of early September. Drenching rains soon came, and with them, disillusion. If Britain was not going to defend Poland, people wondered, why on earth were they still at war? Was there any other reason to continue this supposed conflict? If so, Chamberlain's government never said what it was, despite pleas from Commonwealth leaders and others to tell them what Britain's war aims were. Having tried to avert war until the last minute and still determined to avoid combat, the prime minister and his men simply didn't know what to say on the subject. When Lord Halifax asked Alexander Cadogan what he thought Britain's war aims should be, Cadogan replied that he saw "awful difficulties" in anything that might be proposed. "I suppose the cry is 'Abolish Hitlerism,'" Cadogan wrote in his diary. "But what if Hitler hands over to Goering? Meanwhile, what of the course of operations? What if Germany now sits tight? . . . What do we do? Build up our armaments feverishly? What for? Can we last out the course? Time is on our side. What are the Germans doing meanwhile? Must try and think this out . . ." Such confused and muddled thinking was the target of a limerick making the rounds in Whitehall:

> An elderly statesman with gout
> When asked what the war was about,
> Replied with a sigh
> My colleagues and I
> Are doing our best to find out.

With no enduring sense of purpose or community in Britain, the country's already deep social divisions widened into chasms as the "bore war" ground on. "The war is not popular among the lowest sections of the community," John Colville wrote in his diary. "There is the suspicion that it is being fought in the interests of the rich." The cost of living rose nearly 25 percent in the first six months of the war, but the Chamberlain government, ignoring Labour warnings of possible worker unrest, rejected union demands for wage hikes. (The prime minister "always treated us like dirt," complained Clement Attlee.) At the same time, the government insisted that the upper classes had already made their share of economic sacrifices.

What those sacrifices were, no one knew. There certainly hadn't been any in regard to food. Although the Labour Party pressed for food rationing from the beginning of the war, the government refused to introduce it until early 1940, arguing it was an unnecessary restriction that would be used as propaganda fodder by Germany. When Attlee told Chamberlain he was being deluged by telegrams demanding rationing, the prime minister's parliamentary private secretary, Lord Dunglass, sniffily remarked how astonishing it was that "people grumble when one is doing one's best to let them live normally . . ." But these weren't normal times, and shortages of essential foodstuffs were beginning to develop. There were widespread complaints about hoarding by the wealthy. "The rich people from the West End are coming in to take the poor people's food," a grocer in London's East End complained. One day a wealthy couple and their chauffeur came into his store. The man and woman each scooped up twenty-eight-pound sacks of sugar, while their driver claimed another two sacks. "I made them put it all back again and gave them three pounds each," the grocer said. "I don't think that sort of thing is right . . . They don't give the poor a chance."

While the middle and lower classes had to cope with shortages of virtually everything—sugar, bacon, ham, butter, even coal—life for the wealthy went on much the same as it always had. Nancy Tree discovered that for herself the first weekend after war was declared. She and her husband had been invited to a shooting party at the country home of Lord Camrose. Assuming that the party had been called off because of the war, the Trees didn't go. "To my horror," Nancy Tree later said, "I got a telephone message from Lady Camrose . . . saying, 'What time were we arriving?' They were waiting and they hadn't heard from us; they were still having their shoot. I had to write and apologize and say, 'I thought the war stopped everything.'" In his diary, John Colville described a dinner party at the home of Lord Kemsley, Lord Camrose's brother and the owner of *The Sunday Times*: "None of us dressed (to show it was war-time), but in every other respect it might have been a party of prewar days—there was a galaxy of footmen, the dinner was vast and excellent, and wine flowed like water. Vulgar, perhaps, in these days; but certainly a pleasant relapse into the gilded past."

Many members of the upper class closed their big houses in London (they threw parties called house coolings before they left) and took up residence in the city's luxury hotels. But they still dined on smoked salmon and caviar at the finest restaurants, where shortages were virtually unknown and there was no rationing. Top-hatted doormen still graced the front entrances of the Dorchester and Savoy, although the Savoy's managing director shocked guests there by doffing his top hat and frock coat when war broke out and appearing in a business suit and bowler for the duration. Strawberries and cream were still available for afternoon tea at the Connaught, and eight different varieties of oysters were on the menu at Scott's restaurant in Piccadilly. Early in the war

Evelyn Waugh, after spending one morning in a fruitless search for a war-related job, improved his spirits by lunching at St. James's Club on half a dozen oysters, half a grouse, and a whole partridge, accompanied by half a bottle of white wine and half a bottle of vintage Bordeaux. At about the same time, Chips Channon took his wife and some friends to luncheon at the Ritz, which, as he noted in his diary, had "become fantastically fashionable . . . Ritzes always thrive in wartime, as we are all cookless."

Cinemas and other places of amusement, closed at the beginning of the war, quickly reopened when no bombs fell. Popular nightclubs like the Embassy Club, Café de Paris, and the Four Hundred Club were jammed; in the only concession to the war, formal dress was no longer required, and many of the patrons wore uniforms. In the window of a Rolls-Royce showroom in London, a discreet little sign read BUSINESS AS USUAL. Debutantes still danced at balls, and in the country some of the gentry still rode to hounds, even though the government supposedly had requisitioned all hunting horses for the military. Hunting devotees insisted they were being patriotic; a master of foxhounds wrote to *Horse and Hound* magazine that a complete halt of hunting "would be hailed by the Nazis as a proof that things were not going too well here."

Yet while the upper class carried on much as usual, some of its members objected when those they considered their inferiors tried to join the party. In *The Spectator*, Harold Nicolson described how a "major in a minor regiment" had a man ejected from a posh London restaurant because he was wearing the uniform of a lowly private. In a letter to the editor, the playwright St. John Ervine ignored the slight to the private and attacked Nicolson for having the temerity to suggest that there was such a thing as "a minor regiment."

The wealthy, however, did not entirely escape from encounters with countrymen less privileged than they. Thanks to the massive evacuation of children from the cities at the start of the war, aristocrats and members of the landed gentry found themselves housing youngsters from the slums of London's East End and other large urban areas. Winston and Clementine Churchill, Ronald and Nancy Tree, the Duke and

Duchess of Atholl, the Duke of Connaught, Lady Astor, and Lord Beaver-brook were among those who shared their country estates with the young evacuees. For many in the upper class, it was an eye-opening experience, forcing them to come face-to-face with the extreme poverty in Britain from which most of them had previously been sheltered. Oliver Lyttelton, a rich businessman and Eton schoolmate of Harold Macmillan's, recalled how shocked he was by the behavior of the thirty-one city children placed in his spacious country house in Wiltshire. "I had little dreamt," he wrote, "that English children could be so completely ignorant of the simplest rules of hygiene, and that they would regard the floors and carpets as suitable places upon which to relieve themselves."

In country mansions and provincial middle-class houses throughout Britain, other hosts of children from the slums were similarly horrified by their temporary wards' poor hygiene habits, foul language, nonexistent table manners, bed-wetting, dirty bodies, and lice-ridden clothes. A number of the adults regarded the children's behavior as a personal affront, not realizing that many of them came from tenements with no working toilets or baths and were not accustomed to using either.

Yet as bad as conditions at home might be, most evacuees, feeling lost without their parents, longed to return to the city. "Most of them had never seen the country," Ronald Tree said of the preschool youngsters who stayed at his country house in Oxfordshire. "They were terrified by its silence and the sight of even the most placid cow. They were also desperately homesick for the rest of their families and their friends." The playwright and novelist Bernard Kops recalled decades later how his little sister, Rose, screamed to their mother, "I want to [stay] with you! I want to be killed with you!" as she and he were taken away from their East End neighborhood to the country. "Rose had never been away from home, never been more than six inches away from my mother [in her life]."

For all its good intentions, the government's evacuation program, which included pregnant women and mothers with small children, turned out to be a colossal failure. Officials had been preparing for the possibility of a mass exodus for more than a year before the outbreak of war, but all the planning had been done in secret. The government, hoping to avert conflict right up to September 3, had wanted to avoid the appearance of a country getting ready for war. As a result, the evacuation plan was never debated in Parliament or the press, and no questions were raised about the potential problems of such an unprecedented migration scheme. In their preparations, officials concentrated on the mechanics of getting the evacuees safely away from the cities. Little thought was given to what would happen to the women and children *after* they had left. Several months before the war began, rural towns and villages selected as reception areas had appealed to the government for money to prepare for the influx of evacuees. No funds were disbursed until late in August, and few firm plans were put in place.

The result of such a casual, slapdash approach was chaos. In many cases, when the children boarded trains or buses to flee the cities, neither they, their parents, nor the organizers knew where they would end up. When they arrived at their destinations, siblings were often separated from one another by local evacuation officials, as were students who, along with their teachers, had traveled together as a unit, hoping to reconstitute their schools in new surroundings. The students of one London boys' school ended up being placed in various villages in a fifty-square-mile area, and it took their teachers several days to find out where they all were.

In most reception areas there was no organized process for matching children with temporary guardians and no checks on the guardians' suitability as surrogate parents. Not infrequently after their journeys, the young evacuees, tired and frightened, were brought into the local village hall, where residents gathered to make their choice. The scene, remarked an observer, was "reminiscent of a cross between an early Roman slave market and Selfridge's bargain basement." One evacuee, who was five years old at the time, said she felt like "a sheep on market day." Polite, clean, nicely dressed children were usually taken first, as were older boys and girls who looked as if they might be able to help out on the farm or in the house. Organizers walked the children who were not chosen in a crocodile line from house to house, urging the residents to take in one or more of them.

Occasionally the pairing turned out to be a great success; a number of evacuees grew very attached to their guardians and remained in close touch for years after the war. In many cases, however, the experience was unhappy. Of his guardians, a boy from the East End remarked: "They just wanted the allowance they were given for keeping me. All the food went to their children. It got so bad that when the mother went out, she would measure the loaf of bread with a piece of string." A girl from Birmingham, who was forced to cook and clean for the old woman who had taken her in, later recalled: "I felt alone, frightened, degraded, angry and constantly preached at . . . I wrote home constantly, imploring my father to please come and get me and I would kiss the streets of Birmingham if he did."

Even when hosts received the evacuees with sympathy and kindness, as many of them did, the strain of having complete strangers living in their houses for months on end led, almost inevitably, to an erosion of goodwill. A teacher sent with her students to a village in Hertfordshire wrote home: "We were most warmly received, but now that the newness has worn off, the children do not appear such angels, or the hostesses, such saints." In the end many guardians were as eager to get rid of the evacuees as they themselves were eager to go. A well-known barrister, who lived near Ronald and Nancy Tree in Oxfordshire, used to walk the streets of his village handing out money to evacuees who wanted to return to the city. In *Put Out More Flags*, Evelyn Waugh's satiric look at the phony war, one of the main characters is the wife of a country squire, whose volunteer job as a billeting officer "had transformed her, in four months, from one of the most popular women in the countryside into a figure of terror. When her car was seen approaching, people fled through covered lines of retreat, through side doors and stable yards, into the snow, anywhere to avoid her persuasive, 'But surely you could manage one more.'"

By January 1940, however, the need for fleeing was over; this unprecedented social experiment had come to an end for most of its early participants. With no bombs falling on the cities, a majority of the evacuees decided to go back home. But when many of the children returned, they found their schools closed, some having been requisitioned by the government for other purposes. A number of youngsters did not receive any schooling for the entire school year, despite pleas to local education boards from their parents. As a result, in some cities, gangs of unruly children roamed the streets for months, with little to do but get into trouble.

The first winter of the war in Britain was a dark, gloomy time. Rain fell incessantly in December, and then, in January, a tenacious cold spell gripped the country. It was in fact the coldest winter thus far in the twentieth century. Eight miles of the Thames froze solid, and heavy snows made traveling perilous. Villages and towns were cut off for days; water pipes froze and burst, and there was a severe shortage of coal.

The misery was made even worse by the blackout, the most detested disruption of the war, which, in the words of one historian, "transformed conditions of life more thoroughly than any other single feature of the conflict." During the phony war period it was far more dangerous to walk the streets of London at night than to be at the front in France. By the end of 1939 only three British soldiers had been killed in action, while back home traffic accidents had claimed more than four thousand lives, two-thirds of them pedestrians. A leading surgeon declared in the *British Medical Journal* that by frightening the British government into adopting the blackout, Germany had managed to kill more than six hundred Britons a month without sending over a single bomber. Nearly one Briton in five, according to a Gallup poll, had been involved in a blackout-related accident by the end of December.

The government had ordered curbs, sharp corners, lampposts, steps, and the running boards of cars painted white, while tree trunks were adorned with three white rings of paint. But even with all the precautions, people by the thousands continued to fall off or stumble into these obstacles in the unfamiliar, threatening darkness. "Coming out into the blackout is like falling into an inky well," *The New Yorker*'s Mollie Panter-Downes observed. The writer George Beardmore was reminded of the plague years as he walked home every night in the Stygian dark. "All the streets were deserted as though plague had struck and the death cart had made its daily collection. No children at play, no loungers up against the lamp posts, no sound . . . It all seems very humiliating, this cowering down in expectation of death falling from the heavens."

Critics of the blackout argued that it was causing great loss of life, a reduction in work productivity, and a decline in public morale without providing any benefits. For example, they said, German bombers didn't need the lights of London to pinpoint the city, since the Thames, which bisected London, shone like a silver ribbon at night from the air. (After the war a German pilot agreed that the blackout had been an ineffective method of protection: "Neither a single light, nor a group of lights, was of any help in navigating a plane if there was nothing else to be seen. In any event, London's approximate position was easily detected, even from very far away, owing to the concentration of searchlights.")

One of the blackout's sharpest critics was Winston Churchill, who repeatedly urged the cabinet to ease the lighting restrictions. The government finally made a few concessions. By the end of the year dim street lighting was restored at certain intersections and road crossings, shops and hotels were permitted to have faintly lit OPEN and ENTRANCE signs, and pedestrians were allowed to carry pocket flashlights, to be turned off during air raids. But venturing out on the streets of London and other major cities at night remained a dangerous proposition, not only because of the potential for accidents but also because of the threat of rapes and muggings.

As a result, most Britons stayed inside during the long winter nights, having performed the irksome, time-consuming daily duty of blacking out their windows with heavy dark curtains or some other covering. Those too poor to afford material for curtains often painted their windows black. However they were shrouded, the windows didn't allow even a breath of fresh air to enter, making for gloomy, stuffy homebound evenings. "The black curtains over the windows weighed you down, they oppressed you," Ben Robertson, an American war correspondent, remarked. "I had never realized what light and air meant to a room." Janet Murrow, the wife of the CBS correspondent Edward R. Murrow, recalled that the air in their London flat became so noxious from the smoke of her husband's cigarettes that she could barely stand it.

"There's no place like home," declared the lyrics of a popular song, "but we see too much of it now."

On New Year's Eve 1939, Ed Murrow gave American radio listeners his assessment of how Britain had fared in the first four months of supposed war:

> Homes have been broken up by evacuation . . . Many businesses have been ruined. Prices continue to rise. There are no bright lights this year, and there will be no sirens or horns sounded at midnight tonight, lest they be confused with air raid warnings . . . When war came last September, there was almost a sense of relief. The suspense of waiting was ended, but the waiting hasn't ended. The uncertainty remains, plus a large degree of boredom.

Murrow was understating the popular mood. By the New Year many, if not most, British citizens were fed up with this so-called conflict. Their lives had been seriously disrupted—and for what? What was the point? How were these upheavals and deprivations helping win a war that wasn't even being fought? At the beginning they had accepted the fact that they might soon be dead, but they never realized that war could be so *trivial*.

In this struggle there was no glamour or excitement to relieve the tedium and offset the "intolerable annoyances," no bands, flags, patriotic rallies, or crowds cheering columns of marching men. In their place were "sandbags and khaki and air raid shelters and gas masks, and the cultivated careful voice of the BBC putting the best complexion on the news." To many people, Mollie Panter-Downes wrote, the war was nothing but a "tiresome chore."

Londoners were "waiting, always waiting," complained a young actress named Theodora FitzGibbon. "Waiting for news, for buses, for trains. Waiting for bombs that never fell . . . Worst of all, waiting in queues: for food, for forms to be filled in, for things that would never happen. The misery of doing nothing, waiting to be told what to do." A man in a North London pub asked: "Why don't they begin fighting? Is it a war, or isn't it? Everyone's losing heart."

The general depression extended even to everyday social intercourse. "Something is happening to conversation in London," Murrow told his CBS listeners. "There isn't much of it . . . Nothing seems important, not even the weather. Wit, happiness, manners, and conversation sink gradually. Conversation is about to become a casualty." To Charles Ritchie, London was a "waste of dull desolation"; in the view of Sir Robert Bruce Lockhart, a writer and veteran diplomat, the capital was suffering from "gangrene of the soul." As a newcomer to Britain, Leland Stowe of the *Chicago Daily News* was astonished at the country's continued listlessness in the face of what he saw as the certainty of an eventual German attack. "The outlook was far more black and discouraging than any of us newspapermen could hope to report or permit ourselves to say . . ." he wrote. "How could synthetic leadership produce anything but a synthetic war? Couldn't the British people see?" In November, "filled with forebodings, impatience and mounting wrath," Stowe wrote in his diary: "More and more I think the British national symbol should be a tortoise or an ostrich instead of a lion."

In early 1940 Sir John Reith, now head of the newly formed Ministry of Information, reported to Neville Chamberlain that a "passive, negative feeling of apathy and boredom" was rife in the country. "There is a general feeling," said Reith, "that individuals do not count in the conduct of the war." The morale of Britain was "much lower than anybody . . . ever dared to say," added Kenneth Clark, who worked in Reith's ministry during the war's early days. "But there was obviously nothing that we could do about it, except to hope that, by some miracle, we could win a few battles."

It was one of the ironies of the phony war that the Ministry of Information, whose job it was to promote and sustain civilian morale, only succeeded in making it worse. Housed in the University of London's high-rise campus in Bloomsbury, the new ministry quickly ballooned into a bloated, unwieldy bureaucracy, "a monster . . . so large, so voluminous, so amorphous, that no single man could cope with it," recalled Duff Cooper, who knew about such things, since in May 1940 he became the MoI's third director in less than a year. The hiring of the ministry's huge staff was done willy-nilly, largely through the Oxbridge social network. Dozens of people were hired from academia and the cultural and art worlds—museum curators, historians, writers, artists, philosophers, anthropologists, film producers—all of them eminently successful in their fields but most without any expertise in propaganda, the press, or popular psychology. Kenneth Clark, with nothing much to do at the National Gallery, was put in charge of the MoI's film division, despite the fact that "I had no qualifications for the job, knew absolutely nothing about the structure of the film world, and was not even aware of the difference between producers, distributors, and exhibitors." He finally concluded that his "inexplicable" appointment was due to the fact that in those days films were often referred to as pictures, and as head of Britain's leading art museum he was considered somewhat of a picture authority.

In their brainstorming for ways to bolster public morale, MoI staffers produced some endearingly simple suggestions. On the day of Germany's invasion of Poland, the ministry's Home Publicity Division met to discuss actions that could be taken to counter public panic in the event of air raids. One of the group's members, a Lady Grigg, said that "the most comforting thing—at least where women were concerned—was to have a cup of tea and get together to talk things over." According to the minutes of the meeting, "This was agreed to be a most valuable suggestion and ways for carrying it into effect . . . were considered. It was decided that . . . an appeal should be made to householders to supply tea to anyone in their neighbourhood who needed it during or after an air raid."

While a cup of tea might seem an inadequate response to widespread panic and terror, the idea, at least, was a practical one, meant to offer comfort during a time of trouble. More often, however, the proposals for bolstering public morale that came from the ministry were supercilious and condescending, devised by Eton and Oxford men with no knowledge or understanding of the British public for which they were supposed to be working. A group of MPs and other outsiders, asked to advise the MoI on public morale, declared that the public "was all right and was likely to remain so, and that the one thing that really annoyed it was to feel that it was being kept needlessly in the dark and treated as a child."

The following doggerel, appearing on a government poster urging good behavior in the blackout, shows that the outsiders' advice was not taken:

> Billy Brown's own highway Code
> For blackouts is "Stay off the Road,"
> He'll never step out and begin
> To meet a bus that's pulling in.
> He doesn't wave his torch at night,
> But "flags" his bus with something white.
> He never jostles in a queue,
> But waits and takes his turn. Do you?

Another early government poster, aimed at providing reassurance and inspiration to the British people, was greeted with a torrent of criticism. On a bright red background, with a crown at its top, the poster declared: "YOUR courage, YOUR determination, YOUR resolution will bring us victory." Its creator regarded it as "a rallying war-cry that will . . . put us in an offensive mood at once." The public found it offensive, all right, noting the contrast between "your" and "us" and reading into the message the implication that "resolve on the part of the lower classes will bring victory to the privileged few." The poster was eventually withdrawn, but many other exhortatory messages from the government, featuring characters just as irritating as Billy Brown ("Miss Leaky Mouth," "Miss Teacup Whisper," and "Mr. Glumpot" were a few choice examples), were mounted in railway stations, shops, pubs, factories, libraries, and buses in the months to come. Every day the British people were faced with admonitions like these: "Freedom Is in Peril—Defend It With All Your Might," "We're Going to See It Through," "It All Depends on Me," and "Don't Help the Enemy—Careless Talk Might Give Away Vital Secrets."

Most Britons ignored the posters, just as they disregarded the endless government leaflets they received in the mail ordering them, among other things, to tape their windows, refrain from lighting a cigarette on the street at night, and desist from spitting. "Officialdom run amok," was the disgusted verdict of *Picture Post*. The *Evening Standard* declared: "We are not fighting the big Hitler on the Rhine only to set up little Hitlers here." Charles Ritchie mused: "Living in London is like being an inmate of a reformatory school. Everywhere you turn, you run into some regulation designed for your own protection. The Government is like the School Matron with her keys jangling at her waist . . . Nothing but acute physical danger can make such a regime bearable."

But there apparently was no acute danger, and the public was tired of pretending as if there were. Few British citizens now followed government orders to carry gas masks with them at all times. Nor did they take part in shelter drills. They turned deaf ears to the orders of air-raid wardens, who were viewed as the embodiment of an interfering and incompetent government, busybodies wearing ridiculous tin hats who harassed people about gas masks and the blackout.

In the late fall of 1939 Violet Bonham Carter wrote to her sister-in-law: "I think the public will get demoralized unless something is done soon to make an appeal to their courage & imagination . . . There is no light— no [social] intercourse—no food for the mind and spirit—above all no *news*!" For Lady Violet, as for a number of other Britons, the worst thing about the phony war was not the blackout or the food rationing or the patronizing government regulations. It was the lack of knowledge about what was going on. In the name of national security, the government had imposed a suffocating censorship on all information about the war, resulting in an almost total absence of news about how it was being waged. Even nonmilitary news was quashed; the press, for example, was barred from running stories about the intense winter cold spell for fear of giving away too much weather information to the enemy. Once again the Ministry of Information was blamed for the problem. It was, after all, in charge of releasing government information. But in this case, the hapless MoI, widely regarded as "the gang that couldn't shoot straight," was innocent, at least where military news was concerned.

The armed services were reluctant to part with any war-related information, and the MoI had no power to force them to release information that they wanted to keep secret. The Royal Navy, under Winston Churchill, was the worst offender. "If the Admiralty could have had their way, they would prefer a policy of complete silence," Churchill later wrote. Since that was not a realistic option, his fallback position was that any naval news of importance or interest could be announced only by him. Although, as first lord and later as prime minister, Churchill rallied the British public as few British leaders have ever done, he shared the mentality of the British services that "a civilian's job was to ask no questions, to pay his taxes in order to keep up the Armed Forces, to take off his hat when the Colours marched past . . ."

British and American journalists were barred from covering the BEF in France until more than a month after the war had begun. When a small group of correspondents was finally allowed to visit the nonexistent front, their reporting was generally confined by the government to briefings by press officers "filling us with stories of how good the morale . . . was and how the British and French armies could stand up to any attack." The Royal Air Force was even more restrictive, banning correspondents from all its stations and prohibiting them from talking to pilots or ground crews. None of the services allowed news photographers to take pictures of their forces.

When the American correspondent John Gunther asked a military censor for the text of a leaflet that had been dropped over Germany shortly after the invasion of Poland, he was turned down with this explanation: "We are not allowed to disclose information which might be of value to the enemy." Struggling to keep his temper, Gunther pointed out that the enemy had already seen the leaflet. Wasn't that its point? The official blinked, then stammered, "Yes, something must be wrong there."

Reporters tried to get around the military secrecy by obtaining information from other sources. But when they did so, their stories were often quashed, even when they carried no security risk. Both British and foreign correspondents were outraged by what they considered this "petty, absurd, tyrannical" censorship. *Picture Post* showed its frustration by running a large photo of a sign reading: "KEEP OUT! This is a private war. The War Office, the Admiralty, the Air Ministry and the Ministry of Information are engaged in a war against the Nazis. They are on no account to be disturbed. Nothing is to be photographed. No one is to come near." *Picture Post* had begun the war, its editors declared, with "high hopes, because we felt we had a job to do . . . We felt we could show

the British people what their fighting forces were doing, and show the
world how Britain was reacting to the war. For a few weeks we knew there
would be confusion. But now—two months after the war began—we get
twenty pictures showing the German side of the war for every one showing the British. Is this war? Is this democracy? Is this common sense?"

There was no doubt that Germany, as *Picture Post* indicated, was
winning the battle of propaganda as handily as it had defeated Poland.
While its sophisticated publicity machine, set up by Joseph Goebbels,
churned out dramatic photos and newsreel footage of the German triumph in Poland, cinema audiences in Britain continued to be treated
to hackneyed newsreel shots of "gold keys and cut ribbons and beauty
queens," the novelist Graham Greene wrote in *The Spectator*. To show
there was a war on, the royal family occasionally was seen on the screen
"inspecting something or other," accompanied by the announcer's invari-
able comment that "the Queen has never looked prettier." In the view of
The New York Times, "the British, with the best case in the world, are pre-
senting it far less ably than the Germans, with the worst." Exasperated
by British and French censorship, journalists from the United States and
other neutral countries made their way to Berlin for war news. As a result, newspapers and magazines in the United States and elsewhere
were filled with stories that reflected Germany's viewpoint on the war.

Thanks to a stream of English-language radio programs transmitted
from Germany, Nazi propagandists were able to score points in Britain
as well. So desperate was the British public for news that millions of
people frequently tuned in to German stations. Indeed, according to a
nationwide poll, more than six million Britons, nearly 20 percent of the
population, listened regularly to the most popular Nazi propagandist,
Lord Haw Haw, the nom de plume of William Joyce, a renegade Irishman who broadcast from Berlin. "We nearly always turn him on at 9:15
to try and glean some news that the Ministry of Information withholds
from us," one man told a representative from Mass Observation, a private social research group. "The effect of Haw Haw is considered to be
extremely insidious," an MoI report warned, "and this danger is under-
estimated by the BBC and the Government, who do not fully appreciate to what extent this propaganda is believed."

In early 1940 Sir Richard Acland, a Liberal MP, summed up what he believed to be the feelings of the average British citizen about the war: "We are told nothing. We know nothing. Nobody seems to want us, and we hope that [the government] will soon finish with it." As the phony war dragged on, apathy, cynicism, frustration with the government, and fear over the country's military weaknesses began to eat away many people's resolve. In the words of Harold Macmillan, there was "a smell of peace in the air."

Although a distinct minority, advocates of a negotiated settlement with Hitler, particularly members of the British upper class who had long been pro-German, became increasingly vocal. The Duke of Buccleuch told Lord Dunglass, Chamberlain's PPS, that Britain would have to make peace with Germany sooner or later. Why not do it now when "comparatively little damage has been done and when there is still time to avert economic ruin"? The Duke of Westminster declared that the war was part of a Jewish and Masonic plot to destroy Christian civilization and should be ended, a remark that roused the ire of his friend Winston Churchill, who warned him against "preach[ing] defeatism." Lord Beaverbrook urged the Duke of Windsor to head a peace drive in Britain and promised him the support of his papers. The Duke of Bedford meanwhile was conducting his own personal peace mission, traveling to neutral Ireland to offer initiatives for a settlement to German diplomats in Dublin.

Even the king was "a little *défaitiste*," according to Alexander Cadogan, who visited George VI shortly after war was declared. Cadogan thought the king's depression over the war stemmed from a conversation with Ambassador Joseph P. Kennedy, who insisted that Britain could not hold out against a militarily superior Germany and that the British should come to terms while they still could.

Right-wing aristocrats weren't the only ones urging the end of the war. In the late fall of 1939 a group of Labour MPs signed a statement calling for an international conference to negotiate an armistice as soon as possible, and several trade unions passed antiwar resolutions. In an article in the left-wing *New Statesman*, George Bernard Shaw demanded that Britain make peace with Hitler "instead of making more mischief and ruining our people in the process."

The most prominent left-wing peace advocate, however, was none other than the man who had presided over Britain's victory in 1918. On October 3, 1939, former prime minister David Lloyd George rose in the House of Commons to urge peace negotiations with Hitler. His proposal was greeted in the chamber with shocked murmurs and angry mutters. Red-faced with anger, Duff Cooper shot up from his seat and accused Lloyd George of preaching surrender. He had just handed Germany an enormous propaganda coup, Cooper declared; the Nazis could now say that the man who won the last war was already conceding defeat in this one. In a later conversation with a newspaper editor, Lloyd George gave this reply to Cooper and his other critics: "People call me a defeatist. But what I say to them is: 'Tell me how we can win.'" He noted that the country had no army worthy of the name, adding that if Britain continued to be apathetic about the war, it was heading for certain defeat.

Three days after Lloyd George's speech in the House of Commons, Hitler appeared before the Reichstag to make his own call for peace, basically offering to end the war if France and Britain ceded to Germany the right to control Eastern Europe and also agreed to the restoration of Germany's former colonies in Africa. Chamberlain rejected Hitler's proposals, but in private, he and his government were still chasing the will-o'-the-wisp of a possible peace settlement, just as they had done before the war began.

Still determined not to anger the Germans, British officials urged the BBC and the print media not to broadcast or print reports of the widespread Nazi killings of Jews and other citizens of the countries now under German control. "We have abundant evidence of atrocities in Poland and in Germany itself," Harold Nicolson wrote in his diary. "Appalling assassinations have taken place in both countries, but the Ministry [of Information] will not allow [the news] to be released for fear that an atrocities campaign will antagonize German opinion. I am beginning to believe that . . . we really are playing for an arranged peace." Adding fuel to that suspicion was the revelation that the Foreign Office had encouraged the *New Statesman* to print George Bernard Shaw's demands for peace. The playwright said he was not surprised: "I was sure they would rise up and call me blessed for saying what they wanted to say, but dared not."

For his part, Chamberlain insisted that Hitler would have to be deposed before peace could be considered ("an element of damaged vanity" over being duped by the führer was the basis for this demand, thought John Colville). But the prime minister and Lord Halifax were willing to consider the possibility of dealing with a German government that did not include Hitler in a position of power. Declaring that "we should not absolutely shut the door," Halifax told the War Cabinet in early November about government discussions with a Swedish businessman purportedly acting as intermediary to Hermann Göring, Hitler's deputy, who was being touted as a possible successor to the German leader. According to Halifax, the Foreign Office told the Swede that Britain would never come to terms with a new German government "unless Hitler ceased to hold a position where he could influence the course of events." Alarmed by *any* talk of negotiations with Germany, Churchill privately warned Halifax that such a message would be interpreted as meaning "we are prepared to accept a Government in Germany which reserved a ceremonial and honorable position for Hitler, which would be contrary to the whole basis of our public declarations." He added: "There is great danger in these secret communications. If, for instance, you said anything like what you suggested, the Germans could use it to undermine French confidence in us with possibly fatal effects."

Nonetheless, the British government continued its pursuit of a way to end the war that would not involve fighting. With the backing of Whitehall and Downing Street, two British intelligence operatives met in Holland with several dissident German generals to discuss the possibility of getting rid of Hitler and of Britain's coming to terms with a government headed by Göring. Unfortunately, the dissident generals turned out to be Nazi double agents, who lured the British operatives into a trap, then whisked them off to prison in Germany.

Of course the idea of a new German government was a chimera. Hitler was in full control. And unlike his Western foes, he was *entirely* focused on the waging of war. While Britain and France limped toward rearmament, Germany had taken full advantage of the lull provided by the phony war. German munitions factories, untouched by British bombs, were operating at full capacity, as was Czechoslovakia's Skoda works, second only to Germany's Krupp plant in size. Although Britain was now turning out new Hurricane and Spitfire fighter planes, which were soon to prove crucial in the Battle of Britain, German airplane production continued to outpace that of the Allies. Planes, tanks, and weapons were pouring off German assembly lines; in addition, Germany had in its possession, thanks to its seizure of Czechoslovakia, more than 1,500 Czech planes, 500 antiaircraft guns, 450 tanks, 43,000 machine guns, 1 million rifles, and more than $29 million worth of Czech gold, to help pay for Germany's explosive military growth.

In April 1940 an Allied strategic study noted the favorable position in which Germany found itself as a result of Britain and France's military inactivity: "The Reich appears to have suffered relatively little wear and tear during the first six months of war, and that mainly as the result of the allied blockade. Meanwhile, it has profited from the interval to perfect the degree of equipment of its land and air forces, to increase the officer strength and complete the training of its troops, and to add further divisions to those already in the field."

Less than a month into the phony war, having seen his peace offer rebuffed, Hitler was plotting his next blitzkrieg. He told his generals of plans for a sweep through Western Europe, followed by an air and sea war against Britain. The Western Allies would be forced into a shooting war, whether they liked it or not. "We must get at them," declared Hitler, "as soon as possible."

In late November, Harold Nicolson, at home at Sissinghurst, looked out the window at "a windy night with a scudding moon." His thoughts were as unsettled as the weather: "I think of . . . all those devils in Germany and Rome plotting, plotting, plotting our destruction in the spring."

CHAPTER FIFTEEN

"HE IS ABSOLUTELY LOYAL"

Three weeks after the war began, Ronald Cartland entered the House of Commons and quietly took his usual seat. He had not attended a Commons debate since the day Germany invaded Poland. It felt strange to him to be back in the chamber—almost as if he didn't belong there anymore.

Caught up in preparing for the combat he was sure was coming, Cartland had just finished an army small-arms course in Kent, not far from the English Channel. He had thrown himself into the training with his usual intensity, breaking away only once, when he and a fellow Territorial officer stayed for a weekend at Bob Boothby's rented country house just a few miles from their camp. Boothby and the two young officers spent one long, lazy afternoon picnicking in a nearby meadow. The weather was beautiful, the game pie delicious, the burgundy plentiful, and the conversation sparkling. Both Boothby and Cartland were noted for their wit, and that afternoon they bantered back and forth for hours. "For that brief moment of time, we cast all cares aside," Boothby wrote years later, recalling the afternoon as one of "good companionship and unalloyed happiness." Underlying the fun, however, was "a sense of impending disaster." There was, concluded Boothby, "a touch of desperation in our gaiety."

For Cartland, returning to London and the House of Commons on a few days' leave only accentuated his feeling of looming catastrophe.

Just days before, he'd been learning the most effective ways to kill the enemy. Now he was back with people who seemed to think there was no enemy at all. The war could not be wished away, he told his sister. It was coming. Hitler currently was biding his time, but when he struck, "there will be destruction such as we have never dreamt of. England has got to wake up—or be annihilated."

This war, he knew, would be like no other in history. This one would involve not just sailors, pilots, and soldiers on distant battlefields; it would sweep over the entire nation. Like it or not, everyone would be on the front lines. If Britain was to have any chance of winning, its citizens must be roused from their lassitude and mobilized for the conflict ahead. But how were they to be awakened if their leaders were even more lethargic than they?

One night during his leave, Cartland dined with Harold Nicolson and several other parliamentary colleagues. All were struck by how "extremely pessimistic" their normally buoyant friend seemed. Cartland told them that Neville Chamberlain and David Margesson should be "hung upon lampposts" and that "we are frightfully short of ammunition in every branch, that we have, in fact, no Army, Navy or Air Force."

Now, from his seat on a second-row bench, Cartland watched as Chamberlain stood to deliver his weekly address on the progress of the war. As the prime minister launched into a dry recitation of the latest facts and figures, Harold Nicolson, sitting a few feet from Cartland, felt "the confidence and spirits of the House dropping inch by inch." Like all of Chamberlain's weekly statements, this one was "dull as ditchwater"; Chamberlain himself might have been "the secretary of a firm of undertakers reading the minutes of the last meeting." Nicolson clearly was prepared to think the worst of the prime minister, but in this case, his views were shared by a number of Chamberlain loyalists. "The PM is costive and dull and talks of endurance and victory in the most defeatist tones," noted Thomas Jones, a former deputy secretary to the cabinet, who watched Chamberlain's speech from the gallery. More than a few MPs had fallen asleep. When the prime minister finally finished, only scattered, faint cheers were heard.

Then Winston Churchill rose. He strode to the dispatch box, placed his notes on it, and began his first report to the House on the war at sea. Thumbs in his waistcoat, he talked of the Royal Navy's successes in setting up the convoy system, its triumphs in destroying German submarines, the steady reduction of British merchant shipping losses. Such upbeat news should not spawn complacency, he warned: "One must not dwell upon these reassuring figures too much, for war is full of unpleasant surprises."

The contents of the speech were not particularly memorable, at least by Churchillian standards. There was none of the inspired rhetoric for which he was celebrated. Yet no one was napping now. Throughout the chamber, members and visitors listened intently, many leaning forward, trying to catch every phrase. As Churchill spoke, Nicolson "could feel the spirits of the House rising with every word."

What roused the first lord's audience was not so much what he said but how he said it. His combative, determined manner, combining candor, wit, and confidence, "carried the exhilaration of a spring morning walk along the cliffs," in the words of one observer. Full of gusto, he conveyed a sense of Elizabethan high adventure in relating the navy's exploits, so different from the torpid style of Chamberlain and the other ministers. When he finished, members on both sides of the chamber jumped to their feet with shouts and cheers. Among them was Cartland, whose spirits had suddenly improved. "Winston smashed and confounded the critics who had been whispering that the years had taken their toll," he wrote to his sister. "He revealed to a delighted House all the weapons of Leadership that his armoury contains. I know that the Nation will never let him go now . . ." The day after Churchill's speech the *Daily Telegraph* reported: "Few ministerial statements in recent years have evoked as much enthusiasm in the House as Mr. Churchill's . . . The First Lord stole the afternoon from the Prime Minister."

On October 1, in his first national radio broadcast as first lord, Churchill energized the country just as he had stirred the House a few days before. The Royal Navy was on the offensive, he declared; its ships were hunting German U-boats "night and day—I will not say without mercy, because God forbid we should ever part company with that—but at any rate with zeal and not altogether without relish." He savaged Hitler "and his group of wicked men, whose hands are stained with blood and soiled with corruption," and promised that Britain, as the "defenders of civilization and freedom," would fight to the end.

It was a virtuoso performance—and one that did not go unnoticed in Germany. "The local enthusiasm for peace [is] a little dampened today by Churchill's broadcast last night," William Shirer told CBS listeners from Berlin. Unlike Chamberlain, Churchill had fire in his belly. Instead of shrinking from combat, he seemed eager for more. In this speech, as in later broadcasts to the nation, the first lord "clothed in living language the realities of this war," said Kingsley Martin, editor of *The New Statesman*. In one address, Churchill talked with contempt of the "Nazi gangsters" and described how they were now feeling "the long arm of British sea power on their shoulders." In another, he proclaimed that Britain was ready to "endure the worst malice of Hitler and his Huns." Full of defiance and hope, he was, as the *New Statesman* editor noted, a welcome tonic for a doubting, fearful nation. "We have talked and theorized and argued and hesitated," Martin wrote. "We have . . . seen our own faults, been inhibited by our scruples . . . In Mr. Churchill, we have seen a man of action, who sweeps all this aside and reminds us that, whatever else we are or think we are, we were born and bred British, and British we must now live or die."

Even when he reported on naval setbacks and losses, as he did not infrequently, Churchill managed to invest his account of bad news with an unquenchable feeling of optimism. After relating to the House the sorry story of the sinking of the *Royal Oak*, he warned that "continual losses must be expected. No immunity can be guaranteed at any time . . . We shall suffer and we shall suffer continually . . ." Yet, he added, "I feel no doubt that in the end we shall break their hearts."

At the same time, when there was good news, he exploited it for all it was worth. When the German pocket battleship *Graf Spee* was scuttled by its crew in December 1939 after being damaged by three British cruisers, the first lord ordered the ships' crews home and staged a great public celebration in honor of the country's new heroes. He was determined to bolster British morale, and he would do whatever it took to achieve that goal, even playing tricks with the truth. Within the Admiralty, for example, it was well known that his announcements to the House of German ship and submarine losses were often greatly exaggerated. When the director of antisubmarine warfare raised questions about the figures, Churchill told him: "There are two people who sink U-boats in this war, Talbot. You sink them in the Atlantic, and I sink them in the House of Commons. The trouble is that you are sinking them at exactly half the rate I am."

Whatever his methods, Churchill succeeded in his goal—and more. He not only boosted his countrymen's spirits but gave them a better understanding of why this war was being fought. In doing so, he became the most popular public figure in the nation. Throughout the phony war, movie audiences applauded enthusiastically whenever he appeared in newsreels, while appearances by Chamberlain and most of the other cabinet ministers were usually greeted with silence. After each of his radio broadcasts, attendance at theaters in London's West End rose dramatically. Theater managers concluded that Churchill's vitality had rubbed off on the playgoers, had made them decide to get out of their black-curtained flats and houses for an evening. "How we look forward to the Churchill broadcasts," George Beardmore wrote in his diary. "Everyone adores him."

Well, not quite everyone. Certainly not Chamberlain, Halifax, and most of the rest of the cabinet, who thought Churchill was trying to overshadow the prime minister and put himself in charge of the war. "[E]veryone was very conscious that he was regarded by his colleagues as trying to take the war over," an Admiralty official recalled. "They were pretty sensitive about that." The truth was, Churchill was temperamentally unable to focus only on running his own ministry, vital a task as that was. As first lord of the admiralty in the early months of World War II, he behaved much as he had as first lord in World War I, regarding every aspect of the war as his rightful concern and firing off a seemingly endless volley of questions and opinions to Chamberlain and other members of the cabinet. Trying to infect his colleagues with the same urgency he felt, he repeatedly expressed his anxiety about the shortage of planes and tanks, the delay in bringing the army up to full strength, and, above all, the failure to take any major offensive action against the enemy. "Do you realize that perhaps we are heading for *defeat*?" he wrote to one top-ranking admiral.

Not surprisingly, most of Churchill's fellow ministers reacted to his interference with irritation and dismay. After a broadcast in which Churchill chastised neutral countries in Europe for not having the courage to stand up to Hitler, a greatly annoyed Halifax wrote to him: "Would you think it unreasonable of me to ask that in future, if you are going to speak with particular reference to Foreign policy, you might let me see in advance what you had it in mind to say?"

Yet it was impossible for Churchill to remain silent, not when, in his view, the fate of Britain and the rest of Europe was at stake. On January 27, 1940, in Manchester, he gave what was arguably his most compelling speech of the phony war. Urging the mobilization of the entire nation, he called on his countrymen to throw themselves into the war effort with all their might. All of Britain's labor force must be harnessed for war, he said; trade unions and industry must cooperate in this vital enterprise. At the end of the address, which was broadcast throughout the country, he made one final appeal: "Come then: let us to the task, to the battle, to the toil—each to our part, each to our station. Fill the armies, rule the air, pour out the munitions, strangle the U boats, sweep the mines, plough the land, build the ships, guard the streets, succour the wounded, uplift the downcast, and honour the brave. Let us go forward together in all parts of the Empire, in all parts of the island. There is not a week, nor a day, nor an hour to lose."

This powerful rallying cry roused and thrilled his audience. It was also the kind of speech, many people thought, that should have been given long ago by the prime minister. If it did nothing else, Churchill's Manchester address added impetus to the feeling in some London political circles that Chamberlain must go and the first lord must take his place. Cartland, Boothby, Macmillan, Law, and others had pushed the idea for months. But now even some supporters of Chamberlain were thinking what previously had been unthinkable. Following one of Churchill's speeches in the House, "even Chamberlainites were saying, 'We have now found our leader,'" Nicolson wrote. After listening to a Churchill broadcast, John Colville concluded that the first lord would be prime minister before the war was over, although he was not necessarily happy about it: "[j]udging from his record of untrustworthiness and instability, he may, in that case, lead us into the most dangerous paths."

In London there was growing talk of Churchill's leading a palace coup, of taking advantage of his popularity with the people to mount a revolt and bring down Chamberlain and his government. The talk had no substance. Throughout the phony war Churchill made it clear that he would not participate in any plot to oust Chamberlain, just as he had refused to do so the day before war was declared. Despite his conviction that the country was in great danger and despite his frustration over the government's inertia, he would do nothing to sabotage the prime minister. Boothby, who knew Churchill better than most of the Tory rebels, wrote during this time: "Contrary to the general view, Churchill makes a fetish of personal loyalty . . . Those who are building their hopes on the advent to power of a genuine national government under Churchill are, I think, under a delusion. He will take no action to displace the man who at the twelfth hour gave him his confidence, and put him at the head of a department which absorbs his interests and energies."

As Boothby observed, after so many years in the political wilderness, Churchill now was in his element, his attention focused on running the navy and having a say in directing the war. Despite all his anxieties, he was "buoyant, for he was where he loved best to be—in action and fully extended," said Violet Bonham Carter. In one of his early books Churchill had written about some decision he had made: "I acted in accordance with my feelings, without troubling to square such conduct with the conclusions of thought." Lady Violet considered such words "profoundly self-revealing." Churchill, she said, had a habit of thinking with his heart. In this case, his emotions—gratitude to the prime minister for restoring him to the center of the action—took precedence over his concern that Britain under Chamberlain might be heading for defeat.

Indeed, during the phony war Churchill made no public criticism of the government's policies, even when the Tory whips and other Chamberlain supporters spread rumors designed to undermine him. In his diary Edward Spears noted some of the "whispers" about Churchill that he had heard in the House smoking room and lobbies: "He is tired, not well, feeling his age." Such innuendo, however, had no effect on Churchill's loyalty to the prime minister. Responding to a complaint by Hugh Dalton about Britain's failure to wage real war against Germany, he said that if he were not in the cabinet, he would have "much to say" about the subject, but "I have signed on for this voyage and so I cannot use such arguments now."

In fact, there were times when Churchill became one of Chamberlain's most forceful defenders. When Lady Violet visited him at the Admiralty and talked about "the old appeasers" in the government, Churchill launched into a spirited justification of the prime minister, declaring, "No man is more inflexible, more single-minded. He has a will of steel." (Lady Violet refrained from pointing out that perhaps Chamberlain was using those qualities in pursuit of the wrong goals.) When one of Churchill's children made a joking comment about Chamberlain at lunch one day, he scowled at the offender and barked: "If you are going to make offensive remarks about my chief, you will have to leave the table. We are united in a great and common cause, and I am not prepared to tolerate such language about the Prime Minister."

Arguments by Churchill's supporters that such loyalty, while admirable, was profoundly misplaced, that the survival of the country was more important than the survival of the Chamberlain government, went nowhere. Brendan Bracken was particularly passionate on this score, declaring that "things were rotten and they were getting worse. We were not winning this war, we were on the way to losing it." He argued vehemently with his boss that he was carrying loyalty to absurd lengths. Churchill told him to mind his own business.

Chamberlain meanwhile continued to pursue the nonconfrontational course he had set for the war, confident that he would meet no public opposition from Churchill. "Winston, in spite of his violence and impulsiveness, is very responsive to a sympathetic handling," he wrote his sister. "To me personally he is absolutely loyal and I am continually hearing from others of the admiration he expresses for the PM."

And what of the rebels' other alternative to Chamberlain? What of Anthony Eden, the onetime shining hope of the Tory dissidents and much of the nation? Thanks to his caution and vacillation in the previous two years, Eden was out of action, a virtual nonentity in the government, stuck away in the Dominions Office. For a former foreign secretary, this new job, which did not include membership in the War Cabinet, was a humiliating comedown. Increasingly frustrated and impatient, he attended most War Cabinet meetings, but only as a spectator. "His restless energy could not be tamed to endure the futile inactivity of this strange period," recalled one of Eden's subordinates. "He gave an impression of superficiality, with no profound interest in the problems of the Commonwealth."

After interviewing Eden in March 1940, Cecil King, publisher of the *Daily Mirror*, one of the few newspapers to oppose openly Chamberlain's conduct of the war, described the dominions secretary in his diary as "most charming, most intelligent, but as a future leader, quite pathetic." Eden "has no independent point of view and clearly no intention of upsetting the existing political status quo; is in fact a very small straw on the current of events . . ." King wrote. "Really, as I walked down Whitehall after leaving him, I was nearly in tears."

By early 1940, when Leo Amery and most of the Tory dissidents in his group had decided that Chamberlain must go, as had Clement Davies's and Bob Boothby's Vigilante group, the challenge remained: how to loosen the prime minister's control of the House and convince the Tory majority he had to be toppled. The obstacles seemed no less formidable than before, despite the growing public dissatisfaction with Chamberlain's leadership. Walter Bagehot, the noted British constitutional scholar, once wrote that such public disaffection should logically lead to a change of government: "The distinguishing quality of Parliamentary Government . . . is that, in each stage of a public transaction, there is a discussion; that the public assists at this discussion; that it can, through Parliament, turn out an administration which is not doing as it likes and can put in an administration which will do what it likes." But Chamberlain had turned such constitutional theories on their ear. With his massive majority in the House, he believed he could safely ignore public opinion, while David Margesson and his deputies did their best to extinguish dissent in the Commons. "Everything is done to suppress independence of judgment, wherever it may show its hideous head," Dick Law sardonically observed.

Support for Chamberlain was equated with supporting the troops and the country in a time of war. Even newspapers like *The Daily Telegraph*, highly critical of the government shortly before the war began, were calling for national unity and declaring that MPs must not express opinions that might endanger the government's survival. Lord Camrose, the *Telegraph*'s owner, told a friend he had nothing good to say about any government minister, but he believed it was wrong to say anything to damage the government at this time of crisis and especially did "not want to say anything against the Prime Minister." In the minds of some, the idea of overthrowing a government during wartime was nothing less than treason.

Leland Stowe, like a number of other American correspondents in London, did not understand that mentality. He could not comprehend why anti-Chamberlain MPs were so hesitant. "Why don't you get rid of Chamberlain, Wilson, Hoare and the rest of the appeasers right away?" Stowe demanded of a young Tory rebel. "How can you trust people like that to win the war for you?" The MP shook his head. It didn't work that way in British politics, he said. It was impossible to do anything right now. Not only was the Tory majority too large, but the dissidents weren't even sure that the Labour Party would join an attempt to topple Chamberlain. After flirting with the idea of a cross-party coalition, most of its parliamentary leaders had backed away from the notion. Indeed, it had recently expelled from party ranks a leading member, Sir Stafford Cripps, who had continued to insist on the need for a union of all antigovernment forces. "The only way [the government] can be ousted is on a big issue, with the whole nation aroused," the Tory MP told Stowe. An issue that would rally anti-Chamberlain sentiment in his own party as well as in the Opposition. One that could force a vote of confidence to bring the prime minister down.

On the afternoon of April 4, Leo Amery arrived at 21 Arlington Street, a stately mansion around the corner from the Ritz. He was shown into the drawing room, where the house's owner, Lord Salisbury, and some twenty other men, all Conservative members of the House of Commons or the House of Lords, were waiting. The seventy-eight-year-old marquess was immaculately dressed as usual. In public, he still wore a frock coat and top hat, one of the last figures in London society to do so. But Lord Salisbury was no anachronism of a more genteel, bygone age. Son of a prime minister, a former leader of the House of Lords, and the father of Bobbety Cranborne, he was head of the Cecil clan, and like most of the Cecils, he was known for his iron integrity and sense of honor. People still paid close attention to what he said. What he was saying now was that there must be radical changes in Neville Chamberlain's government, as well as a more confrontational approach toward the war. He had invited those in the room to join him in pressing the prime minister to adopt those goals.

Although Lord Salisbury was far less vocal than his son, he too had been a strong opponent of appeasement. He had spoken out against Munich, been an early advocate of conscription, and been as appalled by the government's inertia in fighting Germany as his son was. After the war began, he peppered Lord Halifax and other government officials with notes and memos urging a more vigorous prosecution of the conflict. His concerns about the government's sluggishness were hardly allayed by Chamberlain's actions in two war-related crises in the early months of 1940. The prime minister had long been urged to make changes in his cabinet to make it more offense-minded. But in January he did the opposite: he fired the war secretary, Leslie Hore-Belisha, second only to Churchill in his desire to take the battle to the enemy and in his popularity with the public.

In his three years at the War Office, Hore-Belisha had worked hard to modernize and enlarge the hidebound British Army, which for centuries had valued class over merit and the gentleman amateur over the professional warrior. The war secretary had sacked three top generals and replaced them with younger men. He raised the pay and allowances of regular soldiers, built them new barracks, and gave them an opportunity to become officers. (Previously, the army officer corps had come almost exclusively from the upper classes.) For more than a year before the war began, he had urged Chamberlain to introduce conscription.

Hore-Belisha's democratic reforms were popular with the public, but they were despised by the army brass, who considered him a pushy interloper and persuaded Chamberlain to get rid of him. There was a strong element of anti-Semitism in this animus toward the Jewish Hore-Belisha, who was called Horeb-Elisha behind his back. The war secretary's dismissal caused the biggest political furor thus far in the war, not a big enough crisis to prompt a vote of confidence but substantial enough to undermine further the government's standing with the British people.

It was damaged even more by Chamberlain's response to the Soviet invasion of Finland in November 1939 and that small country's heroic fight against its aggressors. In Britain, as in the United States, there were calls from the public and press to send Allied troops, planes, arms, and ammunition to help the Finns. In retrospect, the idea of dispatching British forces and matériel to Finland when there were not enough men, planes, and weapons for the front in France and the protection of Britain did not make good strategic sense. But in January, Chamberlain promised aid to the Finns, declaring that they "can rest assured our response will be no mere formality."

Facing overwhelming odds, Finland was forced to capitulate to the Soviets in early March. When Chamberlain told the Commons a few days later that the British government had assisted Finland in its losing fight and then ticked off a long list of arms and supplies that had been sent, Harold Macmillan jumped to his feet and in effect called the prime minister a liar. Macmillan, who had spent a week in Finland during its three-month resistance, said the Finns had told him that their requests for British aid had fallen "almost entirely at first on deaf ears, and were followed at last by materials which were sent always in too small quantities and always too late." He then read from a list of his own figures, given to him by Finnish officials, of the supplies and arms that they, in fact, had received. It did not tally with the prime minister's.

Since September 1939 Macmillan had made several speeches in the Commons attacking the government's conduct of the war. But none of his previous addresses possessed the power and impact of his remarks about Finland. It was one of those rare experiences, he wrote later, of "starting with a hostile audience and winning it over to my side." Even government supporters acknowledged that Macmillan's criticism had dealt a blow to Chamberlain. Dick Law, who made a speech of his own that day that came close to demanding the prime minister's resignation, wrote to a friend: "I still don't understand why Harold didn't bring down the government. Perhaps he has done so, and we shall become aware of it soon." But even if that proved not to be true, Law said, he was convinced "we ought to continue. The more we weaken the government, the more, I honestly believe, we strengthen England."

Macmillan and Law were two of the Conservative MPs present in Lord Salisbury's drawing room on April 4. Salisbury had invited them, Amery, and the others to join what he called the Watching Committee. The purpose of the committee, the marquess said, was to "watch the administration of the war . . . and harass ministers where they ought to be harassed."

More than half of this eclectic collection of Tory parliamentarians came from the House of Lords. There were the "good boys," as Amery called them, most of them pro-Chamberlain, who, while beginning to question the government's running of the war, were still generally supportive of the prime minister. Then there were the "bad boys," several of whom who had been stalwart foes of appeasement since before Munich: Amery, Macmillan, Law, Nicolson, Edward Spears, Duff Cooper, and Paul Emrys-Evans, who was appointed secretary of the new group. (Bobbety Cranborne was ill during this period and did not take an active part in the committee's activities.) The Watching Committee was hardly as radical as Amery's group or the Vigilantes. It was, as the name suggested, a watchdog organization, trying to spur Chamberlain to bring in more dynamic ministers and to become more combative toward Germany. Yet with its moderate tone and its membership list containing several pillars of the Conservative establishment, it made any criticism of Chamberlain more acceptable, just as it conferred a certain respectability on the activities of Amery and the other "bad boys."

In turn, Amery, who was named chairman of the group's military subcommittee, infected the Watching Committee with some of his own pugnacity. What's more, he emerged as the catalyst in what soon was to become a rebellion against Chamberlain, the "essential link," as the historian David Dutton has called him, between the various centers of opposition to the prime minister. Throughout April he spent much of his time going from one meeting to another of the Watching Committee, the Vigilantes, and his own group of Tory rebels.

The spirit of revolt was smoldering. Now all it needed was a "big issue" to force it into flame. Ironically, that issue was to come from Chamberlain's decision, at long last, to take offensive action against Germany. And Winston Churchill, albeit unknowingly, provided the spark.

———

On March 28, one week before the Watching Committee's first meeting, Chamberlain finally signed off on the plan that Churchill had advocated since the beginning of the war: stopping the shipment of iron ore from Sweden to Germany down the coast of Norway. For seven months the cabinet had argued over various permutations of this idea, including mining Norwegian waters, halting German ships, even taking control of the Swedish ore fields. In January it had come close to a decision, informing Norway and Sweden that Britain was considering taking military action to stop shipment of the ore. But when both countries vigorously protested, the idea was temporarily abandoned. In February plans were made to seize the Swedish ore fields and occupy several Norwegian ports as part of an expedition to aid Finland, but that operation too was dropped. Shortly afterward an infuriated Churchill wrote to Halifax: "I feel I ought to let you know that I am v[er]y deeply concerned about the way the war is going. It is not less deadly because it is silent . . . Can we suppose [the Germans] have not been thinking about what to do? Surely they have a plan. We have none. There is no sort of action in view except to wait on events."

According to John Colville, Chamberlain's decision in March to stop the ore, after all the months of vacillation and delays, was not so much because he had changed his mind about confronting Germany but because he believed in "the necessity of throwing occasional sops to public opinion." In concert with French leaders, the prime minister agreed to a plan to mine Norwegian territorial waters. After another postponement, which pushed the operation back three days, it finally was set. At dawn on Monday, April 8, British ships would begin sowing mines in the waters of Norway. The Allies, at long last, were taking control of the war.

Or so they thought.

CHAPTER SIXTEEN

"GAMBLING WITH THE LIFE OF THE NATION"

By early April memories of the harsh winter were fading fast in London. The days were soft and warm, the birds were engaged in their usual spring chatter, and daffodils and tulips had sprung up everywhere. The longer days meant fewer hours spent behind blackout curtains, and people stayed outside as long as possible, enjoying the golden weather. The parks were crowded, as were shops, restaurants, and nightclubs. Everyone, it seemed, wanted to forget the war. During that brief halcyon time, "even the newspaper headlines were unalarming," recalled Virginia Cowles.

The beginning of spring also served as a tonic for Neville Chamberlain. Brimming with new confidence and energy, he refused to let anything disturb him, not even reports from British intelligence of German battleships on the move, of the massing of enemy troops, of communications blackouts. "The accumulation of evidence that an attack [in the west] is imminent is formidable . . . and yet I cannot convince myself that it is coming," he wrote his sister.

For Dick Law, who had become the most outspoken Tory rebel of all, the lovely weather had no such restorative effect. Unlike the prime minister, he was sure it meant that a German offensive was at hand. "It is clear to me that we're going to lose this war unless there is a change," he wrote Bobbety Cranborne. Law's friends told him that he had developed an "obsession" about getting rid of Chamberlain. If so, he replied, it was an obsession that "was shared widely, not only in this country but all over the world."

When the Conservative Party's governing body, the Central Council, met in Westminster Hall on April 4 to approve an expression of confidence in the prime minister and his government, Law decided to attend the session in order to oppose the resolution. Feeling like Daniel in the lion's den, he nervously mounted the stage to make his speech. As he looked out from the podium at the party faithful sitting before him, Law was sure that he was about to "be torn limb from limb." To his astonishment, however, his scathing remarks about the government's lethargy in running the war were greeted with what he later described as "rapturous applause." He was halfway through his speech when Chamberlain himself entered the hall, so Law sat down while he addressed the group.

Chamberlain assured the gathering that Britain now had nothing to fear in its struggle with Germany. Acknowledging that German preparations for the conflict had been "far ahead of our own" when war broke out, he said that since then, the country had been able to "make good and remove our weaknesses . . . and so enormously add to our fighting strength that we can face the future with a calm and steady mind, whatever it brings." He was, he added, "ten times as confident of victory" as he was when the war began. So confident was he that he couldn't resist adding another few words, ones that, like "peace in our time," ended up haunting him for the rest of his life and into history. About Hitler, "one thing is certain," Chamberlain said. "He missed the bus."

According to Law, Chamberlain's remarks received only a "lukewarm" response from the crowd. After the prime minister left the hall, Law continued with his attack on the government. It had its effect: a resolution of confidence was passed, but in an amended form that was much less complimentary of the prime minister than the original.

When Chamberlain made his cocky declaration about Hitler's missing the bus, he knew, as his audience did not, that on the following day a special naval force was to leave Scapa Flow and cross the North Sea on its way to lay mines in Norwegian waters. What he did *not* know was that even as he was speaking, German merchant ships that had carried Swedish iron ore to Germany were now steaming back to Norway with troops, arms, and equipment hidden in their holds. This secret shuttling of German forces to Norway in supposedly empty ships had been under way for almost two weeks. Undetected by British intelligence, the ships anchored in Norwegian ports under various pretexts, with the troops on board awaiting the orders to strike.

In late 1939 Hitler had concluded that Britain intended to land in Norway and decided that "I want to be there before them." His suspicions of British intentions were reinforced by a British destroyer's interception of a German supply ship, the *Altmark*, in Norwegian waters on February 16, 1940. The *Altmark* was carrying about three hundred British merchant seamen taken prisoner after their ships had been sunk; after a brief skirmish British sailors boarded the *Altmark* and rescued their countrymen.

Early in the morning of April 9, the day after British ships had begun laying mines along Norway's southern coast, several thousand German infantry and parachute troops, supported by warships and hundreds of aircraft, launched a lightning attack on Denmark and Norway. Within twelve hours Denmark had been occupied, and German forces had seized the Norwegian capital of Oslo and all of the country's major ports.

The brilliant air and sea operation caught the Chamberlain government by complete surprise. Its initial reaction, like that of the country, was confusion, disbelief, and shock. The Commons scheduled a debate, and Ronald Cartland, whose regiment had been sent to France in early January, obtained leave to return for it. He came back to London determined to raise hell on the floor of the House. The German blitzkrieg in Norway, he was sure, would soon be followed by another in France. His men, along with the other Territorial units sent to bolster the regular BEF forces, were criminally unprepared to face the enemy. They had not been properly trained and still did not have enough arms or equipment or even adequate medical services. "There are innumerable scandals out here," he wrote a friend shortly before returning to Britain. "We want another Miss Nightingale, another Lloyd George, and every soldier I've spoken to wants Churchill in place of the Coroner."

When he got back to London, Cartland had several long, gloomy talks with Dick Law, Jim Thomas, Bob Boothby, Paul Emrys-Evans, and other parliamentary colleagues. He talked of quitting Parliament, of getting out of politics altogether. "I am quite convinced never to support the Tory party again," he had written to Emrys-Evans the week before. "You will never save the soul of England until you destroy the party machine."

In the end Cartland was denied the opportunity to make his case before the Commons. On April 12, two days after he arrived in London, the morning newspapers carried stories of German troop movements near the Belgian border, and he decided he had to return to France. Back with his troops, he wrote a letter to his mother that showed he had regained a bit of his old fire and enthusiasm. He still believed that the future of England was "terrible to contemplate," and he remained "pretty disgusted." Yet, he added, "whatever I *say*, I shall never be able to keep out of public life. After the war—if Chamberlain *still* reigns—[it's] the revolution for me—one last desperate attempt to save England."

It took the Allies almost a week to mount a response to the German invasion of Norway, and from the beginning it was a botched operation. At least half of the hastily assembled, ill-prepared British expeditionary force were Territorial units whose men knew little about combat. In the scramble to get the force on its way, not much thought was given to the rugged, mountainous terrain in which the troops would have to do battle. Winter still held Norway in a firm grip; deep snow and ice covered the ground in much of the country, yet almost no troops had been provided with snowshoes or skis. They had been given no instruction about fighting under such frigid conditions.

On April 13, five days after the German invasion, British, French, and Polish forces began landing at Narvik, in Norway's far north. British troops also put ashore at Namsos and Andalsnes, two small fishing ports several hundred miles apart in central Norway, with orders to conduct a pincer movement against the ancient Norwegian capital of Trondheim. In most cases, the British lacked sufficient quantities of almost everything they needed—transport, artillery, antiaircraft weapons, communications gear, fighter cover, medical equipment, food, even maps of the areas where they were to fight.

At the same time, new German troops, unharried by British bombers, were flooding into Norway to reinforce units already there. "Fortunately, one can always count upon the British to arrive too late," a German colonel remarked to an American correspondent. British pilots were not given permission to attack German-held airfields in Norway until April 11. Even then their assaults were limited to machine guns rather than bombs. *The New York Times* reported one instance in which an RAF reconnaissance aircraft spotted an airfield in Denmark jammed with German troop transport planes. When the Air Ministry asked permission to bomb the field, the War Cabinet debated the request for three days. Permission was finally granted, but by the time British bombers reached their target, the planes, along with their troops, had vanished into Norway.

Such delays and confusion were the rule rather than the exception. Orders were given, then countermanded. British troops dispatched to one front were diverted at the last minute to another. "Senior staff officers [were] asking junior officers what they should do next," one young officer who had been in Norway wrote to Lord Salisbury. "Absolute chaos reigned."

In an operation that called for the utmost cooperation from the three British military services, there was wrangling and a lack of coordination among the various service chiefs and ministers. No single government official was given the authority to make final decisions about the Norway operation and carry them out. In late April, Brendan Bracken complained to Leo Amery and his group of rebels about "the hopeless soviet which at present settles, or doesn't settle our strategy. They have duplicated the three chiefs of staff with deputies, and the whole six of them, with a variety of others, all meet in conclave with Winston or Neville as chairman, but with no one really deciding what the plans should be." Chamberlain had asked Churchill in early April to take over as head of the War Cabinet's Military Coordinating Committee. This new assignment added to Churchill's already heavy responsibilities but, to his great frustration, did not give him any real power since he could not take or enforce any decision on his own.

The Germans meanwhile had no such problems with decision making. Nor did they have the same compunction as the British about attacking the enemy from the air. In their nightmarish introduction to war, the green British troops in Norway had to contend not only with the well-trained, well-equipped forces of the Wehrmacht but also with the merciless strafing and bombing of the Luftwaffe. It was no contest. "We've been massacred! Simply massacred!" a Territorial lieutenant exploded to Leland Stowe, one of the few Western journalists to make it into Norway, after a battle near Namsos that ended in a rout of British forces. "We've got no planes! The Jerries have been bombing us all afternoon . . . It's been bloody awful!" Out of six hundred men in the lieutenant's battalion, more than two hundred had been killed or wounded during four days of fighting. Stretcher bearers attempting to carry the injured to safety were routinely machine-gunned by German dive-bombers.

Stowe interviewed the young British officer, exhausted and covered with mud, as he retreated, along with other survivors, up a road leading north. "We've got no proper clothes for these mountains," the lieutenant said. "We've got no white capes. The Jerries could see us everywhere in the snow. They just mowed our men down. I tell you . . . it's that bloody Chamberlain!" He told Stowe: "I'm glad you're a reporter. For God's sake, tell them we've got to have airplanes and anti-air guns! Tell them everything we've said!" In interviews with several other survivors of the battle, Stowe encountered the same anguish and bitterness toward a government that had sent them to Norway without proper training and protection. "What's the matter with people in London?" a corporal exclaimed. "If only we could get rid of that bloody old Neville Chamberlain, maybe we'd have a chance in this war."

In his dispatches to the *Chicago Daily News*, Stowe did as the lieutenant asked. He told the full story of what he had seen and heard: how the British troops found themselves at the mercy of the Luftwaffe, how they were "dumped into Norway's deep snows . . . without a single anti-aircraft gun, without one squadron of supporting planes, without a single piece of field artillery." His articles, which amounted to a blistering indictment of what he called "one of the costliest and most inexplicable bungles in military history," were reprinted in newspapers throughout the United States and much of the rest of the world.

These newspaper accounts of British blunders only reinforced the strong feelings held by many Americans that the United States should stay clear of the war. "It looks like the typical performance of the Chamberlain government—too little and too late," *The New Republic* declared.

"One thing is more certain every day. The isolationism of Americans is steadily strengthened by the deep conviction that even if it became desirable on other grounds to enter the conflict against Hitlerism, it would be fatal to enlist under this banner. For there is no reason to believe that such leadership could win either a war or a peace."

The British people meanwhile were being told an entirely different story about Norway. Stowe discovered that for himself one night after he and a photographer colleague took shelter in a farmhouse, and the owners of the house tuned in the BBC news for their English-speaking guests. "British expeditionary forces are pressing forward steadily from all points where they have landed in Norway," the BBC announcer reported in a plummy voice. "Resistance has been shattered along the railroad. In the Namsos sector, the British and French are advancing successfully toward Trondheim." The photographer stared at Stowe in bewilderment. "Christ, what's the matter with those mugs?" he burst out. "Are they crazy?"

The "mugs" weren't crazy, just badly misinformed. The conflict in Norway had erupted so quickly that virtually no British correspondents were in place to cover it. So the British press and public had to rely on the army, navy, and air force for information about what was going on. According to early reports provided by the service ministries to newspapers and the BBC, the British forces were meeting success after success. "The British Navy has embarked on a glorious enterprise," trumpeted the *Daily Mail*. "Hitler is shaken by the hammer blows of our sailors and airmen." Some papers couldn't resist embroidering what were already specious accounts of military triumphs. The *Daily Express* published an article about the British storming of Narvik, which had not yet happened, asserting that the action had "an Elizabethan ring to it." Reports by Chamberlain and Churchill to the House of Commons only added to the feeling of confidence that everything was going Britain's way. Two days after the German invasion, Churchill told the House that in his view, "Herr Hitler has committed a grave strategic error" and that "we have greatly gained by what has occurred in Scandinavia."

That was just what the British people wanted to hear. After eight months of nonexistent war, the waiting and boredom were over. British troops and sailors had finally tangled with the enemy and, by most accounts, were doing well. A sense of relief replaced the initial shock over the German invasion of Norway. "The country," remarked Liberal MP Percy Harris, "was suffering from an incorrigible optimism."

But as April slipped by, the early buoyancy gave way to a growing unease. The service ministries gave fewer and fewer press briefings about British successes. In fact, they released little information about Norway at all. At the same time, several British newspapers began running accounts of the debacle near Namsos, based on Leland Stowe's reporting. The War Office dismissed Stowe's reports as "an obvious distortion of the facts," but they, along with other accounts of British failures from sources in neutral countries, contributed to the sense that something had gone very wrong and that information was being suppressed. "There can be no question that the handling by the press and radio in this country of the news from Norway . . . has undermined the confidence of a considerable section of the British public in the integrity and accuracy of its news sources," Edward R. Murrow reported to American listeners on April 22. "The fighting services still have the whip hand and apparently are not concerned about, or are not aware of, the flood of disturbing statement and rumor reaching this country from abroad."

Then, on May 2, Chamberlain went before the House of Commons to make a shocking announcement: the British troops that had landed at Andalsnes and Namsos had been forced to retreat and were now being evacuated. The prime minister admitted that the forces sent to Norway had been insufficiently equipped and had not been given adequate fighter cover or antiaircraft guns. Furthermore, he said, enemy reinforcements had poured in at a much greater rate than expected. This devastating confession of failure rocked the country hard. According to Margery Allingham, the shock "boiled down to nothing more or less than the sudden and paralyzing revelation that Chamberlain was a vain old man who had nothing particular up his sleeve." As the police constable in Allingham's Essex village bitterly put it, "We thought he was getting on with it. Instead, the old blighter was mucking about."

Like many of their countrymen, the people of Tolleshunt D'Arcy had hoped that the seeming inertia of the government during the phony war was a facade, that Chamberlain and his men were using those months of inactivity to "build up a colossal war machine," even if there was no public sign of it. Allingham herself was sure that "the Government was working like a fiend to get ready for a smashing spring offensive, probably in the north, and I thought we were incomparably better equipped, especially in the air, than we turned out to be." Her belief in the imminence of a big push was bolstered by Chamberlain's April 4 quip that Hitler had "missed the bus." She and others in her village interpreted the remark as a wink to the British people, "a little encouraging personal dig in the ribs for which [everyone] had been waiting so long," a sly hint that Britain was about to take care of Herr Hitler. When Chamberlain acknowledged on May 2 that the opposite was true, that Germany had gotten the best of Britain in Norway, Allingham suddenly felt like a passenger in a bus hurtling down a narrow, winding mountain road who makes the horrifying discovery that the driver was "slightly tight and not a brilliant driver at the best." Was he about to drive the bus right off the cliff? "I have never been more abjectly frightened in my life," Allingham wrote.

The stunning realization that the world's greatest sea power had been humiliated by the daunting air power of Germany—that "Hitler had proved his capacity," in Edward Spears's words, "to swallow a whole country under our very noses practically overnight"—ignited a wave of fury as well as fear throughout the country. "We have . . . been heavily beaten—routed," George Beardmore noted angrily in his diary. "All that people like me can understand is that Germany has collected every country she has wanted."

No one, however, was more enraged than Leo Amery. Time and again he had warned the government that its reluctance to confront the enemy—to bomb its airfields, factories, and other economic and military targets—could only lead to disaster. "How differently might the Norwegian campaign have [been] if the total strength of the Luftwaffe had been kept down by the wear and tear of six months of constant fighting, while the greater part of it had to be kept back to defend its home bases and factories . . ." he wrote. On May 2, shortly after the prime minister's speech, Amery phoned Sir Samuel Hoare, recently named the new air minister, and barked: "The government must go!" The time had come, the Tory rebel leader told a friend, for "open warfare."

The bad news from Norway provided, at long last, the spark for rebellion. But Norway wasn't the only issue energizing the dissidents in April. The army had just released a report revealing it would not get modern tanks for at least another year. And the new budget unveiled by Sir John Simon showed that Britain's spending on the war effort over the next year would be almost 40 percent less than Germany's. The government, Amery declared, was "gambling with the life of the nation. We cannot afford to go on in this leisurely fashion."

Most members of Amery's group were poised to revolt. So were the Vigilantes. Throughout April they spent much of their time trying to decide how to put their plans into action. One warm Sunday morning a group of them, including Dick Law, Jim Thomas, and Ronald Tree, were sitting in deck chairs on the lawn of Tree's country house, immersed in their plotting. Nancy Tree, who had been cutting flowers, wandered by and overheard their discussion. "Why all this talk?" she drawled. "You all know what you should do. Now go ahead and do it."

True enough—but the rebels had to be careful. If their conspiracy was to have any chance of success, they needed to muster the support of as many Tories as possible. And in the first days after the German invasion of Norway, several members of Lord Salisbury's Watching Committee, including Salisbury himself, still were insisting that Chamberlain must be given a chance to make changes in his government and in the conduct of the war. The day after the invasion Salisbury went to 10 Downing Street to see Chamberlain. Warning that "a failure in Norway would be fatal to the Government," Salisbury demanded that the prime minister shake up his government and reduce the size of his War Cabinet. The elderly peer also urged a far more vigorous prosecution of the war, specifically an all-out bombing offensive against military targets in Germany. Although friendly, Chamberlain rejected all of Salisbury's proposals. He did not seem "in the least minded to consider the idea of a real War Cabinet or indeed that things wanted conducting with greater vigour and sense of time," Salisbury wrote Bobbety Cranborne. The prime minister told Salisbury that "if people did not like the administration of the present Government, they could change it."

London political circles meanwhile were alive with talk and rumors of the plot to bring the prime minister down and of who would succeed him if, by some miracle, the conspiracy succeeded. There was mention of Lloyd George and even of Amery, but the two most likely candidates were Winston Churchill and Lord Halifax, who, although tainted by appeasement, was known to favor an all-party coalition government and was believed to be more resolute than Chamberlain. Most members of the Amery and Davies groups wanted Churchill and were deeply worried about the impact of the Norwegian fiasco on his chances. He, after all, had been the architect of the offensive in Norway and the cabinet minister who would be held responsible for the Royal Navy's reverses there. The first lord's steadfast allegiance to Chamberlain was another source of concern. To Harold Macmillan and the other rebels, it was clear that "Churchill's loyalty and sense of duty would ensure that he would stand firmly by Neville Chamberlain and urge him to fight on as long as he could command a majority."

Yet his loyalty was hardly reciprocated. During those rumor-filled days Chamberlain and his lieutenants were engaged in plots of their own, including the idea of getting rid of Churchill by making him the scapegoat for Norway. Late in April, Lord Dunglass asked Chips Channon whether he thought "Winston should be deflated. Ought he to leave the Admiralty?" Channon wrote in his diary: "Evidently these thoughts are in Neville's head." At about the same time, Harold Nicolson observed: "The Whips are putting it about that it is all the fault of Winston, who has made another forlorn failure." Caught up in their own intrigues, some of Chamberlain's men refused to believe that Churchill was really as faithful to his chief as he seemed. Channon, for one, noted rumors that Churchill had "now thrown off his mask" and was drawing up plans for an alternative government. John Colville heard that while Churchill himself was loyal, "his satellites (e.g. Duff Cooper, Amery etc.) were doing all in their power to create mischief and ill-feeling." In fact, although Brendan Bracken was conducting his own private campaign to get Chamberlain out, which included meetings with the Tory rebels, there is no evidence that Churchill took part in the maneuvering.

In any event, Churchill had no time for plotting. He was far too busy trying to cope with the disaster in Norway, which he feared would tar his reputation just as the Dardanelles failure had. Juggling his responsibilities at the Admiralty and acting as chairman of the cabinet

Military Coordinating Committee, he was clearly exhausted and seemed, to some of his friends, to have lost his usual verve and energy. After one of Churchill's speeches in the House, Nicolson wrote worriedly that he had seldom seen the first lord "to less advantage . . . He hesitates, gets his notes in the wrong order, puts on the wrong pair of spectacles, fumbles for the right pair . . . and one way and another makes a lamentable performance."

The man considered Churchill's chief rival for the premiership meanwhile was making an even less favorable impression. In one last attempt to convince the government to change its approach to the war, Lord Salisbury and a Watching Committee delegation that included Amery, Emrys-Evans, and Nicolson paid a call on Lord Halifax on April 29. Salisbury warned Halifax that if Hitler succeeded in his conquest of Norway, "the effects on the neutral [countries] would be very serious." To counter this military and propaganda coup, Britain must seize the initiative elsewhere, preferably by launching a bombing campaign against enemy military targets. Halifax's response to Salisbury's proposal was as unreceptive as Chamberlain's had been. "He understands the dangers of the position but does not seem to have any ideas for dealing with it," Emrys-Evans wrote to Bobbety Cranborne. At the end of the meeting Salisbury looked sternly at the foreign secretary. "Lord Halifax," he snapped, "we are not satisfied." Accompanied by his colleagues, he swept from the room.

For Salisbury and most of the rest of the Watching Committee, this meeting with Halifax was the final straw. They now shared the conviction of the other dissidents that if Chamberlain were not ousted immediately, Britain might well lose the war. A true national government—a coalition of Conservatives, Labour, and Liberals that would in turn oversee the collaboration of labor and industry—was now an urgent necessity. With almost everyone in the three dissident groups now on board, the Tory rebels began to make plans for a showdown.

On May 1, over dinner at the Carlton Hotel, the Amery group agreed that Chamberlain and his government must be ousted "at the earliest possible moment." Some members wanted the group to go on record as supporting Churchill as Chamberlain's successor, but Amery balked. Not all the rebels agreed on Churchill, and it was essential that they present a united front to the rest of Parliament, with no differences among themselves. "The essential thing [is] change," Amery told the other MPs. Once Chamberlain was toppled, then the decision about his replacement could be made. But how were they to convince other Tories to oppose the prime minister?

The next day Chamberlain, with his announcement of the troops' evacuation from Norway, handed them the answer. Within hours of his appearance before the Commons, Amery met with Clement Davies to discuss how to exploit this bombshell. They decided to use a two-day parliamentary debate already scheduled for the following week as the vehicle for an all-out attempt to get rid of the government. The May 7 and 8 debate, to be held before Parliament adjourned for the annual Whitsunday holiday, was perfect for the insurgents' purpose, since adjournment debates before parliamentary holidays could be used as forums for wide-ranging discussions of major issues. Thus the motion that "This House do now adjourn" would become the instrument for a no-holds-barred examination of the government and its prosecution of the war. The debate, in some rebels' view, would be Parliament's supreme test. If MPs were not effective in voicing the country's concerns, Ronald Tree wrote Bobbety Cranborne, the House of Commons "will cease to count—and everywhere people will lose faith in the power of Parliamentary institutions."

Once the debate was set, the rebel leaders held talks with Clement Attlee and other members of the Opposition front bench to find out if there was "a sufficient possibility of agreement for a joint move to remove Chamberlain." The two groups were wary of each other: the Tories considered the Labourites weak and overly cautious, and Labour leaders were not convinced that the rebels would rise to the challenge this time and actually vote against the prime minister. Clement Davies, who was close to Attlee and Arthur Greenwood, pressed the two men to use the debate to call for a no-confidence vote in Chamberlain. After discussing the idea with other top Labour figures, Attlee decided against it—at least for the moment. It was too risky, he said. If Chamberlain won the vote, his hold on the office would be immeasurably strengthened.

The government meanwhile finally realized it might be facing serious trouble. "David Margesson says we are on the eve of the greatest political crisis" since the national economic emergency in 1931, Chips Channon wrote on May 3. Chamberlain fought back with all the resources at his command. He spied on his opponents to find out their plans and, in at least one case, let them know what he was doing. After Liberal leader Archibald Sinclair had criticized Chamberlain in a speech, the prime minister phoned him to complain, then informed him his phone conversations were being tapped and, to prove it, repeated to him the contents of a recent exchange between Sinclair and a colleague.

As usual, government efforts to have the BBC and the nation's newspapers rally around the prime minister in a time of national crisis had their desired effect. Even papers that had blasted the fumbling of the Norway expedition and called for a government shakeup were careful not to condemn Chamberlain personally or urge the government's downfall. "It seems clear that complacency will secure another triumph in the House," Robert Bruce Lockhart wrote on Sunday, May 6. "Since Friday, the press and the BBC have been preparing the way— not to mention ministerial speakers . . . Tonight, [Tory] members of the House were on the air to repeat that no one had the right to criticize unless they knew all the facts."

Chamberlain and his men knew they were in for a rough time over the next two days. But they were confident they would emerge as the victors. The debate will be "awkward," John Colville acknowledged on May 6, but "obviously the Government will win through." His assessment was shared by many others, including journalists like Ed Murrow. "Chamberlain's government is in no immediate danger," Murrow reported on CBS the week before the debate. "The British are not in the habit of overthrowing governments because of military defeats."

CHAPTER SEVENTEEN

"'IN THE NAME OF GOD, GO!'"

In the early morning of May 7 a crowd already had begun to gather in Parliament Square. By midafternoon people were spilling out into Great George and Parliament streets. Women carrying market baskets and pushing prams stood alongside soldiers and bowler-hatted businessmen, all watching quietly as cars and taxis carrying MPs, reporters, ambassadors, and other distinguished guests streamed through the gates of the grand Gothic Revival building. The mood of the throng was subdued, even anxious. There was little conversation or laughter on that bright spring day.

In the lobbies and smoking room, dozens of members milled around, talking in low voices. The air was alive with speculation and uncertainty. Would Labour change its mind and press for a vote of confidence at the end of the two days of debate? If so, how many Tories would summon up the courage to defy the threats and cajoling of Margesson and the other whips and vote against the government? What promises or proposals were being made behind the scenes? Who would speak?

Not even the answer to that last question was known for certain. The only speakers scheduled thus far were Chamberlain, slated to make the opening statement defending the government's conduct of the Norway campaign, and Winston Churchill, who would deliver the government's final arguments. The prime minister and his men had finally realized it would be foolhardy to blame the lack of arms and equipment in Norway on a man who had been pressing for full-scale rearmament for more than five years. Besides, they desperately needed Churchill's oratorical skills on their side in this crucial test of Chamberlain's power.

For the last five days the rebels had been working furiously to line up opposition to the prime minister. Clement Davies, the chief leader of the Vigilantes, had not slept for three nights. A director of the manufacturing conglomerate Unilever, he had spent the mornings at his day job, dealing with toothpaste and soap products. In the afternoons and evenings, he focused on deposing Chamberlain. But as Davies and the other dissidents circulated among their colleagues, engaging in some last-minute lobbying, they knew that their odds of success were slim. Taking a few minutes off from wooing fellow Conservatives, a tense Bob Boothby joined Dorothy Macmillan and Baffy Dugdale for tea in the members' tea room. Boothby told the women he feared there would be no change of government, that "the mess is so great and the disasters to be expected . . . so terrible, let those who have sown the wind reap the whirlwind." A couple of days before, Chamberlain had written his sister: "I don't think my enemies will get me this time."

When the prime minister entered the Commons, the chamber was packed. Margesson had issued a three-line whip, a message demanding the presence of all Conservative members. He had sent a special whip to the several dozen Tories on active duty in the military, urging them to do everything possible to attend. Although many, like Ronald Cartland, were with the BEF in France and could not leave their posts, more than twenty heeded the call. As a result, Tory backbenchers, a good many of them wearing uniforms, were jammed together so tightly on the benches that as Edward Spears put it, "some uncertainty" existed as to "the ownership of arms and legs in the immediate vicinity, cramp being the best indication that a limb did, in fact, belong to you." Those who couldn't find space on the benches sat in the Members' Gallery or congregated in the gangways or around the Speaker's chair.

To catcalls of "Missed the bus!" from the 150-plus Labour MPs, Chamberlain rose from his seat shortly before 4:00 p.m. and placed his notes on the dispatch box in front of him. Appearing nervous and dispirited, he began a long recounting of the previous month's events in Norway. He made no call for the creation of a truly national government, as some MPs had predicted, just a halting justification of a military fiasco that was indefensible. He downplayed the defeat of British troops—after all, he said, only a relatively small number of men had been deployed, and they were being successfully withdrawn—and he claimed that the Germans themselves had suffered heavy losses. Appealing for national unity, he stressed the grave perils facing Britain. "This is not a time for quarrelling among ourselves," he argued. "It is rather a time for closing our ranks." Any criticism voiced in the debate, he said, would give comfort to the enemy.

Facing the greatest political challenge of his life, Neville Chamberlain had failed to rise to the occasion. Chips Channon thought the prime minister "spoke haltingly and did not make a good case; in fact, he fumbled his words and seemed tired and embarrassed." The House became increasingly restive as he spoke, with Opposition jeers, boos, and cries of "Missed the bus!" growing louder and more raucous. Chamberlain, Helen Kirkpatrick noted from the press gallery, "was not allowed to finish a single full sentence without interruption." Harold Macmillan, staunch Chamberlain foe though he was, thought the interruptions rude and unfair, "unworthy of a great occasion." Leo Amery, in his customary place in the third row below the gangway on the government benches, sat quietly and listened.

Chamberlain had totally misjudged the mood of the House, Amery thought. Instead of acknowledging the lessons learned from Britain's defeat in Norway, instead of rallying the Commons and the country to battle, he once again had fallen back on lame excuses for failure. But with Britain on the verge of all-out war with Germany, failure could no longer be tolerated. "Speak for England!" Amery had urged Arthur Greenwood eight months before. Now, he had decided, *he* would be the one to speak for the country.

Just as Chamberlain's speech in the Norway debate was unquestionably the most important of his career, the same, Amery well knew, would hold true for him. Painfully aware of his reputation as a boring speaker, he had worked for hours on what he planned to say, poring through books, jotting down ideas, and carefully honing his words. An avid student of British parliamentary history, Amery was particularly interested in the era of Oliver Cromwell and was familiar with many of Cromwell's speeches. Earlier that day, sitting in the book-lined study of

his Eaton Square home, he studied with special care a speech that
Cromwell delivered to Parliament in 1653. He copied down one particular sentence and put it with the rest of his notes. It was "strong
meat" and would give him a powerful conclusion to his speech, but he
was not sure he would use it. The purpose of speaking, after all, was to
bring down the government, and he needed to have the House with
him to do that. Was the Cromwell quotation too forceful? Would it
simply antagonize his fellow MPs? He decided to wait until he gave
the speech before making up his mind whether or not to use it.

After Chamberlain had finished speaking, Clement Attlee rose and
delivered a tepid attack on the government's handling of Norway—"a
politician's speech," someone called it, "willing to wound and yet afraid
to strike." Other speeches, in defense and opposition of Chamberlain,
followed in quick succession. One highlight of the afternoon was an
address by Adm. Sir Roger Keyes, a Tory MP and hero of the Great War
who had won fame for leading a daring raid against German submarine
pens at a Belgian port in 1918. At Duff Cooper's urging, the small,
slender Keyes had come to the chamber that day in the full-dress uniform of an admiral of the fleet, sporting six rows of ribbons and medals,
as well as masses of gold braid on his sleeve that, in Dick Law's words,
"seemed to go right up to the armpit." In a weak, trembling voice, Keyes
unleashed a devastating assault on the government for what he regarded as its lack of nerve in not pressing a naval attack against German
forces in Trondheim. "The fact that he was practically incoherent with
nervousness gave more might to his words," Law remarked. "The hero
of the last war was denouncing the leader of this one."

For Leo Amery, the hours after Chamberlain's address were a time
of "agonized discomfort," as he listened to speeches "which never seem
to end" while rehearsing in his mind the points he himself wanted to
make. "This time," he later wrote, "I knew that what I had to say mattered . . . [and] I was desperately anxious that it should have its intended effect." Yet when he rose to be recognized, the Speaker of the
House, Sir Edward Fitzroy, failed to call on him. As a Privy Counsellor
and former cabinet member Amery had precedence over other Tory
backbenchers and by tradition should have been one of the first speakers to be recognized. But Fitzroy had the power to decide when Amery

would address the House. Again and again the tall, spare figure in white wig and black silk robes looked past Amery as if he weren't there.

Although a member of the government party, the Speaker was supposed to preside over the Commons with impartiality. But Amery knew that Fitzroy's sympathies lay with Chamberlain, and he realized that the Speaker, knowing "I was out to make trouble," probably would not call on him until the dinner hour, when virtually everyone in the chamber had gone out to eat. As the afternoon faded into evening and the House slowly emptied, Amery became more and more concerned. How could he have any influence on the debate if there was no one around to hear him? When Fitzroy finally deigned to recognize him, it was eight o'clock, with barely a dozen members still in the chamber. A frustrated Amery wondered if he should sit down and try again the next day.

Just then Clement Davies slipped behind him. He *must* speak, Davies whispered in his ear; he would make sure Amery had an audience. The Independent MP left the chamber to round up members from the smoking room, lobbies, and library while Amery made a few comments about previous speeches, playing for time. When he finally reached the heart of his address, the chamber was almost full.

"The Prime Minister gave us a reasoned, argumentative case for our failure," Amery said. "It is always possible to do that after every failure. Making a case and winning a war are not the same thing. Wars are won, not by explanations after the event, but by foresight, by clear decision, and by swift action. I confess that I did not feel there was one sentence in the Prime Minister's speech . . . which suggested that the Government foresaw what Germany meant to do, or came to a clear decision . . . or acted swiftly or consistently throughout the whole of this lamentable affair."

Pouring scorn on Chamberlain's claim of heavy German losses, Amery noted that the enemy had lost a score of transports, a few warships, and several thousand men, which meant "nothing to them." In return, they had gained Norway, with "the strategic advantages which outweigh the whole of their losses."

In this debate, Amery told his colleagues, they and Parliament were on trial just as much as the prime minister and his men. "If we lose this war," he said, "it is not this or that ephemeral Government but

Parliament as an institution that will be condemned" for failing to do
its duty. That duty, he made clear, was to oust the current government.
"We cannot go on as we are," he declared. "There must be a change."
A small, strong War Cabinet must be created, with its members given
the authority to oversee the war effort. All three parties must be taken
into the government, joining forces to unite the nation, to draw upon
all its resources and the abilities of all its people.

The leaders of this new administration cannot be "peacetime
statesmen who are not well fitted for the conduct of war," Amery said,
flicking a glance at the men sitting on the government's front bench.
"Compromise and procrastination are the natural qualities . . . of a political leader in time of peace. They are fatal qualities in war. Vision,
daring, swiftness and consistency of decision are the very essence of
victory."

Amery's voice grew quieter as he looked around the chamber. "Somehow or other," he continued, "we must get into the Government men
who can match our enemies in fighting spirit, in daring, in resolution
and in thirst for victory . . . It may not be easy to find these men. They
can be found only by trial and by ruthlessly discarding all who fail . . .
But find them we must—for we are fighting today for our life, for our
liberty, for our all."

Amery paused. The chamber was hushed, his fellow MPs focused
on every word. He thought of the quotation from Oliver Cromwell that
he had jotted down that morning. He had to decide now. Should he
read it? The words were scathing, even brutal. But as Amery studied
the faces of his colleagues that night, he knew he could use them and
carry the Commons along with him. He would quote these words of
Cromwell with "great reluctance," he said, "because I am speaking of
those who are old friends and associates of mine. But they are words
which I think are applicable to the present situation."

Amery glanced down at his notes. "This is what Cromwell said to
the Long Parliament when he thought it was no longer fit to conduct
the affairs of the nation." His voice hardening, he fixed his gaze on
members of the cabinet, sitting stock-still on the front bench. " 'You
have sat too long here for any good you have been doing! Depart, I say,
and let us have done with you!

" 'In the name of God, go!' "

Amery's words ripped the air like bullets. The ministers' faces whitened, and loud gasps swept the chamber. The sense of shock was almost palpable. A stunned Harold Macmillan thought that Amery's closing salvo was "the most formidable philippic which I have ever heard . . ." In Macmillan's view, Amery's "logical, powerful, unanswerable" address had, "with rare skill, put into the frame of a quotation the thought that was forming in every listener's mind." According to Edward Spears, "it was as if Amery were hurling stones as large as himself . . . at the government's glass house. The crash of glass could not be heard, but the effect was that of a series of deafening explosions." Looking down from the press gallery, a *Daily Telegraph* reporter, J. E. Sewell, realized that the government had just suffered its "most damaging assault since before the war."

Long after the House adjourned for the night, MPs packed the smoking room, lobbies, bars, and other popular gathering places in the Palace of Westminster, all of them talking about Amery's electrifying speech. It was clear that his challenge had persuaded a number of Tories who had not openly opposed Chamberlain before that he should resign. But it was still far from certain if they would dare vote against their party's government at a time of national crisis—that is, if the Labour Party actually decided to call for a vote of confidence. As Hugh Dalton and other Labour leaders had pointed out repeatedly, a sizable number of Conservatives would have to shed party loyalty and vote with them and the Liberals if there was to be any chance of ousting Chamberlain. Opposition leaders now had to decide whether to take the risk of demanding a vote.

Ironically, when leading Labour MPs met the following morning to discuss what to do, it was Dalton who turned out to be the most reluctant to call for a vote. He was convinced that although many Tories might abstain, no more than a dozen actually would summon up the courage to vote against the government. Margesson's control was too strong, the tug of party loyalty too great. A vote of confidence was a terrible gamble, Dalton thought. If it backfired, prompting Conservatives to rally to

Chamberlain's support, it would keep this defeatist prime minister securely in power at a time when Britain was facing the greatest danger in its history. But Amery's speech had persuaded Attlee and the others to take the plunge. Overriding Dalton's objections, they decided to demand a division at the end of the debate late that night. If the gamble failed, Arthur Greenwood said, the Tories would bear the blame. "The responsibility for any change lies not with us," Greenwood declared. "It lies with the Conservatives, whose responsibilities are, far and away, greater than ours."

At about the same time that morning, members of Lord Salisbury's Watching Committee were meeting at his Arlington Street mansion to decide their own plan of action. Salisbury's comments would hardly have reassured Dalton and the other Labour leaders. He argued that if Labour called for a division, the Tory rebels should show their displeasure with the government by abstaining. Most of the committee's other members, however, had come to the conclusion that abstention was far too weak a protest. "Amery's words were ringing in our ears," Harold Macmillan recalled.

The government meanwhile was reeling from the impact of those words. Overnight the confident mood of Chamberlain and his men had vanished, replaced by growing anxiety and alarm. "This morning, everybody is at the nadir of gloom, lower than I have yet seen them," John Colville wrote. When the House met again that afternoon, Chamberlain's supporters became even more disturbed when Herbert Morrison stood to announce the Labour Party's demand for a division at the end of the debate—in essence a vote of confidence in the prime minister. "We knew then it was to be war," Channon wrote.

The moment that Morrison finished speaking, Chamberlain jumped to his feet, his face flushed. The speech of his erstwhile friend Amery the night before had shocked and infuriated him, and he was determined to strike back. "I do not seek to evade criticism," he snapped. "But I say to my friends in the House—and I *have* friends in the House—that no Government can prosecute a war efficiently unless it has public and parliamentary support." Turning to face the Tory benches, the prime minister heatedly declared: "I accept this challenge. I welcome it indeed. At least I shall see who is with us and who is against us, and I call on my friends to support us in the Lobby tonight."

Chamberlain was resorting to his familiar tactics, demanding that his "friends"—i.e., loyal Tory MPs—vote for the government and indirectly threatening those who planned to do otherwise. That had always worked for him before: the threats, the bullying, the insistence that fidelity to party and prime minister trumped any other consideration. Once again, just as in the aftermath of Munich and at the outbreak of war, he seemed unable to focus on anything but himself. Again he had transformed a question of the highest national interest into a purely personal issue. "It was so profoundly, so fatally characteristic of him to make this tremendous issue of life and death a matter of who were and who were not his friends," remarked Violet Bonham Carter.

Chamberlain's challenge only served to heighten the hostility and anger on both sides of the chamber. The speeches grew more inflammatory, and the speakers increasingly were interrupted by hoots and jeers from their opponents. Duff Cooper rose to denounce the prime minister and declare that he planned to vote against the government. David Lloyd George, about to turn eighty, held the House spellbound as he mounted a slashing attack against his longtime political enemy for what he termed the prime minister's inept conduct of the war. "It is not a question of who are the Prime Minister's friends. It is a far bigger issue," he declared. Noting Chamberlain's appeal for sacrifice, Lloyd George scornfully flung his notes down on the table in front of him and proclaimed that "the Prime Minister should give an example of sacrifice, because there is nothing which can contribute more to victory in this war than that he should sacrifice the seals of office."

Like Cooper and most of Chamberlain's other foes, Lloyd George was engaged in a delicate balancing act, trying to bring down Chamberlain and his government while at the same time attempting to protect Winston Churchill from the fallout. "I do not think the First Lord was responsible for all the things that happened in Norway," Lloyd George said, only to have Churchill leap to his feet to declare that he took "complete responsibility for everything that has been done by the Admiralty." Such loyalty was misplaced, Lloyd George admonished Churchill. The first lord must not "allow himself to be converted into an air raid shelter to keep splinters from hitting his colleagues."

As the speeches continued throughout the afternoon and evening, the intrigue and lobbying outside the chamber grew more frenetic. "The 'glamour boys' are smacking their lips," Chips Channon remarked, "but their full strength is not yet known." Following Chamberlain's lead, Margesson and the other government whips relentlessly pressured Tory MPs, alternately warning about the personal consequences of voting against Chamberlain and promising a complete overhaul of the government if the prime minister won the vote of confidence.

Shortly before Churchill was to speak, members of Amery's rebel group gathered in a House committee room for a secret session with the Vigilantes. It was the first time the two groups, totaling some eighty MPs, had met together. Joining forces, they designated Amery their leader, then agreed that they would vote against the prime minister. After all the indecision and all the abstaining in previous votes, beginning with Eden's resignation more than two years before, the rebels finally had taken an unequivocal stand.

After the meeting Macmillan stopped by the smoking room, where he found the first lord of the admiralty lighting a cigar. When Churchill beckoned him over, Macmillan wished him luck in his speech but said he hoped his defense of the government would not be too convincing. "Why not?" Churchill asked. "Because," Macmillan replied, "we must have a new prime minister, and it must be you." The first lord growled that he had "signed on for the voyage and would stick with the ship." But, Macmillan wrote later, "I don't think that he was angry with me."

Minutes later Churchill, with Brendan Bracken in his wake, strode into the chamber, in the words of Dick Law, with "fire in his eye and his jaw sticking out like the ram of a battleship." He sat down beside Chamberlain and conferred with him for a moment. Then he rose to deliver a belligerent defense of the prime minister and his government, voicing none of the criticism he had privately leveled at his cabinet colleagues since the early days of the war. The irony of the government's most forceful prewar critic acting now as its most passionate defender was lost on nobody. "One saw at once that he was in a bellicose mood, alive and enjoying himself, relishing the . . . position in which he found himself: i.e., that of defending his enemies, and a cause in which he did not believe," Chips Channon wrote. Channon, however, was wrong on one score. While he may have disagreed with Chamberlain's running of the war, Churchill did not view the prime minister as an enemy. Just a few days before, he had thanked Chamberlain for the faith shown in him, promised him total fidelity in return, and said he would do his best "to make all go smoothly."

To the House, Churchill denied that his views of the war differed from those of other members of the cabinet, demanding that his fellow MPs "dismiss these delusions." He devoted most of his address to a justification of the government's handling of the Norway campaign, which, in Amery's view, was "a quite incomprehensible account" despite being delivered in "his most persuasive manner." The first lord went on to echo Chamberlain's appeal for national unity, as well as to repeat the prime minister's assertion that criticism of the government would be seen as playing into the hands of Germany. Turning around to glare at the Tory rebels, most of whom wanted to make him prime minister, Churchill called for the burying of "prewar feuds" and "personal quarrels." Shoulders hunched, lower lip jutting out, he declared: "Let us keep our hatreds for the common enemy. Let party interests be ignored."

John Peck, a young subordinate of Churchill's at the Admiralty, felt "strangely uneasy" as he listened to the first lord's speech, thinking "it did not ring entirely true." Violet Bonham Carter thought that Churchill's "peroration sounded conscientious and forced. He couldn't throw all his weight in it." Others noted that Churchill carefully limited himself to a defense of the Norway expedition and did not dwell at length on the overall question of the government's fitness to conduct the war, which was, after all, the real focus of the debate. "The major argument, of which Norway was only a part, remained unanswered," observed J. E. Sewell.

Labour and Liberal members agreed with nothing Churchill said. They heckled him so mercilessly that he finally lost his temper, shouting angrily at the Opposition benches while Labourites and Liberals shouted back. In the middle of this verbal brawl, Sewell concluded that Churchill's "audience was in no condition to be influenced by his arguments." Later he wrote: "No speech of his, before or afterwards, made less impression."

In arguably the most important debate in the history of Parliament, it was the oratory of Leo Amery, not Winston Churchill, that in the end was to have the most lasting impact on the fate of Britain.

Churchill finished speaking shortly before 11:00 p.m. The moment for which the Tory rebels had been working had finally arrived. The Speaker commanded, "Clear the lobbies!" and the doorkeepers rang the division bells. Policemen shouted, "Division!" in the corridors outside, alerting any MPs not in the chamber that a vote was about to take place.

Years later Tory MPs remembered those next few minutes as one of the most stressful and traumatic experiences of their lives. For a brief moment even some of the dissidents had second thoughts about voting against the government. Conservatives knew that if they opposed Chamberlain, they would be politically doomed if the government triumphed. They also had to wrestle with the question raised by Chamberlain and Churchill in the debate: whether it was right to vote against their government in time of war and to do so at a particularly critical moment of the conflict.

As members rose from the benches, the strain of the evening exploded into rancor and recrimination. MPs who once had been close friends hurled insults and abuse at one another. "Quislings!" pro-Chamberlain MPs shouted at those who had made clear they planned to vote against the prime minister.* "Yes-men!" the insurgents yelled back. The scene, said Chips Channon, was "bedlam." The government whips continued their lobbying until the last moment, buttonholing Tories as they surged toward the back of the chamber and urging them to vote for the government just once more, with the promise that Chamberlain would accede to their demands for government reconstruction the following day. Charles Taylor, a Chamberlain supporter who had decided to vote against the government, recalled the "terrible pressure" that Margesson put on him to change his mind. "Do you realize Winston Churchill is going to support Neville Chamberlain tonight?"

---

*Chamberlain supporters were using the new synonym for "traitor," which had come into use only the month before, after Vidkun Quisling, a Norwegian fascist leader, collaborated with Germany in the invasion and occupation of his homeland.

Margesson demanded. "Of course he will," Taylor replied. "He must. He is First Lord."

Indeed, as MPs divided at the rear of the chamber, with those backing the government turning right, into the "aye" lobby, and those against Chamberlain turning left, both Churchill and Anthony Eden were among the government supporters who headed to the right. Joining them were their parliamentary private secretaries, Brendan Bracken and Jim Thomas. But the two junior men were doing so only under duress. Both of them were desperate to vote against Chamberlain, but they had been reminded by their bosses and some of their fellow Tory dissidents that if they did so, their votes would be interpreted as reflecting the private views of Churchill and Eden. "It was a sad ending to a day for which I had waited since [Eden's resignation in 1938]," Thomas wrote later to Bobbety Cranborne, who was too ill to attend the debate. "And I am still not sure we were right."

Members stood in single file and waited their turn to pass through the lobbies, which were more like long corridors than rooms. As they entered, they announced their names to two division clerks in each lobby, who ticked the names off a list. The MPs then walked through the lobby and exited through half-closed double doors. The doors were flanked by two colleagues serving as tellers, who counted each MP as he left.

Leo Amery, looking grim, strode through the "no" lobby. Dick Law and Paul Emrys-Evans followed, with Harold Macmillan, Ronald Tree, and Harold Nicolson close behind. The Tories kept coming: Bob Boothby, Jack Macnamara, Duncan Sandys, and even a few former Chamberlain supporters like Lady Astor, who had grown disenchanted with his conduct of the war.

Edward Spears, who followed Duff Cooper into the "no" lobby, saw that David Margesson was one of the tellers at the door. For Spears, it was an excruciating moment. He had served with Margesson in the Great War, and despite their political differences, Spears still considered the chief government whip a friend. He watched Margesson give Cooper a look of "implacable resentment," as Cooper made a slight bow to him (part of the arcane division ritual) and Margesson announced, "one fifty-one," the latest count of those opposing the prime minister. In turn, Spears bowed to Margesson and quickly went through the door, as the chief whip said flatly, "one fifty-two." Voting against the government in the Norway debate, Spears wrote, was "far harder and more difficult than anything that had come my way in the last war." Yet he believed it was necessary for the survival of the nation. His vote, along with those of his fellow rebels, was "our contribution to the war, our way of fighting."

But for more than a score of MPs waiting to vote that night, fighting meant more than involvement in the cut and thrust of Parliament, vital as that was. They were Army, Royal Navy, and Royal Air Force officers on active duty who had been summoned by the whips to participate in this debate. Unlike the young Britons who had fought in the Great War, they were being given the chance to influence their government's conduct of the war. Most of them were Tories who had been staunch Chamberlain supporters. Almost all of them voted against him.

Some, like Roy Wise, a lieutenant colonel in the Queen's Royal Regiment, had been caught up in the debacle in Norway. "I have come straight back from Namsos to vote against the Government," Wise told Hugh Dalton. "I voted on behalf of my men. We were bombed by German planes and had nothing with which to reply, not even a machine gun." Another young Norway veteran, a longtime admirer of Chamberlain's, silently walked through the Opposition lobby, tears streaming down his face. The crusty Dalton found he was crying too as he glanced around the lobby, which "seemed to be full of young Conservatives in uniform—khaki, Navy blue and Air Force blue all intermingled—many of them giving the last vote they would ever give, for their country and against their party."

One young officer spied by Dalton was the baby of the House, twenty-five-year-old John Profumo, who had just been elected to Parliament the month before in a by-election in Northamptonshire. The recent Oxford graduate, whose candidacy had been supported by the Chamberlain machine, had been given leave from his army unit in Essex to take part in the debate, although his fellow officers suspected that the fun-loving Profumo planned to spend the time off at a nightclub rather than in the Commons. But Profumo dutifully showed up in the chamber and, swayed by the arguments of the anti-Chamberlain rebels, decided it was his duty, in the interest of both his country and his regiment, to vote against the government.

As the chamber slowly cleared and the minutes ticked by, several Conservatives stayed in their seats, signifying their intention to abstain. But there was one young Tory remaining on the benches who still had not decided what to do. Ever since his celebrated by-election victory in Oxford in late 1938, Quintin Hogg had been regarded as the embodiment of appeasement. Still a strong supporter of Chamberlain's, he had joined a Territorial Army unit shortly after the war began and had been sent for training in Lincolnshire. Like Ronald Cartland and many other Territorial officers, Hogg soon discovered that the government seemed to have little interest in preparing his men and him for war. "For nine months, I had been in a . . . unit which had neither the equipment, the training, nor the transport to engage in field operations," he later remarked. There were no field exercises, no issuing of weapons (except for a .45 Colt pistol and three dumdum bullets to Hogg himself), no coordinated exercises with tank units or the RAF.

Hogg had arrived in London from Lincolnshire "in a thoroughly bloody-minded mood." After the two-day debate he still was agonizing over how he should vote. He was a firm believer in party loyalty, but he was also convinced of the "total nervelessness" of the government in running the war. His head was telling him to vote for the government or, if he couldn't bring himself to do that, to abstain. His "guts," as he later put it, were telling him that "the present administration had to be brought to an end." He sat on the bench for almost six minutes, the time allotted for a division. Just before the doorkeepers moved to lock the doors of the lobbies, Quintin Hogg rose from his seat. He strode resolutely to the rear of the chamber and turned left—into the "no" lobby.

After the division was over, MPs poured back into the chamber to await the results, all of them "so tense," as Spears remembered it, that "they seemed to be vibrating like taut wire." Once again the room was jammed. Members crowded the gangways and clustered around the Speaker's chair, and every seat in the galleries was taken. After what seemed like an endless wait, the four tellers marched in, took their places in front of the Speaker, and made their ritual bows. David Margesson was on the right, which meant that the government had won. But by how much? There was total silence as the crowd in the chamber focused its attention on the tall, lean figure of the chief government whip. In a calm, even voice, Margesson read out the numbers: ayes, 281; noes, 200. Members gasped, and the hush dissolved into pandemonium. Chamberlain's usual majority of 250 or more had dwindled to only 81! Forty-two Tory MPs had voted with the Opposition, and more than 40 had deliberately abstained as a sign of their displeasure with the government. In all, more than 20 percent of Conservative backbenchers were in open revolt against their prime minister. It was clear to everyone that Chamberlain's ostensible victory was really a stunning defeat.

Labour and Liberal MPs, along with Harold Macmillan and some of the other Tory rebels, leaped to their feet, cheering, shouting, and waving their order papers, while Chamberlain's dumbfounded supporters remained in their seats. Shouts of "Resign!" and "In the name of God, go!" filled the air. Josiah Wedgwood began to sing "Rule, Britannia," and Macmillan, who was sitting next to him, joined in. In the middle of the frenzy, Chamberlain, his face ashen, rose abruptly. As Margesson signaled Tory loyalists to stand and cheer the shaken prime minister, Chamberlain stepped over the feet of his colleagues on the front bench and walked out of the chamber. His wife, in a black coat and hat and wearing a nosegay of violets, watched from the gallery, looking "infinitely sad."

For almost everyone in the room, even for those who had worked so hard for months, even years to make this day a reality, it was a painful moment. Leo Amery, looking on from his seat below the gangway, did not regret his withering attack—it had to be done, he firmly believed—but he was sorry for the personal hurt he had caused his old friend. Bob Boothby, who was standing by the Speaker's chair, watched as Chamberlain's hunched figure, looking "truly sad and pathetic," slowly entered a dark corridor behind the chair and disappeared from sight. Remembering the triumphant Chamberlain after Munich, with crowds surging around him, Boothby couldn't help feeling "very sorry for him in this hour of his fall."

The prime minister's bitter supporters felt no such magnanimity, however, toward the Tory colleagues whom they held responsible for Chamberlain's humiliation. Euan Wallace, the financial secretary to the Treasury, refrained from going into the members' lobby after the House adjourned that night, because if he had, he later said, he would have knocked down Macmillan, who had been his fellow aide-de-camp in Canada twenty years before. The MPs who did venture into the lobby witnessed several hostile confrontations. One pro-Chamberlain MP sneeringly told a Tory rebel that he and his friends were like "enemy parachute troops who had descended behind the lines in Conservative uniform." Ronald Tree was besieged by several government loyalists who upbraided him for his vote. "You've got what you've been working for," one snarled. "I only hope you will regret it for the rest of your life." Indeed, some of the prime minister's supporters were determined to make sure he *did* regret it. Tree had been nominated for membership in the elite Royal Yacht Club, but the day after the vote his nomination was blackballed. Later he was told that a whip was overheard saying, "I'll cook Tree's chances," as he left the House the night before. Tree called his blackballing an act of "childish revenge." Revenge it clearly was. As events soon would prove, he was not the only Conservative dissident targeted for retaliation.

The young military officers who voted against the prime minister were also subjected to threats and recrimination. The morning after the vote, David Margesson gave a savage tongue-lashing to John Profumo, accusing him of betraying every principle he had been elected to support. "And I can tell you this, you utterly contemptible little shit," Margesson spit out. "On every morning that you wake up for the rest of your life you will be ashamed of what you did last night." The chief whip, Profumo noted many years later, couldn't have been more wrong.

When Quintin Hogg was told something similar by a fellow Tory MP who shared his train compartment on the way back to Lincolnshire, Hogg shot back: "Say that to me in six months' time!" He rejoined his army rifle unit, not knowing until later that hundreds of pieces of hate mail from government supporters had descended on his home in the days following the vote. His wife did not send them on.

Six months later Hogg and his unit were fighting the Germans in the Middle East. His Tory colleague never responded to his challenge.

CHAPTER EIGHTEEN

"VICTORY AT ALL COSTS"

———— ⌣ ————

After the House adjourned near midnight on May 8, someone asked an ebullient Hugh Dalton what would happen next. Dalton replied that the answer was clear: "The Old Man must go along to Buckingham Palace and hand in [his resignation]." Thanks to Winston Churchill, however, Chamberlain had decided otherwise.

Immediately after the vote, the prime minister had in fact summoned Churchill to his office at the Palace of Westminster to tell him that he was going to resign, that a new national government must be formed. But again Churchill's generosity and loyalty got the better of him. Astonishingly, he urged Chamberlain to fight to remain in office: "This has been a damaging debate, but you have a good majority. Do not take the matter grievously to heart." Buoyed by Churchill's support, Chamberlain decided to hold on. He went to the palace and told the king that he planned to continue in office and restructure his government.

Chamberlain's parliamentary opponents were stunned by this news and by Churchill's role in it. The prime minister, one Tory dissident said bitterly, was clinging to office "like a dirty old piece of chewing gum on the leg of a chair." How could he possibly think he could remain in power? His foes mobilized to stop that from happening, while he and his supporters worked equally furiously to see that it did. For the next two days Parliament and Downing Street were rife with whispered conversations and secret meetings, intrigue and conspiracy, plots and counterplots.

Told that a number of Tories who abstained or voted against him the previous night were having second thoughts, Chamberlain was on the phone from early morning on May 9, trying to placate the waverers. In his conversations with some MPs, he offered to get rid of the arch-appeasers in his cabinet, including Samuel Hoare, John Simon, and Kingsley Wood, if the members would agree to support his staying on. At one point that day, in a move instigated by Horace Wilson, he summoned Leo Amery to his office and offered him, on the same terms, his pick of any top post in the cabinet, including foreign secretary and chancellor of the exchequer. Amery rejected this attempt to buy him off, noting in his diary that "Neville's advisers" seemed to think that personal advancement was the only motive for his foes' criticism and opposition.

Amery and the other insurgent MPs moved quickly to head off the prime minister's campaign. That morning the Watching Committee approved a resolution declaring that Chamberlain must resign and that either Halifax or Churchill should be selected to form an all-party government. A few hours later Amery's group and the Vigilantes, along with other MPs who had voted against the government, met and reached a similar conclusion. They decided to support any prime minister who could form a truly national government, "appointing its men by merit and not on Whips' lines, and making a real war Cabinet"—in other words, Churchill or Halifax.

As they had before, Macmillan, Boothby, Clement Davies, and several others urged the rebels to come out for Churchill and against Halifax. But again Amery, who was in the chair, disagreed. Their focus now, he said, must be to get rid of Chamberlain. Many of those who voted against the prime minister the night before, including Attlee, Dalton, and other Labour members, as well as a fair number of Tories, preferred Halifax to Churchill. So did Lord Salisbury, most of the peers on the Watching Committee, and the king, whose support of the government's policies had been clear since his appearance with Chamberlain on the balcony of Buckingham Palace after Munich. All these figures continued to have doubts about the first lord, particularly over what they saw as his impetuosity and rash judgment, doubts that were hardly allayed by his behavior during the Norway debacle.

"The Whips are being very active," Amery said, and Chamberlain "has given vast promises of conciliation" to discontented Tories. Time was of the essence. Chamberlain's rearguard action must first be nipped in the bud, and then attention could be given to the question of his successor. The other dissidents finally agreed, and Boothby was dispatched to tell Labour and Liberal leaders what had been decided. The contacts between the rebels and Labour, which had begun with the clandestine meeting between Harold Macmillan and Hugh Dalton after Munich, were finally bearing fruit.

Finding Dalton in Annie's Bar, a popular little gathering place off the Commons lobby, Boothby asked him if the news of the rebels' decision would help bolster the Labour leaders' own opposition to Chamberlain. Dalton said it would, declaring that "no member of our Party would serve under Chamberlain" and agreeing that the press should be told of this joint determination to get the prime minister out. A few minutes later Dalton saw Boothby in the lobby, surrounded by journalists who were jotting down his remarks.

Yet while continuing their maneuvering to oust the prime minister, Boothby, Davies, and the other champions of Churchill did not stop promoting the first lord's candidacy or trying to torpedo Halifax. Davies, in particular, worked relentlessly to press Churchill's cause, using Boothby's flat in Pall Mall as his base. The Independent MP was a close friend of both Attlee's and Greenwood's, and he capitalized on those relationships to try to counter Labour's long-standing antipathy to Churchill. "No Labour leader at any level regarded Churchill as a friend, or even sympathetic to their cause," Robert Rhodes James has noted. Labour's animosity stemmed not just from Churchill's savage criticism of its party over the years. (He once declared that the election of a Labour government in Britain would be "a serious national misfortune" akin to defeat in war.) Many Labourites also believed that as home secretary Churchill had sent troops in 1910 to put down riots by striking mine workers in Tonypandy, Wales. It wasn't true. Churchill had sent troops to help keep the peace *after* the rioting was over. Nonetheless, the Tonypandy myth haunted Churchill for the rest of his political career.

Throughout the day on May 9, Davies lobbied Attlee and Green-wood on behalf of Churchill. He reminded them of Halifax's proap-peasement record and declared that Churchill was the only man with the energy and drive to lead Britain through the war. By early evening, he had made considerable headway, telling Boothby that the Labour leaders were now "unable to distinguish between the P.M. and Halifax, and are *not* prepared to serve under the latter." Brendan Bracken mean-while was also working on Attlee and Greenwood, telling them, on his own authority, that Churchill would not serve under Halifax and urg-ing them not to refuse to serve under Churchill.

When Churchill found out what Bracken had said, he angrily rebuked his PPS, declaring he would indeed be willing to serve under Halifax or, for that matter, under any minister capable of prosecuting the war. Nonetheless, if Chamberlain was not to remain in office, Churchill was convinced that he should be the one to replace the prime minister. He made that clear, without actually pressing his case, at a meeting that Chamberlain called that afternoon at Downing Street. To Churchill, Hal-ifax, and David Margesson, the prime minister acknowledged that the Labour Party must be brought into the government. If Labour leaders refused to join his cabinet, he indicated he was prepared to resign. The next question, of course, was who would take his place.

Churchill knew that Chamberlain wanted Halifax as his successor. Earlier in the day Kingsley Wood had urged the first lord not to agree to serve under Halifax when Chamberlain brought up the subject of his replacement. In fact, said Wood, Churchill shouldn't say anything at all when the question came up, a point that Bracken also apparently made. Considering that Wood had been one of Chamberlain's staunchest supporters, it seemed odd that at the last moment he was throwing his lot in with Churchill. His decision probably had much to do with the fact that Chamberlain had been telling others all day he was willing to dump Wood, among other cabinet members, to save himself.

In any event, Churchill did as Wood and Bracken had suggested. He remained silent at the meeting, letting Halifax carry the conversa-tion. Although Halifax earlier had told his undersecretary, Rab Butler, that he felt sure he could do the job of prime minister, he had no driv-ing ambition to become head of the government. Unlike Churchill, he knew and cared little about military matters or the strategy of war. If he became prime minister, he would have to appoint Churchill minister of defense, thus making Winston the key man in the government for the duration of the war. Halifax had a hard enough time dealing with the irrepressible Churchill as first lord; he was sure Churchill would be unmanageable if he were put in charge of all war operations. And since Halifax was a member of the House of Lords, he, unlike Churchill, would have no voice in the Commons. But Halifax's lack of enthusiasm for the job may also have reflected his awareness of the growing momentum of the pro-Churchill campaign being waged by the Tory dissidents and their allies. Indeed, Margesson noted during the meeting that sentiment in the Commons had started "veering" toward Churchill.

So when Chamberlain told the others that he thought Halifax was the most acceptable candidate, the foreign secretary made clear his reluctance to take the job. "I said it would be a hopeless position," Halifax told Alexander Cadogan. "If I was not in charge of the war and if I didn't lead in the House, I should be a cipher. I thought Winston was a better choice. Winston did not demur. He was very kind and polite but showed that he thought this the right solution."

Later that day Chamberlain met with Attlee and Greenwood and asked if their party would join his government. Churchill, who was also present, urged them to agree. Attlee at first appeared indecisive, but Greenwood said he was sure the answer would be no. The two men told the prime minister they would seek the views of Labour's national executive board, meeting the following day in Bournemouth, for confirmation.

Thus, as the soft, balmy afternoon of May 9 deepened into evening, it appeared virtually certain that Churchill would be named prime minister the following day. Many of those who had previously favored Halifax, among them Lord Salisbury, had now agreed to support Churchill. In a conversation with Macmillan that night, Brendan Bracken was "guarded . . . but seemed happy." Once again, however, Chamberlain complicated matters by having second thoughts about resigning. This time, the impetus for his change of heart came from Adolf Hitler.

Friday, May 10, dawned clear and lovely, another in a seemingly endless string of glorious spring days. It was the last working day before the

Whitsun break, and Britons were looking forward to the holiday. Those who turned on the wireless early that morning, however, were jolted out of their relaxed mood. The BBC announced that German troops had been pouring into Belgium, the Netherlands, and Luxembourg since before dawn. Bombs were raining down on towns and villages throughout the Low Countries and France. After being tested in Poland and Scandinavia, the Nazi blitzkrieg was now slicing through the very heart of Western Europe. On that day, as *Picture Post* later put it, the people of Britain "realized that total war was upon us at last." The Whitsun holiday was canceled, the government ordered all citizens to resume carrying their gas masks, Air Raid Precautions personnel geared up again, and huge crowds massed outside 10 Downing Street.

The House of Commons had adjourned for the holiday, but many MPs remained in London, awaiting word of Chamberlain's resignation. Exhausted after the previous three emotion-filled days at the House, Harold Macmillan spent the morning at his family's publishing firm, trying to catch up on a backlog of work but finding it difficult to focus on editing matters with the world in chaos. Then Bracken phoned him with even more distressing news. As a result of the German invasion, Chamberlain had decided he must remain as prime minister, that a change of government would cause too much difficulty and confusion during this time of national crisis. He planned to ask Labour leaders to support his government, and rumors were already swirling that Labour had agreed. Bracken was furious, as were Macmillan and Chamberlain's other opponents. "The Old Man is an incorrigible limpet," Hugh Dalton fumed, "always trying new tricks to keep himself firm on the rock."

The prime minister's foes swung back into action. Paul Emrys-Evans and Dick Law saw Lord Salisbury, who told them that "we must maintain our point of view, namely that Winston should be made Prime Minister during the course of the day." Clement Davies, working from Boothby's flat, talked to Greenwood after the Labour leaders arrived in Bournemouth for their executive meeting and secured Greenwood's denial of the rumor of Labour's support of Chamberlain. Both the Salisbury and Greenwood statements were released immediately to the press.

Yet Chamberlain continued to believe he had dodged defeat. To members of his cabinet, he seemed energized, even "stimulated," in the view of one, by the news from the Low Countries. Indeed, he acted as if Amery's devastating attack on him and the disastrous House vote had never occurred, even though Kingsley Wood had told him earlier that day that he must resign. Midway through the cabinet meeting, an aide entered the Cabinet Room and handed a piece of paper to Horace Wilson, who glanced at it and, with no change of expression, passed it across the table to Chamberlain. It was a message from Attlee and Greenwood, informing Chamberlain of Labour's decision not to join his government and spelling the end of the prime minister's frantic attempts to stay in power. The cabinet meeting was adjourned, and within an hour the prime minister was on his way to Buckingham Palace.

Accepting Chamberlain's resignation with reluctance, George VI expressed anger toward the prime minister's opponents. "I told him how grossly unfairly I thought he had been treated and that I was terribly sorry that all this controversy had happened," the king recalled. When he said he thought Halifax should replace Chamberlain, the prime minister told him it was to be Churchill.

Early that evening a decidedly unenthusiastic monarch summoned Winston Churchill to the palace. He left as prime minister. Although Hitler had no way of knowing it, he had just suffered his first major defeat. Years later Churchill wrote in his memoirs: "Considering the prominent part I played in [the Norway disaster] . . . it was a marvel that I survived." He could not have done so—and certainly could not have become prime minister—without the help of the Tory rebels and their Labour, Liberal, and Independent allies.

Parliament, the guardian of democracy, had finally triumphed.

From his first days as leader of his country Winston Churchill made clear to the British people, to Germany, and to the rest of the world that at long last appeasement was over. Britain was going to fight. "You ask what is our aim?" he declared to the House of Commons on May 13. "I can answer in one word—victory. Victory at all costs, victory in spite of all terror, victory, however long and hard the road may be; for without victory, there is no survival." As he listened to those words, Leo Amery beamed. "That is what we had been waiting for all those long, depressing, disheartening months," he later wrote. "That for me was the justification of my own efforts to secure leadership worthy of the occasion."

Years later, in his memoirs, Amery reflected on the transformation of his unruly schoolboy comrade into a man of destiny: "Above all, [Churchill] believed in himself and in his countrymen. All his life he had striven for greatness. Now the time and place for greatness were his, and he could rise to the full height of his opportunity." The Churchillian qualities that many before had seen as serious flaws—his combativeness, high-flown rhetoric, soaring romanticism, egotism—became, in these calamitous days, essential virtues. "For once," Amery remarked, "democracy had found a leader who could not only voice its spirit but who was also a great master of war." With understandable pride, he added, "I think I was mainly instrumental in bringing it about."

Within hours of Churchill's taking office on May 10, Downing Street and much of Whitehall were forced to shed their orderly, leisurely routines. The new prime minister "arrived on the scene like a jet-propelled rocket," recalled John Colville, whom Churchill kept on as private secretary. "The pace became frantic . . . . Replies were expected within minutes of questions being asked, staid officials actually took to running, and bells rang continuously." The chiefs of staff and their planning committees were in almost constant session, some government offices worked around the clock, and for most top officials, there were to be no more relaxed country weekends. "We realized," said Colville, that "we were at war." With Churchill's accession, there also was no more talk of the evacuation of Parliament or key Whitehall departments if London was bombed. Under no circumstances, Churchill announced, would top government agencies leave the British capital.

Conventional wisdom has it that at the time of Churchill's assumption of power, the British people were sunk in lethargy and that only in the nick of time did the new prime minister shake them out of their stupor and, as Isaiah Berlin put it, "transform cowards into brave men." In truth, they had never been given the chance to be brave. Many, if not most, Britons were already champing at the bit to fight; for months they had been yearning for someone to lead them in the effort. Shortly before the Norway debate an American diplomat in London told James

Reston of *The New York Times* that "all this country needs is a theme song. The British need somebody to come along and give them a rallying cry—a great personal leader. If they get that, they've got the men and the courage to win the war."

Mass Observation, the British social research organization, echoed that view. "Everywhere, people were eagerly waiting for directions," one of its reports declared. "They were itching for something to do." One young woman told a Mass Observation researcher immediately after Churchill's takeover: "There is no denying that there is a great fount of energy in this country, seething and boiling to get on with things. I do hope that Churchill . . . is going to announce a mobilization of our resources. People are dying for it."

When the new prime minister declared on May 13, "Come then, let us go forward together with our united strength," his countrymen accepted the invitation with gusto. Within days of a government appeal for volunteers for a Home Guard to defend Britain against German invaders, more than 250,000 men offered their services. By the end of June more than half a million had enlisted in the Home Guard ranks. The economy meanwhile was quickly mobilized, with many factories voluntarily adopting seven-day workweeks and ten- to twelve-hour shifts. Disputes between industry and labor showed a dramatic decline.

"Resistance was in the air—on the streets, in the papers, everywhere, and in everything," observed the American journalist Ben Robertson, who arrived in London shortly after Churchill took office. An old woman who lived in South London told him that the people in her neighborhood were getting ready, street by street and house by house, to fight the Germans. "I've got a butcher knife myself," she said, "and I'm going to take one German with me to glory."

As the news on the Continent grew increasingly darker over the next several weeks, the resolve and fortitude of the British people were put to their first real test. Within five days of being invaded, the Netherlands was crushed and Belgium was close to surrender. More than a million German troops and fifteen hundred tanks were tearing through the French countryside, having outflanked the vaunted Maginot Line ("the greatest fraud in modern history," *Picture Post* sourly called the supposedly impenetrable chain of fortifications), striking through the Ardennes Forest and crossing the Meuse River. Cut off from French forces in the south, the vastly outnumbered British and French troops in Belgium and northern France found themselves in a trap, with the enemy about to slam the door of the cage. Their only alternative to surrender was to retreat northwest—to the beaches of Dunkirk and, they hoped, evacuation.

As Churchill, Amery, and the other opponents of appeasement had predicted for years, Britain was now reaping the whirlwind for its previous governments' failure to prepare the country for war. "We were so ill-prepared," Lord Beaverbrook, one of the staunchest appeasers, acknowledged many years later. "Our peril was beyond comprehension." When he heard the news of the May 13 German firebombing of Rotterdam, Leo Amery thought back to Chamberlain's adamant refusal over the course of the phony war to bomb any nonmilitary German targets and his reluctance to bomb any military installations, planes, trucks, or ships as well. "What could have suited the Germans better," Amery wrote, "than to be able to mount that immense [invasion] with the undisturbed use of all their communications by rail, road, canal and river, up to the moment when Hitler showed what he thought of the 'humanitarian' air truce by smothering defenceless Rotterdam in flames?"

The RAF finally was sent into action against the enemy in France, but it was overwhelmed almost immediately by the Luftwaffe's superior force. After ten days of combat, more than 80 percent of the 135 British bombers sent to help defend France had been shot down or destroyed on the ground. The attrition rate for RAF fighter pilots and planes was almost as severe, with more than three hundred fliers killed or reported missing in the first three weeks of fighting. "From the Royal Air Force point of view, the battle for France was a complete and utter shambles," a British pilot later recalled. "There was no intelligence. Communications were poor. Everything appeared to be ad hoc." The same held true for the operations of the British Army.

By the last week of May the German juggernaut seemed unstoppable. British forces had begun their retreat toward Dunkirk, pursued by German troops and strafed by dive-bombers as they fled down dusty roads and lanes leading to the port. Elsewhere in the country French troops were surrendering by the thousands. It was at that critical moment that Lord Halifax, whom Churchill had kept on as foreign secretary, suggested the possibility of peace negotiations with Hitler.

When the War Cabinet met on May 26 to discuss the latest spate of disastrous news from the French fronts, Halifax argued that the war was unwinnable. The day before, the Italian ambassador had told him that Mussolini was willing to serve as an intermediary between the Allies and Hitler to discuss peace terms. Halifax urged acceptance of Mussolini's offer. In exchange for the preservation of the independence and freedom of Britain and, it was hoped, its empire, the foreign secretary was prepared to concede to the führer domination of the European continent.

To Churchill, the idea that Germany would allow Britain its freedom while controlling the rest of Europe was an absurd and profoundly dangerous illusion. "We should become a slave state," he declared, and after four days of debate within the War Cabinet, he rejected this last gasp of appeasement and defeatism. On May 28 the prime minister met with the full cabinet and vowed to the cheering ministers that whatever happened at Dunkirk, "we shall fight it out." Realizing he was beaten, Halifax gave in. "Then and there," the historian John Lukacs has written, Churchill "saved Britain, and Europe, and Western civilization."

A delighted Ronald Cartland heard the news of Chamberlain's resignation and Churchill's accession on May 10, just after he and his unit crossed the French frontier to join the fighting in Belgium. He scribbled a short note to his mother: "A grand new Government, I think. I'm *so* glad . . . now we are justified. And Winston—our hope—he may yet save civilization." Cartland had little time, however, to ponder the ramifications of the change of government. He was a major now, in command of a battery attached to the Fifty-third Anti-Tank Regiment, Royal Artillery, which was very much in the thick of the action. Despite the chaos and carnage of war, Cartland found he liked being a soldier and, indeed, turned out to be very good at it. "He loved the Army," Dick Law recalled. "And he had a boyish delight in the success he was having in it." Churchill's takeover had erased much of Cartland's gloom about the future, and his natural lightheartedness and joie de vivre were once again on full display. "I am extraordinarily fit, and wildly rebellious—in a word, my dear Gilbert, just exactly as you have always known me," he wrote to a friend.

With Belgium collapsing, Cartland and his unit, like the rest of the British Expeditionary Force, were ordered to retreat back into France. About the flight westward, the young MP wrote to a woman acquaintance: "The weather is perfect, and the country looks beautiful. Flowers and gardens are at their very best." But he also told her about the charred bodies he saw, the burning houses, "and all the horrors of war come to life . . . The bombs fall and I hear the drone of the German airplanes. They are after us . . . Our [antiaircraft] guns are most disappointing."

At the same time, his mind was still focused on the new government in London. Two weeks after the changeover, he was impatiently trying to find out more about what was going on. "No letters—no papers," he wrote his mother. "I hardly know who is in the new Cabinet and none of the Ministries and Undersecretaries—which of course I want to know a lot. From all I hear Winston is proving simply first-rate. I am delighted about it—a Govt at last which I can *wholeheartedly* support."

During the last week of May, Cartland's battery was assigned to the defense of Cassel, a small medieval hill town that overlooked a main road leading to Dunkirk, about nineteen miles to the north. Cassel, which boasted spectacular panoramic views of the green and gold fields of northern France, was perhaps the most important strongpoint of a sixty-mile-long escape corridor hurriedly organized by the BEF high command; within this narrow passageway tens of thousands of British troops were retreating north to the coast. The mission of Cartland's battery, along with units of the 145th Infantry Brigade, was to use their hilltop position to hold off for as long as possible the swarms of German panzers and troops pursuing the British.

In the early morning of May 27 the enemy attacked Cassel in force. Tanks, artillery, and mortars battered the town while waves of Stukas swept down, machine guns blazing. Although they suffered heavy casualties, the town's defenders managed to drive the Germans back, destroying more than twenty-five enemy tanks in the process. During the assault, according to one of Cartland's men, the major was "everywhere," keeping up the troops' spirits, helping move guns that had been knocked out of action, and taking up a Bren gun himself against the Germans. A lieutenant in Cartland's unit later described his superior officer as "absolutely magnificent" in the fight, adding that he didn't "know a braver person than Ronnie."

The Cassel defenders held on for two more days, fending off a second German attack and expecting a counteroffensive by British and French troops at any moment. They had no way of knowing that Allied resistance had almost entirely collapsed and that on the morning of May 28 they themselves had been ordered to withdraw to Dunkirk. The BEF communications network was in shambles, however, and the message to the men in Cassel did not reach them until twenty-four hours later—on the morning of May 29. By then the Germans had brought in reinforcements, and the place was surrounded. Luftwaffe aircraft rained leaflets down on the town, calling on the British troops to surrender since all "your generals are gone!"

Cassel's defenders had no intention of doing so. Late that night they destroyed their heavy guns and vehicles and, armed only with rifles and other small arms, managed to slip stealthily out of the burning town on foot. Under cover of darkness, they split up and headed northeast, toward Dunkirk. At eight-thirty the following morning Cartland and the fifty-some men in his battery were only a few miles from Dunkirk, walking, half concealed, in a ditch that bordered a road. A heavy mist had given them protection since dawn, but it was now burning off. Before them was open countryside, and in the distance, about a half mile ahead, they saw German tanks firing on another British unit.

Before they could take cover, they were spotted and came under heavy fire themselves. Cartland rose slightly from the ditch to reconnoiter. As he did so, he was shot in the head. He died instantly, the first member of Parliament killed in World War II. His men, crouching a few yards away, were marched off into German captivity. Although they had made it possible for untold numbers of British troops to reach Dunkirk, virtually none of the men at Cassel made it to the beaches themselves.

Because the other men in Cartland's unit were taken prisoner, his fate remained a mystery for several months. On June 6 his mother received two telegrams from the War Office informing her that both Ronald and her younger son, Tony, a twenty-eight-year-old captain in the Lincolnshire Regiment, were missing in action. In the midst of coping with the debacle in France and the Dunkirk evacuation, Winston Churchill phoned Mary Cartland three times during this period, asking if she had received any further news of Ronald. During one call he told her he planned to give her son a ministry post when—if—he returned. He also wrote her a letter of sympathy, and when she thanked him for it, he sent her a telegram that said simply: "I so often think about him."

Not until January 4, 1941, did the uncertainty end. Mary Cartland received a letter from the mother of one of Ronald's junior officers, who had just heard from her son, now a German prisoner of war. In his letter, the young officer described Cartland's death in detail. When the news was made public, Mary and Barbara Cartland were deluged with more than five hundred letters of condolence.* "It is with very great sorrow that I have heard that you have received news that Ronald was killed in action," Churchill wrote Mrs. Cartland. "Pray accept my deepest sympathy in the loss of so brilliant and splendid a son, whose exceptional abilities would have carried him far, had he not so proudly given his life for his country."

The death of a young man or woman of great potential almost always evokes deep feelings of pain and deprivation when one considers the promise, the hopes and dreams, that will never be fulfilled. But in the case of Ronald Cartland, the outpouring of anguish, the sense of waste, the belief that Britain had suffered a grievous loss with his death were truly remarkable. "The more I think about it, the more conscious I become of the reality of that loss to the country," Dick Law wrote to Leo Amery. Law added: "Politics is a murky and a painful business, and people like Ronald cast a kind of radiance over it to make it all tolerable. I shall always be glad to think that our paths touched, even for so short a time. Don't you feel that?"

---

*A month later Mary Cartland learned that Tony had been killed on May 29, the day before Ronald's death. Tony Cartland and his company had been holding a rearguard trench near Louvain when they were surrounded and ordered to surrender. Cartland refused and continued firing at the enemy until he was cut down by automatic-rifle fire.

Again and again fellow MPs talked of Cartland as the shining hope of his political generation, a man who one day might well have achieved his boyhood goal of becoming prime minister. "Ronald had everything before him," Anthony Eden remarked. "We were all so sure that he had a great part to play in the world after the war . . . Of all the younger men I knew, his was the fairest future . . . He [was the one who] could least be spared." Echoing that sentiment, Bob Boothby wrote: "Ronnie would have been one of the Builders. His loss can scarcely be estimated." And Law later declared: "It is impossible to write adequately of Ronald. I shall always think of him as one of the really great men that I have known."

When he heard of Cartland's death, Amery spent one morning poring through old *Hansard* parliamentary records and reading all of Ronald's speeches in the House, from his 1936 maiden address on. "I was much struck not only by their courage but by their constructive and forward outlook," Amery told Law. In a letter to *The Times*, he noted that "rare" and "shining" courage that he said was on full display in Cartland's passionate fight for social justice and his battle against appeasement.

In *The Spectator*, Harold Nicolson declared that death was "the only surrender of which Ronald Cartland would have been capable." To Nicolson and the other anti-appeasement rebels, Cartland was "more than an example, he was a lesson . . . He was that amazing phenomenon: a young man of the postwar generation who actually believed in himself. He gave us faith." When he heard that Cartland had been killed, Nicolson, like many of his parliamentary colleagues, thought back to the young MP's speech less than a year before, in which he called Chamberlain a dictator to his face and predicted that very soon "we may be going to fight, and we may be going to die." "We shall forever remember him as he was at that moment," Nicolson wrote. "Defiant, faithful, devoted, and brave beyond compare."

On February 18, 1941, six months after the Luftwaffe had begun nightly air raids on London, a memorial service was held for Ronald Cartland at St. Martin-in-the-Fields Church, not far from Trafalgar Square. The church, whose south-side windows had been blown out in one of the raids, was jammed. Brendan Bracken represented the prime minister, and many of the anti-appeasement rebels—Harold Nicolson, Leo Amery, Dick Law, Harold Macmillan, Ronald Tree, Edward Spears, Duncan Sandys, Paul Emrys-Evans—were also there.

Listening to the eulogies, Emrys-Evans recalled a frosty day in early 1939 when he and Cartland went for a hike near Emrys-Evans's country house in Shropshire, not far from the Welsh border. As they walked along a trail, Cartland began talking about his love of his country and his anxieties about the future. He was certain that war was coming and that "all the well-meant endeavors to prevent it would fail." At the same time, he said, he was convinced that Britain and its people would finally prevail. Pausing for a moment, Cartland looked out at the distant mountains of Wales, blue against the gray winter sky. He turned to Emrys-Evans and said, as matter-of-factly as if he had been talking about the weather, that he "would not be there to see these things come to pass."

At the end of the memorial service the choir from Charterhouse, Cartland's alma mater, sang the hymn "O Valiant Hearts Who to Your Glory Came":

> Tranquil you lie, your knightly virtue proved,
> Your memory hallowed in the land you loved.

With that, the young MP's friends and colleagues left the church and returned to the streets of bomb-blasted London—back to Westminster, Whitehall, and the business of fighting the war.

CHAPTER NINETEEN

A QUESTION OF LOYALTY

On June 4, 1940, when British troops were being evacuated from the beaches of Dunkirk, the fall of France was imminent, and a German invasion of Britain was expected to follow soon afterward, Winston Churchill appeared before the House of Commons to proclaim: "We shall go on to the end . . . We shall defend our island, whatever the cost may be . . . We shall never surrender." For the next five years Churchill never wavered in that determination to fight to the death. In the first days of his administration, however, he had appointed to key government posts men who had done their best to keep their country from waging war, even after it had been declared. Virtually every major figure identified with appeasement retained his old job under Churchill or was given a new position, including Chamberlain himself, Halifax, Kingsley Wood, John Simon, Horace Wilson, and David Margesson. (Samuel Hoare was one of the few not given a top job. He was banished to Spain as British ambassador.) Except for the prime minister and a few other ministers, the new regime appeared to be very much like the one it replaced. It was, said one unhappy Tory rebel, "all the old gang."

Indeed, less than two hours after Churchill had taken over as prime minister on May 10, his continuing loyalty to Chamberlain threatened to blow up into a major political crisis. Without consulting the Labour leaders whom he needed to include in his new all-party government, Churchill offered his predecessor the key posts of chancellor of the exchequer and leader of the House of Commons, as well as a seat in the War Cabinet. In effect, the proposal would have made Chamberlain deputy prime minister. Chamberlain announced the new positions himself in his farewell radio address as prime minister that evening.

Many listeners were stunned, and none more so than Attlee and Greenwood. With reluctance, they accepted Chamberlain's inclusion in the War Cabinet, but they would not tolerate his appointment to the other positions. The Tories who had worked so hard to oust Chamberlain were equally appalled. Early on May 10 the Watching Committee, initially the most reluctant to get rid of him, had agreed that Chamberlain must be expelled from the government when Churchill took over. Lord Salisbury was delegated to tell Churchill of the committee's view but didn't get the chance: the new prime minister had already let Chamberlain know he wanted him to remain in the government's inner circles.

On May 11, Boothby, Macmillan, Emrys-Evans, and Law met at Amery's house to discuss what could be done to ward off what they believed was a full-blown political disaster. Clement Davies, who joined them, declared that Attlee and Greenwood now had grave doubts whether Labour should join Churchill's government after all. In the middle of the discussion, Bobbety Cranborne phoned to find out what was going on. When Amery told him of the new crisis, Cranborne put his father on the line. Everyone knew that Churchill respected Salisbury and listened to his views. Salisbury promised to call the new prime minister at once and convey their strong objections, as well as those of Labour, to Chamberlain's appointment. According to Amery, Salisbury's intervention "made all the difference." Churchill now backed down. Instead of chancellor and House leader, Chamberlain was named lord president of the council, a largely honorific, though potentially influential, post, depending on the political importance of its occupant. (Stanley Baldwin had the title of lord president when he and the Conservatives were pulling the strings in Ramsay MacDonald's government in the early 1930s.) But Chamberlain would stay in the small War Cabinet, whose other members were Churchill, Lord Halifax, Attlee, and Greenwood.

As more ministerial appointments were announced over the next few days, Labour leaders and the Tory rebels found many of them to be almost as disturbing as the retention of Chamberlain. It was true that several Labour figures, including Hugh Dalton, Ernest Bevin, and Herbert Morrison, were given high-ranking positions: Dalton became minister of economic warfare; Bevin, minister of labor; and Morrison, minister of supply. Yet of the thirty-six ministerial posts disclosed by May 15, twenty-one were given to men who had served under Chamberlain. Not only did Halifax remain as foreign secretary, but Rab Butler, one of the most aggressive proponents of appeasement in the government, stayed on in the Foreign Office as undersecretary. In the words of the historian Andrew Roberts, Butler had taken to appeasement "with an unholy glee not shared after the Anschluss by anyone else in the Foreign Office. His extreme partisanship against members of his own party, his relish for backroom deals, and his almost messianic opposition to Churchill make [him] seem a thoroughly unattractive figure."

Churchill also wanted Lloyd George in the cabinet as minister of agriculture and tried to persuade Chamberlain not to oppose the appointment. After considerable pressure from the prime minister, a reluctant Chamberlain finally agreed, but Lloyd George, a close friend of Churchill's who nonetheless had opposed him on many policy and political issues over the years, turned the post down, refusing to be in any government that included Chamberlain and Halifax.

Horace Wilson was ejected from his Downing Street office but retained his influential position as head of the Civil Service and permanent secretary to the Treasury. John Simon became lord chancellor, serving as leader of the House of Lords and head of the British judiciary. Kingsley Wood, the onetime devoted friend of Chamberlain's and prominent appeaser, whose idea of waging war as air minister was to drop pamphlets, not bombs, replaced Simon as chancellor of the exchequer. The plump, bespectacled Wood knew nothing about finance, and the gossip in both pro- and anti-Chamberlain political circles was that he had been given this tremendously important position as a reward for switching his allegiance to Churchill at a crucial moment.

But the appointment that most upset the Tory rebels was Churchill's retention of David Margesson as chief government whip. For almost two years Margesson, James Stuart, and the other Tory whips (most of whom also were kept on by Churchill) had done everything in their power to make the rebels' lives miserable. They had spied on them, encouraged other MPs to ostracize them, tried to break them politically. The dissidents could not believe that Churchill would allow Margesson to continue in office, especially since Churchill himself had received similar rough treatment from the whips. While Churchill might have been able to forgive and forget, his wife could not. Furious at Margesson's reappointment, Clementine Churchill told the chief whip exactly what she thought of him during one encounter, and when Churchill invited Margesson for lunch at Admiralty House shortly after he became prime minister, Clementine refused to attend, going out for a walk instead.

There was even more distressing news about Margesson: Churchill, in the midst of coping with the disaster in France, had no time to deal with the lesser ministerial appointments, so he handed them over to the chief whip and to Brendan Bracken, whom Churchill had kept on as parliamentary private secretary. These were the posts for which, under normal circumstances, the younger Tory rebels would be considered. But as Bracken warned Macmillan and the others, Margesson was not inclined to be generous to the dissidents, notwithstanding Churchill's generosity toward him.

At the time of his takeover and, later, in his memoirs, Churchill argued that he had no choice but to retain Chamberlain and his associates in the government because his own position with the Conservative majority in the House, many of whom still considered Chamberlain their leader, was still extremely tenuous. With Britain in such grave danger, it was essential, in Churchill's view, that he do nothing to antagonize the dominant party in Parliament. He was afraid that if he didn't conciliate Chamberlain, Halifax, and the others, they might use their majority to bring him down.

That attitude reflected one of the many complexities in Churchill's character. As confident as he was of his ability to lead the nation in what more and more people were realizing was the darkest moment of its history, he had little self-assurance, at least in the beginning of his premiership, when it came to dealing with his own party in the House of Commons. Having switched parties twice, he'd been a parliamentary loner for much of his career, unpopular with most of his colleagues, whether Tory, Labour, or Liberal, and rarely able to muster much support for the policies and positions important to him. There was a distinct vulnerability about him where Parliament was concerned. "The House of Commons used to frighten him . . . for years, perhaps up to the war," Brendan Bracken later said.

Yet Churchill was also correct in his belief that many Tories had not reconciled themselves to his succeeding Chamberlain, even though he had been steadfastly loyal to *their* leader during the phony war. Many were openly hostile. John Colville later declared: "Seldom can a prime minister have taken office with the establishment so dubious of the choice and so prepared to have its doubts justified." On May 13, when Churchill made his first appearance in the House as prime minister (to deliver his soaring "victory at all costs" speech) he was snubbed by most of the Tory backbenchers, who sat silently when Churchill came in but jumped to their feet and cheered lustily when Chamberlain took his seat next to the new prime minister. Churchill won cheers only from the Tory rebels, Labourites, and Liberals.

Nonetheless, in the view of many of Churchill's supporters, he was exaggerating his political vulnerability and sending the wrong signals to the country and the world by keeping the discredited appeasers in office. Even some of those who agreed that he had to be wary of the Conservative majority thought he had gone too far in retaining in high posts almost all the men responsible for the terrible position in which Britain now found itself. "The Cabinet is deplorable & seems to have been entirely dictated by Party exigencies . . . " Violet Bonham Carter wrote. "Winston will, of course, run it but the others do not even present a surface on which a mind c[ou]ld strike."

The Economist decried most of Churchill's appointments, particularly that of Kingsley Wood, which it termed "a disaster." Under a headline reading "Thank God for Churchill," the *Sunday Pictorial* declared: "Let us pray, too, for an end to the political game and an end to Mr. Chamberlain's perilous regime. Give us a cabinet we can believe in! The world will then see the stoutest nation in its finest, triumphant hour!" The *Sunday Pictorial* and its sister paper, the *Daily Mirror*, had been among the handful of newspapers that in prewar days had consistently opposed appeasement and strongly supported Churchill and his views. Cecil

King, the head of the Mirror newspaper group, unsuccessfully remonstrated with Churchill over what he saw as the folly of keeping Chamberlain, Halifax, and the others in office. Churchill "is strong enough in the country, if not in the Tory Party, to throw them all out and be damned to them," King wrote in his diary. "It seems to me that time and the nation are so clearly against the Tory backbenchers that Churchill can defy them and get away with it." *Nineteenth Century and After*, a literary and current affairs journal, agreed. "What need has Churchill of the Conservative leadership?" it demanded. "The country has put him where he is. He is not there on the sufferance of any sulky Conservatives." A Gallup poll taken that summer revealed that three-quarters of the British public wanted Chamberlain out of the government.

None of that mattered to Churchill. For in addition to his concerns about his political base, there was a strong element of emotion in his decision to retain Chamberlain, if not the others. He believed he and his predecessor had formed a close friendship during the phony war, and he was determined to remain faithful to his friend, regardless of what anyone else said or thought. "Churchill had a certain naivete in his character," Harold Macmillan later remarked. "He hated disbelieving in people." At the end of May the prime minister wrote to Lloyd George: "I have received a very great deal of help from Chamberlain. His kindness and courtesy to me in our new relations have touched me. I have joined hands with him and must act with perfect loyalty."

Yet as Churchill soon discovered, there was a price to be paid for keeping the men of Munich in office: he was forced to spend valuable time and energy putting out brushfires of appeasement. Early in Churchill's tenure Duff Cooper warned him that the "Munich spirit is not dead in this country." Some officials, Cooper said, still believed that "you can defeat your enemies by kind words and courtesy." Chamberlain, for one, although supporting Churchill in his battle with Halifax over peace negotiations in late May, had not given up urging gentle treatment of the enemy, declaring to the War Cabinet two days after he resigned that German oil refineries and factories should not be bombed.

Rab Butler meanwhile came close to disloyalty. In midsummer he told a high-ranking Swedish diplomat in London, in an obvious reference to Churchill, that "no diehards would be allowed to stand in the way" of peace with Germany if "reasonable conditions could be agreed." Butler added that Lord Halifax had asked him to pass on the message that "common sense and not bravado" would dictate British government policy. The Swedish diplomat reported to Stockholm on his meeting with Butler, news of which also made its way to Berlin. It appeared, said a German Foreign Ministry memo, that "sound common sense in authoritative circles in London" had returned.

Thanks to British intelligence Churchill too was informed of the conversation. Although he was angry, he sent a relatively restrained message to Halifax, declaring that the foreign secretary's deputy had "held odd language" with the Swedish diplomat and that "certainly the Swede derived a strong impression of defeatism." An unapologetic Halifax strongly defended Butler: "I should be very sorry if you felt any doubt either about Butler's discretion or his complete loyalty to Government policy, of which I am completely satisfied." Churchill let the matter drop, and Butler kept his job. Yet he showed little gratitude; to his associates, he referred to Churchill as "a half-breed American," talked sneeringly of "Winston and his rabble," and declared that the new administration was "a serious disaster." On the day that Churchill became prime minister, Butler and three other Chamberlain loyalists in the government opened a bottle of champagne and toasted Chamberlain as their "king over the water." Early on, Butler even held out hope that Chamberlain would be brought back as prime minister and made it clear he would do what he could to bring that about.

He was hardly alone. The fact that two-thirds of Chamberlain's top appointees were still in the government did not stop Tories from being outraged that Churchill was now in charge. When she learned that Churchill had become prime minister, Nancy Dugdale, the wife of one of Margesson's junior whips, wrote in fury to her husband, who was then serving with the army in Palestine: "I could hardly control myself . . . W. C. is really the counterpart of Goering in England, full of the desire for blood, 'Blitzkrieg,' and bloated with ego and over-feeding, the same treachery running through his veins, punctuated by heroics and hot air. I can't tell you how depressed I feel about it." Dugdale was even more incensed by the idea that "all those reptile satellites—Duff Cooper–

Bob Boothby–Brendan Bracken, etc.—will ooze into jobs they are utterly unfitted for. All we are fighting to uphold will go out of public life. I regard this as a greater disaster than the invasion of the Low Countries."

That astonishing last statement of Dugdale's reflected the attitude of many pro-Chamberlain Tories at the time. For the next several weeks they devoted their energies to undermining their country's new leader rather than joining forces behind him to defend Britain in its hour of supreme crisis. "When the nation outside Parliament unified to meet the Nazi threat, imposing upon itself an extraordinary self discipline, their elected representatives schemed, criticized and joined cabals to withhold their full-hearted support from the coalition," Andrew Roberts noted. "Parliamentary cabals became more outspoken as the military situation became more desperate." The Tory rebels had put their country before their party. Chamberlain's supporters now were doing the opposite.

It was a shameful situation, and Neville Chamberlain, at least in the early days of Churchill's government, did nothing to stop it. There is no indication that he himself intrigued against Churchill, but there is also no indication that he did anything to halt the intriguing going on in his name. As *Contemporary Review* noted, Margesson and the whips had imposed such tight control on the Conservative majority that except for the Tories who had voted against Chamberlain or abstained, it had become "a solid, unquestioning body of robots, silent, except for the chorus of cheers ever ready to be evoked for their leader." If Chamberlain and Margesson had wanted to put an end to the sniping and plotting against Churchill, there is little doubt they could have done so.

But during those early days Chamberlain was obsessed with the plots that he believed his enemies were hatching against *him*. His fury at Amery, Davies, Boothby, and the others who had helped oust him was unabated, and his letters to his sisters in May and June were filled with suspicions about Churchill's allies and their purported scheming. "I must warn you that the people who have been building up a 'hate' against me have not in any way given it up," he wrote in one letter. In another, he declared, "I discovered a nice little intrigue this week."

It wasn't until the end of June, by which time Italy had declared war on France and Britain, and the French government had capitulated to Germany, that Chamberlain acted to stop his supporters from blatantly showing their resentment and disdain for the new prime minister. For weeks Paul Einzig, the political correspondent for the *Financial News*, had watched from the press gallery as Chamberlain loyalists continued their sullen silence whenever Churchill entered the chamber, rose to make one of his rousing speeches, or sat down after delivering one. Einzig was appalled by these childish displays of pique, but he was even more concerned about the conclusion drawn by American and other foreign journalists after witnessing such scenes: that "the Tory majority was not behind Churchill in his determination to fight on against heavy odds." Einzig wrote a long letter to Chamberlain outlining his worries. "I know for a fact that on more than one occasion several ambassadors and important press correspondents left the House with the impression that the Prime Minister could not rely upon the support of the Conservative majority," he told Chamberlain. The former prime minister wrote back, assuring Einzig of "my determination not to tolerate anything in the nature of half-hearted support."

Finally, if belatedly, he took action. After Churchill rose on July 4 to announce the results of one of his most traumatic decisions of the entire war—the Royal Navy's sinking of French ships anchored at Mers-el-Kebir in Algeria—Margesson stood, turned to the Tory backbenchers, and waved his order papers, a clear indication that they should do the same. On cue, every Tory in the chamber jumped to his feet and loudly cheered the prime minister. Churchill burst into tears.

By that time, however, it should have been clear to even the most diehard Chamberlain supporters that the game was all but over. Over the course of that summer, as the Luftwaffe began its bombing raids against England, Churchill succeeded brilliantly in capturing the hearts and minds of the nation. A Gallup poll taken a few weeks after his July 4 speech showed that 88 percent of the British public approved of him and his leadership. By the end of the summer he clearly was in control. "He is at the very top of his form now," Chips Channon acknowledged in late July, "and the House is completely with him, as is the country."

If Chamberlain's supporters were unable to keep Churchill from succeeding as prime minister, they *were* able to help thwart the ambitions of a number of Tory dissidents, largely through David Margesson. While generous to his former political enemies, Churchill gave few jobs of any consequence to the men who helped put him into office. Anthony Eden became war secretary, but he had long since lost his rebel status and, in any event, was not included in the War Cabinet. Duff Cooper became minister of information, with Harold Nicolson as his undersecretary and Ronald Tree his parliamentary private secretary. But to his shock and dismay, Leo Amery, who arguably was the man most responsible for Churchill's now being prime minister, was asked to head the India Office, a relatively minor cabinet post that had little, at that point, to do with the war.

The day after Amery's speech against Chamberlain there had been speculation in some of the newspapers that he himself might become the next prime minister. That wasn't in the cards, but Amery believed that his extensive past experience in the cabinet and his crucial contribution to Churchill's accession would earn him a top post, perhaps defense minister or chancellor of the exchequer. When Churchill offered him the India job, he accepted it but told the prime minister that "I felt he was side-tracking me from the real conduct of the war . . . that the old gang, and Neville in particular, had succeeded in keeping me not only out of the War Cabinet, but out of any real part of things."

It's not clear whether Chamberlain did, in fact, try to "side-track" Amery. Whether he did or not, it *is* clear in retrospect that Churchill himself had no desire to give Amery a major position in Britain's war effort. Churchill had been denied power so long that once finally given it, he wasn't about to share it with anybody. "It took Armageddon to make me prime minister," he told Boothby in late May. "But now I am here I am determined that power shall be in no other hands but mine." Certainly he wasn't going to share it with someone of equal political stature who had challenged him so vigorously in the past. Churchill, said Violet Bonham Carter, "was by temperament an intellectual autocrat. He never liked having other people's way. He infinitely preferred his own."

The offer of secretary of state for India was deeply wounding to Amery, and after accepting the job he seriously considered telling

Churchill he had changed his mind. But he finally decided it was his duty to take the appointment, acknowledging that "Churchill was the right man to conduct the war, with or without my direct help." Besides, it would bring him "inside the fortress" of government.

When Boothby and Macmillan asked Amery his advice on whether they should take "unattractive" low-ranking posts if offered, Amery said yes, using the same rationale he had given himself: that it would get them "inside the fortress." Like others among the Tory rebels, Boothby and Macmillan had come to view Amery as their mentor, and he did what he could to further their careers. In the days after Churchill became prime minister, Amery repeatedly urged him to give good jobs to "my young men" and to pay attention to their views. Guided by Margesson, Churchill did neither.

Bobbety Cranborne was appointed paymaster general, and Dick Law became financial secretary to the War Office. Jim Thomas was named a junior whip to Margesson, the only rebel to be appointed to the whips' office. ("At least I shall have my foot in the door if . . . not in the room, but it will be unpleasant and uphill work," Thomas wrote glumly to Cranborne.) Macmillan and Boothby were offered undersecretary posts at two of the less notable ministries, Macmillan at the Ministry of Supply and Boothby at the Ministry of Food. Boothby, one of only three MPs to stand by Churchill during his wilderness years, was not even the first choice for the Food Ministry job; the radical Labour MP Emanuel Shinwell had earlier turned it down as a "bloody insult." Boothby was similarly unenthusiastic about the position, and he revealed that lack of enthusiasm when Churchill proposed it to him. The next day, in an apologetic letter to the prime minister, he wrote: "I'm afraid I must have appeared ungracious yesterday . . . I very much appreciate the offer you have been able to make to me, and am particularly glad that I go to a department so closely concerned with our war effort. I will do my best to justify your choice."

At least Boothby was given a job. A number of insurgents were not. Despite the best efforts of Amery and Archibald Sinclair (who was named air minister), Churchill declined to give any post at all to Clement Davies. This was one instance of blackballing in which Chamberlain, who despised Davies and called him "that traitorous Welshman who ratted from the Government," may indeed have played a part. Similarly,

Paul Emrys-Evans, who had been chairman of the House Foreign Affairs Committee and had vigorously opposed appeasement since before Munich, was left out in the cold, despite Amery's appeals. Ronald Cross, the minister of shipping, reportedly wanted Emrys-Evans as his PPS, but even that minor appointment was vetoed by the whips' office.

The exclusion of the rebels from influential positions in Churchill's government startled many in London's political and journalistic circles. "It seems strange tactics to leave out all the elements which have been pressing for a more vigorous conduct of the war, while including a lot of shocking duds," said Cecil King. Years later Boothby wrote: "Strangely Churchill never really forgave the men who had put him in power. In some ways he felt a kind of resentment against those who had helped him to obtain it."

Despite his initial dissatisfaction and hurt over being shunted off to the India Office, it didn't take long for Leo Amery to recover his natural ebullience. "[W]e shall see if this is only a belated sputter of my political candle or the beginning of a real second inning," he wrote in his diary. "Whichever it is I think I shall enjoy it." Macmillan, Boothby, and the rest of Amery's "young men" had similar reactions. While they had hoped for better jobs, at least they were now in the government after years in the wilderness, and for the most part they tackled their assignments with enthusiasm. But they soon discovered that their sense of urgency was not widely shared in the middle and lower reaches of their ministries or, for that matter, in other parts of the government outside Downing Street and the military services. In early June, with Paris about to fall, France close to capitulation, and the threat of a German invasion of Britain looming, all too many civil servants, many of them put in place by Horace Wilson, still operated as if the phony war were a leisurely reality. "The change of Government [at the top] is the beginning, not the end, of the house cleaning that is necessary . . ." remarked *The Economist*. "New blood is wanted in the ministries as well as in the Cabinet . . . It is vital . . . to accelerate and invigorate the whole tempo and atmosphere of Government."

Churchill and those around him may have been working night and day to cope with the cascade of crises facing the country, but the rest

of the War Cabinet, other than Lord Halifax, had been given no spe-
cific assignments in the direction of the government. No high-level officials had been put in charge of "giving the necessary impulsion or
coordination to different administrative departments," as Amery put it.
As titantic a force as he was, Churchill couldn't run the war and the
government by himself. In the view of his supporters and people in his
own circle, he needed to share the responsibility and authority.

On June 17, at Macmillan's instigation, he, Boothby, and several
other junior ministers came to see Amery at his home to tell him how
"gravely perturbed" they were about the ongoing lethargy in their departments and the overall lack of coordination in the government. Accompanying them were Clement Davies and Lloyd George, to whom
Macmillan and Boothby had been close since their firebrand years in
the 1920s. The undersecretaries wanted Amery's help in writing a letter to Churchill communicating their concerns and proposing possible
solutions. Although Amery had deep misgivings about how Churchill
would react to such a letter, he felt strongly that the problems his pro-
tégés cited were serious and that they had the right to express their
views, to "respectfully put it to Winston that the whole machine needed
further tuning up."

That afternoon he drafted a letter incorporating the junior ministers' suggestions that Churchill bestow more power on his top ministers. "Nothing less than a revolutionary change in our administrative
methods will secure the rapidity of decisions and actions which is required," the letter declared. Specifically, it proposed that each member
of the War Cabinet be given the authority to oversee groups of government departments and to give direct orders to the departments' ministers. In turn the ministers should have more authority in the running
of their departments, with the freedom to hire and fire members of
their staffs without regard to the Treasury or Civil Service (i.e., Horace
Wilson). These were ideas, based in part on the organization of Lloyd
George's small War Cabinet from 1916 to 1918, that Amery himself
had long espoused.

The letter also had a line about the need to select members of the
War Cabinet "purely from the point of view of personal fitness for the
task," an indirect but indisputable dig at some of the War Cabinet's
current members. As Amery recalled, "this was a hope—and not, I

think, a definite suggestion—to be put to Winston that there were still too many of the old gang, viz. Neville and Halifax, in the War Cabinet."

After drafting the letter, Amery showed it to Duff Cooper, Lord Salisbury, and colonial secretary George Lloyd. All three opposed sending it to Churchill, with Salisbury declaring that "Winston alone could decide [such things] and if he didn't want to make such extreme changes, he wouldn't be influenced by a letter." While Amery himself did not disagree, he felt that the "extreme gravity of the situation" warranted some sort of intervention. Instead of sending the letter, he said, he would see Churchill and, in an informal way, let him know of his junior ministers' concerns.

But when Amery arrived at 10 Downing Street the following afternoon, he found that Neville Chamberlain had been there before him. Earlier that day Chamberlain had heard from a contact about the undersecretaries' meeting and letter and also about the involvement of two people he considered his archenemies, Davies and Lloyd George. He had immediately gone to Churchill with the claim that the former Tory dissidents, in league with Davies and Lloyd George, were involved in a new conspiracy, this time against both Chamberlain and Churchill.

Although he certainly was wrong that the undersecretaries wanted to unseat the man they had worked so hard to put in power, Chamberlain was correct in his suspicion that they would like to get rid of *him*. It was a desire shared by a majority of the British public. "The resignation of Neville Chamberlain . . . and possibly of Sir Kingsley Wood and Lord Simon now seems inevitable in the face of a widespread feeling in the country that the continued war efforts of Great Britain are deterred by the presence of these men in the government," Helen Kirkpatrick wrote in the *Chicago Daily News* on June 18.

British troops returning from Dunkirk in early June had been scathing in their denunciation of the Chamberlain regime's failure to supply them with sufficient planes, tanks, and arms; their reports in turn had "aroused a storm of indignation" in Britain. "Much as recrimination may be deprecated at this time . . ." *The Observer*'s political correspondent wrote, "a number of Members of Parliament feel that they cannot restrain themselves any longer. They find among the public an intensely bitter feeling that the nation has been let down by past political leaders—some of them still ministers of the crown—who failed to realize the magnitude of the threat to our security and failed to make adequate preparations against it." Several newspapers, including the *Daily Mirror*, *News Chronicle*, *Sunday Pictorial*, and *Daily Herald*, demanded the dismissal of Chamberlain and his associates from the government. So did several trade unions.

Obsessed by this campaign against him, Chamberlain was determined to outmaneuver his critics. He employed a sort of emotional blackmail with the hard-pressed Churchill, indicating on more than one occasion that he *would* resign unless the prime minister made his foes stop their efforts to get rid of him. This Churchill tried to do, by, among other things, demanding that Attlee and Greenwood muzzle the anti-Chamberlain Labour press and unions.

Yet even if Chamberlain had not preceded Amery to Churchill's office on June 18, Amery's visit clearly had no chance of success. His timing could hardly have been worse. France had collapsed the previous day, and just a few hours after meeting with Amery, Churchill was to deliver another of his stirring speeches to Parliament, in which he declared: "The battle of France is over. I expect that the battle of Britain is about to begin." Working eighteen hours a day under crushing pressure, still plagued by political insecurities, Churchill was facing the greatest crisis Britain had ever known. He was in no mood to hear criticism from his subordinates, however constructive their ideas might be, or to consider changes in a government he had just assembled. Indeed, during this perilous time he allowed no challenges to his authority and could be quite unpleasant in making that clear. As Robert Rhodes James wrote, "1940 saw him at his best, but also at his worst, particularly in human relationships, and especially toward those who had been his friends." His irascibility and bad temper had become enough of an issue by late June that Clementine Churchill felt compelled to write a note chiding her vastly overworked, overstressed husband for his "rough, sarcastic & overbearing manner" to those around him. She had been told, she said, that "if an idea is suggested you are supposed to be so contemptuous that presently no ideas, good or bad, will be forthcoming." She added: "My darling Winston, I must confess I have noticed a deterioration in your manner; & you are not as kind as you used to be."

There certainly was no kindness on display in Churchill's meeting with Amery. Noting Chamberlain's suspicions, he furiously accused his longtime associate of intriguing with George Lloyd, the colonial secretary, to force changes in the War Cabinet that would be in "[their] interest." Amery hotly denied the charge, declaring that Lloyd had not even been involved in the discussions at Amery's house and that, in any event, both he and Lloyd "were wholeheartedly interested in the work of our departments and wanted nothing else." He tried to assure Churchill that "there was no plot, certainly no plot to impose change on [him], but certainly a serious desire to make some sort of representation to him as to what junior ministers were finding in their departments."

Churchill would have none of it. He told Amery that the junior ministers were there to do the jobs he had given them, and if they wanted to criticize the government, they should resign and do it from the outside. He would make no changes; that was final. That night Amery noted in his diary that Macmillan, Boothby, and the other undersecretaries had "successfully frightened Attlee, Greenwood, and, above all, Neville, and roused Winston's authoritarian instincts. They had better all resign themselves for the time being to doing their work, however acute their sense of the national danger."

Boothby, who, in the words of one friend, was "drawn to trouble as babies are drawn to milk," was not prepared to follow Amery's advice. Impetuous and outspoken as always (not unlike Churchill), he was convinced that the new government was in grave political peril and, disregarding the sensitivity of the situation, sat down on June 19 to write a letter to his onetime mentor, "telling him how to run the war—what to do with Members of Parliament, where to put the troops, how to deploy the Fleet, the lot." It was, Boothby later admitted, "one of the most foolish things I have ever done." In earlier years he had gotten away with standing up to Churchill, with chiding him and giving him advice. That was true no longer.

Already in a foul temper over Amery's intercession the day before, Churchill was now beside himself. He immediately summoned Boothby to Downing Street, took him into the Cabinet Room, and gave him a tongue-lashing for his effrontery and perceived disloyalty. Accusing his former PPS of continuing to conspire against Chamberlain, Churchill said: "You went to Amery's house the other night. You had no business to go there." If Boothby didn't start minding his own business, the prime minister threatened, he would "perhaps have no business to mind." Greatly shaken by the confrontation, Boothby returned to the House of Commons and gulped down a quadruple whiskey in the smoking room. Many years later he was asked by a journalist if he didn't think Churchill had grounds for his anger. "*Every* ground," he replied. "I was arrogant, conceited. It wasn't the moment to tell him how to win the war." He had made, he said, a "terrible mistake."

For his part, Churchill never forgave or forgot what came to be known as "the undersecretaries' plot." He remained convinced of the truth of Chamberlain's assertion that Amery and the younger men were trying to wrest power away from him and that Lloyd George, whose own War Cabinet was held up to Churchill as a model, was at the center of the conspiracy.

Many years later, Churchill told Violet Bonham Carter that Harold Macmillan, by then chancellor of the exchequer, was "a curious fellow. In some ways you can't depend on him." That wasn't true, Lady Violet protested; in the fight against appeasement, Macmillan had been one of the "most courageous and dependable of [his] adherents." Churchill replied: "Yes, but he did a very curious thing in '40, after I had taken office. He and Leo Amery went [around proposing] some kind of triumvirate government to be headed by Lloyd George."

Meanwhile the man responsible for putting that thought in Churchill's mind had little time to benefit from the prime minister's steadfast loyalty to him. At the end of July, Neville Chamberlain was diagnosed with intestinal cancer and underwent surgery. After a difficult convalescence he resigned as lord president on September 22. Less than two months later, during the height of the Blitz, Chamberlain died at his country house in Hampshire. In the House of Commons, Churchill paid a somewhat restrained tribute to his predecessor as a peace-loving man who had tried to save the world from catastrophe. "This alone," said Churchill, "will stand him in good stead as far as what is called the verdict of history is concerned."

CHAPTER TWENTY

A SON'S BETRAYAL

When Leo Amery was named secretary of state for India, much of the British press shared his surprise and disappointment at not being given a more important post. "Are the brains of L. S. Amery being used to the greatest advantage?" asked the *Sunday Pictorial*. *The Economist* declared: "Amery could be better employed than at the India Office." According to *Contemporary Review*, "Mr. Amery's has long been a voice crying in the wilderness, and many would have preferred to see him either in the War Cabinet or chancellor of the exchequer, but it is a great thing to have so resolute a personality in the Government."

The India position, however, turned out to be much more substantive than either Amery or his supporters expected. As the war spread beyond Europe, India became a vitally important base of operations for Britain, providing thousands of troops for Allied campaigns on the Middle East and Far East fronts. It also presented British officials with one of their biggest political headaches of the war, as Gandhi and the Congress Party announced their intention to rid India of the British raj at the same time that Burma and other Southeast Asian neighbors of India were falling to the Japanese.

Amery's portfolio at the India Office gave ample scope for his prodigious energies, but it also ensured that his already difficult relationship with Churchill would become even stormier as the war progressed. Indeed, it's odd that Churchill gave the India post to Amery since the

future of that British colony was an issue over which the two had differed sharply in the past. In the intervening years their differences
over India had widened. By 1940 Amery was convinced that India
should be given full independence within the Commonwealth, while
Churchill still firmly held that India should continue under British
rule.

As before, they had violent arguments over the issue. Churchill's
force and single-mindedness, so vital for the prosecution of the war and
the inspiration of his countrymen, often made life difficult for those
who worked with him. He did not like disagreement with his views
and, according to Canadian prime minister Mackenzie King, "was very
domineering; he cowed his colleagues . . . He had a way of stifling discussion when it was critical." Unlike most of the cabinet, however,
Amery refused to be intimidated by what he considered Churchill's
bullying, and when the prime minister shouted at him during cabinet
meetings, Amery shouted back. The other cabinet ministers, he wrote,
were "partly shocked and partly delighted that Winston should be spoken to in straight terms." Underlying these contentious exchanges was
their old rivalry dating from the days when they were red-haired,
freckle-faced teenagers at Harrow. Yet Churchill repeatedly made clear
that at long last he had won the competition. Amery was serving at *his*
sufferance.

In the back of Churchill's mind, the suspicion seemed to linger that
his longtime colleague was conspiring against him, just as Amery and
the other rebels had conspired to overthrow Chamberlain. In late July
the prime minister erupted in anger when he discovered that Amery
had been exchanging telegrams with the British viceroy in India about
the possibility of conciliating Mahatma Gandhi and other leaders of
the Congress Party by promising independence for India after the war.
In the opinion of Amery's cabinet colleagues, he had acted within the
purview of his office in sounding out the viceroy on the issue. But
Churchill was adamantly opposed both to Indian independence and to
negotiating with the Indian activists. He accused Amery of trying to
stir up revolution in India and insisted on seeing the private correspon-
dence between him and the viceroy. At one cabinet meeting he denounced Amery so violently that an uncomfortable Alexander Cadogan
got up and left the room.

This was a humiliating experience for Amery, and he told Churchill that if these had been normal times, he would have resigned. After similar confrontations with the prime minister later in the war, he was again to consider—and discard—the idea of resignation. As his diary entries throughout the early 1940s revealed, he was in turn highly critical of Churchill. "It is an awful thing dealing with a man like Winston who is at the same moment dictatorial, eloquent, and muddle-headed," he wrote in 1942. About his colleagues in the cabinet, Amery added: "None of them ever really have the courage to stand up to Winston and tell him when he is making a fool of himself."

Yet he also regretted that he and Churchill could not overcome their differences and seemed destined to remain at odds.

I have never been able to get into any sort of personal touch with Winston. He never consults me if he can help it, and I don't suppose I have had an hour's talk with him altogether since I have been in his government . . . In an odd way, he seems to be afraid of me. Whether it goes back to our relative positions in early youth, or the fact that I used to fight him on Empire questions in Baldwin's cabinet, or defeated him afterwards over India, he is instinctively inclined to disagree with anything I say and to think that I want to mobilize opinion against him, or even that I have, as he once let out, ideas of supplanting him. I wish it were possible to disabuse him of this attitude.

As Bob Boothby noted, Churchill did indeed seem to mistrust and resent Amery and the other Tory rebels who had helped bring him to power. It was one of the many paradoxes of Winston Churchill that although he himself had been viewed as a rebel for years, he was, as Robert Rhodes James pointed out, "fundamentally a very conservative man." Throughout his career he had longed to be part of the power structure, not to bring it down. Even though he, Britain, and the rest of the world benefited from the parliamentary revolt that helped topple Chamberlain from office, Churchill never seemed to accept its necessity or validity. He never acknowledged the vital importance of Amery and the other insurgents in his emergence as prime minister, so crucial to the survival of Britain and the West.

For his part, Amery never regretted the part he played in helping Churchill gain power. "He is a real war leader," he declared shortly after Churchill took over, "and one whom it is worthwhile to serve under." In November 1941, when British forces were on the defensive in the Middle East and Allied shipping losses were skyrocketing, Amery wrote to a beleaguered Churchill: "We may differ on India, but I yield to none in my admiration for what you have done and are doing in the wider field, and am only anxious to give you all the help in my power."

As frustrating and contentious as Amery's relationship with Churchill was, he had a far greater worry during the course of the war. While he and the rest of the British government were working to bring about the defeat of Germany, his elder son, John, was ensconced in Berlin, making pro-Nazi broadcasts and trying to persuade British prisoners of war to switch their allegiance and fight for the Germans.

John Amery, described by one writer as "the ultimate ne'er-do-well," had been in almost constant trouble since childhood. Indulged by his parents, he had been given a sports car at the age of fifteen and, within a few years, had amassed more than seventy driving tickets. Prone to wild temper tantrums and heavy drinking, he ran away from Harrow at sixteen and began to travel aimlessly around Europe, becoming involved in a series of shady business ventures. His parents' many attempts to help him came to naught; by the time he was in his early twenties, he had run up enormous debts that his father felt obliged to cover.

According to Leo Amery, when civil war broke out in Spain in the summer of 1936, John, then twenty-three, volunteered for Franco's forces, working for a few months as a gunrunner for the rebels. He was strongly anti-Communist and, notwithstanding his father's Jewish ancestry and firm support of Zionism, violently anti-Semitic. After leaving Spain, he drifted around Europe and was in France when war was declared in September 1939. The following spring Amery, in Paris after a trip to inspect the Maginot Line, tried to persuade his son to return home and enlist in the British Army. John told his father that he was currently involved in a film production venture; if that didn't work out soon, he would come back to England.

The German conquest of France, however, ended any possibility of John Amery's return; after France fell, he was interned there. When German officials discovered he was the son of a British cabinet minister, they recruited him as a propagandist and eventually brought him to Berlin. His anxious mother and father had heard little from him since the collapse of France. Then, on November 17, 1942, an American reporter told Leo Amery that his son was in the German capital and apparently in the pay of the Nazis; even worse, he reportedly was preparing to make a pro-German broadcast to England. "A friend tells me that the Germans keep a whole bevy of people like [P. G.] Wodehouse, etc., at the Hotel Adlon to use for their wretched purposes, and it looks as if they had netted John to join them," Amery wrote in his diary.

When he accompanied Churchill to Harrow on November 18 for a concert at their old school, Amery told the prime minister about his son, adding he was ready to resign if the situation became too much of an embarrassment to Churchill and his government. "Good God!" Churchill exclaimed. "I wouldn't hear of such a thing!" The prime minister, whose own son, Randolph, had been a worry to his parents on more than one occasion, assured Amery that no one could blame him for "the aberrations of a grown-up son." For all their quarreling over the years, Churchill was demonstrating loyalty and compassion when it most counted. For that, Amery was forever grateful.

The following night Leo and Florence Amery turned on the wireless in their Eaton Place drawing room and braced themselves for a miserable ordeal. For more than half an hour they listened as their son, in a harangue transmitted by Berlin Radio, denounced Jews, Russians, and Americans and urged the British public to overthrow their government. "It is up to you to decide that this has lasted long enough, that our boys are dying to serve no British interests, that the civilians are suffering not for Britain, but for the interests of a small clique of utterly unscrupulous men," he declared. "It's up to you, to your common sense—you, the man in the street—you alone can stop this crime. You alone can overthrow the men who have brought our country so low . . . who against every British interest allied our country to the Bolsheviks and Americans."

Listening to the broadcast was a shattering experience for the Amerys, and they dealt with it by deciding that an impostor using John's name had actually been the speaker. "My dear Winston," Amery wrote to Churchill the next day, "I listened in twice to what the German radio announced as my son's broadcast, and both my wife and I are convinced that it was not his voice but a voice of entirely different character and that of a practiced speaker and broadcaster." But it *was* John Amery's voice, and over the next two years he made several more broadcasts and speeches similar to the one his parents had heard. He also toured Allied prisoner of war camps to recruit British servicemen to fight with the Germans against the Soviet Union, describing his appeal as "a call to arms in the defence of all civilization against Asiatic and Jewish bestiality." (Only one British POW answered the call.)

Thanks to the intervention of Brendan Bracken, who replaced Duff Cooper as minister of information in 1941, most British newspapers printed little or nothing about John Amery's broadcasts. But Leo Amery knew his son's treachery was a topic of gossip in London, and although his friends and colleagues rallied around him, he was shamed and humiliated. He also was haunted by the knowledge that the War Office and MI6, Britain's foreign intelligence agency, were gathering evidence against John in order to charge him with treason after the war was over. "I wonder whether the influence of his unfortunate and much-to-be-pitied father will save young Amery from the fate he so richly deserves," a War Office staffer wrote in late 1942.

In the final months of the war John Amery resettled in Italy, where he was captured in the spring of 1945 by partisans and turned over to British authorities. He was brought back to England on July 9 and taken to Wandsworth Prison, a bleak dark-stone Victorian structure in the middle of a shabby district in South London. It soon became obvious that the British government planned to make an example of him. About 140 British subjects were prosecuted during and after the war for collaborating with the Germans; a number of them, like Amery, had made pro-German broadcasts. Yet only Amery and William Joyce, the infamous "Lord Haw Haw," were charged with high treason, which was punishable by death. The others were accused of lesser crimes, and most spent only a few years in prison.

On November 28, 1945, John Amery, his face gaunt and unshaved and his long dark hair curling over the collar of his coat, stepped into a dock at the Old Bailey. Three tables in front of the judge's bench were filled with black-gowned barristers, special police, and military intelligence officers, revealing the importance the government attached to the case. The chief prosecuting counsel was Britain's attorney general, Sir Hartley Shawcross, just returned home from his duties as the leading British prosecutor at the trials of Göring and other German war criminals in Nuremberg. The only member of Amery's family in the courtroom was his younger brother, Julian, who had worked hard over the previous four months on John's defense.

After reading the eight-count indictment, the court clerk asked Amery how he pleaded. In a weak voice he replied, "I plead guilty to all counts." His response shocked virtually everyone in the courtroom; they knew that the thirty-two-year-old defendant had just sentenced himself to death. There was no other possible sentence and no appeal. The elderly judge, in his white wig and red and purple robes, leaned forward. "I never accept a plea of guilty on a capital charge without assuring myself that the accused thoroughly understands what he is doing and what the immediate result will be," he said. Amery's defense counsel answered, "I can assure you of that, My Lord." With that, a square of black cloth was placed on the judge's head. Looking straight at Amery, he proclaimed: "You now stand a self-confessed traitor to your King and country, and you have forfeited your right to live."

Amery later said he pleaded guilty to spare his family the pain and humiliation of a prolonged trial. His father, tormented by the belief that John would not be facing death if it were not for his own former status as cabinet minister, lobbied hard for clemency. "I feel a certain responsibility for the position in which he finds himself," he wrote to the Home Office, "because it was the fact that he was my son that made it worthwhile for the Germans to approach him, and subsequently to give his utterances and actions a prominence which they would not otherwise have received."

At Leo Amery's request, Lord Horder, a prominent doctor and friend of the Amerys, submitted a report to the Home Office testifying to John Amery's mental instability over the years and declaring he could not tell right from wrong. After examining the prisoner, two psychiatrists appointed by the Home Office agreed with Horder. They concluded that John Amery could not form moral judgments about his own conduct and that therefore, he should not be executed. Both reports fell on deaf ears, and the appeal for clemency was denied. "Capital punishment in this country is tolerated as a deterrent because the man in the street believes that the law is administered without fear or favour," a Home Office memo stated. "If Amery were reprieved it would be difficult to convince the ordinary man that [he] had not received exceptional and privileged treatment."

On the night before their son's execution, Leo and Florence Amery visited him in his cell at Wandsworth. "You have given me a fine send-off," he told them. The following morning, shortly before the scheduled execution time of nine o'clock, the Amerys gathered their household staff together at their house in Eaton Place. Leo Amery read a poem he had written about John, and everyone present recited the Lord's Prayer. At about the same time, Britain's famed chief executioner, Albert Pierrepoint, entered John Amery's cell at Wandsworth. The prisoner extended his hand. "Mr. Pierrepoint," he said, "I've always wanted to meet you, although not, of course, under these circumstances." The surprised Pierrepoint shook his hand, then gently turned him around, bound his arms behind him, and led him to the gallows. Outside Wandsworth, Julian Amery sat, waiting, in a car. At 9:08 a.m. a warden pinned a notice on the prison's outer wall: "Judgment of death was this day executed on John Amery."

Amery's body was buried on the prison grounds. The following year his mother requested permission to visit his grave, but her request was denied. In 1948 the vicar of the Anglican church attended by the Amerys asked the Wandsworth chaplain, who counseled John before his death, if he would meet with Mrs. Amery to talk about her son. Again the government refused permission. "Visits to the relatives of an executed man are felt to be undesirable," a Home Office report stated. "There must be no appearance of preference for the family of an ex-Cabinet minister."

CHAPTER TWENTY-ONE

AFTERMATH

When Churchill became prime minister, most of Leo Amery's "young men," having been assigned to low-ranking government posts or no posts at all, had little reason to expect they would be given more challenging work for the duration. But for some, this in fact was soon to change.

Shortly after Churchill took office, Brendan Bracken made what amounted to a backhanded apology to Bob Boothby and the others who had been excluded from important government positions. Acknowledging that "many glaring misfits" had been appointed to key jobs, Bracken assured Boothby that when "this whizzing crisis is over, I dare say some improvements can be made."

By December 1940 the "whizzing crisis" to which Bracken referred, the immediate threat to Britain's security and independence, had ended. Against all odds, the RAF had bested the Luftwaffe in the Battle of Britain, and even though Germany's bombing of London and other British cities continued into 1941, the danger of an imminent German invasion of Britain was over. The threat to Churchill's own political security had also receded; by the end of the year he was in firm control in the House of Commons and in the country. He now felt confident enough to move some of the men of Munich out of the top ranks of his government.

The unexpected death in December of Lord Lothian, the British ambassador to the United States, provided Churchill with the opportunity for a major reshuffle. A very reluctant Lord Halifax was pressed to take Lothian's place. With Halifax banished to Washington, the prime minister installed Anthony Eden as his foreign secretary, a post that Eden held until the end of the war. Dick Law moved from his junior post in the War Office to replace the notorious Rab Butler as foreign affairs undersecretary.* And shortly before Lothian's death, Bobbety Cranborne was named dominions secretary. Cranborne in turn persuaded Churchill to appoint Paul Emrys-Evans his undersecretary.

For a time it appeared that Bob Boothby's political future was also on the rise. After he gave up trying to tell Churchill how to run the war and settled down to do his job at the Ministry of Food, he turned out to be surprisingly good at it. Like Leo Amery, Boothby discovered that his position was more significant than he or anyone else had expected. Indeed, the Ministry of Food was the most important civilian department during the war, and its head, Lord Woolton, a prominent former businessman, was the best-known and most popular minister in the government, with the exception of Churchill himself. As Woolton's second-in-command, Boothby became almost as well known and well liked as his boss. He and Woolton were responsible for proposing and implementing a government program that provided free milk for poor children and nursing mothers. When the Blitz began, Boothby was in charge of setting up portable canteens in the bombed-out East End of London, where food and hot drinks were served to residents who had lost their homes. On mornings after air raids, with the acrid smell of smoke still in the air, he would arrive on the scene, stepping over broken glass and piles of rubble, offering help, sympathy, tea, and laughter to dazed survivors. Boothby also was given high marks for his adept performance on behalf of the ministry in Parliament. In the opinion of the *New Statesman*, he demonstrated "just that kind of drive and enthusiasm which government departments need."

Then, in January 1941, Boothby's promising political future came to an abrupt end. The catalyst was a scandal over his involvement two years before in a campaign to aid Czech citizens living in Britain.

---

*Named education secretary in 1941, Butler became an ardent domestic reformer. He was responsible for the 1944 Education Act, which guaranteed every child the right to a secondary education and was a cornerstone of the postwar welfare state.

When Germany seized Czechoslovakia in March 1939, the bank accounts and investments of Czech expatriates were frozen in their homeland. At about the same time, the British government blocked Czech government assets held on deposit in Britain, to prevent the Germans from looting them. A month later a private committee, with Boothby as its unsalaried chairman, was set up to lobby the British government to help the Czechs in Britain, who were trying to regain their frozen savings and investments, by paying them from the blocked Czech assets. Boothby, who had worked for several years as a stockbroker in the City, did not reveal at the time that he had a personal stake in the effort. A friend of his, a wealthy Czech businessman, had asked him to help negotiate the unfreezing of his wife's Czech bonds, promising Boothby 10 percent of any amount she received. Casual about money all his life, Boothby was heavily in debt and accepted the offer.

He had done nothing illegal—he had long been a champion of the Czechs and had worked vigorously for a settlement for all Czech claimants—but rumors and reports of his personal interest prompted allegations of impropriety. In August, Sir John Simon, then chancellor of the exchequer, summoned Boothby to his office to question him about the committee and its purposes. He alleged that Boothby had become its chairman for the sole purpose of financial gain. Boothby, quite truthfully, denied the accusation but never revealed to Simon, or to any of the other officials who later questioned him, that he did in fact have a personal interest in the matter.

A year later, in September 1940, Boothby's Czech friend was arrested and interned as an alien, a fate suffered by thousands of foreigners in Britain at the time. When police found in the man's papers evidence of the financial arrangement between him and Boothby, that information was brought to the attention of Churchill, who immediately ordered Boothby to Downing Street. The prime minister icily informed his former PPS that he had decided to create a select House committee to inquire into his conduct.

In setting up the committee, Churchill unwittingly provided the pro-Chamberlain Tories with an instrument of revenge against a foe whom, with his extravagant and unconventional lifestyle and his caustic outspokenness in the fight against the former prime minister, they particularly despised. Now the antagonism toward him could finally be unleashed. The Tory MP chosen to chair the select committee was John Gretton, chairman of Bass brewery and a fervent supporter of Chamberlain and appeasement. (Boothby and his supporters believed that Gretton's selection was the doing of James Stuart.) Most of the rest of the select committee also was heavily pro-Chamberlain. It was, concluded Hugh Dalton, "a hangman's committee."

Boothby was suspended from his post at the Food Ministry while the committee conducted its investigation. In January 1941 it concluded that he had aided the Czechs in Britain for the sole purpose of financial gain and that his conduct was "derogatory to the dignity of the House and inconsistent with the standards which Parliament is entitled to expect from its Members." Boothby was stunned, as were many others, by the findings. Ellen Wilkinson, a Labour MP who was undersecretary for the Ministry of Home Security, wrote: "The feeling I meet everywhere is 'Why on earth couldn't this be settled by a private wigging if he had stepped over the line an inch . . . We can't afford to lose a man like that from the M/Food!" In his diary, Hugh Dalton observed that Boothby "is a far better man than most of those who judged him on the Select Committee. Unfortunately he has broken the Eleventh Commandment, whereas many a financial rascal in Parliament has not—'Thou shall not be found out.'"

Boothby knew that the committee's findings meant he would have to resign his office, but at the same time, he fought to keep his House seat. When the Commons was presented with the committee's report on January 28, 1941, he acknowledged that he should have made public his personal interest in the settlement of Czech claims, but he vehemently denied that he had done anything wrong. "I helped the Czechs because I did not want them to be robbed by the Germans, not because I wanted to rob them myself," he told a hushed House. "Folly I have admitted: guilt I cannot admit."

Boothby's eloquence swayed the House in his favor. It did not press for his resignation, and his loyal constituents in East Aberdeenshire gave him their full support; he remained in the Commons until he himself decided to leave it almost twenty years later. But he was never given another government job during the war, and his hopes for political advancement were gone. What hurt him most, however, was what he perceived as Churchill's willingness to throw him to the wolves. "Why did he bother, at intervals, to hate me?" Boothby once asked Maj. Gen. Sir Hastings Ismay, Churchill's chief military aide during the war. According to Boothby, Ismay thought for a moment and then replied: "You wrote him one or two very tactless letters, which angered him, and you were apt to tell him things he didn't want to hear."

All that may have been true, but Churchill, having been informed of an alleged impropriety by a government minister, clearly had no choice but to order an investigation. He had no intention of giving any of his old political enemies an opportunity to attack him over the indiscretions of a former close associate. Yet the prime minister seemed discomfited by the violently partisan nature of the proceedings, telling John Colville that he could not "endure a man hunt." In a speech to the House, Churchill called Boothby's resignation from the government "a heartbreaking business." He added: "Especially it is a great source of pain to me, because Mr. Boothby was for many years one of my personal and trusted friends, and often a supporter at lonely and difficult moments, and for whom I have always entertained a warm personal regard. He is a loss to all."

At the same time, however, Churchill in private made clear he wanted nothing more to do with Boothby. When one MP asked him what Boothby should do now, Churchill replied that he should "join a bomb disposal squad as the best way of rehabilitating himself in the eyes of his fellow men." After a pause, he reportedly added: "After all, the bombs might not go off." James Stuart and Boothby's other parliamentary enemies, who were delighted by his downfall, made sure that Churchill's remark was well circulated in the lobbies and smoking room of the Commons. Stuart even mentioned it years later in his memoirs.

Why did Churchill, who was known for his tolerance of his friends' peccadilloes, distance himself so thoroughly from Boothby? In the midst of the affair, the prime minister told Woolton that Boothby "had much capacity but no virtue." Yet Churchill never cut his ties to close associates like Lord Beaverbrook, Lord Birkenhead, and the Duke of Westminster, whose financial dealings and personal behavior were even more questionable than Boothby's. Churchill "liked bounders," Roy Jenkins, his biographer, noted. But most of those "bounders"—Beaverbrook, Birkenhead, and the rest—were men whom

Churchill considered his social and political equals. He didn't have the same forbearance toward men he regarded as his subordinates, especially those, like the undisciplined Boothby, who treated politics and the pursuit of power as a sport, a game to be played, rather than as the principal focus of their lives.

And while, as Churchill himself pointed out, Boothby had been a strong supporter of the older man when he was out of political favor, he never had given him the unquestioning loyalty that Churchill demanded from his followers. Emotional, sentimental, and magnanimous as he often was, Churchill at times revealed a hardness to his character, an insensitivity to allies who had outlived their usefulness. "The idea of having a friend who was of no practical use to him, but being a friend because he liked him, had no place," said Sir Desmond Morton, a close wartime adviser to Churchill who himself was later cast out of the inner circle.

For the other anti-appeasement Tories who had been brought, however belatedly, into Churchill's government, it was exciting at last to be near the center of things. But the experience of working for the savior of Britain, as Amery and several of the others found out, could be difficult and frustrating as well. Throughout the war Churchill clung fast to his power, determined, as he had told Boothby in May 1940, that it "shall be in no other hands but mine." No one was more hamstrung by the prime minister's refusal to delegate authority than Anthony Eden, who, having repeatedly muffed his own chances of succeeding Neville Chamberlain, was relegated to the wartime role of Churchill's loyal lieutenant and heir presumptive, with little real say in how the war was waged. "What troubles me," Eden wrote to Bobbety Cranborne in April 1942, "is that I—and I suppose other members of the War Cabinet—are regarded by the public as those running the war, & we don't one little bit . . . Altogether I am most unhappy."

In that same year, however, one former Tory dissident managed to escape the conflicts and dissatisfactions of working in Whitehall and, in the process, found himself with far more wartime influence than any of his parliamentary colleagues. After the Anglo-American invasion of North Africa in late 1942, Churchill asked Harold Macmillan to go to Algiers as the prime minister's representative to the new Allied headquarters there. Macmillan feared that the Algiers job would be a political dead end, but he took it anyway, hoping it would give him more direct work in the war effort.

As it turned out, the war that occupied Macmillan in North Africa had little to do with fighting the Germans. Two French generals, Charles de Gaulle and Henri Giraud, were at each other's throats over who should head the French provisional government. Algiers was an American sphere of influence, and President Franklin Roosevelt, who, like Churchill, detested de Gaulle, wanted Giraud as leader. Macmillan, who spoke perfect French and was familiar with French politics, knew that de Gaulle, prickly and infuriating as he was, was the only one with the will and strength of character to lead the French forces. With calm and great diplomatic skill, Macmillan mediated between the two feuding generals, as well as arbitrated the disagreements among de Gaulle, Roosevelt, and Churchill. Thanks in part to Macmillan's efforts, de Gaulle emerged victorious and went on to claim the leadership of France after its liberation.

Algiers proved to be the turning point of Harold Macmillan's life. For the first time in his career he had a mandate to act on his own, and he took full advantage of it. He gained the confidence and trust of the Allied commander, Gen. Dwight D. Eisenhower, and other American officials, often persuading them to adopt his point of view while making them think it had been their idea all along. "I suspect it was in Algiers, where he could do all the thinking and make all the decisions while Ike took all the credit, that Harold Macmillan first realized his own capacity for supreme leadership," said Richard Crossman, a former Oxford don and future Labour MP who headed Allied psychological warfare operations in North Africa.

Unlike Boothby, Eden, and other colleagues, Macmillan was content to have the spotlight shine elsewhere. "I recall how brilliantly he disguised his power," said John Wyndham, Macmillan's private secretary. "Kudos he seldom sought—give him the power and he would be perfectly content if others gained the credit . . . Power for power's sake was what he enjoyed." Macmillan once advised Crossman that in working with Americans he should permit his colleagues "not only to have a superior rank to yourself and much higher pay, but also the feeling that [they are] running the show. This will enable you to run it yourself."

With his success in North Africa, the shy, inhibited Macmillan began to loosen up, shedding his pomposity and pedantic ways and becoming more relaxed and self-confident. Indeed, within months of arriving in Algiers, he had transformed himself into a "dashing man of action," flitting calmly in and out of war zones, once escaping from a burning plane in the North African desert and then plunging back inside to rescue a trapped passenger. In Algiers he was not denigrated or pitied as a cuckold, nor was he the target of mocking gossip. There he could shed the humiliation of the affair between his wife and Boothby. Yet his pain over that relationship persisted. Throughout the war he continued to have spells of gloom and depression, and to a few select friends he revealed the anguish he still suffered. Many years later friends speculated that his wife's affair was "the grit in the oyster" that spurred Macmillan on in his surprising rise to power during and after the war.

In the summer of 1943 Macmillan was sent to Italy as Churchill's representative to the Allied headquarters there after the Allied invasion of Sicily in July. After Mussolini fell, Macmillan helped negotiate terms of the Italian armistice with the Badoglio government and over the next two years was involved in setting up a new, more liberal, and broadbased Italian regime. In reality, he was framing Allied policy for occupied Italy, as he was later to do in Greece, Lebanon, Syria, and Yugoslavia. After so many years of powerlessness as a Tory backbencher, Macmillan was now rewriting constitutions and rebuilding countries and, in doing so, affecting the lives of millions. The power he wielded was immense, but as in North Africa, he tried to operate as much as possible behind the scenes. He was, said Wyndham, "the Viceroy of the Mediterranean by stealth."

In July 1945, two months after the Allied victory in Europe, Britain held its first general election in ten years. When the votes were tallied,

Winston Churchill, so inspirational in wartime, had been swept out of office by weary, war-sick voters who decided they preferred the Labour Party to manage their crippled economy. In the crushing Labour land-slide, Macmillan, Amery, and Harold Nicolson were among the anti-appeasement rebels who lost their parliamentary seats. Neither Amery nor Nicolson ever returned to the House, but Macmillan was more fortunate; a few months after the general election he won a by-election in the London suburb of Bromley and rejoined his colleagues in the Commons.

The Tory dissidents who had helped oust Neville Chamberlain had never been a tight-knit band of brothers, and the tensions and rivalries that divided them in the two years before Chamberlain's ouster were still on display in the dealings of those who survived the 1945 electoral debacle. Anthony Eden, for one, was furious that Macmillan, in his war-time posts in North Africa and Italy, had been allowed to report directly to Churchill rather than to him and the Foreign Office. Now he saw Macmillan as a threat to his position as Churchill's successor in the Tory leadership, a view shared by others. "Harold may yet succeed Win-ston," Robert Bruce Lockhart wrote in his diary in early 1946. "He has grown more in stature during the war than anyone . . . He was always clever, but was shy and diffident, had a clammy handshake and was more like a wet fish than a man. Now he is full of confidence and is not only not afraid to speak but jumps in and speaks brilliantly. He has a better mind than Anthony." Of Eden, Lockhart mused: "I think that he is a little jealous of Harold. In this respect he is like a woman; he fears a potential rival."

No longer a party outsider, Macmillan was now a major figure in Tory inner circles. His parliamentary colleagues were taken aback by how much he had changed. The sensitive, emotional idealist, who once had thumbed his nose at his party, proposed innovative and daring legis-lation, and worked to form cross-party alliances with the Opposition, was gone. In his place was a languid, cynical, insouciant toff, who, with his hands clutching the lapels of his jacket, delivered overly pol-ished speeches in the House of Commons and baited Prime Minister Clement Attlee and the other Labour ministers with cheerful malice. The protective emotional shell he had fashioned to hide his pain over

Dorothy's decades-long affair with Boothby had hardened into a rock-like carapace; no one quite knew any more who the real Macmillan was. "He's a great performer," Violet Bonham Carter observed, "but the performance sometimes obscures the man."

In the late 1940s Macmillan became an ally of Rab Butler's in his efforts to modernize the Conservative Party. Butler, whose metamorphosis from despised appeaser to forward-thinking domestic reformer was now complete, was instrumental in moving the Conservatives away from their old, reactionary policies and fashioning a progressive new Tory program that pledged to keep and improve the comprehensive social services of Labour's welfare state while restoring economic prosperity to Britain. In a country still beset by food and fuel shortages and rationing, Labour's socialism was losing its appeal, and in 1951 British voters returned the seventy-seven-year-old Churchill and his Tory colleagues to office.

In Churchill's second administration, several of the former anti-appeasement rebels were given important posts in the cabinet. Anthony Eden became foreign secretary once more. Bobbety Cranborne, now Lord Salisbury, was appointed Commonwealth secretary. Jim Thomas, who had served in the whips' office during the war, was named first lord of the admiralty. Macmillan became minister of housing and, within two years, fulfilled a key Churchill campaign promise to build three hundred thousand new houses in Britain. In October 1954, six months before Churchill finally—and very reluctantly—relinquished his job to Eden, the prime minister rewarded Macmillan for his success by promoting him to defense minister.

If he had been willing to fight for it, Anthony Eden might well have been prime minister seventeen years before he finally made it to the top. At the time of his resignation as foreign secretary in February 1938, the odds were good that he could have toppled Chamberlain. But Eden had not had the strength of will to rebel—not against Chamberlain then and not against an increasingly debilitated Churchill more than a decade and a half later.

As a consequence, he captured the prize of the prime ministership in April 1955 without ever involving himself much in the political intriguing that he found so distasteful. Yet his adroitness in avoiding the dirty work of political life now made it impossible for him to meet the myriad challenges facing him. As foreign secretary he had been a brilliant negotiator, but having stayed away from the rough-and-tumble of parliamentary politics for most of his career, he was unskilled in the tough backroom maneuvering of the Commons with which a prime minister has to deal. As the longtime "golden boy" of British politics he also was unused to criticism, which he regarded as a personal affront. Eden "lacked the broad shoulders which every occupant of No. 10 needs to have," said the journalist W. F. Deedes, a junior government minister in his administration. Eden's difficulties in coping with the pressures of his new office were heightened by frequent bouts of bad health, stemming from a botched gallbladder operation in 1953.

Less than a year after Eden took over from Churchill, Britain's economy began to sour. Wages and prices escalated, as did inflation; then a tightening of credit sent the economy into recession. Eden's government came under intense criticism, and his popularity ratings plummeted. A front-page headline in the *Daily Mirror* proclaimed: "Even the Tories Are Saying It Now: Eden Is a Flop." It was at this point that the new prime minister was confronted with the most formidable challenge of his administration.

In July 1956, angered by the withdrawal of American and British aid for construction of the Aswan Dam, Egypt's president, Gamal Abdel Nasser, suddenly nationalized the Suez Canal, which had been operating under British and French control since its construction. Nasser never closed the canal, and British and French ships continued to be able to use this vital link to the Middle East, India and the Far East. But Eden was enraged by what he viewed as an unpardonable affront to British prestige and a serious threat to his nation's security. Determined to prove his toughness, he vowed to get the canal back—not through diplomatic means, which the Foreign Office was urging, but by force.

The prime minister and several members of his cabinet, including Macmillan, then chancellor of the exchequer, and Lord Salisbury, lord president of the council, drew parallels between the current crisis and the dire situation in which Britain and France found themselves in the late 1930s. The year 1956 was the twentieth anniversary of Hitler's remilitarization of the Rhineland, and Eden and the others were quick to compare the Rhineland with Suez, and Hitler with Nasser. "We all know this is how fascist governments behave," Eden declared, "and we all remember, only too well, what the cost can be in giving in to fascism." Not for the first time, and certainly not for the last, the lessons of Munich and appeasement were wrongly applied to a later international crisis. Hitler had been a real threat to Britain's security and survival. Nasser was not. Indeed, some legal experts believed that Nasser had not even breached international law by seizing the canal. In any event, he had not blocked its operation, and he was willing to negotiate its future.

Nonetheless, Eden and several of his ministers, including Macmillan and Salisbury, were determined to pursue military action. In October the British signed a secret agreement with France and Israel calling for an Israeli attack on Egypt followed by a British-French invasion. On October 29, Israel began its assault, and British and French troops attacked a week later. The U.S. government was outraged by the operation, and Britain and France found themselves condemned as aggressors in the United Nations.

The affair was a total disaster for Eden. There was a run on the pound, and Britain, facing bankruptcy, needed a loan from the International Monetary Fund to bail it out. The trouble, as Macmillan explained to Eden and the rest of the cabinet, was that the United States wouldn't permit authorization of the loan unless the invasion of Egypt was called off. Having pressed hard for military intervention, Macmillan now reversed himself and advocated a cease-fire. Eden had no choice but to comply.

The repercussions of the Suez crisis were eerily similar to those of Munich almost twenty years before. Once again families were divided, close friendships ended, and dinner parties erupted in acrimony. During one debate in the House of Commons tempers became so heated that the Speaker was forced to halt the session. In the House of Lords, Lord Tedder, a former RAF chief of staff, said he knew of families "who are giving up their Christmas gathering because they know there will be fighting over the issue."

Yet despite the discord in the country, Eden, like Chamberlain in 1938, kept tight control of his Tory majority in the Commons. Violet

Bonham Carter, who was as furious over what she called the "shame" of Suez as she had been over Munich, buttonholed her Tory MP friends to demand: "Is there not one of you with the courage to come out against the government?" Of the thirty or so Tories who opposed military intervention, only eight dared defy the cajoling and threats of the party whips and abstain in a November 8 vote of confidence in Eden's government. One of them was Bob Boothby, the only Conservative to ignore his party's dictates over both Munich and Suez. Another was Nigel Nicolson, the son of Harold Nicolson, who knew he was probably committing political suicide by abstaining. In the debate before the vote, Nicolson denounced the Suez action as "not only unwise but highly immoral." In a haunting echo of Ronald Cartland and the other young Tory rebels almost two decades before, Harold Nicolson's son accused Eden, Macmillan, and the other ministers of "breaking all the rules you made for yourself in the conduct of foreign affairs all your career—which was being true to alliances and treaties and telling the truth to the House of Commons. You did not tell the truth."

Nicolson was right in thinking that his opposition over Suez would mean the end of his political career. In the 1930s the Tories who rebelled over Munich were saved by the war. There was no such salvation for the Suez rebels: five of the eight, including Nicolson, were denied support by their constituency associations and lost their seats in the next election. The unsinkable Boothby was among the three who survived.

For Nicolson and other young left-leaning Tories elected in the early 1950s, the Suez crisis was a profoundly disillusioning experience, made even more so by Harold Macmillan's conduct during it. A number of them had regarded him as their mentor, a role model to follow in his progressivism and passion for social reform. "The leaders of our truancy" were Butler and Macmillan, but "it was Macmillan who delighted us most," Nicolson said. "He had been [our] favorite Minister, speaking to our small group as if we were already trusted colleagues."

But the man who had been such a firebrand in the 1930s, who demonstrated the courage of his convictions during the Munich crisis, was now advising his young associates not to do the same over Suez. When Anthony Nutting, a junior minister in the Foreign Office, resigned in protest of the government's actions, Macmillan urged him not to give the customary speech in the House explaining why he was quitting. After reading the statement that Nutting had prepared, the chancellor of the exchequer shook his head and declared: "This is very damaging. It could easily bring down the Government, and for you, dear boy, it will do irreparable harm. Why say anything at all? You have already been proved right and we have been proved wrong. You have also done the right thing by resigning, and if you keep silent now, you will be revered and rewarded." Disgusted with Macmillan and the cynical hypocrisy of politics, Nutting picked up the text of his speech and silently left the room. Outside 11 Downing Street, he tore the pages to shreds and stuffed them down a storm drain. He did not make the speech.

Two weeks after the vote of confidence, Anthony Eden, emotionally and physically broken, stunned the country by leaving for a lengthy recuperation in Jamaica. In January 1957, after only twenty-one months in office, he resigned the post for which he had hungered most of his political life. Almost everyone expected Rab Butler, who had presided over the government while Eden was in Jamaica, to be chosen to succeed him. Yet in the early afternoon of January 10 it was Harold Macmillan who received the summons from Buckingham Palace. Less than an hour later Macmillan was on his way to 10 Downing Street as the new prime minister.

When the sixty-three-year-old Macmillan took office, the betting in political circles was that he wouldn't last six weeks. The British economy was in a shambles. The country's international prestige had been severely damaged, as had its relationship with its most important ally, the United States. The Conservative Party was demoralized and badly split, and it appeared that Labour would win the next election by a landslide.

As it turned out, however, Macmillan, who unlike Eden, Boothby, Cartland, or Duff Cooper had never been touted in his youth as a possible prime minister, remained in office for more than six years. In that time he left an indelible stamp on the country. He presided over the birth of Britain's new affluent society, winning reelection in 1959 with the slogan "Most of our people have never had it so good." A tough-minded pragmatist, he acknowledged that Britain's days as a world power were over and began the dismantling of what was left of the British Empire, shocking many in his party. His historic 1960 "winds of change" speech in South Africa, conceding the inexorability of African nationalism, helped accelerate the movement toward independence of Britain's African colonies and protectorates. In addition, Macmillan improved British relations with the United States and pressed President John F. Kennedy, whose sister had been married to Dorothy Macmillan's nephew, to negotiate a nuclear test ban treaty with the Soviet leader Nikita Khrushchev. When the Limited Test Ban Treaty finally was signed in August 1963, Kennedy, who called Macmillan Uncle Harold, gave the British prime minister credit for being its midwife.

Macmillan's private life, however, remained fraught with tension. Three decades after Dorothy Macmillan first clasped Bob Boothby's hand on the Scottish moors, their relationship still was a central part of their lives. For the most part, the British public had no clue that the prime minister's immensely popular wife, now grown stout and white-haired, the image of everyone's favorite grandmother, had been having an adulterous affair since the late 1920s with a close colleague and former friend of her husband. The strange, divided lives of Boothby and the Macmillans continued much as they had for years. Although they were considerably more discreet about their relationship, Boothby and Lady Dorothy met frequently for lunch and dinner and exchanged phone calls or letters almost daily. Yet Dorothy Macmillan remained the quintessentially loyal political wife, at her husband's side for every election outing, every foreign trip, every state dinner. Still much more at ease than he with the hurly-burly of politicking, she devoted herself to furthering his career, while he relied heavily on her political advice.

Only occasionally did outsiders detect the emotional strain underlying this odd arrangement. In the 1950s Anne Glyn-Jones, a researcher for Macmillan, found in his personal files an old newspaper clipping about Sarah Macmillan's love of horses when she was a little girl. It was a charming story, and Glyn Jones, not realizing that Sarah was Boothby's daughter, showed it to the Macmillans and other members of their family one night when they were having cocktails before dinner. No sooner had she said, "I've got a paper here from the 1930s about Sarah," she recalled, than "an icy silence fell, and Mr. Macmillan crossed the room in an absolute flash and tore the paper out of my hand. It was the only occasion I ever knew him to behave in a brusque or discourteous way."

As part of Macmillan's determined effort to conceal the strain caused by the affair between Lady Dorothy and Boothby, he maintained a surprisingly amicable relationship with Boothby, at least on the surface. But the relationship haunted him throughout his term as prime minister and indeed, by many accounts, affected his response to the notorious Profumo scandal, which helped bring his administration to an abrupt and premature end in 1963. The revelation that the war secretary John Profumo, who as a young MP had voted against Chamberlain in 1940, had lied about his liaison with a party girl named Christine Keeler was one of several recent political reverses suffered by the Macmillan government, following a remarkably long honeymoon with the country.

For months before news of the Profumo affair broke, rumors of the cabinet secretary's relationship with Keeler, who also was involved with a Soviet military attaché, had swirled around London. Yet Macmillan's staff had hesitated to raise the issue with the prime minister because they knew how distasteful and painful he found the subject of adultery. "I don't think he wanted to know about that sort of gossip, and therefore he neglected perhaps to take it as seriously as he should have," said one of his private secretaries. In June 1963 Profumo resigned from his office and Parliament, and four months later the sixty-nine-year-old Macmillan stepped down as well. According to his biographer Alistair Horne, he "never quite got over the Profumo scandal: he suddenly seemed older, and more alone, and never regained his former deftness." When, in Ocober, he developed serious prostate problems, Macmillan came to the erroneous conclusion that he had cancer and decided he must quit as prime minister. After undergoing surgery, he returned to Birch Grove with Dorothy and, following a long recuperation, went back to work as chairman of his family's publishing company.

Less than three years later Dorothy Macmillan collapsed in the entry hall of Birch Grove and died of a massive heart attack. Both her husband and Boothby were shattered. After her death Macmillan buried himself in his work at Macmillan's and, when he was home at Birch Grove, retreated to a small apartment in the attic. "When [Dorothy] was around, you felt the house was full," said an acquaintance. "When she died, Birch Grove suddenly seemed quiet." Boothby, for his part, drank heavily and seemed, in the words of a friend, "to go to pieces." Whenever the phone rang, he jumped up to answer it, half expecting to hear Dorothy's voice. Slowly, however, he recovered his bearings, and more than a year after Dorothy's death, he married Wanda Senna, a young Sardinian woman whom he had known for more than ten years and who was thirty-two years his junior. His marriage brought Boothby a significant measure of happiness and contentment. Yet he could never put Dorothy completely behind him.

Shortly after his wife's death, Macmillan found a huge cache of Boothby's letters to her at Birch Grove and decided to burn them. He took the hundreds of letters out to the incinerator in the back of the garden and began to stuff them in. But a sudden wind snatched them out of his hands, and they went whirling about the garden, with Macmillan in frantic pursuit. With comic flair, he told the story to Boothby one day, taking great pains to poke fun at himself, this dignified, myopic former prime minister chasing down the letters of his dead wife's lover.

Yet neither Macmillan nor Boothby laughed at the end of the story. They sat there in silence, two elderly men whose youthful idealism and quest for social justice had first brought them together more than forty years before. "And so it all ended," Macmillan finally said. Again, there was silence. "And so it all ended," Boothby echoed.

When Harold Macmillan died in 1986 at the age of ninety-two, one newspaper headline proclaimed him "A Giant of Post-War Politics." Several newspaper obituaries called him Britain's most successful prime minister since Churchill. "He brought the country years of prosperity, peace and progress," the *Daily Mail* declared. Other accounts of his life focused on his weary cynicism and his well-deserved reputation for wily, ruthless political infighting in the postwar years. Yet whatever the judgments of him as politician and statesman, Macmillan himself, with his patrician drawl, languid air, Edwardian manners, and fondness for grouse shooting, was remembered, for the most part, as a man from a bygone age, an irrelevance in modern times.

In the flood of stories after his death, the young Macmillan—the dreamer, the passionate idealist, the crusader who battled appeasement—was largely overlooked. Yet unlike the rest of his life, there was a timeless relevance and appeal about this early chapter, for it demonstrated how a small band of men, lacking much political power or influence, could change the course of history by standing up for what they believed.

It was the actions of these individuals—not impersonal historical forces, not "parliamentary spontaneous combustion," not some intangible deus ex machina—that resulted in Neville Chamberlain's resignation and Winston Churchill's accession to power in May 1940. However cynical, jaded, opportunistic, or politically wrongheaded they might have become later in life, Macmillan and the other parliamentary rebels showed resoluteness and moral courage when it mattered most, during the greatest crisis in Britain's history. "Politics, it is truly said, is the 'art of the possible,'" Paul Emrys-Evans once observed. "But great causes have only [prevailed] through the vigour and energy of resolute men who attempted—and succeeded—in making the impossible possible."

The rebels' cause certainly had seemed impossible at the time. They were defying a seemingly omnipotent prime minister and political establishment, whose success at shutting down dissent and dispute within the government and the press had been unparalleled. In the course of their two-year struggle the dissidents, with a rare exception like Ronald Cartland, were not untarnished heroes. They were timid and cautious on occasion, susceptible to intimidation and appeals to loyalty made by Chamberlain and his men, worried about their careers and being branded as parliamentary pariahs. But when their country's future hung in the balance in May 1940, they put all those considerations aside. In the end, they did what Leo Amery had urged Arthur Greenwood to do eight months before.

They spoke for England.

NOTES

INTRODUCTION

3 "jitterbugs": Robert Boothby, *Boothby: Recollections of a Rebel*, p. 133.

3 "without arms": Ibid., p. 135.

4 "the machine is out of control": Edward R. Murrow, *This Is London*, p. 52.

6 "nobody thought": "Warlord for Peacemaker," *Time*, May 20, 1940.

6 "You ask what": Winston Churchill, *The Gathering Storm*, p. 26.

6 "Looking back": Paul Addison, *The Road to 1945: British Politics and the Second World War*, p. 92.

7 "like battering one's": Boothby, *Recollections of a Rebel*, p. 121.

7 "parliamentary political spontaneous": Larry L. Witherell, "Lord Salisbury's 'Watching Committee' and the Fall of Neville Chamberlain, May 1940," *English Historical Review*, November 2001.

7 "Rebellion": Catherine Drinker Bowen, *Biography: The Craft and the Calling*, p. 108.

7 "No government": Ronald Cartland, *The Common Problem*, p. 61.

1: "WE MAY BE GOING TO DIE"

8 But the highlight: Angela Lambert, *1939: The Last Season of Peace*, p. 167.

9 "gay, young, brilliant": Robert Rhodes James, ed., *"Chips": The Diaries of Sir Henry Channon*, p. 205.

9 "Taxi-cab drivers": Virginia Cowles, *Looking for Trouble*, p. 257.

9 "Afterwards, when they": Helen P. Kirkpatrick, *Under the British Umbrella*, p. 301.

10 "Darling, the thing is": Lambert, *1939*, p. 184.

10 According to *The New York Times*: Lynne Olson and Stanley Cloud, *A Question of Honor: The Kosciuszko Squadron: Forgotten Heroes of World War II*, p. 38.

10 "of great urgency": John Harvey, ed. *The Diplomatic Diaries of Oliver Harvey, 1937–1940*, p. 301.

11 "we are being treated": Harold Macmillan, *Winds of Change: 1914–1939*, p. 518.

11 Churchill told Edward Spears: Sir Edward L. Spears, *Assignment to Catastrophe*, vol. 1, *Prelude to Dunkirk: July 1939–May 1940*, p. 2.

11 "if there were ever": Nicolson diaries, July 27, 1939.

12 While the scarlet and gold: David Cannadine, *In Churchill's Shadow: Confronting the Past in Modern Britain*, pp. 7–8.

13 "There are much greater": Julian Amery, *Approach March: A Venture in Autobiography*, p. 46.

13 "Last September the House": "British Commons Votes for Holiday," *New York Times*, August 3, 1939.

13 "At this moment": William Manchester, *The Last Lion: Winston Spencer Churchill: Alone, 1932–1940*, p. 486.

14 "suffers from a curious vanity": John Colville, *The Fringes of Power: Downing Street Diaries*, p. 117.

14 "you distrust": *Hansard* parliamentary debates, August 2, 1939.

14 "very badly in need": Ibid.

15 As a small boy: Barbara Cartland, *Ronald Cartland*, p. 27.

15 "had very little": Richard Law, letter to *The Times*, January 7, 1941.

15 "We are near": Ronald Cartland, p. 23.

15 "Men who hold views": Barbara Cartland, *Ronald Cartland*, p. 197.

16 "a cross between": Ibid., p. 190.

16 "The liberty of": Ronald Cartland, p. 53.

16 "Well," Cartland remarked: Barbara Cartland, *Ronald Cartland*, p. 227.

16 "Do no more": Ibid.

16 "You must speak": Nicolson diaries, August 2, 1939.

16 "I am sorry": Barbara Cartland, *Ronald Cartland*, p. 221.

17 "Cartland had committed": Harold Nicolson, "Marginal Comment," *Spectator*, May 1, 1942.

17 "The right honorable": Barbara Cartland, *Ronald Cartland*, pp. 222–23.

17 "It is all very well": Ibid., p. 223.

18 "Its effect was galvanic": Nicolson diaries, August 2, 1939.

18 "had profound": *Hansard*, August 2, 1939.

18 "Well done": Barbara Cartland, *Ronald Cartland*, p. 225.

18 "Ronald Cartland!": Ibid., p. 225.

19 "their actions [will be]": Ibid., p. 226.

19 "An attempt will be made": Ibid., p. 228.

19 "Mr. Ronald Cartland": *Evening News*, August 3, 1939.

19 "severe measures": Neville Thompson, *The Anti-Appeasers: Conservative Opposition to Appeasement in the 1930s*, p. 218.

19 "Ronald Cartland's": R. H. Edwards to Neville Chamberlain, August 3, 1939, Chamberlain Papers.

20 "As for Master": Neville Chamberlain to Ida Chamberlain, August 5, 1939, Chamberlain Papers.

20 "I regret nothing": Barbara Cartland, *Ronald Cartland*, p. 227.

2: PLAYING THE GAME

21 More than a third: Kirkpatrick, *Under the British Umbrella*, p. 42.

22 "What surprised me": Cowles, *Looking for Trouble*, p. 103.

22 "it was easier": Noel Annan, *Our Age: English Intellectuals Between the World Wars*, p. 8.

22 "as unrelated": Drew Middleton, *These Are the British*, p. 234.

23 "their Lord of the Flies": Quentin Crewe, *Well, I Forget the Rest: The Autobiography of an Optimist*, p. 29.

23 "might do something": Rupert Wilkinson, *Gentlemanly Power: British Leadership and the Public School Tradition*, p. 80.

24 "one matter": J.R.J. Macnamara, *The Whistle Blows*, p. 142.

24 "every amenity": Christopher Hollis, "Parliament and the Establishment," in *The Establishment*, ed. Hugh Thomas, p. 176.

25 "A veritable": Macnamara, *The Whistle Blows*, p. 144.

25 "despised culture": Frances Leggett, *Late and Soon: The Transatlantic Story of a Marriage*, p. 247.

25 "He adored": Gay Charteris to John Hill, November 1978, Margesson Papers.

25 Indeed, Lloyd George: Frank Owen, *Guilty Men*, p. 106.

26 "limitations as well": Gay Charteris to John Hill, November 1978, Margesson Papers.

26 "You were either": Sir Percy Harris, *Forty Years in and out of Parliament*, p. 152.

26 "If you are busy": Patrick Donner, *Crusade*, p. 80.

26 "applies to the House": Owen, p. 107.

27 "extremely strong": Josiah Wedgwood, *Memoirs of a Fighting Life*, p. 157.

27 "work (or gossip)": Ibid., p. 120.

27 "Nothing is more": Hollis, in Thomas, *The Establishment*, p. 176.

27 "He disdained": Richard Law, letter to *The Times*, January 7, 1941.

27 Four years: Barbara Cartland, *Ronald Cartland*, p. 28.

28 "I want you": Ibid., p. 39.

28 "I shall get": Ibid, p. 41.

28 "I used to listen": Gwen Robyns, *Barbara Cartland*, p. 81.

29 "have almost": Barbara Cartland, *We Danced All Night*, p. 286.

29 "If [Ronald]": Barbara Cartland, *Ronald Cartland*, p. 45.

29 When millions: Barbara Cartland, *We Danced All Night*, p. 287.

30 "two nations": Quoted in Richard Critchfield, *An American Looks at Britain*, p. 16.

30 "Socialism would": Barbara Cartland, *Ronald Cartland*, p. 76.

30 "I must be": Ibid., p. 86.

31 "by the older": Richard Law, letter to *The Times*, January 7, 1941.

31 "Most of the House": Barbara Cartland, *Ronald Cartland*, p. 111.

31 "good and very demure": Macnamara, p. 143.

31 "I am afraid": Barbara Cartland, *Ronald Cartland*, p. 121.

32 "I was always": Ibid., p. 12.

32 "No one could": Ibid., p. 165.

32 "When he leaves": Nicolson diaries, September 20, 1939.

32 "a knight": Elizabeth Longford, *The Pebbled Shore: The Memoirs of Elizabeth Longford*, p. 173.

33 "Cartland is ambitious": *Sunday Express*, May 24, 1936.

33 "I can't tell": Barbara Cartland, *Ronald Cartland*, p. 136.

33 "Ronald approached": Ibid., p. 13.

33 "taking on the role": Ibid., p. 188.
33 "If you are going": Ibid., p. 135.
33 "Mr. Cartland": Ibid.
34 In August 1935: Ibid., p. 102.
34 "follow his conscience": Ibid., p. 182.
34 "We must make": Ibid., p. 183.
34 "an independent character": Paul Emrys-Evans unpublished memoir, Emrys-Evans Papers.
35 "It seems to me": Barbara Cartland, *Ronald Cartland*, p. 122.

3: "TROUBLESOME YOUNG MEN"

36 "a tiresome fellow": Ronald Tree, *When the Moon Was High*, p. 53.
36 "a bit of a bore": Arthur Baker, *The House Is Sitting*, p. 237.
36 "Mr. Harold": Alistair Horne, *Harold Macmillan*, vol. 1, *1894–1956*, p. 109.
37 "I always felt": Harold Macmillan, *Winds of Change: 1914–1939*, p. 41.
37 "I learnt books": Anthony Sampson, *Macmillan: A Study in Ambiguity*, p. 16.
37 "to escape from": Horne, *Macmillan*, vol. 1,, p. 10.
37 "no sympathy": Macmillan, *Winds of Change*, p. 57.
37 "devotion and support": Horne, *Macmillan*, vol. 1, p. 11.
37 "if you failed": Macmillan interview, *The Macmillans: Portrait of a Political Marriage*, BBC documentary, March 14, 1996.
37 "I admired her": Horne, *Macmillan*, vol. 1, p. 12.
37 "a home where": Ibid., p. 21.
38 "spoilt darlings": James Stuart, *Within the Fringe*, p. 20.
39 "a city of the dead": Macmillan interview, *The Macmillans*, BBC.
39 "an obligation": Macmillan, *Winds of Change*, p. 98.
39 "gentlemen of England": Sampson, p. 23.
39 "dedicated": Colin R. Coote, *A Companion of Honour: The Story of Walter Elliot*, p. 18.
39 "as if they were": Richard Davenport-Hines, *The Macmillans*, p. 331.
39 "extraordinary zest": Horne, *Macmillan*, vol. 1, p. 54.
39 "you knew": Ibid., p. 55.
40 "I love her": Ibid., p. 56.
40 "A million men": Barbara Cartland, *We Danced All Night*, p. 13.
40 "escape the problems": Horne, *Macmillan*, vol. 1, p. 57.
40 "an unpleasant woman": John Pearson, *The Serpent and the Stag*, p. 259.
40 "She wouldn't speak": Ibid., p. 264.
40 "Uncle Harold": Cherie Booth and Cate Haste, *The Goldfish Bowl: Married to the Prime Minister 1955–1997*, p. 38.
40 As unpretentious: Horne, *Macmillan*, vol. 1, p. 66.
41 "soft heart for": Sampson, p. 28.
41 "almost as remote": Macmillan, *Winds of Change*, p. 181.
41 the offspring: Duchess of Devonshire, *The House: Living at Chatsworth*, p. 66.
42 A languid man: Horne, *Macmillan*, vol. 1, p. 67.
42 "He gave": Booth and Haste, p. 36.
42 "a simple": Macmillan interview, *The Macmillans*, BBC.

42 "a rather sad": Horne, *Macmillan*, vol. 1, p. 67.

42 "Whereas Uncle": Duke of Devonshire interview, *The Macmillans*, BBC.

43 "wait for Doomsday": J. B. Priestley, *English Journey*, p. 238.

43 "the heckling and din": Sampson, p. 29.

43 "manner was": Horne, *Macmillan*, vol. 1, p. 348.

43 "She was a wizard": Booth and Haste, p. 40.

44 "She was the greater": Horne, *Macmillan*, vol. 1, p. 73.

44 "a period of tranquility": Sampson, p. 29.

44 " a natural gift": Robert Rhodes James, *Robert Boothby: A Portrait of Churchill's Ally*, p. 38.

45 "A natural storm": Virginia Cowles, *Winston Churchill: The Era and the Man*, p. 5.

45 "Winston was very": *Times Saturday Review*, Jan. 22, 1969.

46 "walks in": Neville Thompson, p. 24.

46 "All doors": Boothby, *Recollections of a Rebel*, p. 44.

46 "He was an adventurer": Interview with Marie Ridder.

47 "on the borderland": Robert Boothby, *I Fight to Live*, p. 53.

47 "Herrings again!": James, *Boothby*, p. 60.

47 "Ye should've": Ibid., p. 54.

47 "unique, wayward": Macmillan, *Winds of Change*, p. 176.

47 "In the drawing-room": Boothby, *I Fight to Live*, p. 45.

48 The decision on whom: John Colville, *Winston Churchill and His Inner Circle*, p. 24.

48 "nothing . . . shall": Colin R. Coote, *The Other Club*, p. 20.

48 "We were a very": Wedgwood, p. 117.

48 "I hope": Boothby to Churchill, December 7, 1928, Churchill Papers.

48 On at least: James, *Boothby*, p. 88.

48 "I loved serving": Boothby interview with Martin Gilbert, Churchill Papers.

49 "half-baked sentimentalism": James, *Boothby*, p. 87.

49 "Most Tories": Horne, *Macmillan*, vol. 1, p. 75.

49 "I wish you": Winston Churchill to J.C.C. Davidson, November 8, 1927, Churchill Papers.

50 "To sit": Horne, *Macmillan*, vol. 1, p. 80.

50 "I should . . . like": Harold Macmillan to Winston Churchill, January 1, 1928, Churchill Papers.

50 "But my unhappy": Harold Macmillan, *The Past Masters*, p. 64.

51 On the second: James, *Boothby*, p. 113.

51 "We were young": Macmillan, *Winds of Change*, p. 118.

51 one of the Macmillans': Booth and Haste, p. 41.

51 "He could be": Horne, *Macmillan*, vol. 1, p. 81.

51 "society made": Critchfield, p. 55.

51 "From the moment": Barbara Cartland, *We Danced All Night*, p. 59.

52 "would continue": Victoria Glendinning, *Vita: The Life of V. Sackville-West*, p. 209.

53 "women would call": W. F. Deedes interview, *The Macmillans*, BBC.

53 "an ability": Interview with Marie Ridder.

53 "he was forever": James, *Boothby*, p. 114.

53 "I told her": Horne, *Macmillan*, vol. 1, p. 89.

54 "The commandments": Barbara Cartland, *We Danced All Night*, p. 67.

54 "Society used": *Times Saturday Review*, November 22, 1969.

54 "it would have": Lord Stockton interview, *The Macmillans*, BBC.

54 "I never loved": Horne, *Macmillan*, vol. 1, p. 89.

55 "[I]n spite of": Booth and Haste, p. 44.

55 "She was desperately": Ibid., p. 42.

55 "a period in paradise": Robert Rhodes James interview, *The Macmillans*, BBC.

55 "Why did you": James, *Boothby*, p. 116.

55 When Dorothy's: Ibid., p. 120.

55 "The reverberations": Janet Aitken Kidd, *The Beaverbrook Girl*, p. 137.

55 "Keep it quiet": John Dale, "My Darling Dorothy," *Daily Mail*, May 10, 1978.

55 "What [my father]": Horne, *Macmillan*, vol. 1, p. 88.

55 "The greatest men": Cecil Beaton, *Self-Portrait with Friends*, p. 106.

55 "It has become": James, *Boothby*, p. 115.

56 "I am passionately": Ibid., p. 118.

56 "that bloody": Ibid.

56 "does not hang": Nicolson diaries, November 29, 1930.

56 "Went down": Nick Smart, ed., *Diaries and Letters of Robert Bernays 1932–1939*, p. 77.

56 "The gloom": Simon Ball, *The Guardsmen: Harold Macmillan, Three Friends, and the World They Made*, p. 130.

56 "It was only": Susan Barnes, "The Hon. Member, the Star of Television," *Sunday Times*, April 1, 1973.

57 "I was a self-satisfied": Boothby interview, *Good Afternoon,* Thames Television, April 9, 1975.

57 "His charm": James, *Boothby,* p. 95.

57 "You can't have": *Daily Mail*, November 10, 1978.

57 "drew the conclusion": James, *Boothby,* p. 128.

58 "He was fond": *Sunday Times,* April 1, 1973.

58 "It was important": Glyn-Jones interview, *The Macmillans,* BBC.

58 One friend: Horne, *Macmillan*, vol. 1, p. 98.

59 "intense poverty": Quoted in Piers Brendon, *The Dark Valley: A Panorama of the 1930s*, p. 196.

59 "I think there": Sampson, p. 43.

4: "DICTATORS ARE VERY POPULAR THESE DAYS"

61 "I am going": Boothby, *I Fight to Live*, p. 102.

62 "You have been": Ibid.

62 "along the Kurfürstendamm": Quoted in Manchester, p. 55.

62 "homosexuality was": Boothby, *Recollections of a Rebel*, p. 107.

63 "Somehow Hitler": Ibid., p. 111.

63 "nice, innocuous sermon": Ibid., p. 118.

63 "I tell you": Boothby, *I Fight to Live*, pp. 130–31.

64 "We were preparing": Quoted in Brendon, p. 15.

64 "We were determined": Annan, p. 10.

64 "the bomber": Manchester, p. 95.

64 "Picture if you can": Stuart Hylton, *The Darkest Hour: The Hidden History of the Home Front*, p. 32.

65 "we thought": David Reynolds, "Churchill's Writing of History: Appeasement, Autobiography and *The Gathering Storm*," Transactions of the Royal Historical Society, series 6, vol. 11, 2001, p. 234.

65 "I will not": Andrew Roberts, *Eminent Churchillians*, p. 6.

66 "Food!": Brendon, p. 197.

66 "tender to the Nazis": Kenneth Rose, *The Later Cecils*, p. 179.

66 "they would prefer": Nicolson diaries, May 18, 1938.

66 "People of the governing": Nicolson diaries, June 6, 1938.

66 "it was no business": Kenneth Young, ed., *The Diaries of Sir Robert Bruce Lockhart*, vol. 1, *1915–1939*, p. 263.

66 "is going the dictator": James, *"Chips,"* p. 84.

66 "served largely": Ian Kershaw, *Making Friends with Hitler: Lord Londonderry and Britain's Road to War*, p. 143.

67 At one fellowship: Nicolson diaries, January 25, 1938.

67 "formidable and capricious": Loelia Lindsay, *Grace and Favour*, p. 181.

67 "with elaborate secrecy": Ibid., p. 189.

68 "[T]here were a lot": Lambert, *1939*, p. 79.

68 "with the best intentions": Quoted in Kershaw, p. 64.

68 "The central fact": Manchester, p. 80.

68 "an Austrian Joan": Ibid., p. 81.

68 "my dear little": Barbara Cartland, *The Isthmus Years*, p. 142.

69 "a born leader": Manchester, p. 80.

69 Tree had visited: Tree, p. 56.

69 "was persuaded": Ibid., p. 59

69 "I have never": Macnamara, p. 14.

69 "we were drifting": Paul Emrys-Evans to Julian Amery, May 22, 1956, Emrys-Evans Papers.

70 "If we are weak": James Lees-Milne, *Harold Nicolson: 1886–1929*, p. 340.

70 "the nicest men": Boothby, *Recollections of a Rebel*, p. 33.

71 "scorched and cynical": Boothby, *I Fight to Live*, p. 39.

71 "methodical, respectable": Charles Ritchie, *The Siren Years: A Canadian Diplomat Abroad, 1937–1945*, p. 51.

72 "great and noble": Macnamara, p. 206.

73 "The rape of Abyssinia": Robert Rhodes James, *Victor Cazalet: A Portrait*, p. 172.

73 "regarded as among": Macmillan, *Winds of Change*, p. 421.

73 "that small group": Sampson, p. 50.

74 "The feeling in the House": Nicolson diaries, March 23, 1936.

74 "The forty-eight": Manchester, p. 175.

74 "After all": Ibid, p. 179.

74 "there were quite": Max Egremont, *Under Two Flags: The Life of Major-General Sir Edward Spears*, pp. 134–35.

75 "You made some": Martin Gilbert, *Winston S. Churchill*, vol. 5, *The Prophet of Truth, 1922–1939*, p. 300.

76 "almost demented": Ibid., p. 355.

76 "a foul race": Norman Rose, *Churchill: The Unruly Giant*, p. 266.

76 "alarming and nauseating": Ibid.

76 "a crime against": Geoffrey Best, *Churchill: A Study in Greatness*, p. 138.

76 "reactionary and unrealistic": Macmillan, *Winds of Change*, p. 291.
76 "The public looks": Brian Gardner, *Churchill in His Time: A Study in a Reputation 1939–1945*, p. 1.
77 "You must be": Bonham Carter interview with Kenneth Harris, *The Listener*, undated.
78 "stories of a neighbour": Crewe, p. 56.
78 "a woman of such": Mark Pottle, *Champion Redoubtable: The Diaries and Letters of Violet Bonham Carter 1914–1941*, p. xxi.
78 "Had she been": Walter Terry, *Daily Mail*, November 20, 1969.
78 "for the first time": Bonham Carter interview, *The Listener*.
78 "Words were": Ibid.
79 "His wife": Pottle, *Champion*, p. xxviii.
79 She took him: Ibid., p. xxiv.
79 "Neutrality is not": Bonham Carter obituary, *Daily Express*, November 20, 1969.
79 "In Germany": Pottle, *Champion*, p. xxviii.
80 "Where are my": James, *Cazalet*, p. 171.
80 "Unless we": Pottle, *Champion*, p. 189.
80 "So they go": Churchill, *The Gathering Storm*, p. 215.
81 "gone to the country": Ibid., p. 216.
81 "We had the feeling": Ibid., p. 217.
81 "the last believer": Manchester, p. 223.
81 "filled with emotion": Boothby, *Recollections of a Rebel*, p. 125.
81 "It was": Manchester, p. 232.
81 "In five fatal": Boothby, *Recollections of a Rebel*, p. 125.
82 "What happened": Boothby to Churchill, December 7, 1936, Churchill Papers.
82 "It was frightfully": Boothby interview with Martin Gilbert, Churchill Papers.
82 "you are the only": Boothby to Churchill, December 11, 1936, Churchill Papers.
82 "undermined the reputation": Macmillan, *Winds of Change*, p. 442.
82 "no man ever": Nicolson diaries, May 27, 1939.

5: "I LACK THE 'SPUNK'"
84 "We are still": *Daily Telegraph*, January 15, 1977.
84 "the darling of": Kenneth Clark, *Another Part of the Wood: A Self-Portrait*, p. 223.
84 "Paradoxically": Bonham Carter Notebook, "The Thirties," Bonham Carter Papers.
85 Affectionately called: Robert Rhodes James, *Anthony Eden*, p. 38.
85 "deprived him": D. R. Thorpe, *Eden: The Life and Times of Anthony Eden First Earl of Avon, 1897–1977*, p. 45.
86 "outstanding success": Ibid., p. 120.
86 "the fourth best": Ibid.
87 "Anthony Eden": David Dutton, *Anthony Eden: A Life and Reputation*, p. 7.
87 "My God": Noel Busch, "Anthony Eden," *Life*, August 30, 1943.
87 "Eden's appointment": Mary Soames, *Speaking for Themselves: The Personal Letters of Winston and Clementine Churchill*, p. 402.
87 "I think you": Norman Rose, *Churchill*, p. 288.
87 "Dare I confess": James, *Eden*, p. 135.

87 "I think we": Ibid., p. 136.

88 "suppose that": Manchester, p. 180.

88 "There are many": Winston Churchill, *Collier's*, October 16, 1937.

88 "I should have": Dutton, p. 67.

89 "he would have": Macmillan, *The Past Masters*, p. 132.

90 "led to the creation": Winston Churchill, *Collier's*, October 16, 1937.

90 "Only a few": L. S. Amery, *My Political Life,* vol. 3, *The Unforgiving Years 1929–1940*, p. 226.

90 "His face seemed": Francis Williams, *Nothing So Strange*, p. 144.

90 "with unconvincing conviviality": Harold Nicolson, "People and Things," *Spectator*, May 17, 1940.

90 "my sharp tongue": David J. Dutton, "The Neville Chamberlain Diary Letters, Vol. II," Institute of Historical Research, March 2002.

90 "He was always": Tree, p. 70.

91 "[His] vanity": Colville, *The Fringes of Power*, p. 117.

91 When Pakenham: Longford, p. 133.

91 "I am myself": David Dilks, ed., *The Diaries of Sir Alexander Cadogan 1938–1945*, p. 107.

92 "A boxer": Quoted in Cowles, *Churchill*, p. 102.

92 Most of the budget: David Carlton, *Anthony Eden: A Biography*, pp. 117–18.

92 "a very depressing": Young, *Lockhart Diaries*, vol. 1, p. 364.

92 "He thought": Macmillan interview, *The Past Masters*, BBC, October 30, 1975.

93 "Prime Minister": Helen Kirkpatrick Milbank oral history, Washington Press Club Foundation, April 3, 1990.

93 "A man who is": Andrew Roberts, *"The Holy Fox": The Life of Lord Halifax*, p. 131.

93 "He is the most": Clark, *Another Part of the Wood*, p. 224.

94 "build a bridge": Unpublished article by J.P.L.Thomas, Cilcennin Papers.

94 "foreign policy was": Ibid.

94 "was becoming": Ibid.

94 "ridiculous . . . but": Simon Ball, p. 5.

95 "The Cecils": Kenneth Rose, *The Later Cecils*, p. 33.

95 "He saw so": Simon Ball, p. 165.

95 "The Government is living": Carlton, p. 119.

95 "the situation": Duff Cooper, *Old Men Forget: An Autobiography of Duff Cooper*, p. 212.

96 In between: Simon Ball, p. 168.

96 "The newspapers": Nicolson diaries, February 21, 1938.

96 "doubtless think": Arthur Mann to Forbes Adam, February 30, 1938, Avon Papers.

96 In a nationwide: Richard Cockett, *Twilight of Truth: Chamberlain, Appeasement & the Manipulation of the Press*, p. 190.

96 "The whole country": James, *"Chips,"* p. 145.

97 Just hours: Churchill to Eden, February 21, 1938, Churchill Papers.

97 They were so bland: Macmillan, *Winds of Change*, p. 485.

97 "surrender to blackmail": Simon Ball, p. 170.

98 "took the House": *Daily Telegraph*, February 22, 1938.

98 "is at this hour": "Anthony Eden's Temptation in the Wilderness," February 26, 1938, printed in *Yorkshire Post*, Avon Papers.

98 "the one strong": Churchill, *The Gathering Storm*, p. 257.

98 "We assumed": Dutton, p. 3.

98 "I truly hate": James, *Eden*, p. 203.

99 "the move": Thorpe, p. 218.

99 "too shrewd": James, *"Chips,"* p. 147.

99 "Germany neither intends": Geoffrey Cox, *Countdown to War*, p. 220.

99 "hung in the air": Cowles, *Looking for Trouble*, p. 111.

100 "public opinion was": Manchester, p. 287.

100 "has been in": Ronald Cartland to Jim Thomas, March 22, 1938, Cilcennin Papers.

100 "In my wildest": Franklin Reid Gannon, *The British Press and Germany 1936–1939*, p. 152.

100 "the behavior": Manchester, p. 281.

101 "at the top": Jim Thomas to Paul Emrys-Evans, March 1938, Emrys-Evans Papers.

101 "public settled": Cowles, *Looking for Trouble*, p. 111.

101 "certainly nothing": Emrys-Evans to Paul Addison, June 3, 1965, Emrys-Evans Papers.

102 "The events": Emrys-Evans to David Margesson, July 13, 1936, Emrys-Evans Papers.

102 "blazingly honest": Interview with Alistair Henderson.

102 "It is fashionable": Emrys-Evans to Leo Amery, July 1, 1954, Emrys-Evans Papers.

102 "a libel": Emrys-Evans to Anthony Eden, November 29, 1961, Emrys-Evans Papers.

102 "It was a humiliating": Emrys-Evans to Anthony Eden, May 16, 1962, Emrys-Evans Papers.

102 "pressing on": Emrys-Evans to Leo Amery, August 3, 1954, Emrys-Evans Papers.

103 "a calamity": *Hansard*, February 21, 1938.

103 "country which": Ibid.

104 "He seemed marked": Lees-Milne, *Nicolson, 1886–1929*, p. 366.

104 "It is so odd": Ibid., p. 92.

105 "I have lost": Harold Nicolson, *Diaries and Letters*, vol. 1, *1930–1939*, p. 55.

105 "Most certainly": Ibid., p. 212.

105 "shouts and laughter": Ibid., p. 222.

105 "I do not": Nicolson diaries, December 31, 1937.

106 "I have come": Nicolson, *Diaries and Letters*, vol. 1, p. 326.

106 "I wish": Sir Robert Doncaster to Emrys-Evans, April 12, 1938, Emrys-Evans Papers.

106 "Why is it": Nicolson, *Diaries and Letters*, vol. 1, p. 332.

6: "QUITE SIMPLY, HE TOLD LIES"

107 It was after: Ben Pimlott, ed., *The Political Diary of Hugh Dalton: 1918–40; 1945–60*, p. 225.

108 "Nothing delights": Ben Pimlott, *Hugh Dalton*, p. 190.

108 "still terrified": Hugh Dalton, *The Fateful Years: Memoirs 1931–1945*, p. 162.

108 After Hitler's annexation: Ibid.

109 In late March: Ronald Tree to Anthony Eden, March 23, 1938, Avon Papers.

109 "I, for one": Duncan Sandys to Anthony Eden, April 28, 1938, Avon Papers.

109 "While I wish": Anthony Eden to Bobbety Cranborne, June 8, 1938, Avon Papers.

110 Although he would not promise: Roberts, *"Holy Fox,"* pp. 95–96.

111 A believer: John Barnes and David Nicolson, eds., *The Empire at Bay: The Leo Amery Diaries 1929–1945*, p. 370.

111 "not prepared": L. S. Amery, *My Political Life*, vol. 3, p. 175.

111 "the straightest": William Roger Louis, *In the Name of God, Go!: Leo Amery and the British Empire in the Age of Churchill*, p. 39.

111 In a letter: L. S. Amery, *My Political Life*, vol. 3, p. 23.

111 What Amery: Amery obituary, *Manchester Guardian*, September 17, 1955.

112 "He consistently": Charles Eade, ed., *Churchill by His Contemporaries*, p. 19.

112 "Now you're": Winston Churchill, *My Early Life: A Roving Commission*, p. 18.

113 He never became: Ibid., p. 20.

113 "always had": Martin Gilbert, *Winston S. Churchill, Companion Volume V, 1922–1939*, Part 2, p. 34.

113 "one of the finest": Amery obituary, *Birmingham Post*, September 17, 1955.

114 For lack: L. S. Amery, *My Political Life*, vol. 1, *England Before the Storm 1896–1914*, p. 117.

114 "Keep cool": Brian Roberts, *Churchills in Africa*, pp. 173–74.

115 "the early worm": L. S. Amery, *My Political Life*, vol. 1, p. 117.

115 "I owe it": John Barnes and David Nicholson, eds., *The Leo Amery Diaries 1886–1929*, p. 78.

115 "Winston Churchill": Julian Amery, p. 44.

115 "All through life": Amery obituary, *Manchester Guardian*, September 17, 1955.

116 "semi-enemy": Roy Jenkins, *Churchill: A Biography*, p. 381.

116 "a brilliant talker": Amery to Stanley Baldwin, April 10, 1927, Amery Papers.

116 "My diary": L. S. Amery, *My Political Life*, vol. 2, *War and Peace 1914–1929*, p. 504.

116 "I had been": Ibid., p. 99.

117 "at all costs": Ibid., p. 103.

117 "And so to": Barnes and Nicholson, *Amery Diaries 1929–1945*, p. 383.

117 "If only": Ibid., p. 288.

117 If he were only: Louis, p. 30.

117 "ye haven't": L. S. Amery, *My Political Life*, vol. 2, p. 65.

118 "had not been": Cooper, p. 204.

118 "After the Anschluss": Margery Allingham, *The Oaken Heart*, p. 18.

118 They were told: Cockett, p. 189.

119 At most: Robert Graves and Alan Hodge, *The Long Weekend: A Social History of Great Britain 1918–1939*, p. 432.

119 "real power": Cox, p. 66.

119 "From the moment": James Margach, *The Abuse of Power: The War Between Downing Street and the Media from Lloyd George to Callaghan*, p. 50.

119 "the press in": Roberts, *"Holy Fox,"* p. 74.

119 "If only": Cockett, p. 41.

119 "Assuming that": Brendon, p. 58.

120 In the middle: Robert Shepherd, *A Class Divided: Appeasement and the Road to Munich 1938*, p. 112.

120 From the day: Cockett, p. 6.

120   Steward, meanwhile: Ibid., p. 5.

120   "the most shy": Margach, p. 51.

121   Everyone present: Ibid., p. 52.

121   "Jewish-Communist": Ibid., p. 53.

121   "I tell you": Ibid., p. 59.

121   "honorary members": Ibid., p. 129.

122   "I do my": Cockett, p. 27.

122   "I spend my": Margach, p. 54.

122   "I urged": Basil Liddell Hart, *The Liddell Hart Memoirs*, vol. 2, p. 130.

122   "I had been": Ibid., p. 197.

123   While *The Times*: Kershaw, p. 58.

123   "all Western Europe": Gannon, p. 26.-

123   "loyal support": Anne Chisholm and Michael Davie, *Lord Beaverbrook: A Life*, p. 348.

123   "Frank, be": Ibid.

123   "your views": Manchester, p. 298.

124   "I was acutely": Cockett, p. 45.

124   "Most of the office": Ibid., p. 65.

124   "It is hard": A. J. Davies, *We, the Nation: The Conservative Party and the Pursuit of Power*, p. 415.

124   "habit of suppressing": Brendon, p. 432.

124   When the two: Cowles, *Looking for Trouble*, p. 127.

125   "kept quiet": Martha Gellhorn, "The Lord Will Provide for England," *Collier's*, September 1938.

7: "OUR OWN SOUL IS AT STAKE"

126   "the greatest performance": Boothby, *I Fight to Live*, p. 155.

126   "you had to feel": Ibid.

127   "They are undoubtedly": Herbert von Dirksen, *Documents and Materials Relating to the Eve of the Second World War*, pp. 36–37.

127   If Britain went: Dilks, p. 64.

127   "In the circumstances": Williamson Murray, *The Change in the European Balance of Power, 1938–1939*, p. 88.

128   "cannot at the present": Manchester, p. 293.

128   "things had gone": Ibid., p. 308.

128   But a few: Murray, *Change*, p. 190.

129   Cooper argued: John Charmley, *Duff Cooper*, p. 115.

129   "a year or so": Murray, *Change*, p. 190.

129   "written down": Cockett, p. 76.

129   "I feel strongly": James Lees-Milne, *Harold Nicolson: 1930–1968*, p. 109.

129   "very angry": Cockett, p. 112.

129   "We must warn": Lees-Milne, *Nicolson 1930–1968*, p. 110.

130   Incredibly: Murray, *Change*, p. 196.

130   "would have": Manchester, p. 331.

131   "we shall simply": Dirksen, p. 46.

131   "We were being told": Cooper, p. 228.

131 "British press": Harvey, p. 180.
131 "I got the impression": Manchester, p. 336.
131 "frightful": Cooper, p. 229.
131 "From beginning": Ibid., p. 230.
132 Stanley argued: Murray, *Change*, p. 201.
132 "the most terrible": Manchester, p. 338.
132 "not Czechoslovakia alone": Ibid., p. 340.
132 "You have abandoned": Shepherd, p. 191.
132 "More telephone": Nicolson diaries, September 21, 1938.
132 "not lead a revolt": Nicolson diaries, September 19, 1938.
132 "until popular favor": Harold Nicolson, *Diaries and Letters 1930–1939*, p. 354.
133 "were such": Duff Cooper manuscript on Munich, Cooper Papers.
133 "the great mass": Manchester, p. 342.
133 "As I understand it": Leo Amery to Neville Chamberlain, September 25, 1938, Chamberlain Papers.
134 "The issue has": L. S. Amery, *My Political Life*, vol. 3, p. 277.
134 "the latter trusted": Murray, *Change*, p. 207.
134 "or even advised": Cooper, p. 239.
134 "a nation of slaves": Manchester, p. 345.
134 "became frankly hysterical": Allingham, p. 32.
135 "obscene, elephant-foetus": Ibid., p. 37.
135 "the sense of impending": Ibid., p. 33.
135 "is like a": Smart, *Diaries and Letters*, p. 78.
135 "very wild": Barnes and Nicholson, *Amery Diaries 1929–1945*, p. 519.
135 "this Cabinet must": N. R. Rose, *Baffy: The Diaries of Blanche Dugdale 1936–1947*, p. 104.
135 "I poured cold": Barnes and Nicholson, *Amery Diaries 1929–1945*, p. 519.
136 "If Chamberlain rats": Harold Nicolson, *Diaries and Letters 1930–1939*, p. 361.
136 "How horrible": Manchester, p. 250.
136 "speech more devoid": Baker, p. 66.
136 Chamberlain had: John W. Wheeler-Bennett, *Munich: Prologue to Tragedy*, p. 169.
137 "Thank God": Ibid., p. 170.
137 Although he was: Macmillan, *Winds of Change*, p. 506.
137 "incredible, almost": Shepherd, p. 217.
137 In a surprising: Macmillan, *Winds of Change*, p. 506.
137 "Stand up": Nicolson diaries, September 28, 1938.
137 "If you have": Wheeler-Bennett, p. 171.
137 "hard as steel": Rose, *Baffy*, p. 107.
137 "While sharing": Bonham Carter Notebook, "The Thirties," Bonham Carter Papers.
138 "he would have": Robert Rhodes James, *Churchill: A Study in Failure 1900–1939*, pp. 336–37.
138 "like a man": Bonham Carter Notebook, "The Thirties," Bonham Carter Papers.
138 "Isn't it glorious?": Pottle, *Champion*, p. 191.
139 "sordid, subhuman": Coote, *The Other Club*, p. 89.
140 "And Mr. Cooper": Kenneth Young, *Lockhart Diaries*, vol. 1, p. 156.

141 As war secretary: Charmley, p. 97.

141 "I was sure": Cooper, p. 204.

141 As first lord: Charmley, pp. 108–109.

141 "Veiners": Cooper, p. 9.

141 Cooper and Boothby: Charmley, p. 124.

141 "everybody insulted": Ibid.

141 "honour demanded vindication": Bonham Carter Notebook, "The Thirties," Bonham
     Carter Papers.

142 "obvious anger": Coote, *Other Club*, p. 91.

142 "humiliation": Coote, *Companion of Honour*, p. 174.

8: "'TERRIBLE, UNMITIGATED, UNPARALLELED DISHONOR'"

143 In two-inch: Cox, p. 75.

143 "No conqueror": Wheeler-Bennett, p. 180.

143 "Thanks to Chamberlain": Graves and Hodge, p. 445.

143 "received a great": Cockett, p. 79.

143 Also spiked: Ibid.

144 "One knew": Williams, *Nothing So Strange*, p. 145.

144 "the biggest": Brendon, p. 625.

145 "You might think": John Colville, *Footprints in Time: Memories*, p. 63.

145 "feeling very lonely": Cooper, p. 242.

145 "Of the various": Ibid., p. 207.

145 "I can bear": Colville, *Footprints in Time*, p. 63.

145 "peace with honor": Manchester, p. 358.

146 "It was 'peace with honor'": Cowles, *Looking for Trouble*, p. 180.

146 "as glad to": Cooper, p. 243.

146 "Most honourable": Philip Ziegler, *Diana Cooper*, p. 189.

146 "I think you": Maureen Stanley to Duff Cooper, undated, Cooper Papers.

146 "my heart leapt": Robert Boothby to Duff Cooper, October 2, 1938, Cooper
     Papers.

146 "We want": Rob Bernays to Duff Cooper, October 3, 1938, Cooper Papers.

146 "May I say": Admiral Cork to Duff Cooper, October 4, 1938, Cooper Papers.

147 "I expect": Louis Mountbatten to Duff Cooper, October 4, 1938, Cooper Papers.

147 "count for nothing": N. R. Rose, *Baffy*, p. 98.

148 "The Munich terms": Ibid., p. 112.

148 "for both our sakes": Ibid., p. 109.

148 "All these men": Macmillan, *Winds of Change*, p. 511.

148 "I should never,": Cooper, p. 248.

149 "profound feeling": Manchester, p. 365.

149 "obviously tired": Ibid.

149 "Wednesday's glow": James, *"Chips,"* p. 173.

149 "to question": Macmillan, *Winds of Change*, p. 509.

149 "clung like a limpet": Unpublished Richard Law (Lord Coleraine) reminiscences
     of Winston Churchill.

149 "normally a most": Ibid.

149 "distaste for what": Cockett, pp. 96–97.
150 "spoke with the burning": Anthony Eden, *The Reckoning: The Memoirs of Anthony Eden Earl of Avon*, p. 39.
150 "junior partner": *Hansard*, October 3, 1938.
150 "wicked mockery": *Hansard*, October 4, 1938.
150 "shame and humiliation": *Hansard*, October 4, 1938.
150 "the situation": Sampson, p. 55.
150 "we have sustained": Manchester, p. 366.
150 "a great and *terrible*": N. R. Rose, *Baffy*, p. 111.
151 "one of the most disastrous": *Hansard*, October 5, 1938.
151 "threats were used": N. R. Rose, *Baffy*, p. 111.
152 "would be marked": Dalton, p. 199.
152 "all proposals": Pimlott, *Hugh Dalton*, p. 258.
153 "a large-scale Tory": Pimlott, *Dalton Diary 1918–1940*, p. 247.
153 "half-agreed": Harold Nicolson, *Diaries and Letters 1930–1939*, p. 369.
153 "He seemed willing": *The Times*, October 4, 1938.
153 "were disappointed": Quoted in Simon Ball, p. 186.
154 "Neville's performance": Barnes and Nicholson, *Amery Diaries 1929–1945*, p. 526.
154 "None of them": Ibid., p. 528.
154 "must enrage": Nicolson diaries, October 6, 1938.
155 "All the world": Gilbert, *Winston S. Churchill*, vol. 5, *1922–1939*, p. 1009.
155 "there was some": Dalton, p. 201.
155 "they would not": Ibid., p. 202.
155 "get rid of": Neville Chamberlain to Hilda Chamberlain, December 11, 1938, Chamberlain Papers.
155 "He is much": Pimlott, *Hugh Dalton*, p. 259.
155 "be prepared": Dalton, p. 202.
156 "A good deal": Gilbert, *Winston S. Churchill*, vol. 5, *1922–1939*, p. 1014.
156 "Forty per cent": Martha Gellhorn, "Obituary of a Democracy," *Collier's*, December 1938.
156 "If we had": Ibid.
156 "What possible advantage": Tom Shachtman, *The Phony War: 1939–1940*, p. 105.
156 "A month ago": Jim Thomas speech to constituents, Cilcennin Papers.
157 "Certainly His Majesty's": Carlton, p. 147.
157 "Poor worms": Stephen Howarth, *August '39: The Last Four Weeks of Peace in Europe*, p. 131.
157 "I said the": Gene Smith, *The Dark Summer*, p. 113.

9: RETRIBUTION
158 Toy shops: "State of the World," *Time*, October 31, 1938.
158 "divinely led": Shepherd, p. 1.
158 "were sent": Clark, *Another Part of the Wood*, p. 224.
158 "almost canonized": Bonham Carter Notebooks, "The Thirties," Bonham Carter Papers.
159 "If you argued": Cox, p. 80.
159 "birds fouling": Charles Loch Mowat, *Britain Between the Wars 1918–1940*, p. 623.

159 "Neville Chamberlain's": Gilbert, *Winston S. Churchill*, vol. 5, *1922–1939*, p. 1009.

159 "vaporous effusions": Cooper, pp. 253–54.

159 "will do anything": Cockett, p. 56.

159 "The jitterbugs": Robert Kee, *1939: The World We Left Behind*, p. 99.

160 "would make Tammany": Kirkpatrick, *Under the British Umbrella*, p. 42.

160 "Conservative party machine": Liddell Hart, p. 228.

160 "in complete agreement": Charmley, p. 132.

160 "breathing fire": Bobbety Cranborne to Jim Thomas, October 8, 1938, Cilcennin Papers.

161 "shows how wise": Bobbety Cranborne to Anthony Eden, October 9, 1938, Avon Papers.

161 "no white sheet": Boothby, *I Fight to Live*, p. 169.

161 "did not there": Unpublished reminiscences of Richard Law (Lord Coleraine).

161 "unconstitutionalism run": Ronald Cartland, p. 23.

161 "Quite recently": Barbara Cartland, *Ronald Cartland*, p. 186.

162 "the greatest attention": Paul Emrys-Evans to Sir Robert Doncaster, January 2, 1939, Emrys-Evans Papers.

162 To underscore: Paul Emrys-Evans to Clement Attlee, April 24, 1957, Emrys-Evans Papers.

162 The affair: Paul Emrys-Evans unpublished memoir, Emrys-Evans Papers.

163 In a very real: Pamela Brookes, *Women at Westminster*, p. 20.

163 "men whom I": Ibid., p. 22.

163 "Because I find": Christopher Sykes, *Nancy: The Life of Lady Astor*, p. 208.

164 "There is no place": Cooper, p. 251.

164 Although women MPs: Susan Pedersen, *Eleanor Rathbone and the Politics of Conscience*, p. 222.

164 "if I could": Brookes, p. 42.

164 "Never can": S. J. Hetherington, *Katharine Atholl: Against the Tide*, p. 170.

165 An English translation: James J. Barnes and Patience P. Barnes, *Hitler's Mein Kampf in Britain and America*, p. 5.

165 "Sometimes the warlike": Gilbert, *Winston S. Churchill*, vol. 5, *1922–1939*, p. 704.

165 Like Churchill: Hetherington, p. 159.

166 "the Red Duchess": Pedersen, p. 286.

166 In a preemptive: Brookes, p. 120.

167 Night after night: Hetherington, p. 211.

167 "there will be": Ibid.

167 Rumors circulated: Beverly Parker Stobaugh, *Women and Parliament 1918–1970*, p. 12.

167 Shortly before: Hetherington, p. 216.

168 "it surely should": Bonham Carter Notebook, "The Thirties," Bonham Carter Papers.

168 He wrote Kitty: Hetherington, pp. 213–14.

168 "You are no doubt": Gilbert, *Winston S. Churchill*, vol. 5, *1922–1939*, p. 1011.

169 "overjoyed": Graham Stewart, *Burying Caesar: The Churchill-Chamberlain Rivalry* p. 338.

169 "Am delighted": Hetherington, p. 218.

169 "I naturally": Gilbert, *Winston S. Churchill*, vol. 5, *1922–1939*, p. 1032.

170 "in the seamy": Cockett, p. 9.
170 "the government spy": James, *"Chips,"* p. 180.
170 "dirty tricks": Margach, p. 102.
170 The *Whitehall Letter*: Cockett, p. 101.
170 "We pointed out": Helen Kirkpatrick Milbank oral history, Washington Press Club Foundation.
171 Did he know: Tree, p. 76.
171 "the Government thought": Ibid.
171 "of course": Neville Chamberlain to Ida Chamberlain, October 9, 1938, Chamberlain Papers.
171 "Among Conservatives": Churchill, *The Gathering Storm*, p. 324.
171 "had the gall": Tree, p. 76.
172 "husbands and wives": Manchester, p. 370.
172 "In every case": Cooper, p. 251.
172 "my mother": Andrew Devonshire, *Accidents of Fortune*, p. 24.
172 "I should like": Shepherd, p. 228.
172 "shot or hanged": Gardner, p. 11.
172 "hostile silence": Shepherd, p. 228.
172 "had become such": Julian Amery, p. 121.
173 "I look forward": Shepherd, p. 229.
173 "those traitors": Barbara Cartland, *Ronald Cartland*, p. 185.
173 "I know you": Bonham Carter Notebook, "The Thirties," Bonham Carter Papers.
173 Lady Astor: James Fox, *Five Sisters: The Langhornes of Virginia*, p. 436.
173 The Wallaces: Robert Becker, *Nancy Lancaster: Her Life, Her World, Her Art*, p. 245.
173 When several: Soames, p. 450.
174 "Ombrello!": Violet Bonham Carter to Harold Macmillan, December 23, 1965, Bonham Carter Papers.
174 "Some of our": Ibid.
175 "A vote for": Julian Amery, p. 113.
175 "Vote for Hogg": Lord Hailsham, *A Sparrow's Flight: The Memoirs of Lord Hailsham of Marylebone*, p. 123.
175 At Birch Grove: Macmillan, *Winds of Change*, p. 520.

10: "WAITING FOR A STIRRING LEAD"

176 On a summer day: Richard Law to Anthony Eden, July 13, 1939, Avon Papers.
176 "Time can seldom": Barbara Cartland, *The Isthmus Years*, p. 178.
177 After a while: Richard Law to Anthony Eden, July 13, 1939, Avon Papers.
177 "sat mute": Eleanor Rathbone to editor, *Spectator*, January 13, 1940.
178 "I'm rather annoyed": Becker, p. 245.
178 "would dominate": Paul Emrys-Evans to Leo Amery, July 1, 1954, Emrys-Evans Papers.
178 "The general feeling": Paul Emrys-Evans to Anthony Eden, May 16, 1962, Emrys-Evans Papers.
178 "Several of my": Gilbert, *Winston S. Churchill*, vol. 5, *1922–1939*, pp. 1022–23.
178 "Winston greatly": Paul Emrys-Evans to Leo Amery, July 1, 1954, Emrys-Evans Papers.

179 "to put yourselves": Richard Law to Anthony Eden, July 13, 1939, Avon Papers.

179 In late October: Cockett, p. 101.

179 "I fear that": Ibid.

180 "madness": Nicolson diaries, November 14, 1938.

180 In the October Gallup: *News Chronicle*, October 28, 1938.

180 "if Mr. Eden": Ibid.

180 "a slow crumbling": Ferdinand Kuhn, Jr., "Chamberlain Keeps His Hold on Voters," *New York Times*, January 22, 1940.

180 "unrepresentative junta": *Manchester Guardian*, October 24, 1938.

180 "is plunging us farther": *Manchester Guardian*, November 8, 1938.

181 "It seemed": Gilbert Murray, "The Life of Anthony Eden," *Picture Post*, October 7, 1939.

181 "the destiny": Juliet Rhys-Williams to Anthony Eden, November 29, 1938, Avon Papers.

181 "Thank you": Anthony Eden to Juliet Rhys-Williams, December 2, 1938, Avon Papers.

181 "It is ridiculous": Timothy Eden to Anthony Eden, November 10, 1938, Avon Papers.

181 "as leader": Timothy Eden to Anthony Eden, October 25, 1938, Avon Papers.

181 "The whole youth": Nicolson diary, November 15, 1938.

182 "I agree": Bobbety Cranborne to Jim Thomas, October 30, 1938, Avon Papers.

182 Eden had dropped: Liddell Hart, p. 211.

182 "saved the day": Ibid.

182 "With such gifts": Barnes and Nicholson, *Amery Diaries 1929–1945*, p. 538.

182 "I think": Anthony Eden to Arthur Mann, December 1, 1938, Avon Papers.

182 "Here was Anthony": Bonham Carter Notebook, "The Thirties," Bonham Carter Papers.

183 "agreed with 90": David J. Dutton, "Power Brokers or Just Glamour Boys," *English Historical Review*, April 2003.

183 "lying pretty": Harvey, p. 236.

183 "Our Anthony": Neville Chamberlain to Hilda Chamberlain, March 12, 1939, Chamberlain Papers.

183 "I have had": Neville Chamberlain to Hilda Chamberlain, October 15, 1938, Chamberlain Papers.

183 "There is an intense": Thomas Horabin to Winston Churchill, April 3, 1939, Churchill Papers.

184 "There is a great": Gilbert, *Winston S. Churchill*, vol. 5, *1922–1939*, p. 971.

184 "Do you claim": Alastair Forbes to Winston Churchill, November 8, 1938, Churchill Papers.

184 "At Chartwell": Gilbert, *Winston S. Churchill*, vol. 5, *1922–1939*, p. 1006.

184 "did not seem": Ibid., p. 1019.

184 "the inarticulate": Ibid., p. 1024.

184 "in danger": Dalton, p. 202.

185 "Winston found": Violet Bonham Carter, *Winston Churchill as I Knew Him*, p. 245.

185 "impression of": Dilks, pp. 166–67.

185 "Britain is better": Ferdinand Kuhn, Jr., "British Still Lag in the Arms Race," *New York Times*, January 8, 1939.

186 "There is a total": Soames, p. 448.

186 "when, judging": Janet Flanner, *London Was Yesterday: 1934–1939*, p. 135.

186 Basil Liddell Hart: *New York Times*, January 24, 1939.

186 "to a level": Gilbert, *Winston S. Churchill*, vol. 5, *1922–1939*, p. 1014.

186 By early 1939: David Fraser, *And We Shall Shock Them: The British Army in the Second World War*, p. 16.

187 The regular: David French, *Raising Churchill's Army: The British Army and the War Against Germany*, p. 52.

187 "no more intention": Kee, p. 114.

187 Not long afterward: Stewart, p. 348.

187 In January 1939: *New York Times*, January 8, 1939.

187 "would arouse": Nicolson diaries, November 24, 1938.

187 "Give us three": *New York Times*, January 8, 1939.

188 The journalists: Williams, *Nothing So Strange*, p. 146.

188 "whole policy": James, *"Chips,"* p. 186.

188 "A chap like": George Beardmore, *Civilians at War: Journals 1938–1946*, p. 26.

188 "symbolic": Kershaw, p. 269.

188 "Surely": Wheeler-Bennett, p. 357.

189 "open challenge": Ferdinand Kuhn, Jr., "British Conscription Rejected," *New York Times*, March 29, 1939.

189 "The feeling": Nicolson diaries, March 17, 1939.

189 "meant business": Liddell Hart, p. 229.

189 "In the event": Wheeler-Bennett, p. 374.

190 "tantamount": Liddell Hart, p. 221.

190 Two days before: Manchester, p. 422.

190 "eyewash": L. S. Amery, *My Political Life*, vol. 3, p. 311.

190 "if Herr Hitler": Flanner, p. 142.

191 Anthony Eden: Sir Robert Bruce Lockhart, *Comes the Reckoning*, p. 238.

191 Ronald Tree: Tree, p. 84.

191 "Those old men": Ronald Cartland, "Parliament and the People," *Headway*, May 1939.

11: "HERE IS THE TESTING"

192 "seemed to think": Liddell Hart, p. 226.

192 "Neville still": Ibid., p. 227.

193 "bind Great Britain": Manchester, p. 411.

193 "It is we": Gilbert, *Winston S. Churchill*, vol. 5, *1922–1939*, p. 1053.

193 "The public are": Harold Nicolson, "People and Things," *Spectator*, May 5, 1939.

193 "a war mentality": Cockett, p. 110.

193 "it is definitely": Brendon, p. 527.

193 "hostility toward": Dirksen, p. 65.

193 "Chamberlain's personality": Ibid., p. 66.

193 When Hitler: Kee, p. 171.

194 "We in Poland": Olson and Cloud, p. 37.

194 "Surely the whole": Ibid., p. 38.

194 "sell the Poles": Pimlott, *Dalton Diary 1918–1940*, p. 262.

194 "enable Britain": Dirksen, p. 71.

194 "If anything": Ibid., p. 120.

194 Wilson presented: Ibid., p. 183.

195 Word of the talks: Murray, *Change*, p. 307.

195 "Dick Law": Nicolson diaries, June 27, 1939.

195 "thinks that all": Ibid., April 11, 1939.

195 "If Chamberlain says": Ibid.

195 "The real fact": Harold Nicolson to Robert Boothby, Nicolson Diaries, June 6, 1939.

196 "I have never": Robert Boothby to Harold Nicolson, Nicolson Diaries, June 9, 1939.

196 "a revolution": Ronald Cartland, "Parliament and the People," *Headway*, May 1939.

196 "The men": Barbara Cartland, *Ronald Cartland*, p. 181.

197 "No more": Manchester, p. 425.

197 "Anthony is terrified": Nicolson diaries, June 30, 1939.

197 "The plain fact": "Winnie for Sea Lord?," *Time*, July 17, 1939.

197 "Mr. Amery": *Picture Post*, July 29, 1939.

197 "Both in ability": *Manchester Guardian*, July 4, 1939.

198 "strong desire": Jenkins, p. 541.

198 "I have taken": Gilbert, *Winston S. Churchill*, vol. 5, *1922–1939*, p. 1092.

198 "Nothing could be": *Time*, July 17, 1939.

198 "a message": Gilbert, *Winston S. Churchill*, vol. 5, *1922–1939*, p. 1065.

198 "It's common talk": Flanner, p. 136.

199 "Chamberlain has resisted": "The Parliamentary Session," *Contemporary Review*, May 1940.

199 "The Prime Minister": Nicolson diaries, July 31, 1939.

199 "makes my mouth": Gilbert, *Winston S. Churchill*, vol. 5, *1922–1939*, p. 1097.

200 "had no defences": Spears, p. 5.

200 "he couldn't ask": Barbara Cartland, *Ronald Cartland*, p. 141.

201 "put pressure": Nancy Harvison Hooker, ed., *The Moffat Papers: Selections from the Diplomatic Journals of Jay Pierrepont Moffat*, p. 253.

201 "felt that they": Joseph P. Lash, *Roosevelt and Churchill 1939–1941*, p. 22.

201 "As we saw it": Hooker, p. 253.

201 "Somehow": Barbara Cartland, *Ronald Cartland*, p. 230.

201 "Here is the testing": Barbara Cartland, *The Isthmus Years*, p. 187.

12: "SPEAK FOR ENGLAND"

202 "It has begun!": Nicolson diaries, September 1, 1939.

202 Near his seaside: Cooper, p. 257.

202 "That," Cooper wrote: Ibid.

202 Ronald Cartland: Barbara Cartland, *Ronald Cartland*, p. 231.

203 "dim aquarium": Nicolson diaries, September 1, 1939.

204 "The Polish Government": Edward Raczyński, *In Allied London*, p. 26.

204 "fine words": Spears, p. 16.

205 "after all": Cooper, p. 259.

205 Eros, the famed: Murrow, p. 33.

205 "It is an odd": Nicolson diaries, September 2, 1939.

206 Duff Cooper: Ibid.

206 "But there has": Dalton, p. 268.

206 "like a lion": Manchester, p. 521.

206 "I hope": Raczyński, p. 29.

206 "He sounded": Ibid.

207 "technical difficulties": Dalton, p. 271.

207 "The amount of alcohol": Gilbert, *Winston S. Churchill*, vol. 5, *1922–1939*, p. 1108.

207 "In their own": *New York Times*, September 3, 1939.

207 "Bob said": N. R. Rose, *Baffy*, p. 149.

207 "I had never": Spears, p. 18.

208 "exactly like a court": Harold Nicolson, *Diaries and Letters 1930–1939*, p. 412.

208 "consideration of a proposal": J. E. Sewell, *Mirror of Britain*, p. 12.

208 Even his staunchest: Spears, p. 20.

208 Two Tory: Ibid., p. 22.

208 "For two": L. S. Amery, *My Political Life*, vol. 3, p. 324.

208 Sensing the mounting: Manchester, p. 524.

209 When he stood: Spears, p. 21.

209 "I am speaking": Sewell, p. 14.

209 "Speak for England": L. S. Amery, *My Political Life*, vol. 3, p. 324.

209 Chamberlain's head: N. R. Rose, *Baffy*, p. 150.

209 "I am gravely": Sewell, p. 14.

210 "And our honour!": Manchester, p. 525.

210 "Let me finish": Ibid.

210 "a speech that": Spears, p. 21.

210 "The tension became": Harold Nicolson, *Diaries and Letters 1930–1939*, pp. 412–13.

210 "Chamberlain": Dalton, p. 265.

210 "Winston": Bonham Carter Notebook, "The Thirties," Bonham Carter Papers.

210 "The familiar voice": N. R. Rose, *Baffy*, p. 150.

211 "All the old": James, *"Chips,"* p. 213.

211 "It must be war": Ibid., p. 214.

211 "the strongest": Manchester, p. 525.

211 "Conspiracy": Martin Gilbert and Richard Gott, *The Appeasers*, p. 320.

211 Boothby was the leading: Cooper, p. 260.

212 "he, Churchill, and": Raczyński, p. 29.

212 Shortly after 11:00 a.m.: *New York Times*, September 4, 1939.

212 He had to remind: Gene Smith, p. 272.

213 One of them: Nicolson diaries, September 3, 1939.

213 "purple in the face": Ibid.

213 "I felt no regrets": Spears, p. 23.

213 One of the MPs: Nicolson diaries, September 3, 1939.

214 "went quite dead": Juliet Gardiner, *Wartime Britain 1939–1945*, p. 3.

214 In London: Gene Smith, p. 271.

214 "a breathless feeling": Allingham, p. 86.

214 "Well, it's come": Ibid., p. 87.

214 "crumpled, despondent": Howarth, p. 228.

214 "You can imagine": Shepherd, p. 287.

214 "personal note": Harold Nicolson, *Diaries and Letters 1930–1939*, p. 414.

214 "They ought": Ibid.

214 By that time: Ibid.

215 As Spears: Spears, p. 25.

215 "Mind those": Gardiner, p. 7.

215 "vast explosions": Ibid.

215 "We were absolutely": Ibid.

215 Violet Bonham Carter: Bonham Carter Notebook, "The Thirties," Bonham Carter Papers.

216 "feeling like": Wedgwood, p. 241.

216 "lament of a man": Eden, *Reckoning*, p. 73.

217 "We are fighting": Manchester, p. 537.

217 "It would perhaps": Harold Macmillan, *The Blast of War: 1939–1945*, p. 3.

217 "the speech": L. S. Amery, *My Political Life*, vol. 3, p. 326.

217 "Your immediate task": Robert Boothby to Winston Churchill, September 3, 1939, Churchill Papers.

217 They lustily cheered: *New York Times*, September 4, 1939.

217 One of them was Macmillan: Macmillan, *Blast of War*, p. x.

13: PLAYING AT WAR

219 "Of course": Olson and Cloud, p. 58.

219 "Long live": Ibid.

220 "Within a day": Kee, p. 304.

220 "Loathing war": L. S. Amery, *My Political Life*, vol. 3, p. 328.

220 "close your hearts": Olson and Cloud, p. 55.

220 "military objectives": L. S. Amery, *My Political Life*, vol. 3, p. 329.

220 "It is like": Dalton, p. 275.

220 "machine gunning": Olson and Cloud, p. 60.

220 R. A. Butler: Raczyński, p. 32.

220 At a meeting: Olson and Cloud, p. 60.

221 "not have the means": Kee, p. 308.

221 "Do you mean": *Picture Post*, September 25, 1939.

221 "the Leaflet-of-the-Month Club": Mollie Panter-Downes, *London War Notes, 1939–1945*, p. 6.

221 "ignominous": Spears, p. 31.

222 "How can we": Ibid.

222 "Today I regret": Ibid.

222 "Are you aware": L. S. Amery, *My Political Life*, vol. 3, p. 330.

222 "greatest danger": Lash, p. 82.

223 "In the agony": Kee, pp. 315–16.

223 "All the world": Ibid., p. 316.

223 "When will": Ibid.

223 "To have devoted": Colville, *The Fringes of Power*, p. 25.

223 "This is a terrible": Kee, p. 317.

224 "What kind of": Stanley Cloud and Lynne Olson, *The Murrow Boys: Pioneers on the Front Lines of Broadcast Journalism*, p. 72.

224 "an ignoble contrast": Ronald Lewin, *The War on Land: The British Army in World War II*, p. 15.

224 "a mere parade-ground": Nick Smart, *British Strategy and Politics During the Phony War*, p. 50.

224 As Maj. Gen. Bernard Law Montgomery: *Memoirs of Field Marshal the Viscount Montgomery of Alamein*, p. 47.

224 "in the depths": Alex Danchev and Daniel Todman, eds., *War Diaries 1939–1945: Field Marshal Lord Alanbrooke*, p. 4.

225 "The most depressing": Ibid., p. 6.

225 "scandalous": Montgomery, p. 54.

225 "My soul revolted": Ibid.

225 "disgustingly early": Colville, *The Fringes of Power*, p. 39.

225 "the opening hours": Manchester, p. 538.

226 "cannot possibly": Martin Gilbert, *Winston S. Churchill*, vol. 6, *Finest Hour, 1939–1941*, p. 18.

226 "the supreme naval offensive": Ibid., pp. 25–26.

226 "Based on false": Ibid., p. 91.

226 "This idea": Churchill, *The Gathering Storm*, p. 574.

227 At various times: Shachtman, p. 116.

227 "aggressive action": Churchill, *The Gathering Storm*, p. 574.

228 "bring Hitler": Gilbert and Gott, p. 346.

228 According to Sir: Colville, *The Fringes of Power*, p. 78.

228 "I am alarmed": Ibid., p. 48.

229 "Father is sunk": Ibid., p. 28.

229 "a sense of great": Leland Stowe, *No Other Road to Freedom*, p. 19.

229 "extraordinary number": Ibid.

230 "with the speed": Angus Calder, *The People's War: Britain 1939–1945*, p. 51.

230 Gen. Hastings: John Colville, *Winston Churchill and His Inner Circle*, p. 165.

230 "what agony": Neville Chamberlain to Hilda Chamberlain, May 17, 1940, Chamberlain Papers.

230 "the war": Ibid.

230 "I was never": Neville Chamberlain to Hilda Chamberlain, October 15, 1939, Chamberlain Papers.

230 "sickened": Neville Chamberlain to Ida Chamberlain, December 20, 1939, Chamberlain Papers.

230 "I don't think": Montgomery, p. 54.

231 "It is probable": E. S. Turner, *The Phoney War*, p. 143.

231 "have voluntarily": Kirkpatrick, *Under the British Umbrella*, p. 357.

231 "A lot of my": Sewell, p. 46.

231 "I secretly feel": James, *"Chips,"* p. 226.

232 "I would tell Hitler": Wedgwood, p. 241.

232 "If there is danger": Ibid., p. 242.

232 "an irritated snort": Eden, *Reckoning*, p. 84.

233 "At the beginning": Cooper, p. 260.

233 "Hitler is the only": Nicolson diaries, September 22, 1939.

233 "As autumn fades": Cooper, p. 261.

233 "Say something": Lovat Dickson, *House of Words*, p. 219.

234 "I have in the past": Robert Boothby to Winston Churchill, September 7, 1939, Churchill Papers.

234 "did not seem likely": Macmillan, *Blast of War*, p. xiii.

234 "It is absurd": Louis, p. 120.

235 "offensive fighting spirit": Leo Amery to Winston Churchill, September 4, 1939, Churchill Papers.

235 "if I can be": Ibid.

235 "a civilian": L. S. Amery, *My Political Life*, vol. 3, p. 353.

236 "I am for taking": Leo Amery to Robert Bower, October 7, 1939, Amery Papers.

236 "MAKE THEM FIGHT!": *Daily Mirror*, January 24, 1940.

236 "great stir": "L. S. Amery," *Picture Post*, June 1, 1940.

236 "Mr. L. S. Amery": *Western Mail*, December 27, 1939.

237 "Amery remains": *Daily Mail*, January 23, 1940.

237 "rather flat": Jubie Lancaster to Bobbety Cranborne, April 4, 1940, Cranborne Papers.

237 "harass the government": Barnes and Nicholson, *Amery Diaries 1929–1945*, p. 558.

237 "Let Chamberlain remain": Harold Nicolson, *The War Years: Diaries and Letters*, vol. 2, *1939–1945*, p. 50.

238 the Vigilantes: Alun Wyburn-Powell, *Clement Davies: Liberal Leader*, p. 91.

238 Indeed, the Vigilantes: Pedersen, p. 308.

238 "are at sixes": Robert Skidelsky, *John Maynard Keynes: Fighting for Britain 1937–1945*, p. 48.

239 "Today I noticed": James, *"Chips,"* p. 222.

239 "Dear David": Boothby, *I Fight to Live*, p. 199.

14: "THE MISERY OF DOING NOTHING"

240 Millions: Peter Lewis, *A People's War*, p. 11.

240 Hospital patients: Turner, p. 12.

240 "One's friends": Ritchie, p. 43.

241 "You have to": Frederick T. Birchall, *The Storm Breaks*, p. 354.

241 "One feels": *Nineteenth Century and After*, October 1939.

241 "changed into determination": Brendon, p. 632.

241 "The spirit of cooperation": Oswald Garrison Villard, "Issues and Men," *Nation*, September 16, 1939.

242 "awful difficulties": Dilks, p. 219.

242 "An elderly statesman": Lockhart, p. 78.

242 "The war is not": Colville, *The Fringes of Power*, p. 116.

242 "always treated us": Addison, p. 61.

242 At the same: Murrow, p. 47.

242 "people grumble": Colville, *The Fringes of Power*, p. 49.

243 "The rich people": E. R. Chamberlin, *Life in Wartime Britain*, p. 75.

243 "To my horror": Becker, p. 246.

243 "None of us": Colville, *The Fringes of Power*, p. 42.

243 Early in the war: Michael Davie, ed., *The Diaries of Evelyn Waugh*, p. 446.

244 "become fantastically": James, *"Chips,"* p. 221.
244 BUSINESS AS USUAL: Murrow, p. 42.
244 "would be hailed": Turner, p. 164.
244 "major in a": Harold Nicolson, *Diaries and Letters: 1939–1945*, p. 57.
245 "I had little": Calder, p. 41.
245 "Most of them": Tree, p. 91.
245 "I want to [stay]": Gardiner, p. 20.
246 No funds: Calder, p. 39.
246 The students: Ibid., p. 38.
246 "reminiscent of a": Ibid., p. 40.
246 "a sheep": Ben Wicks, *The Day They Took the Children*, p. 39.
247 "They just wanted": Ibid., p. 8.
247 "I felt alone": Ibid., p. 97.
247 "We were most": Oswald Garrison Villard, "Issues and Men," *Nation*, October 7, 1939.
247 A well-known barrister: Tree, p. 90.
247 "had transformed": Evelyn Waugh, *Put Out More Flags*, pp. 95–96.
248 "transformed conditions": Calder, p. 63.
248 By the end of 1939: Gardiner, p. 52
248 A leading surgeon: Ibid.
248 Nearly one Briton: Calder, p. 63.
248 "Coming out": Panter-Downes, p. 27.
248 "All the streets": Beardmore, p. 42.
249 "Neither a single": Hylton, pp. 84–85.
249 "The black curtains": Ben Robertson, *I Saw England*, p. 10.
249 Janet Murrow: Cloud and Olson, p. 94.
249 "There's no place": Calder, p. 63.
250 "Homes have been": Murrow, p. 63.
250 "sandbags and khaki": Ritchie, p. 45.
250 "tiresome chore": Panter-Downes, p. 19.
250 "waiting, always waiting": Theodora FitzGibbon, *With Love: An Autobiography 1938–46*, p. 30.
250 "Why don't they": Philip Ziegler, *London at War*, p. 79.
250 "Something is happening": Murrow, p. 39.
251 "waste of dull desolation": Ritchie, p. 45.
251 "gangrene of the soul": Lockhart, p. 72.
251 "The outlook": Stowe, p. 32.
251 "filled with forebodings": Ibid., pp. 32–33.
251 "passive, negative": Lewis, p. 5.
251 "much lower": Ian McLaine, *Ministry of Morale: Home Front Morale and the Ministry of Information in World War Two*, p. 10.
251 "a monster": Ibid., p. 17.
252 "I had no": Kenneth Clark, *The Other Half: A Self-Portrait*, p. 10.
252 "the most comforting": McLaine, p. 27.
252 "was all right": Francis Williams, *Press, Parliament and People*, p. 7.
253 "Billy Brown's": Turner, p. 69.
253 "a rallying war-cry": McLaine, p. 31.
253 "Miss Leaky Mouth": Gardiner, p. 130.

253 "Freedom Is": McLaine, p. 54.

253 "Officialdom run amok": *Picture Post*, October 28, 1939.

253 "We are not": Quoted in *Picture Post*, October 14, 1939.

254 "Living in London": Ritchie, p. 45.

254 Few British citizens: Robert Mackay, *Half the Battle: Civilian Morale in Britain During the Second World War*, p. 56.

254 "I think the public": Pottle, *Champion*, p. 206.

254 "If the Admiralty": McLaine, p. 36.

255 "a civilian's job": Ibid., p. 2.

255 "filling us": "The Seventh Week," *Picture Post*, November 4, 1939.

255 "We are not": Nicolson diaries, September 13, 1939.

255 "petty, absurd": McLaine, p. 40.

255 "KEEP OUT!": "The Seventh Week," *Picture Post*, November 4, 1939.

256 "gold keys": Fiona Glass and Philip Marsden-Smedley, eds., *Articles of War: The Spectator Book of World War II*, p. 59.

256 "the British": "Lag in Propaganda Disturbs British," *New York Times*, November 19, 1939.

256 more than six million: Calder, p. 65.

256 "We nearly always": Lewis, p. 5.

256 "The effect": John Lukacs, *Five Days in London: May 1940*, p. 101.

257 "We are told": Sewell, p. 89.

257 "a smell of peace": Quoted in Williams, *Nothing So Strange*, p. 155.

257 "comparatively little": Colville, *The Fringes of Power*, p. 83.

257 "preach[ing] defeatism": Gilbert, *Winston S. Churchill,* vol. 6, *1939–1941,* pp. 27–28.

257 Lord Beaverbrook: Chisholm and Davie, p. 371.

257 The Duke of Bedford: David Cannadine, *The Decline and Fall of the British Aristocracy*, p. 623.

257 "a little *défaitiste*": Dilks, p. 215.

257 In the late fall: Calder, p. 58.

257 "instead of making": Skidelsky, *Keynes: Fighting for Britain*, p. 49.

258 former prime minister: Cooper, p. 267.

258 "People call me": Cecil H. King, *With Malice Toward None: A War Diary*, p. 13.

258 "We have abundant": Nicolson diaries, September 27, 1939.

258 "I was sure": Skidelsky, *Keynes: Fighting for Britain*, p. 49.

259 "an element": Colville, *The Fringes of Power*, p. 35.

259 "we should not": Manchester, p. 559.

259 "unless Hitler ceased": Gilbert, *Winston S. Churchill,* vol. 6, *1939–1941,* p. 72.

259 "we are prepared": Winston Churchill to Lord Halifax, November 3, 1939, Churchill Papers.

259 With the backing: Dilks, p. 230.

260 "The Reich appears": Williamson Murray and Allan R. Millett, *A War to Be Won: Fighting the Second World War*, p. 62.

260 "We must get": Ibid., p. 54.

260 "a windy night": Nicolson diaries, November 26, 1939.

15: "HE IS ABSOLUTELY LOYAL"

261 It felt strange: Barbara Cartland, *Ronald Cartland*, p. 232.
261 "For that brief": Boothby, *I Fight to Live*, p. 197.
262 "there will be": Barbara Cartland, *Ronald Cartland*, p. 250.
262 "extremely pessimistic": Harold Nicolson, *Diaries and Letters 1939–1945*, p. 36.
262 "the confidence and spirits": Ibid., p. 37.
262 "The PM is costive": Gilbert, *Winston S. Churchill*, vol. 6, *1939–1941*, p. 46.
263 "One must not": Ibid., p. 45.
263 "could feel the spirits": Harold Nicolson, *Diaries and Letters 1939–1945*, p. 37.
263 "carried the exhilaration": Sewell, p. 35.
263 "Winston smashed": Barbara Cartland, *Ronald Cartland*, p. 232.
263 "Few ministerial statements": Quoted in "Fourth Week," *Picture Post*, October 14, 1939.
263 "night and day": Gilbert, *Winston S. Churchill*, vol. 6, *1939–1941*, p. 50.
264 "The local enthusiasm": Quoted in Gardner, p. 23.
264 "clothed in living": Kingsley Martin, *Picture Post*, June 1, 1940.
264 "continual losses": Gilbert, *Winston S. Churchill*, vol. 6, *1939–1941*, p. 77.
264 "There are two people": Paul Addison, "Winston Churchill," *Dictionary of National Biography*.
265 Throughout the phony war: Ziegler, *London at War*, p. 80.
265 Theater managers: "Blackouts and the Theatre," *New York Times*, March 24, 1940.
265 "How we look": Beardmore, p. 49.
265 "[E]veryone was very": Gilbert, *Winston S. Churchill*, vol. 6, *1939–1941*, p. 156.
265 "Do you realize": Jenkins, p. 567.
266 "Would you think": Gilbert, *Winston S. Churchill*, vol. 6, *1939–1941*, p. 139.
266 "Come then": Ibid., p. 143.
266 "even Chamberlainites": Nicolson diaries, September 26, 1939.
266 "[j]udging from his record": Colville, *The Fringes of Power*, p. 29.
267 "Contrary to the general": James, *Boothby*, p. 237.
267 "buoyant": Bonham Carter, p. 34.
267 "I acted in accordance": Churchill, *My Early Life*, pp. 113–14.
267 "profoundly self-revealing": Bonham Carter, p. 34.
267 "He is tired": Spears, p. 88.
267 "much to say": Dalton, p. 278.
268 "No man": Gardner, p. 21.
268 "If you are": Cowles, *Winston Churchill*, p. 311.
268 "things were rotten": Charles Edward Lysaght, *Brendan Bracken*, p. 170.
268 "Winston, in spite": Gilbert, *Winston S. Churchill*, vol. 6, *1939–1941*, p. 203.
268 "His restless energy": Carlton, p. 160.
269 "most charming": King, p. 27.
269 By early 1940: Macmillan, *Blast of War*, p. 52.
269 "The distinguishing": Quoted in W. L. Burn, "The Renaissance of Parliament," *Nineteenth Century and After*, April 1940.
269 "Everything is done": Richard Law to *Daily Telegraph*, April 1, 1940, Emrys-Evans Papers.
270 "not want to say": Cockett, p. 169.

270 "Why don't you": Stowe, p. 31.

270 "The only way": Ibid., p. 32.

270 On the afternoon: L. S. Amery, *My Political Life*, vol. 3, p. 355.

272 "can rest assured": *Time*, January 22, 1940.

272 "almost entirely": Macmillan, *Blast of War*, p. 44.

272 "starting with a hostile": Ibid., p. 42.

272 "I still don't": Richard Law to Paul Emrys-Evans, April 1, 1940, Emrys-Evans Papers.

273 "watch the administration": Smart, *British Strategy and Politics*, p. 205.

273 "good boys": Barnes and Nicholson, *Amery Diaries 1929–1945*, p. 585.

273 "essential link": Dutton, "Power Brokers," *English Historical Review*, April 2003.

274 "I feel I": Gilbert, *Winston S. Churchill*, vol. 6, *1939–1941*, p. 189.

274 "the necessity of throwing": Colville, *The Fringes of Power*, p. 97.

16: "GAMBLING WITH THE LIFE OF THE NATION"

275 "even the newspaper": Cowles, *Looking for Trouble*, p. 336.

275 "The accumulation of evidence": Murray and Millett, p. 63.

275 "It is clear": Richard Law to Bobbety Cranborne, March 22, 1940, Lord Cranborne Papers.

276 "be torn limb": Unpublished reminiscences of Richard Law (Lord Coleraine).

276 "far ahead": Raymond Daniell, "Chamberlain Feels '10 Times' More Sure of Stifling Reich," *New York Times*, April 5, 1940.

276 "lukewarm": Unpublished reminiscences of Richard Law (Lord Coleraine).

277 "I want to be there": Liddell Hart, p. 278.

277 "There are innumerable": Ronald Cartland to Sybil Colefax, March 30, 1940, Colefax Papers.

278 "I am quite": Ronald Cartland to Paul Emrys-Evans, April 1, 1940, Emrys-Evans Papers.

278 "terrible to contemplate": Barbara Cartland, *Ronald Cartland*, p. 251.

278 "Fortunately": Stowe, p. 151.

279 British pilots: L. S. Amery, *My Political Life*, vol. 3, p. 332.

279 *The New York Times*: James Reston, "The British Character: Test by War," *New York Times Magazine*, May 12, 1940.

279 "Senior staff officers": Confidential memo by anonymous writer to Lord Salisbury, April 1940, Salisbury Papers.

279 "the hopeless soviet": Barnes and Nicholson, *Amery Diaries 1929–1945*, p. 588.

280 "We've been massacred!": Stowe, p. 143.

280 "We've got no proper": Ibid., p. 144.

280 "What's the matter": Ibid., p. 149.

280 "dumped into Norway's": Philip Knightley, *The First Casualty*, p. 227.

280 "It looks like": "Can the British Tories Win?," *New Republic*, May 6, 1940.

281 "British expeditionary forces": Stowe, p. 147.

281 "The British Navy": Manchester, p. 634.

281 "an Elizabethan ring": Ibid.

281 "Herr Hitler": Ibid., p. 630.

282 "The country": Harris, p. 148.

282 "an obvious distortion": Laurence Thompson, *1940*, p. 57.

282 "There can be": Murrow, p. 89.

282 The prime minister: "Postmortem," *Newsweek*, May 13, 1940.

282 "boiled down": Allingham, p. 165.

282 "We thought": Ibid.

282 "build up": Ibid., p. 157.

283 "a little encouraging": Ibid., p. 166.

283 "Hitler had proved": Spears, p. 111.

283 "We have": Beardmore, p. 51.

283 "How differently": L. S. Amery, *My Political Life*, vol. 3, p. 332.

283 "The government must": Manchester, p. 641.

284 "gambling with": L. S. Amery, *My Political Life*, vol. 3, p. 356.

284 "Why all this": Becker, p. 261.

284 "a failure in Norway": Kershaw, p. 317.

284 "in the least minded": Lord Salisbury to Bobbety Cranborne, April 13, 1940, Salisbury Papers.

284 "if people did not": Kershaw, p. 317.

285 "Churchill's loyalty": Macmillan, *Blast of War*, p. 53.

285 "Winston should be": James, *"Chips,"* p. 242.

285 "The Whips are": Nicolson diaries, April 30, 1940.

285 "now thrown off": James, *"Chips,"* p. 242.

285 "his satellites": Colville, *The Fringes of Power*, p. 116.

286 "to less advantage": Harold Nicolson, *Diaries and Letters 1939–1945*, p. 70.

286 "He understands": Paul Emrys-Evans to Bobbety Cranborne, May 5, 1940, Cranborne Papers.

286 "Lord Halifax": Paul Emrys-Evans diary, April 29, 1940, Emrys-Evans Papers.

286 "at the earliest": L. S. Amery, *My Political Life*, vol. 3, p. 358.

287 "The essential thing": Barnes and Nicholson, *Amery Diaries 1929–1945*, p. 590.

287 They decided to use: L. S. Amery, *My Political Life*, vol. 3, p. 358.

287 "will cease to count": Ronald Tree to Bobbety Cranborne, May 2, 1940, Cranborne Papers.

287 "a sufficient possibility": David Freeman, "Who Really Put Churchill in Office?," The Churchill Center (www.winstonchurchill.org).

287 "David Margesson says": James, *"Chips,"* p. 244.

288 After Liberal leader: Harris, p. 149.

288 Even papers: Addison, p. 93.

288 "It seems clear": Kenneth Young, ed., *The Diaries of Sir Robert Bruce Lockhart*, vol. 2, *1939–1965*, p. 54.

288 "awkward": Colville, *The Fringes of Power*, p. 117.

288 "Chamberlain's government": Murrow, p. 93.

17: "'IN THE NAME OF GOD, GO!'"
289 Women carrying: "Warlord for Peacemaker," *Time*, May 20, 1940.

289 The air was alive: Macmillan, *Blast of War*, p. 54.

290 Clement Davies: Wyburn-Powell, p. 99.

290 "the mess is so": N. R. Rose, *Baffy*, p. 168.

290 "I don't think my": Neville Chamberlain to Hilda Chamberlain, May 4, 1940, Chamberlain Papers.

290 "some uncertainty": Spears, p. 123.

290 He made no: Macmillan, *Blast of War*, p. 55.

291 "This is not": Sewell, p. 154.

291 "spoke haltingly": James, *"Chips,"* p. 244.

291 The House: "House Is Hostile," *New York Times*, May 8, 1940.

291 "was not allowed": Helen Kirkpatrick, *Chicago Daily News*, May 8, 1940.

291 "unworthy": Macmillan, *Blast of War*, p. 55.

291 Chamberlain had totally: L. S. Amery, *My Political Life*, vol. 3, p. 359.

292 "strong meat": Barnes and Nicholson, *Amery Diaries 1929–1945*, p. 592.

292 "a politician's speech": Sewell, p. 158.

292 "seemed to go": Unpublished reminiscences of Richard Law (Lord Coleraine).

292 "agonized discomfort": L. S. Amery, *My Political Life*, vol. 3, p. 359.

293 "I was out": Ibid., p. 360.

293 Just then: Ibid.

293 "The Prime Minister": Ibid.

293 "nothing to them": Ibid., p. 361.

293 "If we lose": Ibid., pp. 361–62.

294 "Somehow or other": Ibid., p. 364.

294 But as Amery: Ibid., p. 365.

294 "great reluctance": Ibid.

294 "This is what": Ibid.

295 "the most formidable": Macmillan, *Blast of War*, p. 56.

295 "it was as if": Spears, p. 120.

295 "most damaging": Sewell, p. 164.

295 Long after: Macmillan, *Blast of War*, p. 58.

295 It was clear: L. S. Amery, *My Political Life*, vol. 3, p. 365.

295 He was convinced: Dalton, p. 305.

296 But Amery's speech: Barnes and Nicholson, *Amery Diaries 1929–1945*, p. 593.

296 He argued: Paul Emrys-Evans diary, May 8, 1940, Emrys-Evans Papers.

296 "Amery's words": Macmillan, *Blast of War*, p. 59.

296 "This morning": Colville, *The Fringes of Power*, p. 118.

296 "We knew then": James, *"Chips,"* p. 245.

296 "I do not seek": Manchester, p. 653.

297 "It was so": Bonham Carter Notebook, "The Thirties," Bonham Carter Papers.

297 "It is not": Gilbert, *Winston S. Churchill*, vol. 6, *1939–1941*, p. 293.

297 "I do not think": Ibid., pp. 293-94.

298 "The 'glamour boys' ": James, *"Chips,"* p. 244.

298 Following Chamberlain's: Macmillan, *Blast of War*, p. 59.

298 "Why not?": Ibid., p. 61.

298 "fire in his eye": Unpublished reminiscences of Richard Law (Lord Coleraine).

298 "One saw": James, *"Chips,"* p. 246.

299 "to make all": Smart, *British Strategy and Politics*, p. 229.

299 "dismiss these delusions": Sewell, p. 177.

299 "a quite incomprehensible": Quoted in Stewart, p. 412.

299 Turning around: Spears, p. 128.

299 "Let us keep": Gilbert, *Winston S. Churchill,* vol. 6, *1939–1941,* p. 298.

299 "strangely uneasy": Manchester, p. 656.

299 "peroration sounded": Pottle, *Champion,* p. 210.

299 "The major argument": Sewell, p. 177.

299 "audience was": Ibid.

299 "No speech": Ibid.

300 For a brief: Spears, pp. 124–25.

300 "Quislings!": James, *"Chips,"* pp. 246–47.

300 "terrible pressure": Gilbert, *Winston S. Churchill,* vol. 6, *1939–1941,* p. 299.

301 "It was a sad": Quoted in Roberts, *Eminent Churchillians,* p. 139.

301 "implacable resentment": Spears, p. 129.

302 "far harder": Ibid.

302 "I have come": Dalton, p. 343.

302 Another young: Cooper, p. 279.

302 "seemed to be": Pimlott, *Dalton Diary 1918–1940,* p. 342.

302 The recent Oxford: Jenkins, p. 582.

303 "For nine months": Hailsham, p. 135.

303 "in a thoroughly": Ibid., p. 136.

303 "total nervelessness": Ibid.

303 "so tense": Spears, p. 129.

304 Josiah Wedgwood: Macmillan, *Blast of War,* p. 62.

304 "infinitely sad": James, *"Chips,"* p. 369.

304 "truly sad": Spears, p. 130.

304 "very sorry": James, *Boothby,* p. 244.

304 Euan Wallace: Simon Ball, p. 212.

305 "enemy parachute troops": Roberts, *Eminent Churchillians,* p. 145.

305 "You've got": Tree, p. 114.

305 "I'll cook": Ibid.

305 "And I can tell": Jenkins, p. 583.

305 "Say that": Hailsham, p. 139.

18: "VICTORY AT ALL COSTS"

306 "The Old Man": Dalton, p. 306.

306 "This has been": Churchill, *The Gathering Storm,* p. 661.

306 "like a dirty": Dalton, p. 308.

307 In his conversations: Ibid.

307 At one point: Ibid.

307 "Neville's advisers": Barnes and Nicholson, *Amery Diaries 1929–1945,* p. 612.

307 That morning: L. S. Amery, *My Political Life,* vol. 3, p. 370.

307 "appointing its men": Ibid., p. 371.

307 As they had: Macmillan, *Blast of War,* p. 63.

308 "The Whips are being": Harold Nicolson, *Diaries and Letters 1939–1945,* p. 81.

308 Finding Dalton: Pimlott, *Dalton Diary, 1918–1940,* p. 343.

308 Davies, in particular: James, *Boothby,* p. 245.

308 "No Labour leader": James, *Churchill*, p. 331.
309 "unable to distinguish": Robert Boothby to Winston Churchill, May 9, 1940, Churchill Papers.
309 Brendan Bracken: L. S. Amery, *My Political Life*, vol. 3, pp. 371–72.
309 When Churchill: Barnes and Nicholson, *Amery Diaries 1929–1945*, p. 595.
309 To Churchill: Dilks, p. 280.
309 Earlier in the day: James, *Eden*, p. 226.
309 Although Halifax: Roberts, *"Holy Fox,"* p. 199.
310 "veering": Dilks, p. 280.
310 "I said": Ibid.
310 Later that day: Ibid.
310 "guarded": Macmillan, *Blast of War*, p. 63.
311 "realized that total": "Invasion," *Picture Post*, May 20, 1940.
311 Exhausted: Macmillan, *Blast of War*, p. 64.
311 "The Old Man": Pimlott, *Dalton Diary, 1918–1940*, p. 344.
311 "we must maintain": Harold Nicolson, *Diaries and Letters 1939–1945*, p. 82.
311 Clement Davies: Barnes and Nicholson, *Amery Diaries 1929–1945*, p. 613.
311 "stimulated": Manchester, p. 672.
312 Wilson, who glanced at it: Ibid., p. 673.
312 "I told him": Gilbert, *Winston S. Churchill*, vol. 6, *1939–1941*, p. 313.
312 "Considering the": Churchill, *The Gathering Storm*, pp. 649–50.
312 "You ask": Manchester, p. 678.
312 "That is what": L. S. Amery, *My Political Life*, vol. 3, p. 375.
313 "Above all": Ibid., p. 400.
313 "I think": Ibid., p. 376.
313 "arrived on the scene": Colville, *Footprints in Time*, p. 75.
313 "The pace became": Ibid., pp. 75–76.
313 Under no circumstances: Harris, p. 155.
313 "transform cowards": Olson and Cloud, p. 95.
314 "all this country": James Reston, "The British Character: Test by War," *New York Times Magazine*, May 12, 1940.
314 "Everywhere": Mackay, p. 61.
314 "There is no denying": Ibid.
314 Within days: Ibid.
314 "Resistance was": Robertson, p. 17.
314 "I've got": Ibid., p. 67.
315 "We were so": Lukacs, p. 210.
315 "What could": L. S. Amery, *My Political Life*, vol. 3, p. 332.
315 After ten: Smart, *British Strategy and Politics*, p. 162.
315 "From the Royal": Olson and Cloud, p. 102.
316 "We should become": Pimlott, *Second World War Diary of Hugh Dalton: 1940–1945*, p. 28.
316 "we shall fight it out": Ibid.
316 "Then and there": Lukacs, p. 2.
316 "A grand new": Barbara Cartland, *Ronald Cartland*, p. 252.
316 "He loved": Richard Law, letter to *The Times*, January 7, 1941.
317 "I am extraordinarily fit": "Tribute to Ronald Cartland," February 9, 1941.

317 "The weather is perfect": Ronald Cartland to Sybil Colefax, May 23, 1940, Colefax Papers.

317 "No letters": Barbara Cartland, *Ronald Cartland*, p. 254.

317 During the last week: D. R. Guttery, "The Queen's Own Worcestershire Hussars 1922–1956," www.ph012b2086.pwp.blueyonder.co.uk/harry/cassel.htm#guttery.

317 In the early: Brig. Gen. N. F. Somerset to *Daily Telegraph*, February 19, 1948.

317 "everywhere": Barbara Cartland, *Ronald Cartland*, p. 256.

318 The Cassel defenders: "The Queen's Own Worcestershire Hussars 1922–1956."

318 "your generals": Brig. Gen. N. F. Somerset to *Daily Telegraph*, February 19, 1948.

318 At eight-thirty: Barbara Cartland, *Ronald Cartland*, p. 258.

318 Although they: Brig. Gen. N. F. Somerset to *Daily Telegraph*, February 19, 1948.

319 In the midst: Gilbert, *Winston S. Churchill*, vol. 6, *1939–1941*, p. 463.

319 "I so often": Barbara Cartland, *The Isthmus Years*, p. 176.

319 "It is with": Winston Churchill to Mary Cartland, January 6, 1941, Churchill Papers.

319 "The more I": Richard Law to Leo Amery, January 8, 1941, Amery Papers.

320 "Ronald had everything": Barbara Cartland, *Ronald Cartland*, p. 11.

320 "Ronnie would": Robert Boothby to Leo Amery, January 12, 1941, Amery Papers.

320 "It is impossible": Barbara Cartland, *Ronald Cartland*, p. 13.

320 When he heard: Leo Amery to Richard Law, January 7, 1941, Amery Papers.

320 In a letter: Leo Amery to *The Times*, January 6, 1941.

320 "the only surrender": Harold Nicolson, "Marginal Comment," *Spectator*, May 1, 1942.

320 On February 18: Unidentified newspaper clipping, Cartland scrapbooks.

321 Listening to the eulogies: Barbara Cartland, *Ronald Cartland*, p. 201, and interview with Carline Henderson.

321 At the end: Unidentified newspaper clipping, Cartland scrapbooks.

19: A QUESTION OF LOYALTY

322 "We shall go": Jenkins, p. 611.

322 "all the old": Roberts, *Eminent Churchillians*, p. 153.

323 Early on May 10: Simon Ball, p. 213.

323 Clement Davies: L. S. Amery, *My Political Life*, vol. 3, p. 374.

323 "made all the difference": Barnes and Nicholson, *Amery Diaries 1929–1945*, p. 614.

324 Yet of the thirty-six: Calder, p. 86.

324 "with an unholy": Roberts, *"Holy Fox,"* p. 140.

324 But the appointment: Tree, p. 116.

325 Furious: Exchange of letters between David Margesson and Clementine Churchill, June 1940, Margesson Papers.

325 Clementine refused: Tree, pp. 116–17.

326 "The House": Lord Moran, *Churchill: The Struggle for Survival: Taken from the Diaries of Lord Moran*, p. 793.

326 "Seldom can": Manchester, p. 677.

326 On May 13: Roberts, *Eminent Churchillians*, p. 144.

326 "The Cabinet": Pottle, *Champion*, pp. 212–13.

326 "a disaster": "National Inquest," *Economist*, May 18, 1940.

326 "Thank God": *Sunday Pictorial*, July 7, 1940.

327 "is strong enough": King, p. 48.

327 "What need": H. Boardman, "Conservatism, Its Future and Mr. Churchill," *Nineteenth Century and After*, August 1940.

327 A Gallup: Barnes and Nicholson, *Amery Diaries 1929–1945*, p. 602.

327 "Churchill had": Horne, *Macmillan*, vol. 1, p. 165.

327 "I have received": Lukacs, p. 121.

327 "Munich spirit": Charmley, p. 143.

327 Chamberlain, for one: Barnes and Nicholson, *Amery Diaries 1929–1945*, p. 616.

328 "no diehards": Anthony Howard, *RAB: The Life of R. A. Butler*, p. 97.

328 "held odd language": Ibid., pp. 97–98.

328 "I should be": Ibid., p. 98.

328 "a half-breed": Colville, *The Fringes of Power*, p. 122.

328 "king over the water": Jenkins, p. 591.

328 Early on: Roberts, *Eminent Churchillians*, p. 144.

328 "I could hardly": Ibid., pp. 141–42.

328 "all those reptile": Ibid., p. 146.

329 "When the nation": Ibid., pp. 209–10.

329 "a solid, unquestioning": "Parliament and the War," *Contemporary Review*, July 1940.

329 "I must warn you": Neville Chamberlain to Hilda Chamberlain, June 1, 1940, Chamberlain Papers.

329 "I discovered": Neville Chamberlain to Ida Chamberlain, June 21, 1940, Chamberlain Papers.

330 "the Tory majority": Paul Einzig, *In the Centre of Things* p. 210.

330 "I know for": Paul Einzig to Neville Chamberlain, June 29, 1940, Chamberlain Papers.

330 "my determination": Einzig, p. 214.

330 After Churchill rose: Ibid., p. 217.

330 A Gallup poll: Roberts, *Eminent Churchillians*, p. 174.

330 "He is at": James, *"Chips,"* p. 262.

331 "I felt": Barnes and Nicholson, *Amery Diaries 1929–1945*, p. 617.

331 "It took Armageddon": Boothby, *Recollections of a Rebel*, p. 145.

331 "was by temperament": Lash, p. 56.

332 "Churchill was": L. S. Amery, *My Political Life*, vol. 3, p. 375.

332 When Boothby: Barnes and Nicholson, *Amery Diaries 1929–1945*, p. 616.

332 "At least": Roberts, *Eminent Churchillians*, p. 154.

332 "bloody insult": Ben Pimlott, ed., *The Second World War Diary of Hugh Dalton 1929–1945*, p. 16.

332 "I'm afraid": Robert Boothby to Winston Churchill, May 18, 1940, Churchill Papers.

332 "that traitorous": Neville Chamberlain to Hilda Chamberlain, June 1, 1940, Chamberlain Papers.

333 Ronald Cross: Paul Addison to Paul Emrys-Evans, May 3, 1965, Emrys-Evans Papers.

333 "It seems strange": King, p. 40.

333 "Strangely": James, *Boothby*, p. 246.

333 "[W]e shall see": L. S. Amery, *My Political Life*, vol. 3, p. 376.

333 "The change of Government": "National Inquest," *Economist*, May 18, 1940.
334 "giving the necessary": L. S. Amery, "My Political Life," vol. 4, unpublished, Amery Papers.
334 "gravely perturbed": Ibid.
334 "respectfully put it": James, *Boothby*, p. 258.
334 "Nothing less": Amery draft letter to Churchill, June 17, 1940, Amery Papers.
334 "purely from": Ibid.
334 "this was a hope": James, *Boothby*, p. 258.
335 "Winston alone": Barnes and Nicholson, *Amery Diaries 1929–1945*, p. 625.
335 "extreme gravity": Ibid.
335 "The resignation of Neville": Helen Kirkpatrick, *Chicago Daily News*, June 18, 1940.
335 "aroused a storm": Helen Kirkpatrick, *Chicago Daily News*, June 6, 1940.
335 "Much as recrimination": Quoted by Helen Kirkpatrick, *Chicago Daily News*, June 18, 1940.
336 He employed a sort: Neville Chamberlain to Ida Chamberlain, June 8, 1940, Chamberlain Papers.
336 "1940 saw him": James, *Boothby*, p. 252.
336 "rough, sarcastic": Soames, p. 454.
337 "were wholeheartedly": Barnes and Nicholson, *Amery Diaries 1929–1945*, p. 625.
337 "there was no plot": James, *Boothby*, p. 259.
337 "successfully frightened": Barnes and Nicholson, *Amery Diaries 1929–1945*, p. 626.
337 "drawn to trouble": W. F. Deedes, *Dear Bill: A Memoir*, p. 205.
337 "telling him": Boothby, *Recollections of a Rebel*, p. 166.
337 "one of the most": Ibid.
337 "You went to": N. R. Rose, *Baffy*, p. 173.
338 *Every* ground": Susan Barnes, "The Hon. Member, the Star of Television," *Sunday Times*, April 1, 1973.
338 "a curious fellow": Mark Pottle, *Daring to Hope: The Diaries and Letters of Violet Bonham Carter 1946–1969*, p. 161.
338 "This alone": Gilbert, *Winston S. Churchill*, vol. 6, *1939–1941*, p. 903.

20: A SON'S BETRAYAL
339 "Are the brains": *Sunday Pictorial*, July 7, 1940.
339 "Amery could": "National Inquest," *Economist*, May 18, 1940.
339 "Mr. Amery's": "Parliament and the War," *Contemporary Review*, July 1940.
340 By 1940 Amery: Louis, p. 127.
340 "was very domineering": Moran, p. 330.
340 "partly shocked": Barnes and Nicholson, *Amery Diaries 1929–1945*, p. 993.
340 In the opinion: Louis, p. 132.
340 He accused: Ibid., pp. 130–31.
340 At one cabinet: Dilks, p. 316.
341 "It is an awful": Louis, p. 165.
341 "None of them": Ibid.
341 "I have never": Barnes and Nicholson, *Amery Diaries 1929–1945*, p. 758.
341 "fundamentally a very": James, *Churchill*, p. 36.

342 "He is a real": Barnes and Nicholson, *Amery Diaries 1929–1945*, p. 619.

342 "We may differ on": Leo Amery to Winston Churchill, November 29, 1941, Churchill Papers.

342 "the ultimate ne'er-do-well": Geoffrey Wheatcroft, "A Fanatic and a Cad United in Treachery," *Daily Mail*, June 29, 2001.

342 According to Leo: Leo Amery affidavit on John Amery, Home Office report (HO 144/22823/238), National Archives, Kew.

343 "A friend tells": Barnes and Nicholson, *Amery Diaries 1929–1945*, p. 843.

343 "Good God!": Ibid., p. 844.

343 The following: Ibid., p. 845.

344 "My dear Winston": Leo Amery to Winston Churchill, November 20, 1942, Churchill Papers.

344 "a call to arms": Transcript of Amery speech, November 1942, KV 2/78, National Archives.

344 "I wonder whether": D.C. Orr, War Office, to MI5, November 19, 1942, KV 2/78, National Archives.

344 About 140: Adrian Weale, *Patriot Traitors: Roger Casement, John Amery and the Real Meaning of Treason*, p. xvii.

345 Three tables: Rebecca West, "The Crown vs. John Amery," *New Yorker*, December 15, 1945.

345 "I plead": Ibid.

345 "I never accept": Ibid.

345 "You now stand": Ibid.

345 "I feel a certain": Weale, pp. 272–73.

345 At Leo Amery's: Ibid., pp. 240–41.

346 "Capital punishment": Home Office report (HO 144/2283), National Archives.

346 "You have given": Florence Amery to Ian Hamilton, January 1, 1946, Ian Hamilton Papers, Liddell Hart Center for Military Archives, King's College.

346 "Mr. Pierrepoint": Weale, p. xii.

346 At 9:08 a.m.: "The End of Amery," *Time*, December 31, 1945.

346 "Visits to the relatives": Home Office file, June 14, 1948, National Archives.

21: AFTERMATH

347 "many glaring misfits": James, *Boothby*, p. 256.

348 "just that kind": Ibid., p. 286.

349 He had done: Ibid., p. 208.

349 Boothby, quite truthfully: Ibid., p. 226.

350 (Boothby and his supporters: Ibid., p. 274.

350 "derogatory to the dignity": Ibid., p. 283.

350 "The feeling": Ibid., p. 286.

350 "is a far better": Pimlott, *Dalton Second World War Diary 1940–1945*, p. 146.

350 "I helped the Czechs": *The Times*, January 29, 1941.

351 "Why did he": Boothby, *Recollections of a Rebel*, p. 57.

351 "endure a man hunt": Colville, *The Fringes of Power*, p. 126.

351 "a heartbreaking business": *The Times*, January 29, 1941.

351 At the same time: James, *Boothby*, p. 275.

351 "join a bomb": Stuart, p. 90.

351 "had much capacity": Roberts, *Eminent Churchillians*, p. 190.

351 "liked bounders": Jenkins, p. 188.

352 "The idea": James, *Boothby*, p. 85.

352 "What troubles me": Thorpe, *Eden*, p. 271.

353 "I suspect": Sampson, p. 70.

353 "I recall": Lord Egremont, *Wyndham and Children First*, p. 193.

354 "not only to have": Davenport-Hines, p. 223.

354 "dashing man": Ibid., p. 222.

354 Throughout the war: Horne, *Macmillan*, vol. 1, p. 178.

354 "the Viceroy": Lord Egremont, p. 194.

355 "Harold may yet": Young, *Lockhart Diaries*, vol. 2, pp. 519–20.

355 "I think that": Ibid., p. 539.

356 "He's a great": Unidentified newspaper clipping, June 28, 1959, Bonham Carter Papers.

357 "lacked the broad": W. F. Deedes, *Brief Lives*, p. 45.

358 "We all know": *A Rather English Statesman*, BBC, June 6, 2000.

358 Indeed, some: Robert Blake, "Lord Avon," *Sunday Times*, January 16, 1977.

358 The trouble: Anthony Nutting, *No End of a Lesson: The Story of Suez*, p. 146.

358 "who are giving": "The Chosen Leader," *Time*, January 21, 1957.

359 "Is there": Nigel Nicolson, *Long Life*, p. 164.

359 "not only unwise": Interview with Nigel Nicolson, *A Rather English Statesman*, BBC, June 6, 2000.

359 "breaking all the rules": Ibid.

359 "The leaders of our": Nigel Nicolson, *Long Life,* p. 148.

360 "This is very": Nutting, p. 162.

362 "I've got a paper": Glyn-Jones interview, *The Macmillans*, BBC, March 14, 1996.

362 "I don't think": Interview with Sir Frederick Bishop, *The Macmillans*, BBC, March 14, 1996.

362 "never quite got over": Horne, *Macmillan*, vol. 2, *1957–1986*, p. 496.

363 "When [Dorothy] was": Booth and Haste, p. 69.

363 "to go to pieces": James, *Boothby*, p. 425.

363 Whenever the phone: Ibid., p. 120.

363 "And so": Ibid., p. 129.

364 "Politics": Emrys-Evans unpublished memoirs, Emrys-Evans papers.

BIBLIOGRAPHY

ARCHIVAL MATERIAL

BALLIOL COLLEGE, OXFORD
Harold Nicolson Diaries

BODLEIAN LIBRARY, OXFORD
Violet Bonham Carter Papers
Sybil Colefax Papers
Harold Macmillan Papers

BRITISH LIBRARY
Paul Emrys-Evans Papers

CARMARTHENSHIRE ARCHIVES SERVICE, CARMARTHEN, WALES
Lord Cilcennin (James P. L. Thomas) Papers

CHURCHILL COLLEGE, CAMBRIDGE
Leo Amery Papers
Winston Churchill Papers
Duff Cooper Papers
David Margesson Papers

HATFIELD HOUSE, HERTFORDSHIRE
Cranborne Papers
Salisbury Papers

LIDDELL HART CENTRE FOR MILITARY ARCHIVES, KING'S COLLEGE, LONDON
Ian Hamilton Papers
Basil Liddell Hart Papers

NATIONAL ARCHIVES, KEW
War Office and Home Office records concerning John Amery

SMITH COLLEGE, NORTHAMPTON, MASSACHUSETTS
Helen Kirkpatrick Papers

UNIVERSITY OF BIRMINGHAM
Lord Avon (Anthony Eden) Papers
Neville Chamberlain Papers

PUBLISHED SOURCES

Addison, Paul. *The Road to 1945: British Politics and the Second World War*. London: Pimlico, 1994.

Allingham, Margery. *The Oaken Heart*. London: Michael Joseph, 1941.

Amery, Julian. *Approach March: A Venture in Autobiography*. London: Hutchinson, 1973.

Amery, L. S. *In the Rain and the Sun*. London: Hutchinson, 1946.

———. *My Political Life*. Vol. 1, *England Before the Storm 1896–1914*. London: Hutchinson, 1953.

———. *My Political Life*. Vol. 2, *War and Peace 1914–1929*. London: Hutchinson, 1953.

———. *My Political Life*. Vol. 3, *The Unforgiving Years 1929–1940*. London: Hutchinson, 1955.

Annan, Noel. *Our Age: English Intellectuals Between the World Wars*. New York: Random House, 1991.

Atholl, Katharine. *Working Partnership*. London: Arthur Barker, 1958.

Baker, Arthur. *The House Is Sitting*. London: Blandford Press, 1958.

Ball, Simon. *The Guardsmen: Harold Macmillan, Three Friends, and the World They Made*. London: HarperCollins, 2004.

Ball, Stuart, ed. *Parliament and Politics in the Age of Churchill and Attlee: The Headlam Diaries 1935–1951*. Cambridge, U.K.: Cambridge University Press, 1999.

Balsdon, Dacre. *Oxford Life*. London: Eyre & Spottiswoode, 1957.

Barnes, James J., and Patience P. Barnes. *Hitler's Mein Kampf in Britain and America*. Cambridge, U.K.: Cambridge University Press, 1980.

Barnes, John, and David Nicholson, eds. *The Leo Amery Diaries 1886–1929*. London: Hutchinson, 1980.

———. *The Empire at Bay: The Leo Amery Diaries 1929–1945*. London: Hutchinson, 1980.

Barrow, Andrew. *Gossip: A History of High Society from 1920 to 1970*. New York: Coward, McCann & Geoghegan, 1979.

Beardmore, George. *Civilians at War: Journals 1938–1946*. London: John Murray, 1984.

Beaton, Cecil. *Self-Portrait with Friends*. New York: Times Books, 1979.

Becker, Robert. *Nancy Lancaster: Her Life, Her World, Her Art*. New York: Knopf, 1996.

Bennett, Daphne. *Margot: A Life of the Countess of Oxford and Asquith*. New York: Franklin Watts, 1984.

Best, Geoffrey. *Churchill: A Study in Greatness*. New York: Oxford University Press, 2003.

Biffen, John. *Inside the House of Commons: Behind the Scenes at Westminster*. London: Grafton, 1989; New York: HarperCollins, 1989.

Birchall, Frederick T. *The Storm Breaks*. New York: Viking, 1940.

Bloch, Michael. *Ribbentrop: A Biography*. New York: Crown, 1992.

Bogdanor, Vernon, and Robert Skidelsky, eds. *The Age of Affluence: 1951–1964*. London: Macmillan, 1971.

Bonham Carter, Violet. *Winston Churchill as I Knew Him*. London: Eyre, Spottiswoode & Collins, 1965.

Booth, Cherie, and Cate Haste. *The Goldfish Bowl: Married to the Prime Minister 1955–1997*. London: Chatto & Windus, 2004.

Boothby, Robert. *Boothby: Recollections of a Rebel*. London: Hutchinson, 1978.

———. *I Fight to Live*. London: Gollancz, 1947.

Bowen, Catherine Drinker. *Biography: The Craft and the Calling*. Boston: Atlantic Monthly Press, 1968.

Boyle, Andrew. *"Poor, Dear Brendan": The Quest for Brendan Bracken*. London: Hutchinson, 1974.

Brandreth, Gyles. *Breaking the Code: Westminster Diaries*. London: Weidenfeld & Nicolson, 1999.

Brendon, Piers. *The Dark Valley: A Panorama of the 1930s*. New York: Knopf, 2000.

Brookes, Pamela. *Women at Westminster*. London: Peter Davies, 1967.

Calder, Angus. *The People's War: Britain 1939–1945*. New York: Pantheon, 1969.

Cannadine, David. *The Decline and Fall of the British Aristocracy*. New Haven: Yale University Press, 1990.

———. *History in Our Time*. New Haven: Yale University Press, 1998.

———. *In Churchill's Shadow: Confronting the Past in Modern Britain*. London: Allen Lane, 2002; New York: Oxford University Press, 2003.

———. *The Pleasures of the Past*. London: Collins, 1989; New York: Norton, 1990.

Carlton, David. *Anthony Eden: A Biography*. London: Allen Lane, 1981.

Cartland, Barbara. *The Isthmus Years*. London: Hutchinson, 1942.

———. *Ronald Cartland*. London: Collins, 1942.

———. *We Danced All Night*. London: Hutchinson, 1970.

Cartland, Ronald. *The Common Problem*. London: Hutchinson, 1942.

Cecil, David. *The Cecils of Hatfield House*. Boston: Houghton Mifflin, 1973.

Chamberlin, E. R. *Life in Wartime Britain*. London: Batsford, 1972.

Charmley, John. *Duff Cooper*. London: Weidenfeld & Nicolson, 1986.

Chisholm, Anne, and Michael Davie. *Lord Beaverbrook: A Life*. New York: Knopf, 1993.

Churchill, Winston. *The Hinge of Fate*. Boston: Houghton Mifflin, 1950.

———. *The Gathering Storm*. Boston: Houghton Mifflin, 1948.

———. *My Early Life: A Roving Commission*. London: Butterworth, 1930.

Clark, Kenneth. *Another Part of the Wood: A Self-Portrait*. New York: Harper & Row, 1974.

———. *The Other Half: A Self-Portrait*. New York: Harper & Row, 1977.

Cloud, Stanley, and Lynne Olson. *The Murrow Boys: Pioneers on the Front Lines of Broadcast Journalism*. Boston: Houghton Mifflin, 1996.

Cockett, Richard. *Twilight of Truth: Chamberlain, Appeasement & the Manipulation of the Press*. New York: St. Martin's, 1989.

Colville, John. *Footprints in Time: Memories*. London: Century, 1985.

———. *The Fringes of Power: Downing Street Diaries*. New York: Norton, 1985.

———. *Winston Churchill and His Inner Circle*. New York: Wyndham Books, 1981.

Cooper, Duff. *Old Men Forget: An Autobiography of Duff Cooper*. London: Century, 1986.

Coote, Colin R. *A Companion of Honour: The Story of Walter Elliot*. London: Collins, 1965.

———. *The Other Club*. London: Sidgwick & Jackson, 1971.

Cowles, Virginia. *Looking for Trouble*. New York: Harper, 1941.

———. *Winston Churchill: The Era and the Man*. London: Hamilton, 1953.

Cox, Geoffrey. *Countdown to War*. London: Hodder & Stoughton, 1990.

Crewe, Quentin. *Well, I Forget the Rest: The Autobiography of an Optimist*. London: Quartet, 1994.

Critchfield, Richard. *An American Looks at Britain*. New York: Doubleday, 1990.

Dalton, Hugh. *The Fateful Years: Memoirs 1931–1945*. London: Muller, 1962.

Danchev, Alex, and Daniel Todman, eds. *War Diaries 1939–1945: Field Marshal Lord Alanbrooke*. Berkeley: University of California Press, 1998; London: Weidenfeld & Nicolson, 2001.

Davenport-Hines, Richard. *The Macmillans*. London: Mandarin, 1993.

Davie, Michael, ed. *The Diaries of Evelyn Waugh*. London: Weidenfeld & Nicolson, 1976; New York: Little, Brown, 1977.

Davies, A. J. *We, the Nation: The Conservative Party and the Pursuit of Power*. London: Little, Brown, 1995.

Deedes, W. F. *Brief Lives*. London: Macmillan, 2004.

———. *Dear Bill: A Memoir*. London: Macmillan, 2005.

Devonshire, Andrew. *Accidents of Fortune*. London: Michael Russell, 2004.

Devonshire, Duchess of. *The House: Living at Chatsworth*. New York: Holt, Rinehart and Winston, 1982.

Dickson, Lovat. *House of Words*. New York: Atheneum, 1963.

Dilks, David, ed. *The Diaries of Sir Alexander Cadogan 1938–1945*. New York: Putnam, 1971.

Dirksen, Herbert von. *Documents and Materials Relating to the Eve of the Second World War*. Moscow: Foreign Languages Publishing House, 1948.

Donner, Patrick. *Crusade*. London: Sherwood Press, 1984.

Dutton, David. *Anthony Eden: A Life and Reputation*. London: Edward Arnold, 1997.

Eade, Charles, ed. *Churchill by His Contemporaries*. London: Hutchinson, 1953.

Eden, Anthony. *The Reckoning: The Memoirs of Anthony Eden Earl of Avon*. Boston: Houghton Mifflin, 1975.

Egremont, Lord. *Wyndham and Children First*. London: Macmillan, 1968.

Egremont, Max. *Under Two Flags: The Life of Major-General Sir Edward Spears*. London: Weidenfeld & Nicolson, 1997.

Einzig, Paul. *In the Centre of Things*. London: Hutchinson, 1960.

Feiling, Keith. *The Life of Neville Chamberlain*. London: Macmillan, 1946.

Fischer, Louis. *Men and Politics: An Autobiography*. New York: Duell, Sloan and Pearce, 1941.

FitzGibbon, Theodora. *With Love: An Autobiography 1938–46*. London: Pan Books, 1983.

Flanner, Janet. *London Was Yesterday: 1934–1939*. New York: Viking, 1975.

Foot, Michael. *Loyalists and Loners*. London: Collins, 1986.

Foreman, Amanda. *Georgianna, Duchess of Devonshire*. New York: Modern Library, 2001.

Fox, James. *Five Sisters: The Langhornes of Virginia*. New York: Simon & Schuster, 2000.

Fraser, David. *And We Shall Shock Them: The British Army in the Second World War*. London: Hodder & Stoughton, 1983.

French, David. *Raising Churchill's Army: The British Army and the War Against Germany*. Oxford: Oxford University Press, 2000.

Gannon, Franklin Reid. *The British Press and Germany 1936–1939*. Oxford: Clarendon Press, 1971.

Gardiner, Juliet. *Wartime Britain 1939–1945*. London: Headline, 2004.

Gardner, Brian. *Churchill in His Time: A Study in a Reputation 1939–1945*. London: Methuen, 1968.

Gellhorn, Martha. *The View from the Ground*. New York: Atlantic Monthly Press, 1988.

Gilbert, Martin. *Winston S. Churchill*. Vol. 5, *The Prophet of Truth, 1922–1939*. Boston: Houghton Mifflin, 1977.

———.*Winston S. Churchill*. Vol. 6, *Finest Hour, 1939–1941*. Boston: Houghton Mifflin, 1983.

———. *Winston S. Churchill, Companion*. Volume V, parts 1–3. London: Heinemann, 1981.

———. *The Churchill War Papers, September 1939–December 1940*. New York: Norton, 1993. 2 vols.

Gilbert, Martin, and Richard Gott. *The Appeasers*. London: Phoenix, 2000.

Glass, Fiona, and Philip Marsden-Smedley, eds. *Articles of War: The Spectator Book of World War II*. London: Grafton, 1989.

Glendinning, Victoria. *Vita: The Life of V. Sackville-West*. New York: Knopf, 1983.

Graves, Robert, and Alan Hodge. *The Long Weekend: A Social History of Great Britain 1918–1939*. London: Faber and Faber, 1940.

Gunther, John. *Inside Europe*. London: Harper & Bros., 1940.

Hailsham, Lord. *A Sparrow's Flight: The Memoirs of Lord Hailsham of Marylebone*. London: Collins, 1990.

Hamilton, Nigel. *The Full Monty: Montgomery of Alamein*. London: Allen Lane, 2001.

Harris, Sir Percy. *Forty Years in and out of Parliament*. London: Melrose, 1947.

Harvey, John, ed. *The Diplomatic Diaries of Oliver Harvey, 1937–1940*. London: Collins, 1970.

Hetherington, S. J. *Katharine Atholl: Against the Tide*. Aberdeen: Aberdeen University Press, 1989.

Hooker, Nancy Harvison, ed. *The Moffat Papers: Selections from the Diplomatic Jour-*

nals of Jay Pierrepont Moffat. Cambridge, Mass.: Harvard University Press, 1956.

Horne, Alistair. *A Bundle from Britain*. New York: St. Martin's Press, 1993.

———. *Harold Macmillan*. Vol. 1, *1894–1956*. London: Penguin, 1989.

———. *Harold Macmillan*. Vol. 2, *1957–1986*. New York: Viking, 1989.

Howard, Anthony. *RAB: The Life of R. A. Butler*. London: Cape, 1987.

Howarth, Stephen. *August '39: The Last Four Weeks of Peace in Europe*. London: Hodder & Stoughton, 1989.

Hylton, Stuart. *Their Darkest Hour: The Hidden History of the Home Front*. Stroud, U.K.: Sutton, 2001.

James, Robert Rhodes. *Anthony Eden*. London: Weidenfeld & Nicolson, 1986.

———. *Churchill: A Study in Failure 1900–1939*. New York: World Publishing Co., 1970.

———. *Robert Boothby: A Portrait of Churchill's Ally*. New York: Viking, 1991.

———. *Victor Cazalet: A Portrait*. London: Hamish Hamilton, 1976.

James, Robert Rhodes, ed. *"Chips": The Diaries of Sir Henry Channon*. London: Phoenix, 1999.

Jenkins, Roy. *Churchill: A Biography*. New York: Farrar, Straus & Giroux, 2001.

Kee, Robert. *1939: The World We Left Behind*. Boston: Little, Brown, 1984.

Keegan, John. *Winston Churchill*. New York: Viking, 2002.

Kershaw, Ian. *Making Friends with Hitler: Lord Londonderry and Britain's Road to War*. London: Allen Lane, 2004.

Kidd, Janet Aitken. *The Beaverbrook Girl*. London: Collins, 1987.

King, Cecil H. *With Malice Toward None: A War Diary*. London: Sidgwick & Jackson, 1970.

Kirkpatrick, Helen P. *This Terrible Peace*. London: Rich & Cowan, 1939.

———. *Under the British Umbrella*. New York: Scribner's, 1939.

Knightley, Philip. *The First Casualty*. New York: Harcourt Brace Jovanovich, 1975.

Lambert, Angela. *1939: The Last Season of Peace*. London: Weidenfeld & Nicolson, 1989.

———. *Unquiet Souls*. London: Macmillan, 1984.

Lash, Joseph P. *Roosevelt and Churchill 1939–1941*. New York: Norton, 1976.

Leckie, Robert. *Delivered from Evil: The Saga of World War II*. New York: Harper and Row, 1987.

Lees-Milne, James. *Harold Nicolson: 1886–1929*. London: Chatto & Windus, 1980.

———. *Harold Nicolson: 1930–1968*. London: Chatto & Windus, 1981.

Leggett, Frances. *Late and Soon: The Transatlantic Story of a Marriage*. Boston: Houghton Mifflin, 1968.

Lewin, Ronald. *The War on Land: The British Army in World War II*. New York: Morrow, 1970.

Lewis, Peter. *A People's War*. London: Thames Methuen, 1986.

Liddell Hart, Basil. *The Liddell Hart Memoirs*. Vol. 2. New York: Putnam, 1966.

Lindsay, Loelia. *Grace and Favour*. New York: Reynal, 1961.

Lloyd George, Robert. *David & Winston: How a Friendship Changed History*. London: John Murray, 2005.

Lockhart, Sir Robert Bruce. *Comes the Reckoning*. London: Putnam, 1947.

Longford, Elizabeth. *The Pebbled Shore: The Memoirs of Elizabeth Longford*. London: Weidenfeld & Nicolson, 1986.

Lord, Walter. *The Miracle of Dunkirk.* New York: Viking, 1982.

Louis, William Roger. *In the Name of God, Go!: Leo Amery and the British Empire in the Age of Churchill.* New York: Norton, 1992.

Lukacs, John. *Five Days in London: May 1940.* New Haven: Yale University Press, 1999.

Lysaght, Charles Edward. *Brendan Bracken.* London: Allen Lane, 1979.

Mackay, Robert. *Half the Battle: Civilian Morale in Britain During the Second World War.* Manchester, U.K.: Manchester University Press, 2002.

Macleod, Iain. *Neville Chamberlain.* New York: Atheneum, 1962.

Macmillan, Harold. *Winds of Change: 1914–1939.* New York: Macmillan, 1962.

———. *The Blast of War: 1939–1945.* New York: Harper & Row, 1967.

———. *The Past Masters.* New York: Harper & Row, 1975.

Macnamara, J.R.J. *The Whistle Blows.* London: Eyre & Spottiswoode, 1938.

Maillaud, Pierre. *The English Way.* New York: Oxford University Press, 1946.

Manchester, William. *The Last Lion: Winston Spencer Churchill: Alone, 1932–1940.* New York: Dell, 1988.

Margach, James. *The Abuse of Power: The War Between Downing Street and the Media from Lloyd George to Callaghan.* London: W. H. Allen, 1978.

Margetson, Stella. *The Long Party: High Society in the Twenties and Thirties.* Famborough, U.K.: Saxon House, 1971.

Martel, Gordon, ed. *The Times and Appeasement: The Journals of A. L. Kennedy 1932–1939.* Cambridge, U.K.: Cambridge University Press, 2000.

Masters, Brian. *Great Hostesses.* London: Constable, 1982.

McLaine, Ian. *Ministry of Morale: Home Front Morale and the Ministry of Information in World War Two.* London: Allen & Unwin, 1979.

Middleton, Drew. *These Are the British.* New York: Knopf, 1957.

Montgomery, Bernard Law. *Memoirs of Field Marshal the Viscount Montgomery of Alamein.* London: Collins, 1958.

Moran, Lord. *Churchill: The Struggle for Survival: Taken from the Diaries of Lord Moran.* Boston: Houghton Mifflin, 1966.

Mosley, Nicholas. *Rules of the Game and Beyond the Pale: Memoirs of Sir Oswald Mosley and Family.* Elmwood Park, Ill.: Dalkey Archives Press, 1991.

Mowat, Charles Loch. *Britain Between the Wars 1918–1940.* Boston: Beacon Press, 1971.

Murray, Williamson. *The Change in the European Balance of Power, 1938–1939.* Princeton: Princeton University Press, 1982.

Murray, Williamson, and Allan R. Millett. *A War to Be Won: Fighting the Second World War.* Cambridge, Mass.: Belknap/Harvard University Press, 2000.

Murrow, Edward R. *This Is London.* New York: Simon and Schuster, 1941.

Nicolson, Harold. *Diaries and Letters.* Vol. 1, *1930–1939.* New York: Atheneum, 1966.

———. *Marginal Comment: January 6–August 4, 1939.* London: Constable, 1939.

———. *The War Years: Diaries and Letters.* Vol. 2, *1939–1945.* New York: Atheneum, 1967.

Nicolson, Nigel. *Long Life.* London: Weidenfeld & Nicolson, 1997.

———. *Portrait of a Marriage.* New York: Bantam, 1974.

Nutting, Anthony. *No End of a Lesson: The Story of Suez.* New York: Clarkson Potter, 1967.

Olson, Lynne, and Stanley Cloud. *A Question of Honor: The Kosciuszko Squadron: Forgotten Heroes of World War II.* New York: Knopf, 2003.

Owen, Frank. *Guilty Men.* New York: Stokes, 1940.

Panter-Downes, Mollie. *London War Notes, 1939–1945*. New York: Farrar, Straus & Giroux, 1973.

Pearson, John. *The Serpent and the Stag*. New York: Holt, Rinehart and Winston, 1984.

Pedersen, Susan. *Eleanor Rathbone and the Politics of Conscience*. New Haven: Yale University Press, 2004.

Pimlott, Ben. *Hugh Dalton*. London: Jonathan Cape, 1985.

Pimlott, Ben, ed. *The Political Diary of Hugh Dalton: 1918–40; 1945–60*. London: Jonathan Cape, 1986.

———, ed. *The Second World War Diary of Hugh Dalton: 1940–45*. London: Jonathan Cape, 1986.

Ponting, Clive. *1940: Myth and Reality*. London: Hamish Hamilton, 1980.

Pope-Hennessy, James. *The Houses of Parliament*. London: Batsford, 1953.

Pottle, Mark. *Champion Redoubtable: The Diaries and Letters of Violet Bonham Carter 1914–1941*. London: Weidenfeld & Nicolson, 1998.

———. *Daring to Hope: The Diaries and Letters of Violet Bonham Carter 1946–1969*. London: Weidenfeld & Nicolson, 2000.

Priestley, J. B. *English Journey*. New York: Harper and Bros., 1934.

Raczyński, Edward. *In Allied London*. London: Weidenfeld & Nicolson, 1962.

Richards, Peter. *The Backbenchers*. London: Faber and Faber, 1972.

Ritchie, Charles. *The Siren Years: A Canadian Diplomat Abroad, 1937–1945*. Toronto: Macmillan of Canada, 1974.

Roberts, Andrew. *Eminent Churchillians*. New York: Simon and Schuster, 1994.

———. *"The Holy Fox": The Life of Lord Halifax*. London: Phoenix, 1997.

Roberts, Brian. *Churchills in Africa*. London: Hamish Hamilton, 1970.

Robertson, Ben. *I Saw England*. New York: Knopf, 1941.

Robyns, Gwen. *Barbara Cartland*. London: Sidgwick & Jackson, 1984.

Rogers, Barbara. *Men Only*. London: Pandora, 1988.

Rose, Kenneth. *The Later Cecils*. New York: Harper & Row, 1975.

Rose, N. R. *Baffy: The Diaries of Blanche Dugdale 1936–1947*. London: Valentine Mitchell, 1973.

Rose, Norman. *Churchill: The Unruly Giant*. New York: Free Press, 1995.

———. *The Cliveden Set: Portrait of an Exclusive Fraternity*. London: Pimlico, 2001.

Sampson, Anthony. *Macmillan: A Study in Ambiguity*. London: Pelican, 1968.

Searing, Donald D. *Westminster's World*. Cambridge, Mass.: Harvard University Press, 1994.

Sewell, J. E. *Mirror of Britain*. London: Hodder & Stoughton, 1941.

Shachtman, Tom. *The Phony War: 1939–1940*. Lincoln, Neb.: BackinPrint.com, 2000.

Shepherd, Robert. *A Class Divided: Appeasement and the Road to Munich 1938*. London: Macmillan, 1988.

Shirer, William. *Berlin Diary*. New York: Knopf, 1941.

Skidelsky, Robert. *John Maynard Keynes: The Economist as Savior 1920–1937*. London: Allen Lane,1994.

———. *John Maynard Keynes: Fighting for Britain 1937–1945*. London: Macmillan, 2000.

Smart, Nick. *British Strategy and Politics During the Phony War*. Westport, Conn.: Praeger, 2003.

Smart, Nick, ed. *Diaries and Letters of Robert Bernays 1932–1939*. Lewiston, N.Y.: E. Mellen Press, 1996.

Smith, Gene. *The Dark Summer*. New York: Collier, 1989.

Smith, Malcolm. *Britain and 1940: History, Myth and Popular Memory*. New York: Routledge, 2000.

Soames, Mary. *Speaking for Themselves: The Personal Letters of Winston and Clementine Churchill*. New York: Doubleday, 1998.

Spears, Sir Edward L. *Assignment to Catastrophe*. Vol. 1, *Prelude to Dunkirk: July 1939–May 1940*. New York: A. A. Wyn, 1954.

Stewart, Graham. *Burying Caesar: The Churchill-Chamberlain Rivalry*. London: Weidenfeld & Nicolson, 1999.

Stobaugh, Beverly Parker. *Women and Parliament 1918–1970*. Hicksville, N.Y.: Exposition Press, 1978.

Stowe, Leland. *No Other Road to Freedom*. New York: Knopf, 1941.

Stuart, James. *Within the Fringe*. London: Bodley Head, 1967.

Sykes, Christopher. *Nancy: The Life of Lady Astor*. New York: Harper & Row, 1972.

Taylor, A.J.P., ed. *Off the Record: Political Interviews 1933–1943: W. P. Crozier*. London: Hutchinson, 1973.

Thomas, Hugh, ed. *The Establishment*. London: Anthony Blond, 1959.

Thompson, Laurence. *1940*. New York: Morrow, 1966.

Thompson, Neville. *The Anti-Appeasers: Conservative Opposition to Appeasement in the 1930s*. Oxford: Clarendon Press, 1971.

Thorpe, D. R. *Eden: The Life and Times of Anthony Eden First Earl of Avon, 1897–1977*. London: Chatto & Windus, 2003.

Tree, Ronald. *When the Moon Was High*. London: Macmillan, 1975.

Turner, E. S. *The Phoney War*. New York: St. Martin's Press, 1961.

Watt, Donald Cameron. *Personalities and Appeasement*. Austin, Texas: Harry Ransom Humanities Research Center, 1991.

Waugh, Evelyn. *Put Out More Flags*. Boston: Back Bay Books, 2002.

Weale, Adrian. *Patriot Traitors: Roger Casement, John Amery and the Real Meaning of Treason*. London: Viking, 2001.

Wedgwood, Josiah. *Memoirs of a Fighting Life*. London: Hutchinson, 1941.

Wheeler-Bennett, John W. *Munich: Prologue to Tragedy*. New York: Duell, Sloan and Pearce, 1948.

Wicks, Ben. *The Day They Took the Children*. Toronto: Stoddart, 1989.

Wilkinson, Rupert. *Gentlemanly Power: British Leadership and the Public School Tradition*. London: Oxford University Press, 1964.

Williams, Francis. *Nothing So Strange*. New York: American Heritage, 1970.

———. *Press, Parliament and People*. London: Heinemann, 1946.

Winchester, Simon. *Their Noble Lordships: Class and Power in Modern Britain*. New York: Random House, 1982.

Wyburn-Powell, Alun. *Clement Davies: Liberal Leader*. London: Politico's, 2003.

Young, Kenneth, ed. *The Diaries of Sir Robert Bruce Lockhart*. Vol. 1, *1915–1939*. New York: St. Martin's Press, 1975.

———. *The Diaries of Sir Robert Bruce Lockhart*. Vol. 2, *1939–1965*. London: Macmillan, 1985.

Ziegler, Philip. *Diana Cooper*. New York: Knopf, 1982.

———. *London at War*. New York: Knopf, 1995.

ACKNOWLEDGMENTS

In the middle of my research for *Troublesome Young Men*, I wrote to Nigel Nicolson to ask if I could visit him at Sissinghurst Castle to talk about his father, Harold Nicolson. In a polite and graceful reply, Nicolson wrote that at the age of eighty-seven he was "too weak in body and memory" to provide any useful information. In any case, he added, he was sure I knew that "written and contemporary evidence is worth ten times the value of oral reminiscences." I recalled his comment a few weeks later as I sat in the library of Oxford's Balliol College, poring over Harold Nicolson's wonderfully candid and revealing diaries before and during World War II. In an era of cell phones and e-mails, when thoughts, feelings, and insights disappear into the ether almost as fast as they are communicated, it was a distinct treat for me, as it is for other writers and researchers, to immerse myself in a period when people poured out their beliefs, loves, hatreds, doubts, regrets, joys, and opinions of others on paper.

Delving into primary material has always been my greatest pleasure in writing books. It was especially true in my work on *Troublesome Young Men*, thanks to the wealth of letters, journals, and diaries kept by Nicolson and many of the other men and women who play major roles in this book. Although much of the material that I examined has been available to researchers for years, some, like Leo Amery's recently opened papers in the Churchill archives in Cambridge, offer fresh insights into the people on whom they focus. I felt a particular sense of adventure and discovery as I sat in the study of Camfield Place, Barbara Cartland's home in Hertfordshire, and sifted through a massive collection of scrapbooks and letters that helped bring Ronald Cartland to life for me.

My appreciation goes to the librarians and archivists of the various collections for their help. Thanks to Colin Harris and his staff in the Modern Papers Reading Room of Oxford's Bodleian Library; Penelope Bulloch at the Balliol Library; Sandra Marsh and Ieuan Hopkins in the Churchill Archives Centre at Churchill College, Cambridge; and Christine Penney and her staff in the Special Collections Department at the University of Birmingham. My gratitude also to the Marquess of Salisbury and Robin Harcourt Williams for allowing me to consult the papers of the fourth and fifth marquesses of Salisbury at Hatfield House in Hertfordshire.

Thanks to the staffs of the British Library; the Carmarthenshire Archives in Carmarthen, Wales; the Liddell Hart Centre for Military Archives at King's College, London; the National Archives in Kew; the manuscripts division at Smith College in Northampton, Massachusetts; and the British Film Institute, which allowed me to view documentary footage of several of the key figures in the book. Thanks too to Dr. Gerald Anderson, professor of history at North Dakota State University, for sending me his paper "The Last Dance: British High Society in the Summer of 1939."

I owe a particular debt of gratitude to Ian and Glen McCorquodale, the nephews of Ronald Cartland, for talking to me at length about their uncle and their mother, Barbara Cartland, and for granting me access to Ronald Cartland's scrapbooks and letters. My thanks to Lord Coleraine for letting me see excerpts of the unpublished reminiscences of his father, Richard Law, and to Carline Henderson, the daughter of Paul Emrys-Evans, and her former husband, Alistair Henderson, for sharing their memories of Emrys-Evans. Thanks also to Marie Ridder for her insightful comments about her unofficial godfather, Robert Boothby, and to Jeff McAllister and Ann Olivarius for their help and hospitality during my trips to London.

I had the great good fortune to have two of the finest editors in publishing today—John Glusman and Elisabeth Sifton—overseeing this book. John's suggestions helped improve the book considerably, and when he left Farrar, Straus, and Giroux, Elisabeth's elegant comments sharpened it even more. I am deeply grateful to both of them—and to my British editor, Bill Swainson, at Bloomsbury. A special note of appreciation to my agent, Gail Ross, for her encouragement, advice, and friendship.

Thanks to my daughter, Carly, who is, as she has always been, a great source of joy. Above all, I want to thank and acknowledge my husband and frequent collaborator, Stanley Cloud. We began this book together, and when he left for another writing project, he nonetheless continued to work with me in researching *Troublesome Young Men* and, through it all, to provide unstinting counsel and support. He is my inspiration.

INDEX

Simon, Sir John, 68, 91, 92–93, 94, 136,
  228, 284, 307; in Churchill
  government, 322, 323, 349;
  "undersecretaries' plot" and, 335
Simpson, Wallis, 81–82
Sinclair, Archibald, 135–36, 138, 239;
  as air minister, 332; tapping of phone
  conversations, 288
Sissinghurst Castle, 104
Skoda works, 259
Smuts, Jan, 48
Snadden, William McNair, 167–69
socialism, 30, 49
South Africa, 114–15, 361
Soviet Union: Five-Year Plan, 71;
  Germany viewed as counterweight to,
  65; invasion of Finland, 272; invasion
  of Poland, 223; nonaggression pact
  with Germany, 200, 228
Spanish civil war, 124, 165–66, 238, 342
Spears, Edward, 11, 74, 97, 101,
  199–200, 204, 210; air raids and,
  214–15; anti-appeasement stance, 74;
  Ronald Cartland's death and, 321;
  Czechoslovakia crisis and, 135–36;
  delay in aiding Poland and, 207,
  221–22; Eden group and, 177,
  213; May 1940 events leading to
  Chamberlain's resignation and, 290,
  295, 301–302, 303; Norway debacle
  and, 283; Watching Committee and,
  273
Spectator, The, 82, 177, 193, 244, 256,
  320
Speer, Albert, 212
Spencer-Churchill, Lady Sarah, 8–9
Stalin, Joseph, nonaggression pact with
  Germany, 200, 228
Stamp, Lord, 228
St. Andrews University, 180
Stanley, Oliver, 129, 131, 132, 148; wife
  of, 146
Steward, George, 120
St. James's Club, 244
St. Margaret's, Westminster, 41
Stowe, Leland, 229, 251, 270; battle for
  Norway, coverage of, 280, 281, 282

St. Stephen's Club, 120
Stuart, James, 42, 57; retribution against
  Tory rebels, 159–60, 167, 168, 169,
  324–25, 350, 351
Suez Canal, 357–59
Sunday Express, 33, 123, 143
Sunday Pictorial, 196, 326, 336, 338
Sunday Times, The (London), 9, 73, 120,
  213, 243
Sweden, shipping of iron ore to
  Germany by, 226, 236, 274
Swinburne, Algernon, 105
Swinton, Lord, 94
Sybil (Disraeli), 30
Syria, 354

Talleyrand, 140
Taylor, Charles, 300–301
Tedder, Lord, 358
Tennyson, Alfred Lord, 37, 105
Thomas, James P. L. "Jim," 32, 93–94,
  95, 96, 100–101, 156–57, 160, 182;
  appointment to whip's office, 332;
  Eden group and, 177; as first lord of
  the admiralty, 356; spring of 1940,
  efforts to replace Chamberlain in,
  277, 284, 301
Thorpe, D. R., 99
Thost, Dr. Hans Wilhelm, 165
Time magazine, 6, 140, 198
Times, The (London), 81, 100, 111, 122,
  143, 149n, 156, 160, 182, 187,
  192–93, 197, 223, 320; Amery
  as correspondent for, 114–15;
  Czechoslovakia crisis and, 130, 134,
  153; self-censorship by, 122; as Tory
  publication, 123
Titmuss, Richard, 59
Tonypandy, Wales, mine workers' strike
  of 1910 in, 308
Tory rebels: abstention from vote of
  confidence on Munich, 152–55, 159,
  162; adjournment of Parliament in
  1938, 10–19, 199; Churchill group,
  178, 238; Churchill's cabinet and
  ministerial appointments and,